Praise for

WHY?

"[Hayes] show[s] a sophisticated and judicious mastery of the most up-to-date historical scholarship. . . . This timely, level-headed book is a model of public engagement."
— Robert Eaglestone, *Times Higher Education*

"Hayes has written a valuable book for today's challenges, with perspective and sensitivity, that is, indeed, authoritative, readable and revealing."
— *St. Louis Post-Dispatch*

"Explain? Impossible. But Hayes's timely, accessible book sheds light on the horror. In certain circumstances it reminds us that humans can rationalize anything."
— *People*

"I recommend this book for a lucid, well-crafted introduction to the history of the Holocaust. Unlike most works on the history of the Holocaust . . . Hayes' book concentrates . . . on helping readers to understand why the Holocaust occurred when it did, in the manner it did and with the results it produced. It offers readers a window onto how historians go about finding answers to these questions."
— David Engel, professor of Holocaust studies and chair of Hebrew and Judaic studies at New York University, Jewish Telegraphic Agency

"A fascinating, remarkably lucid, compulsively readable explanation of how the mass murder of Europe's Jews came about and how it transpired in the middle of the twentieth century."

—David I. Kertzer, Pulitzer Prize–winning author of
    The Pope and Mussolini

"Calmly argued, alert to the most recent scholarship about the Holocaust, and full of good sense, Peter Hayes's new book carries an essential title asked universally: Why? Why did such a thing happen? Taking up this most difficult of challenges, his pages answer questions that many analysts dare not even ask, let alone answer. That is why this work should be required reading, both for specialists and for those who seek more recently to understand."

—Michael R. Marrus, Chancellor Rose and Ray Wolfe
    Professor Emeritus of Holocaust Studies at the University
    of Toronto, and author of *Lessons of the Holocaust*

"This book is outstanding—beautifully written, with enviable clarity of argument, countless instructive details, and memorable, evocative images. On every issue around which there has been either controversy or confusion—from the interrelationships between the Holocaust and the mass murder of individuals with disabilities to the motivations of the perpetrators, the economics of the killing operations, the special situation of Poland, the experiences of slave laborers, or the dimensions of Jewish resistance—Peter Hayes helpfully distills the debates and provides judicious, orienting assessments. A masterful, indispensable, landmark work."

—Dagmar Herzog, Distinguished Professor of History and
    the Daniel Rose Faculty Scholar at the Graduate Center,
    City University of New York

ALSO BY PETER HAYES

How Was It Possible? A Holocaust Reader (editor)

*Frankreichforum XI: Universitätskulturen/L'Université
en perspective/The Future of the University* (coeditor)

The Oxford Handbook of Holocaust Studies (coeditor)

*Das Amt und die Vergangenheit: Deutsche Diplomaten im
Dritten Reich und in der Bundesrepublik* (coauthor)

From Cooperation to Complicity: Degussa in the Third Reich

The Last Expression: Art and Auschwitz (coeditor)

*"Arisierung" im Nationalsozialismus: Volksgemeinschaft,
Raub und Gedächtnis* (coeditor)

*Lessons and Legacies III: Memory, Memorialization,
and Denial* (editor)

*Lessons and Legacies I: The Meaning of the Holocaust
in a Changing World* (editor)

Industry and Ideology: IG Farben in the Nazi Era

Imperial Germany (coeditor)

WHY?

Explaining
the Holocaust

PETER HAYES

W. W. NORTON & COMPANY

Independent Publishers Since 1923

New York | London

Copyright © 2017 by Peter Hayes

For information about permission to reproduce selections from this book,
write to Permissions, W. W. Norton & Company, Inc.,
500 Fifth Avenue, New York, NY 10110

For information about special discounts for bulk purchases, please contact
W. W. Norton Special Sales at specialsales@wwnorton.com or 800-233-4830

Manufacturing by LSC Harrisonburg
Book design by Marysarah Quinn
Production manager: Anna Oler

Library of Congress Cataloging-in-Publication Data

Names: Hayes, Peter, 1946 September 7– author
Title: Why? : explaining the Holocaust / Peter Hayes.
Description: First edition. | New York ; London : W. W. Norton & Company,
independent publishers since 1923, [2017] | Includes bibliographical
references and index.
Identifiers: LCCN 2016031588 | ISBN 9780393254365 (hardcover)
Subjects: LCSH: Holocaust, Jewish (1939–1945) | Holocaust, Jewish
(1939–1945)—Causes. | Antisemitism—Germany—History—20th century. |
Jews—Germany—History—20th century. | Jews—Persecutions—
Europe—History—20th century. | Germany—History—1933–1945. |
Germany—Ethnic relations.
Classification: LCC D804.3 .H387 2017 | DDC 940.53/1811—dc23
LC record available at https://lccn.loc.gov/2016031588

ISBN 978-0-393-35546-8 pbk.

W. W. Norton & Company, Inc.
500 Fifth Avenue, New York, N.Y. 10110
www.wwnorton.com

W. W. Norton & Company Ltd.
15 Carlisle Street, London W1D 3BS

5 6 7 8 9 0

IN GRATEFUL MEMORY OF INSPIRING TEACHERS:

Mary Faherty

James McGillivray

Athern Park Daggett

John C. Rensenbrink

Timothy W. Mason

Henry Ashby Turner Jr.

CONTENTS

LIST OF FIGURES

Why Another Book
on the Holocaust?

SEVENTY YEARS AFTER the Holocaust ended, it continues to resist comprehension. Despite (or maybe because of) the outpouring of some sixteen thousand books cataloged at the Library of Congress under the heading, despite the proliferation of museums and memorials, despite the annual appearance of new cinematic treatments, and despite the spread of educational programs and courses devoted to the subject, a coherent explanation of why such ghastly carnage erupted from the heart of civilized Europe in the twentieth century seems still to elude people. Indeed, perhaps the adjectives most frequently invoked in connection with the Holocaust are "unfathomable," "incomprehensible," and "inexplicable." These words attest to a distancing reflex, an almost instinctive recoiling in self-defense. To say that one can explain the occurrence of the Holocaust seems tantamount to normalizing it, but professing that one cannot grasp it is an assertion of the speaker's innocence—of his or her incapacity not only to conceive of such horror but to enact anything like it. Small wonder that incomprehension is the default position in the face of the enormity of the Holocaust, even though that stance blocks the possibility of learning from the subject.

Self-protection is not the only reason for the enduring difficulty of coming to intellectual grips with the Holocaust, however. Another is the complexity of the task. To understand the Holocaust requires solving multiple puzzles that surround it. In the course of teaching the subject to American undergraduates for almost three decades and lecturing widely to both academic and general audiences, I have come to recognize eight central issues that people grappling with the subject find most perplexing. Some of these issues involve acts of commission, some concern acts of omission, and still others entail both. All require interlocking clarification before a mind can comprehend and account for the cataclysm. Each chapter of this book examines one of those eight central issues, raised in the form of a question, and the book as a whole reflects my conviction that the Holocaust is no less historically explicable than any other human experience, though the job is not easy.

In answering these questions, I bring to bear expertise that is unusual among students of the Holocaust. I am by training an economic historian. That does not mean that I foreground material motivations for murder (in fact, I contend that they were secondary to ideological motives). My background makes me, however, alert to numbers and their significance, and I deploy them frequently in order to demonstrate their powerful interpretive effects. A second distinguishing feature of my account is its dialectical origins. This is not a book driven by a thesis that the author wants to prove but rather a work that emerged out of the give-and-take of many years of teaching and public speaking, during which I learned which aspects of the subject people most want clarified and why, directed my reading and thinking toward identifying the most reliable responses that scholarship can offer, and then honed ways to make that knowledge as accessible and memorable as I could.

Alongside its explanatory purpose, this book also has another goal: to set the record straight. As the late historian Tony Judt observed, "Impossible to remember as it really was, [the Holocaust] is inherently vulnerable to being remembered as it wasn't." Numerous myths have grown up around the subject, many designed to console us that things could have gone much differently if only some person or entity had acted more bravely or wisely, others intended to cast new blame on favorite or surprising villains or even on historians of the subject. This book dispels many such legends—from the notion that antisemitism brought Adolf Hitler to power in Germany to the belief that a large number of major perpetrators of the Holocaust escaped punishment afterward—and the final chapter reviews and debunks the most prevalent ones, including the loud and recurrent claim that the Holocaust never happened.

The arc of the book's argument is as follows. The Holocaust was the product of a particular time and place: Europe in the aftermath of the Industrial Revolution and the upheavals of World War I and the Bolshevik Revolution. These were the contexts in which ancient hostilities toward Jews and Judaism, deeply rooted in religious rivalry but updated with the trappings of modern science, turned into a fixation on removing Jews from civil society as a magical solution to all social problems. Germany was where the fault lines of disruption lifted this belief to power during the 1930s, but the murder of the Jews of Europe was neither pre-programmed by German history nor an exclusively German project. The massacre took shape under specific political and military conditions and intensified in part because it suited the objectives of many other Europeans, at least during the short, ferocious period when most of the killing occurred. In the face of the slaughter, the victims were largely powerless and the onlookers preoccupied with their own, to them more pressing concerns. The parts of the trap that clicked into place around European Jews during the Nazi era fit so tightly that only a minority could escape, most only just barely and in the nick of time. Afterward, most countries of the old continent delayed acknowledging what they had participated in yet also constructed numerous barriers to its repetition, barriers that now, seventy years later, are under stress.

The pace of specialist research on the Holocaust has outrun most people's ability to keep up and to integrate new findings into a general interpretive picture. Even as misleading notions about the subject have gained ground, antiquated ones linger. Given this, people interested in the subject need a comprehensive stocktaking directed squarely at answering the most central and enduring questions about why and how the massacre of European Jewry unfolded. That is what this book offers.

WHY?

CHAPTER I

TARGETS:
Why the Jews?

OUTBREAKS OF HOSTILITY against minorities are almost always rooted both in ideas—what the majority thinks about the minority—and circumstances: the ways in which or the terms on which the two groups are interacting at a particular time. In order to explain why the Jews became objects of murderous intentions in the twentieth century, one has to look at both sorts of roots.

ANTISEMITISM

Nowadays the term usually used to describe hostility to Jews is antisemitism. A professor of mine in graduate school used to say that the problem with the word is that it is a single term for lots of different attitudes—covering everything from telling crude jokes about Jews to desiring to kill them. He had a point, but a working definition is nonetheless possible. Mine goes like this: Antisemitism is a categorical impugning of Jews as collectively embodying distasteful and/or destructive traits. In other words, antisemitism is the belief that Jews have common repellent and/or ruinous qualities that set them apart from non-Jews. Descent is determinative; individuality is illusory.

That attitude has a long history; indeed, a famous book by Robert Wistrich and a widely seen documentary film on the subject are called *The Longest Hatred*. But that title is misleading for two reasons. First, if Jews have long been hated in Western culture, they have not been equally hated at all times and in all places; and second, the hatred has exhibited a good deal of shape-shifting. In fact, the name that we now use to describe prejudice against or hatred of Jews illustrates both points. The word "antisemitism" appeared only in 1879, and its popularization is usually ascribed to Wilhelm Marr, a German agitator who intended it to describe something new and different from previous forms of hostility toward Jews. Like other "-ism" words that appeared in abundance in the nineteenth century, the word was chosen to suggest that this new hostility was about politics and science. Note what the word claimed to be against: Not Jews but something called Semitism. What was that? Unlike the other targets of nineteenth century "anti-" movements (for example, antisocialism, anticommunism, anti-Catholicism, antivivisectionism, even antidisestablishmentarianism), this term did not combat a belief system that had named itself, but instead invented the phenomenon being opposed. Self-styled "antisemites" borrowed a category from linguistics, and they did so misleadingly. They claimed to combat Semites—speakers of the Semitic family of languages, which differed in syntax and grammatical structure from the so-called Indo-European family of languages that predominated in Europe. But actually not all Semites were targeted, since Arabs generally were not included, though Arabic is a Semitic language. Neither were the modern speakers of Aramaic, the language Jesus spoke, though it is also a Semitic tongue. In the late 1930s and early 1940s, the Nazi regime implicitly conceded that the new term was a lie, as Germany took pains to reassure Arab governments that it regarded their inhabitants as neither threatening nor inferior.

The target of the new "-ism" was Jews, and by focusing on their ancestral language and using an abstract, pseudoscientific euphe-

mism to group them, the antisemites purported to (a) differenti-
ate Jews authoritatively from everyone else, (b) root their difference
in their very nature and thought processes, and thus (c) assert that
opposition to Jews was not a mere prejudice, but a response to a
demonstrable reality that had to be dealt with politically.

Until recently, English spelling has unwittingly accepted the antisemites' case, since the customary insertion of a hyphen and a capital letter in "anti-Semitism" implies that there is something called
"Semitism" somewhere. The original language of the term, German, doesn't make this mistake; the spelling is *Antisemitismus*, all
one word. Nowadays, people and institutions alive to this subtle fact,
such as the United States Holocaust Memorial Museum, insist on the
one-word spelling of antisemitism. Neither Microsoft Word's spell-
check function nor the *Oxford English Dictionary* has caught on yet.

The principal way in which antisemitism has evolved and varied
over time has to do with the relative strength of its xenophobic
and chimerical forms, as identified by Gavin Langmuir, a distinguished medievalist, but slightly redefined here. The xenophobic
form sees Jews as *different* from others in some *observable* respects,
and its adherents exhibit varying degrees of *discomfort* with this difference. The chimerical form sees Jews as *dangerous* to others in some
imagined ways, and its exponents advocate *doing something* in response.
The origins of the words highlight the distinction: *Xenos* is Greek for
"stranger, guest;" *chimera* is Greek for a mythical fire-breathing mon-
ster with a lion's head, a goat's body, and a serpent's tail.

Ancient Roman attitudes toward Jews best illustrate the consequences of the distinction. The Roman writer Tacitus criticized the
Jews for a supposedly "stubborn attachment to one another . . . which
contrasts with their implacable hatred for the rest of mankind,"
and the Romans did not like or understand such Jewish customs as
monotheism, which entailed refusing to worship the emperors as
gods; the Sabbath, which amounted to taking only one and the same
day off from work every week; endogamy, which mandated marry-

ing only other Jews; and circumcision of male infants as a symbol and reminder of a special arrangement with God. But the Romans did not see the Jews as especially or intrinsically dangerous, except when they resisted the empire's authority. Even after the destruction of the temple in Jerusalem in 70 CE by the army of the future Emperor Titus and the suppression of the three successive revolts against Roman rule that led to the almost complete dispersal of the Jews from ancient Judaea after 136 CE, individual Jews could and did still become Roman citizens, and they populated many different walks of life.

Although some ancient Egyptian and Greek texts express animosity toward Jews, the rise of intense hostility to and fear of them largely coincides with the rise of Christianity. The relationship between adherents of the two religions always has reflected a paradox: The two faiths were both very similar and very different, which created intense competition. Jews saw the new religion as essentially a heresy, an erroneous variation on their theology. Christians saw themselves as embracing a new, improved version of that theology, one that superseded the old, which should be cast off as a relic of an earlier era.

Christians both took over and then deviated from the central tenets of Judaism. First, they proclaimed monotheism but declared Jesus the son of God and thus divine and advanced the doctrine of the Trinity, one God in three forms. Second, Christians accepted the Hebrew Bible as revealing the word of God and incorporated it into their Bible as the Old Testament, but then added the Gospels (the "Good News") and other books as new revelations of God's will. Third, Christianity adapted the Jewish ideas of election and the Covenant between God and His people to new purposes. Jews believed that they and God had concluded a series of special agreements or pacts, the most famous of which are the ones with Abraham and Moses in which God promised to make the Jews his Chosen People and "a light unto the nations" in return for obedience to his laws.

These consisted initially of the Ten Commandments, but became elaborated into the 613 central laws or *mitzvot*—actually 248 commandments and 365 prohibitions—set forth in the Torah, the first five books of the Bible, which Christians call the Pentateuch. These laws covered everything from what one may eat or wear to how one should wash and worship. Christianity declared that Jesus heralded a new Covenant that replaced Moses's, that the old laws were now obsolete, and that election to the status of Chosen People was now open to anyone who accepted Christ and the teachings of the Bible and the new scriptures.

One way of understanding what followed is to recall that Jews were the people who said no. Offered a new form of relationship with God, they said they preferred the one they had, and this rejection set off several hundred years of rivalry and mutual recrimination, as the two groups competed for followers until the fourth century of the common era, when Christianity became the official religion of the Roman Empire and thus seemed to win the battle.

That brings us to figure 1, which tries in schematic fashion to capture three interwoven matters: (1) the evolving and overlapping forms of animosity to Jews that developed in Europe during successive eras once Christianity had become dominant, (2) the changing definitions of the problem Jews supposedly represented, and (3) the shifting prescriptions for fixing the situation.

The time frames specified on the chart indicate that distinct frameworks for criticizing Jews developed in those periods, but that does not mean that the new ones erased the old ones entirely. Some people remained antisemitic in the 1940s for reasons devised during the first period; in fact, some people are still antisemites for these supposed reasons. One of the most interesting recent books on the Holocaust, Alon Confino's *A World Without Jews* (2014), in fact argues that a secularized version of the Christian claim to historical supersession was at the heart of the Nazi drive to eradicate

FIGURE 1: THE OVERLAPPING LAYERS OF ANTISEMITISM

PARADIGM/AGE	CONCERN/ PROBLEM	SOLUTION	NOTES
Faith/Church (fourth–eighteenth centuries)	religion/beliefs	segregation, then conversion	rooted in rejection and rivalry and in competing claims to revelation; schizophrenic: preserve/punish, survive/suffer; degradation and separation; demonization during crises: blood libel, Luther; enduring, esp. in Orthodox lands
JEWS BENIGHTED			
Reason/ Enlightenment (eighteenth–nineteenth centuries)	culture/ traditions (law/ritual/dress)	emancipation, then absorption	Voltaire: freedom from past and dogma; liberalism/Code Napoléon
JEWS BACKWARD			
Science (nineteenth–twentieth centuries)	race (blood/genes)	quarantine, then elimination	non-volitional, material, immutable; Darwinian essentialism; veterinary politics: peoples=breeds
JEWS BACTERIAL			

the Jews. Instead of advancing a new religion of supersession, the Nazis saw themselves as promoting an entirely new conception of morality. Confino's claim is not entirely original. Sigmund Freud and Maurice Samuel argued similarly about the roots of antisemitism on the eve of the Holocaust, Léon Poliakov and Norman Cohn about those of Nazi racism shortly afterward. But these thinkers understood that the Nazis were not so much trying to supersede Judeo-Christian morality as to nullify or repeal it. Nazi morality was of the "back to the future" sort; it demanded acknowledgment that the only governing principle of life is the primordial law of the jungle and that the only measure of goodness is physical survival.

That the justifications of antisemitism changed over time also does not mean, despite the prestige of science, that the prejudice became more intellectually sophisticated—that the later phases were more informed and intelligent. They only posed as such.

The first horizontal block in figure 1 concerns the long era of European history in which the dominant framework of thought was religious and the central question that determined or legitimized ideas and policies was "What does God want or demand?" The governing dilemma of Christianity during this long period of discrimination against Jews is that the Church had to do a theological balancing act between two contradictory obligations toward them, as stipulated in the "doctrine of Jewish witness" devised by St. Augustine, the Bishop of Hippo in North Africa, in the early fifth century: persecution and preservation. On the one hand, Augustine taught that the Church had to demonstrate "the negation of the Jews" and "the election of the Christians" by, first, emphasizing the Jews' responsibility for Christ's death as alleged in the later Gospels and, second, making the Jews' existence on earth ever more isolated and miserable as a physical representation of the consequences of rejecting Christianity. Thus, according to this part of Christian theology, the Jews had to suffer because they were religiously benighted—spiritually in darkness.

On the other hand, Jesus was a Jew, and the Jews once had been God's Chosen. Augustine taught that they could not be massacred, unlike every other religious group that denied or deviated from the claim to truth of Catholic or Orthodox Christianity. Indeed, they had to be allowed to live, albeit in misery, until the wondrous day when they saw the light and converted, for that development would herald the Last Judgment and the coming of the Kingdom of Heaven. This is the explanation for a remarkable irony of this story, the survival of the Jews. They were the only religious minority whose faith remained legal in Christian Europe, whose adherents were not automatically and always slaughtered, as the Cathars, Lollards, and other dissenters were, until the Reformation split Western Christendom, and the catastrophically bloody and ultimately stalemated Wars of Religion of the sixteenth and seventeenth centuries taught Catholics and Protestants the necessity of coexistence.

The results of Augustine's dicta included, for hundreds of years, Christian condemnation of the Jews, supplemented by constant establishment of barriers to contact with Christians so that their faith could not be subverted. The relegation of Jews to pariah status, the Church hoped, would induce them to convert. In the final centuries of the Roman Empire, Jews lost the rights, first, to acquire, and later even to hold, Christian slaves, which broke the back of Jews' wealth. One after another, new laws barred Jews from proselytizing, from reversing baptisms, from cohabiting with or marrying Christians, from holding public office, and from building synagogues. Enforcement of separation between Christians and Jews was uneven in Christian Europe, but it steadily increased, eventually creating a pattern of occupational and residential ghettoization that confined Jews to certain usually despised or dangerous activities, such as moneylending or leather tanning, and certain permissible locations, also usually less than desirable ones.

As all this unfolded, the Church found that it could not quite get away with simultaneously fostering hostility to Jews and forbidding violence toward them. Ordinary people periodically lost sight of the theological reasons why adherents of this religion that denied Christ's divinity should be treated differently from all other heretics and infidels and therefore periodically lashed out at Jews, especially in times of adversity. Forced conversions and expulsions flared up as early as the seventh century, then faded away until a rash of outbreaks following the millennial year 1000 and a widespread surge of attacks surrounding the First and Second Crusades (1095–1149). These were generally mob actions opposed by local priests and nobles, but they became common responses to crisis events, and in twelfth-century England they acquired a legitimizing legend, namely the blood libel or ritual murder accusation that ascribed disappearances or deaths of Christian children to an alleged Jewish need for their blood to make matzoh bread for Passover or other ritual purposes. Precisely because the charge was a blatant projection onto Jews of a corrupted form of the Catholic belief in transubstantiation—the creed that the communion wafer and wine become the real flesh and blood of Christ during the Mass—the charge stuck, and it became the pretext for numerous massacres, first in England and later in much of Europe.

By the late Middle Ages, a correlation between social crisis and the slaughter and expulsion of Jews had become firmly established. Whenever adverse developments occurred that people could not otherwise account for, they identified Jews as the agents of Satan who had caused the problems. Massacres of Jews followed the Italian famine of 1315–17 and the outbreak of the Black Death in the Rhineland in 1347, for example. Such popular panics, combined with monarchical desires to confiscate Jewish property, resulted in expulsions of Jews from England and southern Italy in 1290, from France in 1306 and again in 1394, from Spain and Portugal in 1492 and 1497, and from many German cities during the fifteenth century.

As segregation and degradation increased, so did the penetration of popular culture by denigrating images of Jews. The Passion Plays performed at Easter across Christian Europe highlighted the supposed role of Jews, rather than that of Pontius Pilate, in ordering Christ's crucifixion. Chaucer's *Canterbury Tales*, written around 1386, include a story of ritual murder by Jews in "The Prioress's Tale." The story of Shylock seeking his pound of flesh that is at the core of Shakespeare's *The Merchant of Venice*, written in the final years of the sixteenth century, had appeared in Italy more than two hundred years earlier. After 1400, church decorations included an increasing number of depictions of Jews being nursed by sows, and the first printed version of what later became the stereotypical caricature of a Jew with a beaked nose and hunched back appeared in a book of 1493.

By the time of the Reformation in the sixteenth century, hatred of Jews was widespread, and it had crystallized around two central generalizations: (1) that Jews were parasitic profiteers, intent on extracting wealth from Christians, and (2) that Jews were incorrigible instruments of Satan, intent on serving his purposes and afflicting the pious. Martin Luther gave the most extreme voice to these prejudices when he discovered that Jews were no more willing to convert to his version of Christianity than the one he claimed to have reformed. He urged Christians to burn Jews' synagogues, schools, and homes and subject Jews who would not convert to forced labor. In fact, as David Nirenberg has pointed out, "Like so many prophets before him," Luther literally "died in combat with the Jews." In the winter of 1546, he traveled to Eisleben, the city of his birth, in order to dissuade the town from giving refuge to Jews who had fled other cities. He promptly came down with a chill, nonetheless delivered several angry sermons that turned out to be the last ones of his life, and passed away. Even Luther's contemporary, the learned sixteenth-century humanist Erasmus, a man generally regarded as one of the most open-minded thinkers of his day, wrote, "If hatred of Jews makes the Christian, then we are all plenty Christian."

And yet, we all were not, so to speak. In the mid-1500s, the Netherlands welcomed the Jews expelled from Spain, just as the kings of

Poland earlier had encouraged the Jews driven from the Rhineland to migrate eastward. In the 1600s, England reversed its policy and opened its borders to Jews again. Despite the exiles from many of the territories that today compose Italy and Germany, Jews never entirely disappeared from all of them. And for all of Luther's fury, other Protestants, especially Calvinists, were respectful toward the people they saw as their religious forebears.

In other words, if hostility toward Jews was sometimes xenophobic and sometimes chimerical, it was also sometimes dormant. By the eighteenth century, hostility to Jews on various religiously rooted grounds, now fortified by centuries of segregation and condemnation, was widespread and habitual in Europe but not universal. And it was at least theoretically not murderous. The perceived problem was what the Jews believed or chose not to believe; the solution was for them to change their minds, to convert. The means to get them to do so was cruelty toward them, but generally not murder. They were to suffer, but they were also to survive.

That brings us to the second horizontal block in figure 1, the era in which the domination of thought by religion began to come to an end in the European world. The transition is beautifully and best expressed in a couplet from Alexander Pope's poem "An Essay on Man" (1734): "Know then thyself, presume not God to scan; / The proper study of mankind is man." This is a fitting epigraph for the Age of Enlightenment, also known as the Age of Discovery, and the precursor to the Age of Revolution. In these new eras, the driving question was "How can people improve the world?" Of course, labels and generalizations of this sort should be treated warily, but, broadly speaking, the eighteenth century ushered in an age whose watchwords were freedom and liberation or, as the French Revolution's slogan went, "liberty, equality, fraternity." Liberty not only from political tyranny, however, but also from intellectual restrictions, such as those set by religious authority and tradition. Alexander Pope's admonition amounted to a call to stop concentrating intellectual energy on matters like theology and to focus attention instead on the human and natural world. Of course, distinguished individuals had been doing that to some degree since the beginning of the Renaissance, but Pope's clarion call heralded a shift in emphasis, a change in the intellectual center of gravity in the Western world.

The emblematic figure in this sense was the French philosopher François-Marie Arouet, better known by his pen name of Voltaire, who mocked those who believed they inhabited "the best of all possible worlds" and goaded his readers to use their heads to improve society. A fierce critic of all traditional religions, he attacked both the Catholic Church and traditional Judaism with equal vehemence for confining people's thinking and insisting on the continued practice of ancient rituals. In championing the human capacity for improvement, Voltaire embodied the optimism of the age. He also endorsed a new form of hostility to Jews, one that hoped in a figurative sense to "kill them with kindness"—to end their difference from the rest of society by freeing them from inherited restrictions, such as ghettos and confinement to certain occupations.

In theory, this form of hostility to Judaism closely resembled its predecessor in everything but its religious foundation and method. The problem was no longer what Jews believed, though many eighteenth-century thinkers criticized Judaism as overly fixated on obeying old laws and rituals. The problem was the supposedly backward culture of intense Talmud study and rigid observance of traditional practices that prevented Jews from being free and full contributors to society. And the remedial method was no longer cruelty and suffering but kindness and opportunity—the carrot, not the stick. Jews were to be enticed out of their distinctness and into a secular form of conversion: not necessarily a change of religion but a change of everything unique about the religion's adherents, until they became indistinguishable from everyone else. Making them useful was the initial goal of Emancipation— the abolition of residential and occupational restrictions on Jews—

by the Austrian Emperor Joseph II in the 1780s, and by the French Revolution and Napoleon Bonaparte in subsequent decades, but making them similar was the ultimate purpose.

This strategy had notable successes, at least in Western Europe. But even there Judaism and differences between the customs and marriage patterns of Jews and non-Jews did not disappear. Many emancipators were disappointed with the results, even as many people who disliked Jews were, too, though for entirely different reasons.

That brings us to the third horizontal bar in figure 1, the bar concerning the period following the invention of the new word *antisemitism*. The invention marked an ominous qualitative change, in that the new form of hostility focused not on what Jews believed or how they behaved but on what they intrinsically and unchangeably supposedly are. Antisemites generally agreed, as the classification of Jews by their original language implied, that the nature of Jews, their inherited and common qualities, made them not only incapable of becoming like other people, but also fundamentally subversive of other peoples and their societies. Jews could not be changed, but only contained and then eliminated. We might call this the biologization of antisemitism, and it coincided with a shift in the central questions of intellectual and public life from "What does God want?" and its successor "How can people improve the world?" to "What material or physical laws govern us?"

Proponents of this depiction of Jews drew on both old and new forms of science. The old one was basically animal husbandry, the science of breeding. Such people argued that peoples or nationalities were essentially like breeds of horses or dogs, each with special qualities that were passed on from generation to generation and that could be enhanced by selective mating. Thus Germans, like their German shepherds, were good fighters; the French, like their poodles, were showy; and the British, like their bulldogs, were tenacious. The nineteenth century was the great age of generalization of this sort, as each competing European nationality strove to define what made it distinct and great and what made its rivals inferior. As the historian Albert Lindemann has pointed out, "beliefs in racial or ethnic determinism were the norm in most countries" in the nineteenth century, even among Jews.

This old science was reinforced by vulgarized understandings of a new one, Darwinism, the science that argued that animal and plant species survive by random, perhaps accidental, but definite adaptations to their environments. As populations of flora or fauna spread out, they become increasingly different from each other by virtue of this adaptation. Many nationalists argued that their fellow Frenchmen or Germans or Jews and so on were like species, specifically adapted to their historically different surrounding conditions and profoundly different from each other as a result. As Julius Langbehn, a widely read German antisemite, put the matter: "A Jew can no more become a German than a plum can turn into an apple."

The other newer sciences were often belief systems that we no longer consider scientific at all, but until they were invalidated, they also sustained a line of thought that exaggerated the differences among groups of human beings. These belief systems played to a widespread desire in Europe during the heyday of colonialism to show that descriptive or horizontal differences among peoples in such things as skin color and eye shape in fact denoted qualitative or vertical differences in ability—that is, superiority and inferiority. Arthur de Gobineau's three-volume *Essay on the Inequality of the Human Races*, which appeared from 1853 to 1855, became the authoritative text of this sort. It divided humanity into three great racial blocs: the white peoples, who were supposedly spiritual and creative; the yellow peoples, who were allegedly materialist and imitative; and the black ones, who were reputedly sensual and primitive. Even worse than this sort of global categorization, if that is possible, were Gobineau's warnings against race mixing. He linked the existence and endurance of a civilization with the purity of its dominant race and thus, although he was not an antisemite, provided arguments that such people later could use.

What Gobineau's and other nineteenth-century pseudosciences had in common was the claim that external qualities indicated internal ones. Among the other prototypical schools of thought were: physiognomy, the invention of Johann Lavater (1741–1801), who claimed that the shape of faces, notably the straightness of the line from brow to chin, denoted superior traits; and phrenology, the creation of Franz Joseph Gall (1758–1828), who claimed that the shape of heads did the same thing because that shape determined the configuration of the brain, and the size of its various parts determined humans' capacities. Gall's follower Anders Retzius (1796–1860) devised a system of measuring skulls and a formula for expressing the relationship between his findings that he called the cephalic index. Unsurprisingly, given his European origins, Retzius concluded that the longer and narrower the head, the more superior the person. Finally, a more legitimate field of study called philology focused not on people's appearance but on their speech. As practiced in the nineteenth century, philology traced the origins and historical relationship of languages. By the beginning of that era, scholars had established that most European languages—the exceptions are Basque, Hungarian (Magyar), and Finnish—descended from ancient Sanskrit, which had been carried from southern Asia to Europe by a people called Aryans. The point of origin and the destination are what account for titling this family of languages Indo-European.

The person who turned the descriptive classification of tongues into a hierarchical one was the German philologist Friedrich Schlegel (1772–1829), who became the godfather of the Aryan theory of transmission in a book published in 1808. He and his followers described the grammar of Sanskrit-based languages as more precise and subtle than that of other language families, especially the Semitic one that included Arabic and Hebrew, and thus as proof of higher imagination, reasoning, and intellectual growth potential on the part of those who spoke Indo-European tongues. The basis of modern antisemitism became the claim that Jews had been shaped over time—not only by their language but also by their original desert environment—into a species of people fundamentally and unchangeably different from all Europeans, who had been molded differently by the wooded and fertile setting that most of Europe provided. Moreover, because Jews were immutably alien, they had to be contained and expelled, not converted or absorbed, because— this is where the animal husbandry and Darwinism got mixed into a witches' brew—peoples could thrive, compete, and adapt only by preserving their purity, by inbreeding. Ethnic mixing inevitably corrupted the special qualities associated with each breed or nation and led to decline because the traits of the inferior partner always predominated in the offspring.

Of course, this is nonsense as genetics; even as aesthetics, it is accurate only for the sort that prevail at the Westminster Kennel Club, where a winning dog must conform perfectly to an idealized image of its breed. Nowadays we know, partly as a result of such thinking, that inbreeding actually can be harmful. Pursued obsessively, it leads in humans, as in dogs, not to greater perfection but to a host of congenital ailments and to heightened vulnerability to illness.

But the appeal of breeding as a form of public policy increased in the final decades of the nineteenth century because of widespread anxiety over what industrialization and urbanization were doing to European populations. A buzzword of the time was "degeneration," and its signs were supposedly everything from the mounting incidence of tuberculosis, alcoholism, and venereal diseases that went with crowded and poor urban conditions to the supposed brutishness and ineducability of the rapidly multiplying working classes. In this climate, support for ideas of improving the human stock by selective breeding increased rapidly; indeed, such ideas were considered the cutting edge of sophistication. Their chief proponent in the

English-speaking world was Francis Galton (1822–1911), who coined the term "eugenics" for his program of human betterment. In Germany, the equivalent figure was Alfred Ploetz (1860–1940), who preferred the term "racial hygiene" to describe his system of defending the development of the "West Aryan" or "Germanic race" from the supposedly counterproductive consequences of what he termed the "growing protection of the weak." Chief among the protective measures he advocated was the killing of deformed or handicapped children, so that they would not burden healthy people or reproduce physical or mental defects.

Although these doctrines spoke a language of racial "improvement," the measures they proposed were profoundly fatalistic and reactionary. The message of Galton and Ploetz was that throwing money at poor people's problems was pointless; they existed because poor people were less able or, in pseudo-Darwinian language, "fit" for survival in life's struggles. Thus, if one wanted to improve humanity, these eugenicists or racial hygienists contended, the way forward was not to help the downtrodden by building better housing, improving working conditions, and raising the level of public health, for example, but instead to reduce reproduction by the poor and diseased and to increase it by their betters. Galton's successors labeled these two processes "negative" and "positive" eugenics.

Neither these doctrines nor their founders were necessarily or explicitly antisemitic, but their conceptions of what needed to be improved in various populations and what needed to be bred out of them swiftly spilled over into the arguments of racists and became adapted to their purposes. This reinforced the pseudoscientific pose that bigotry toward Jews assumed with the coinage of the word "antisemitism." Once Jews were defined as distinct from others, then their presence could be depicted as an invitation to destructive cross-breeding; once they were declared the embodiments of unwanted characteristics, their removal from the national body could be justified as a form of racial hygiene.

Thus, by the late nineteenth century, European antisemitism had a long and varied history. The persecution of Jews had been recurrent but far from universal or continuous. Attacks on them had evolved over time from ones ostensibly inspired by religious differences to ones that expressed physical fear. Of course, the overlapping phases of Jewish stigmatization always had one constant element: a depiction of Jews as contaminating or corrupting. Their proximity was seen as potentially undermining: first to Christians' faith, then to liberals' belief in human improvement, and finally to the strength and health of other populations.

Yet persecution appeared to be on the wane at the end of the nineteenth century, even though new justifications for it had come into being. The expansion of Jews' rights contained the seeds of boisterous backlash that reinforced old prejudices but failed to erase Jews' gains. At the same time that antisemitism seemed to surge and swell, it remained politically largely impotent.

EMANCIPATION AND BACKLASH

In order to explain why Jews encountered a resurgence of agitation against them in the late nineteenth and early twentieth centuries, we must shift our attention away from the ideas that supposedly legitimated hostility and toward the circumstances that made certain groups of people receptive to it. The result is an ironic and somewhat contradictory story of widening opportunities and rights for Jews accompanied by ever more fervent and frustrated attempts to reverse this process.

Until what historians call the "long nineteenth century"—the 125-year period between the outbreak of the French Revolution in 1789 and the onset of World War I in 1914—most Jews lived in very confined worlds. Jews could be moneylenders, tavern keepers, itinerant peddlers, or cattle buyers who came in contact with non-Jewish customers; in parts of Eastern Europe Jews often managed estates for noblemen and thus dealt with tenants; and observant Jews may have had a reliable non-Jewish employee who came in to light their fires and do any other work that was forbidden on the Sabbath by the 613 laws. Otherwise Jews had very limited interaction with and visibility to non-Jews.

Both of these circumstances began to change in the 1780s. The first crack in the wall of religiously inspired restrictions on Jews came via the succession of Patents of Toleration issued by Austrian Emperor Joseph II for disparate parts of his realm between 1781 and 1789. Of these, the most famous was the Edict of Tolerance of January 2, 1782 governing Vienna and its environs, which set forth the general purpose of "making the Jews useful to the state." To that end, the edict opened Christian schools and universities to Jews, along with numerous trades and commercial occupations previously denied to them; permitted them to employ Christian servants; and relieved them of two conspicuous burdens: a special tax and the obligation of men to wear beards. But the edict also severely restricted Jews' abilities to settle and worship in and around the Austrian capital and to enforce documents written in Hebrew or Yiddish. The point of that last prohibition was to make Jews learn to read and write German, and it succeeded to a remarkable degree. In the German-speaking lands of the early nineteenth century, Jews enjoyed a higher literacy rate than even their gentile neighbors, who were relatively well educated by European standards.

Much more far-reaching than Joseph II's edict was the enactment of the Declaration of the Rights of Man on August 26, 1789, during the heady first days of the French Revolution. That document declared, "Men are born and remain free and equal in rights. Social distinctions may be founded only upon the general good," and went on to proclaim that all citizens are equal in the eyes of the law and therefore equally entitled to hold office and to do "everything that injures no one else." But it took another two years, until September 27, 1791, for the National Assembly to pass a law making Jews full citizens of France. Although Napoleon backtracked to some degree on Jewish equality in France over the next few decades, his armies spread French ideas and practice across much of Europe, tearing down ghetto walls and removing occupational and political restrictions. He thus set in motion both the modern process of Jewish emancipation and the backlash against it that produced the modern form of antisemitism. As noted earlier, the roots of modern antisemitism are in religious differences: Christianity caused Jews both to suffer and to survive for centuries in Europe. But the form of hostility toward Jews that arose in the late nineteenth century and that called itself antisemitism is fundamentally a political movement, an expression of resistance to the emancipation of Jews that began in the late eighteenth century, gathered strength throughout Western and to a lesser degree Central Europe in the nineteenth century, and then reached even into the eastern parts of the continent with the Russian revolution in 1917.

Formally speaking, emancipation was the process by which Jews were freed of all occupational, residential, and political restrictions and placed on a legal status of equality with all other citizens of a state. But to put it that way is too abstract; that definition ignores what emancipation meant in human, day-to-day terms, including what it felt like to the non-Jews who experienced it. It meant the emergence of Jews from pariah status; it meant almost literally their "entrance" into society and into regular contact with non-Jews; and, above all, it meant two possibilities that aroused opposition: first, people who had previously been kept from competing with the practitioners of certain trades and professions now could do so; and second, people who had previously been derided as benighted and backward, as dirty and superstitious, could ascend to positions of authority over non-Jews, over people accustomed to seeing themselves as "better" than Jews. Fear of this second possibility was particularly pronounced in a by no means unusual Bavarian petition of January 10, 1850, opposing equality for Jews. In that document, eighty-three citizens of the town of Hilders in the province of Lower Franconia, which eighty years later became a Nazi stronghold, pleaded for the repeal of emancipation and, in particular, "that . . . no Jew be admitted to a judicial or revenue office, lest we have to humble ourselves before the Jews."

These emotional and practical effects of emancipation go a long way toward explaining the intense resistance it encountered and the halting and erratic nature of its course. After the fall of Napoleon in 1815, the Austrian Empire retained the reforms that Joseph II had introduced, but France was the only other state in Europe that did not turn the clock back; the only legal difference that remained there between Christians and Jews was that the state paid priests and ministers, but not rabbis. In 1830, that distinction disappeared, too. But everywhere else where the French had brought emancipation the new or restored rulers rolled it back, even if sometimes only briefly. Then, between 1830, when Belgium established civil equality upon achieving its independence, and 1871, when newly unified Germany did so, every state that had once been under French domination, along with a few countries in Western and northern Europe that had not, such as Great Britain, Sweden, and Switzerland, reversed the rollback and completed the emancipation process.

Emancipation did not extend, however, to the lands of the Russian Empire, including the largest population of Jews in Europe in the Pale of Settlement, the parts of today's Poland, Lithuania, Belarus, and Ukraine to which most Jews were confined until the revolution that overthrew the tsars in 1917. Neither were the Jews emancipated in Romania until the end of World War I, and then only at the insistence of the victorious Allies. The late onset of emancipation in these regions and the strong resistance to it there are significant, for these are the areas where the Nazis later found most of their victims and received the most widespread local assistance in their murder.

Emancipation was the political project of people called liberals, and it rose or fell everywhere according to their strength. Who were they? The word "liberal" derives from the Latin word *liber*, which means "free." They were the advocates of political and economic freedom, of (a) the rule of law, as created through constitutions and popular elections, not by royal fiat; (b) open and competitive markets, as opposed to guilds that restricted access to an economic activity and tolls and tariffs that restricted the movement of goods; and (c) the importance of ability over birth, as opposed to the aristocratic principle. Uniting the liberals' political and economic tenets was a general openness to change expressed by the French phrase *laissez faire*, "allow to do" or, more figuratively, "let happen," the phrase connoting a willingness to permit economic events to take their course and to generate a continuous process of what Joseph Schumpeter later dubbed "creative destruction."

The liberals' heyday in Europe was exactly the period when emancipation triumphed, the years between 1830 and 1870, but the strength of liberalism, like the pace of emancipation, declined from west to east, from Britain and France to Russia. The farther west, the quicker the liberals' ascent to power, and the quicker emancipation came; the farther east, the less influence they exerted and the less change occurred in the legal position of Jews and their interaction with gentiles. In England, a man of Jewish descent, Benjamin Disraeli, could become prime minister in the 1860s. But in the Russian Empire such a thing was unthinkable, the religiously rooted condemnation of Jews remained the official doctrine of the state, and violent attacks on Jews remained an ever-present possibility. As we shall see, Germany was "the land in the middle," both geographically and with regard to the pace and extent of emancipation.

The liberals' triumph was gradual and incomplete because it encountered resistance almost everywhere, though to varying degrees. To understand why, we need to look at what else was happening while emancipation was spreading. In the nineteenth century, six sweeping trends transformed European society.

First, Europe experienced a population explosion from about 190 million people in 1800 to about 420 million in 1900. In some places, the increases were even greater: The total inhabitants of England,

Scotland, and Wales tripled from 1821 to 1911; the populations of the Netherlands, Denmark, Norway, and Germany almost did so from 1816 to 1909/10; and those of Belgium and Sweden grew by 250 percent. Amid this massive upheaval, the European Jewish population multiplied even faster, from 1.5 million in 1800 to 8.7 million in 1900 (an almost sixfold increase). And it multiplied fastest where it was poorest and most persecuted, in the Russian Empire, which created enormous pressure on Jews to get out somehow to somewhere.

Second, Europe underwent widespread industrialization, which transformed landscapes, created massive factories, provided employment for those surging numbers of people, multiplied goods, and in the process extinguished entire lines of work. Factories, not cobblers, came to produce most shoes. Textile mills turned out cloth far more rapidly and cheaply than individual weavers at home. Whole trades disappeared—how many people today know what a "cooper" is or a "wainwright"?—and the skilled workers who populated them, known as artisans, lost their livelihoods and social standing. But mass production was sensitive to fluctuations of supply and demand, and mill owners tended to push the consequences of these fluctuations onto workforces, with the result that industrialization created cycles of boom and bust, widespread resentment, efforts to push back in the form of unions and organized socialist movements, and enormous social tensions.

Third, with industrialization came urbanization: The population of London grew from 900,000 to 4.7 million between 1800 and 1900, that of Paris from 600,000 to 3.6 million, and that of Berlin from 170,000 to 2.7 million. In 1800, only two European cities had more than half a million inhabitants, London and Paris; in 1900, twenty-three cities did, including seven with more than one million people. Everywhere Jews were conspicuous participants in this migration from the countryside to the cities, and their share in the urban populations, along with their visibility, generally rose dramatically, especially in Vienna, Berlin, Warsaw, and Budapest.

Fourth, extensive improvements in transportation, notably the railroad and steam shipping, accelerated trade and opened Europe to increased competition, especially in agriculture, from newly developing regions, such as the Great Plains of the United States and the pampas of Argentina. This put substantial downward pressure on the prices European farmers could get for their harvests. It also meant that the handicrafts of some regions could be wiped out by the industrial production of others. Increasing exposure to market forces bred widespread insecurity and free-floating desire to blame someone for it.

Fifth, increasing democratization occurred in the forms of successive extensions of voting rights, though as yet only to men, and progressive though incomplete reductions in the privileges and political powers of aristocrats. The results included the rise of mass politics and political parties and of the popular press, much of it of the tabloid sort. Political agitation became a more regular feature of life, as newspapers sought to whip up circulation through sensational accounts, especially of mysterious, behind-the-scenes wire pulling. The term "muckraking" is a creation of the era, and there was plenty of it going on in the last thirty years of the nineteenth century, when one financial and/or political scandal after another occurred.

Sixth, though religious observance remained important, the nineteenth century saw considerable secularization in thought and education, and the trends were resisted fiercely by the papacy, many Protestants, and the Orthodox Church in the East. In fields as disparate as theology, where David Friedrich Strauss launched the critical historical study of Jesus, or biology, where Darwin advanced his theory of the long-term evolution of all life through adaptation, the Christian worldview and traditional piety came under attack and became increasingly regarded in sophisticated quarters as passé. Perhaps the most advanced state of secularization was reached in France, which passed the Ferry Laws between 1879 and 1886, removing elementary education from the purview of the Catholic Church and setting up an explicitly anticlerical school system.

In short, the nineteenth century was an era of rapid, constant, and often bewildering change, and change always unnerves and/or harms some people. The "losers" were clear: clergy who experienced declining deference to their persons and views; nobles who no longer monopolized office or found their lands a guarantee of great relative wealth; conservatives who disliked change in principle and parliamentary government in practice; farmers who faced international competition and thus downward pressure on their incomes; artisans driven out of business by factory production; property owners who feared the growing strength, as the century progressed, of workers' unions and workers' political movements, notably socialism; and even university graduates, who faced steep competition for professional positions. Of course, not every member of these groups experienced a decline of wealth or status during the nineteenth century, but a good many of them did.

Members of all these groups sought explanations for what was happening, and more importantly for what was going wrong for them. In such a context, conspiracy theories found an audience. They were easy to understand, and, then as now, no matter how convoluted, such theories were precise about who to blame for events, namely whoever is apparently benefiting from them. The perpetual motto of conspiracy mongers is the Latin phrase *cui bono*. Who benefits? Or in modern parlance, "Follow the money."

Many Jews were among the conspicuous and principal beneficiaries of the open and competitive universe that liberalism fostered. Many Jews also remained grindingly poor, especially the farther east one looked in Europe. But the number who became prosperous during the nineteenth century, the number who seized on the opportunities that came with emancipation, was real and striking. This was especially true in the spheres of banking and commerce and the professions of law and medicine. In a sense, the Jews of nineteenth-century Europe engaged in what sociologists and historians think of as classic first-generation, upwardly mobile "immigrant" behavior in the United States. Newly emancipated Jews sought out and strove for places in lucrative and secure walks of life, activities that would make their and their children's existences reliably better than their parents'. And, indeed, most of these Jews were immigrants or at least internal ones. Massive numbers of Jews from the far eastern provinces of the Austro-Hungarian monarchy (Galicia, Ruthenia, and Bukovina) migrated to Vienna and its environs, where their traditional garb and their Yiddish speech, which sounded to German ears like a corrupted and grammatically simplified form of their language, later aroused the ire of Adolf Hitler. In Paris, much of the Jewish population arrived in the nineteenth century from Alsace, the border province that Germany took away from France in 1871. In Berlin, a similar inflow came from Posen, a largely rural eastern province that Prussia had stripped from Poland in the late eighteenth century.

Invisible among college students, lawyers, and doctors and rare among business leaders in 1800, Jews seemed disproportionately present in all these prized roles by the 1880s in many places, and even more so by the early 1900s. Here are some illustrative figures from Central Europe:

In the 1880s, Jews accounted for only 3–4 percent of the Austrian population, but 17 percent of all university students and one-third of those at the University of Vienna; in Hungary, Jews constituted 5 percent of the population, but 25 percent of the university students and 43 percent of those at the leading technological university; in Prussia, the biggest state in the German Empire, Jews made up less than 1 percent of the population in 1910–11, but 5.4 percent of the university students, and 17 percent of those at the University of Berlin.

At the turn of the century in Vienna, 62 percent of the lawyers, half the doctors and dentists, 45 percent of the university medical faculty, and one-fourth of the total faculty were Jews; so were some

55 percent of the professional journalists, 40 percent of the directors of publicly traded banks, and 70 percent of the board members of the Vienna stock exchange. In Hungary at the same time, Jews accounted for 34 percent of the lawyers and 48 percent of the physicians.

In 1912, 20 percent of the millionaires in Prussia were Jews; in Germany as a whole, Jews came to 0.95 percent of the population but made up 31 percent of the wealthiest families.

Of course, this surge of success was not simply explicable as standard, upwardly mobile immigrant behavior; it also had specific cultural origins. Much of Jews' initial success in commercial activities represented an extension of the few economic roles previously permitted to them. Moneylenders became bankers; peddlers became shopkeepers and later owned and ran department stores; and cattle traders became brokers of commodities and stocks. And the ascent of Jews in the professions certainly drew on the premium their families and faith placed on learning. The discipline in childhood of religious study with heavy doses of memorization and debate over the meaning of texts is not bad training for going into medicine and law. That may have been what Albert Einstein had in mind when he supposedly quipped that the extent of Jewish academic success in nineteenth-century Europe suggested that the Jews had spent the last two thousand years preparing for university entrance exams.

In nineteenth-century Europe, most Jews did not become successful and/or rich in the ways just listed, but the number and percentage of Jews rose among the people who did achieve these forms of success. This pattern was noticed, envied, and resented by the social groups that felt and often were disadvantaged or threatened by the change and competition that liberalism favored. Unlike some disappointed emancipators who thought Jews had not taken enough advantage of liberalism by becoming just like everyone else, members of the declining groups argued that Jews had taken too much advantage of the opportunities liberalism opened up. The tendency within these groups often was to confuse correlation with cause, to conclude that the rise of some Jews resulted from a conspiracy by all Jews. A group that benefited from modernization became pilloried as its destructive driving force. Of course, one can hear in these charges echoes of the medieval tradition of blaming Jews for plagues or other catastrophes. But the linkage also echoed the modern socialist movement, which posited a conspiracy on the part of the capitalists to maximize their wealth at the expense of the proletariat. In fact, leftists derided antisemitism as "the socialism of fools," the belief system of people who mistook the identity of their real exploiters by focusing on Jews instead of capitalists. Whatever its medieval or modern inspirations, the connection between the incidence of antisemitism and the extent of perceived economic crisis is close; a cliché of the subject is that the appeal of antisemitism rises and falls in inverse relationship with the stock market.

Countering the antisemites' association of Jews with commercial corruption was made more difficult by the fact that many of the late nineteenth century's worst economic and political scandals did involve noticeable numbers of Jews. The most notorious instance in France, the Panama Scandal of 1888–92, centered on widespread bribery of French officials and parliamentarians in order to obtain loans to finance a French company seeking to build a canal through Panama. In the end, more than one hundred deputies, senators, ministers, and ex-ministers were exposed as corrupt, and thousands of small investors lost their savings. The bagmen who bought and paid these politicians were almost exclusively Jews, and the case was grist for antisemitic propaganda that attacked their supposed greed and selfishness.

In sum, the more liberalism triumphed, the more visible and successful Jews became, and the more groups that felt endangered or harmed by economic and political trends lent an ear to a convenient explanation of their troubles. That explanation blamed the Jews and promised relief by repealing emancipation and relegating them to their former contained status. The prevalence of such views seemed to grow with the rise of mass politics and the popular press, both of which encouraged agitators and ideologues. Antisemitism became vocal and loud in many parts of Europe after 1879, and the number of its spokespersons multiplied. Wherever they appeared, such figures as Édouard Drumont in France, Georg von Schoenerer in Austria, and Hermann Ahlwardt in Germany had one thing in common. They came from and spoke to the social groups described here as susceptible to discontent with the direction of the modern world. Wilhelm Marr, the man most responsible for popularizing the word "antisemitism," almost prototypically embodied the frustration and downward mobility that characterized those who found solace in attacking Jews. By the late 1870s, he had failed in succession as a businessman, a journalist, a politician, and a husband, in the last case to a succession of Jewish and half-Jewish wives.

And yet the story of emancipation during the long nineteenth century ends with a paradox. Despite their volubility, antisemitic political parties and movements had very little to show for their agitation prior to World War I. Yes, Karl Lueger campaigned on an antisemitic platform, got elected Lord Mayor of Vienna repeatedly, and served from 1897 till his death in 1910. But he also did the Jews of the city no practical harm—in fact, they experienced a sort of golden age during his time as mayor—and his popularity was atypical. At the same time, Budapest elected a Jewish mayor, Adam Vazsonyi, and in 1895, the Hungarian parliament enacted a law that placed the Jewish and Christian faiths on the same legal footing. Indeed, after 1870, emancipation was not rolled back in a single European state. And in some countries, such as France, Italy, and Austria, Jews gained access to the historic bastions of the aristocracy in the diplomatic and officer corps and the university professorships. The reason for this is that, despite all the disruptive effects of modernization and change, the trajectory for most people in Western and Central Europe during the decades preceding World War I was steadily upward as standards of living improved. Occasional recessions were sharp but usually brief or merely sectoral; they hit particular economic sectors, usually farmers, harder than others, but scarcely affected everyone else. In this context, the laments of the pessimists and their claims that the Jews were at the root of all evil never stopped, but these cries also never gained a wide enough following to change laws.

Whatever the popular strength of antisemitism anywhere, it proved really dangerous to Jews only when powerful officials or elites set out to exploit it or harness it to their purposes. The most famous examples are the Dreyfus affair of 1894–1906, in which conservative and self-serving army officers tried to pin spy charges on a Jewish colleague, and the ritual murder trial of Mendel Beilis in Kiev in 1913. But Dreyfus ultimately was exonerated, though the effort took years, and a jury of non-Jews, half of whom belonged to an antisemitic organization called the Union of the Russian People, actually acquitted Beilis. Even when power holders sought to exploit antisemitism for their own purposes, an aroused or embarrassed public could and did fight back successfully.

Still, the message conveyed by both the Dreyfus and the Beilis affairs regarding the strength of antisemitism was ambiguous. The evidence is strong, as Barbara Tuchman pointed out in the 1960s and several other scholars have since, that Captain Alfred Dreyfus of the French army General Staff did not come under suspicion of being a spy for the German embassy in Paris solely or even primarily because he was a Jew. Equally important in leading to his indictment were two other facts: His handwriting strongly resembled that of the most incriminating document in the matter, the famous *bordereau* found in a wastebasket of that embassy by a cleaning woman; and he was a rather remote and condescending person, much given to bragging about his wealth. The French officer corps was monarchist, Catholic, and antiliberal, but an average of 3 percent of the officers were Jews at any given time during the half-century leading up to World War I, which was thirty to sixty times their share in the total French population in that era, so the institution was not overtly antisemitic. In other words, Dreyfus's military peers and superiors turned on him initially and impetuously in 1894 because they needed a culprit, the handwriting evidence seemed plausible, and they disliked him personally. They persisted in professing his guilt because they feared that backtracking would embarrass the army to whose prestige they were devoted. The antisemitic gutter press turned Dreyfus's heritage into the central issue in the case, not the army, and the prosecutors at his trial did not even mention the subject. At the moment of Dreyfus's conviction in shamelessly manipulated proceedings, even prominent Jewish leaders, as well as Jean Jaurès, the leading French socialist who later was one of Dreyfus's most vigorous defenders, believed in his guilt.

Another disconcerting fact is that the man who first identified another, more plausible spy within the General Staff and whose efforts ultimately led to Dreyfus's vindication was exactly the sort of person usually depicted as having persecuted him. The hero's name was Colonel Georges Picquart, and he was a conservative Catholic with distinctly negative attitudes toward Jews. So were Captain Louis Cuignet and Minister of War Godefroy Cavaignac, the men who later exposed the perjurer who had deflected attention from Picquart's alternative suspect. Finally, Émile Zola, the famous writer who led the crusade to free Dreyfus, articulated crude forms of racial determinism of the sort discussed earlier in this chapter, and these sometimes bordered on antisemitism. He fought for Dreyfus not to defend a Jew from persecution but to combat the Catholics, reactionaries, and militarists he held responsible for Dreyfus's prosecution. In the words of one sharp observer, Zola and the leading Dreyfusards were "enemies of the antisemites, not of antisemitism." The Dreyfus affair stirred up and bequeathed a great deal of antisemitism, but it did not play out along strict party lines, and its resolution was not an unqualified victory over prejudice.

Mendel Beilis appears to have been set up by a local group of prosecutors interested in placating public opinion in Kiev and by several ministers in Moscow who were playing to the deep-seated antisemitism of Tsar Nicholas II. These people connected Beilis to the murder of a thirteen-year-old boy named Andrei Yushchinsky, whose body was discovered in a cave just outside Kiev, for two purely circumstantial reasons: first, the body had been stabbed in ways that supposedly facilitated the draining of blood, as in the sort of ritual murder connected to the blood libel, and second, Beilis managed a brick factory located near the cave and was a Jew. But, unlike in the Dreyfus case, the frame-up took in almost no one. From the beginning, local newspapers questioned the allegations, and a municipal detective swiftly produced evidence that linked a local gang to the murder. Apparently, that gang had gathered up a great deal of loot during the pogroms in Kiev in 1905–06 and hoped to instigate a new round by butchering a body in a manner intended to suggest a ritual murder and cast suspicion on a Jew. Once again, as in the Dreyfus affair, many of Beilis's local defenders were antisemites who simply hated those attacking Beilis more than they hated Jews and thought that the integrity of their own kind was more at stake than the rights of Jews.

In the decades leading up to World War I, the prevailing combination of constant antisemitic agitation, on the one hand, and general growth of Jews' rights and opportunities, on the other, goes a long way toward explaining twin developments among Jews that were the mirror image of what was happening among other Europeans. I am referring to the launching by Theodor Herzl in 1897 of the movement called Zionism, the drive for a Jewish homeland that soon centered on Jerusalem, which occurred in reaction to enduring antisemitism, and to the very limited success of this movement in winning support from Jews in the early decades of this century. Although obsessive and noisy, antisemitism not only generally failed to bend governments to its will, but also generally failed to panic Jews into thinking that their only sustainable future lay in founding their own country. Persistent antisemitism drove millions of Jews to leave Eastern Europe between 1880 and 1910, but rarely for Palestine. Instead, they came overwhelmingly to the United States.

To return to the question with which this chapter began: Why the Jews? Because an ancient tradition of blaming them for disasters, both present and prospective, a tradition deeply rooted in religious rivalry and superstition, persisted into the modern world and even assumed new forms during the eighteenth and nineteenth centuries. That tradition and its adaptations remained available to wax and wane as the impulse to blame did. In the decade immediately preceding World War I, the blaming impulse seemed to course primarily through other channels, especially those of class warfare, and antisemitic outbursts generally were held in check. At the middle of the continent, the territories that became the German Empire in 1871 and the Republic of Austria in 1918 remained for antisemites epicenters of agitation but also of frustration. We will see next why that was so and why the situation changed for the worse during that war and in its aftermath.

CHAPTER 2

ATTACKERS:
Why the Germans?

ANY EUROPEAN ASKED in the immediate aftermath of the Drey-fus and Beilis affairs to identify the country most likely to persecute Jews in the future surely would have named France or Russia. Yet Germans became the principal tormenters of Europe's Jews in the second quarter of the twentieth century. Explaining how this happened involves examining a highly contradictory history.

NATION AND *VOLK*

Perhaps one way of approaching the contradictions is to remember that Germany is the land in the middle of Europe. In the nineteenth century, this was true not only geographically, looking west to east, but also with regard to political structure and the relative strength of antisemitism. The states to Germany's west, notably Great Britain, France, Holland, and Belgium, were all more democratic countries than the German Empire that came together in January 1871. They were constitutional monarchies or republics in which parliaments elected by steadily expanding sectors of the population chose the cabinets and prime ministers that made the major decisions, not kings or queens. To the east, the Russian Empire, on the other hand, was the last great autocracy in Europe, a state in which the tsar claimed to rule alone by divine right, and where a parliament did not exist until 1906. Even thereafter, the tsar claimed the right to dismiss that body whenever he chose and to appoint his ministers without regard to its preferences.

Under the German constitution of 1871, that nation was a political and constitutional hybrid, a mix of these two systems. On the one hand, it had a parliament (the Reichstag) chosen by the broadest electorate then allowed in Europe, all male citizens over the age of twenty-five voting by nominally secret ballot. On the other hand, the parliament had very restricted powers: it could set the national budget annually, but the 75–80 percent of expenditures that went to the military could be debated and authorized only once every seven, later five, years, and the government could take out loans without parliament's permission. In other words, the power of the purse that is the foundation of legislative authority was severely circumscribed. Parliament did not select the prime minister, called the chancellor; the kaiser (emperor) did, and he had exclusive power to declare war in response to an attack and to command the army. In short, the German Empire that lasted from 1871 to 1918 was an authoritarian, militarized country with the trappings of democracy, one that blended elements of the form of governance that had prevailed in Europe before the French Revolution and still prevailed in Russia with the newer form of parliamentary rule that had developed in Great Britain during the eighteenth century and on the continent after 1789.

Something similar can be said about antisemitism in this newly unified state. If we describe the period of post-Napoleonic emancipation as extending from 1815 to 1918, then Germany's enactment of equality for Jews before the law, which occurred in 1869 for the northern two-thirds of the country and in 1871 for the entire realm, falls almost precisely at the midpoint. The breakthrough came after emancipation in virtually every country to Germany's west or north and before emancipation in most of the lands to its south and east, Austria-Hungary being the exception. Germany occupied a middle point not only temporally but also in the forms and extent of emancipation, which were more complete than to the country's east but less than to its west or south.

Another distinct feature of nineteenth-century Germany both determined the timing and influenced the extent of emancipation there. Germany was not only the land in the middle, it was also, in the eyes of its citizens, *"die verspätete Nation,"* the delayed nation. Like Italy, which also completed national unification only in 1870, the word "Germany" was only a geographical term prior to that year. An entity called, in English, the "Holy Roman Empire of the German Nation" had existed until 1806, but a truer description of reality would have been "of the German nations." It was a very loose association under a single monarch of many highly autonomous entities, 1,789 of them, in fact, in 1789. Most Germans thought of themselves as Bavarians, Prussians, Swabians, Hessians, Westphalians, and so on, and most of these names of duchies and kingdoms derived from the Latin names of the tribes that had inhabited each centuries earlier. Bavaria comes from *Bajuvarii*, and Prussia from *Borusii*. Insofar as a sense of German nationalism developed during the nineteenth century, it did so in reaction to and rejection of the French conquest and occupation under Napoleon, and it crystallized around the only idea that could unite so much difference, the notion that all the tribes were related and parts of a common people, or *Volk*.

The founding father of this line of thought was Johann Gottfried Herder, who did his most significant work before the armies of the French Revolution got to Germany and died while they were there. He maintained that nationalities are "wonderfully separated . . . by languages, inclinations, and characters," and that each has an essence, a special set of core characteristics possessed by nearly all people born into it. He was not hostile to Jews, and though he insisted on enduring national differences rooted in different languages, he refused to postulate hierarchies of languages and peoples. "Every nation bears within itself the standard of its perfection," he said. But his sentimental glorification of the unchanging virtues of the German *Volk*, along with his insistence that "every human perfection is national," encouraged a self-exalting quality in German nationalism.

Establishing precisely what this *Volk* had in common was the great task of German nationalist thinkers during the early nineteenth century. They labored to identify, some would say "invent," a collective German nature, and they began by defining it around what Germans in the early 1800s were collectively against: the conquering French and the ideas they had brought with them and stood for. Since emancipation of the Jews was a French import, many German nationalists rejected it as the product of an alien spirit. One of the earliest exponents of this rejection was Johann Gottlieb Fichte, a philosopher who in 1808 delivered a series of lectures published under the title *Addresses to the German Nation*. Fichte's animosity toward Jews predated his nationalism; in the late 1790s, he had called Jews "a state within a state" and had spoken out against their emancipation. Now he flatly argued that "making Jews free German citizens would hurt the German nation" and identified antisemitism with German patriotism. As for the nature of Germanness, he located it in the heroic and martial virtues that Tacitus had ascribed to the German tribes seventeen centuries earlier.

During the later years of the French occupation, the Brothers Grimm began collecting folktales as sources for the essence of Germanness. Though not explicitly anti-French or antisemitic, their enterprise was implicitly exclusionist. The goal was to establish the human qualities that were intrinsically, continuously, and definitively German, qualities that, drawing on Herder, could not be possessed or combined in the same way by any other nationality. Ironically, the most famous tales that the Grimms reproduced—

the ones known as Snow White, Red Riding Hood, and Sleeping Beauty—were, in fact, French in origin. The brothers learned them from Hessians descended from Huguenots—that is, from French Protestant immigrants. This telling fact highlights the artificiality of the Grimms' quest to maximize national and ethnic differences. Nonetheless, by the middle of the nineteenth century, this sort of thinking produced Richard Wagner's pamphlet "Jewishness in Music." It asserted that genuine musical works of art were products of the profound German spirit, to which Jews had no access, which is why they supposedly could produce only shallow and artificial works. The very notion of "German culture" (*Kultur*) had become a prized family birthright that no outsider could inherit or exercise.

All of this made the German sense of nationality somewhat different from that which developed in Britain and France. In Great Britain, the cohering principle was a Protestant monarchy, and it embraced and pulled together different ethnicities—English, Scottish, Welsh, and Scotch Irish. In France, the glue after 1789 was allegiance to the nation—whether it was republic, empire, or kingdom—and citizenship was open to any free person, regardless of race, creed, or color. French reading primers may have begun with the words "Our ancestors the Gauls," but loyalty, not lineage, determined citizenship, and anyone born on the soil of France was, in principle, equal in its eyes. In Germany, and in the multiple states that preceded its unification, citizenship was more exclusive; it derived from one's parents, not the accident of where one was born, and was generally difficult for immigrants or outsiders to acquire.

These conceptual developments help explain the contested status of emancipation in Germany after Napoleon's fall, and the halting and relatively slow pace of its progress between 1828 (when the Kingdom of Württemberg became the first German state to enact lasting emancipation) and 1864 (when the city of Frankfurt became the last to do so before the spread of civil equality to all of the north of Germany in 1869 and to the south two years later). The process required forty-three years from beginning to end because resistance was considerable. It sometimes took violent form, as in the Hep-Hep riots, which began in Würzburg and Frankfurt in 1819, spread to thirty other cities, and lasted for two months. The instigators were small-scale craftsmen and merchants angry at the prospect of competition if Jews were made citizens. One of the rioters' spokesmen, the writer Hartwig von Hundt-Radowsky, declared that the Jews' "freedom to choose their own trades . . . is also a license to plunge Christians into misery." Usually the resistance remained rhetorical; nonetheless, it was impassioned. Representative examples are some of the poems of Heinrich Hoffmann von Fallersleben, who also wrote the words to what has been Germany's national anthem ever since 1922, and the numerous petitions against Jewish equality that were submitted to the Frankfurt parliament when it met in 1848 to write an ultimately abortive constitution for a united Germany. Most of these pleas came from small towns and rural farming communities, and most emphasized traditional complaints about supposed Jewish profiteering. Wherever and whenever it occurred, however, resistance to emancipation had a unifying theme: They are fundamentally different from us—less honest and less spiritual—and can never become like us.

But emancipation came, and it came in tandem with national unification in 1867–71, because liberals were the chief parliamentary patrons of both causes. Achieving one meant, to liberals, insisting on the other. Otto von Bismarck, the conservative Prussian leader who masterminded the three wars against Denmark, Austria, and France that forged German unification, initially found working with the liberals convenient, so he accepted the establishment of full civil and political equality for Jews at the time. But Bismarck was no liberal himself, and he was no fan of political equality in general. He was a fierce defender of his aristocratic caste, the Prussian Junkers, and determined to protect its economic interests and to preserve its near monopoly on leading positions in the government and the military.

If emancipation rode to success on the back of national unification, the backlash against emancipation gained strength when the
economic consequences of unification began to look adverse. In
1873, the German stock markets, which had been driven upwards by
an inflow of investment capital in the form of enormous indemnity
payments from the defeated French, abruptly plummeted. The event
has gone down in German history as the founders' crash (*Gründer-
krach*), since it came so soon after the founding of the unified empire.
The trigger was the collapse of some railroad shares promoted by
a baptized entrepreneur of Jewish descent named Bethel Henry
Strousberg. A year later, a journalist named Otto Glagau published
a series of articles in the popular weekly magazine *Die Gartenlaube*
(The Garden Bower) alleging that the crisis had been brought on
by stock manipulators, "ninety percent" of whom were Jews. The
Catholic newspaper *Germania* soon spread the charges, and in 1877
Glagau republished his articles as a book, adding an introduction
that read, in vitriolic part:

> No longer should we tolerate Jews pushing themselves
> everywhere to the foreground. . . . They push us Chris-
> tians continuously aside, they press us to the wall, they
> take away the air we breathe. In fact, they exercise domi-
> nation over us . . . and they exert an extremely unwhole-
> some influence. . . . The whole history of the world knows
> no other example of a homeless, definitively physically
> and psychically degenerate people, simply through fraud
> and cunning . . . ruling over the orbit of the world.

Meanwhile, Germany's leading conservative newspaper, the *Kreuz-
zeitung*, had gotten into the act. In mid-1875, it published a series
of five articles that purported to disclose how the policies of German government and business were conducted "almost exclusively in favor of our co-citizens of the Mosaic faith and Jewish

nationality," largely because these policies were secretly directed by a Jewish banker in Berlin, Gerson von Bleichröder, who was Bismarck's personal advisor. And, finally, in 1876, the first general secretary of the German Conservative Party, the political vehicle of landowners and agricultural regions, a man named Carl Wilmanns, gave this school of antisemitism a popular catchphrase when he titled a book *The "Golden" International*. Accusing the Jews of constituting a rich, self-interested, unpatriotic, and transnational conspiracy to promote their own wealth, the work went through six editions within a few months.

In short, the 1870s illustrated the force of the remark that antisemitism rises and falls in inverse relationship to the stock market. In that decade, when the market crashed, bigotry rose. The economic fallout of the stock market crash, in the forms of increased unemployment and lost savings, was substantial. The downturn coincided with a crisis in German agriculture brought on by an influx of cheap wheat and corn from the United States that pushed prices down and made large landowners and marginal farmers clamor for tariff protection. All of this created an audience for simple explanations, and the antisemitic agitation of the 1870s provided them. Thus the emergence in February 1879 of Wilhelm Marr and the new word "antisemitism" came as the culmination of a decade of rising reaction against emancipation.

Two other significant events in the history of antisemitism also occurred in 1879. In September, Adolf Stoecker, the Protestant chaplain to the Emperor and his court, added an antisemitic plank to the platform of the Christian Social Workers' Party, which he had formed to strengthen religious feeling and combat socialism among the working classes of Berlin. His motive was more pragmatic than ideological. His party had failed to win a large following through religious appeals, so he now sought a more attractive vote-catching strategy—namely, the claim that an alien minority of greedy and immoral materialists was threatening to take over and corrupt Germany. In December,

Heinrich von Treitschke, a professor of history at the University of Berlin, published an essay that praised the antisemitic agitation of the 1870s as a "natural reaction of the Germanic national consciousness against an alien element that has taken too much space in our life." Near the end of his text he lamented, *"Die Juden sind unser Unglück!"* "The Jews are our misfortune!" Antisemites soon turned the phrase into an accusation. In their hands, the words came to convey something like "The Jews are the cause of our misfortune," and that was the message heard when the Nazis turned the phrase into a slogan emblazoned on the mastheads of their newspapers and the banners at Party rallies during the 1920s and 30s.

The repeated invocation of Treitschke's words demonstrates the lasting legacy of the antisemitic wave of the 1870s, but its immediate impact was not so great. In 1880–81, 265,000 German men signed the Antisemites' Petition, the centerpiece of a campaign to repeal emancipation by prohibiting immigration by Jews, compiling a census of those in the country, and removing all Jews as teachers, judges, and civil servants. But the drive was a political failure. Chancellor Bismarck refused even to respond to the petition, and the number of signatures collected disappointed its initiators. That Treitschke declined to sign showed that the document went too far for even critics of Jewish influence. Stoecker's party was overwhelmed in Berlin in the election of 1881 by the pro-emancipation Progressive Party, whose popular vote nationally almost doubled that of the previous elections in 1878 and raised the party's delegation to the second largest in the Reichstag.

That was the story of antisemitism in Germany before World War I in microcosm: The movement was loud, quotable, recurrent, but it had little political traction or legislative success. From 1887, when Otto Böckel won election to the Reichstag from the city of Marburg, to 1912, the last election prior to World War I, a bewildering series of leaders and political parties dedicated to reversing emancipation came and went without attracting very large followings or enacting a single restriction on Jews' civil rights. At the polls, these parties largely flopped, as shown in figure 2. In seven parliamentary elections from 1887 to 1912, antisemites won only 78 out of a total of 2,779 seats, or 2.8 percent of the whole. They never won more than 4 percent of the popular vote or more than 5.5 percent of the parliamentary seats in any single election. Not

FIGURE 2: ANTISEMITIC VOTING IN IMPERIAL GERMANY

for the Reichstag (the national Parliament)

ELECTION	ANTISEMITES				CONSERVATIVES	TOTAL
	Votes	%	Seats	%	% of votes	% of votes
1887	12,000	.2	1	.3	15.2	15.4
1890	48,000	.7	5	1.3	12.4	13.1
1893	264,000	3.4	16	4.0	13.5	16.9
1898	284,000	3.7	13	3.3	11.1	14.8
1903	245,000	2.6	11	2.8	10.0	12.6
1907	249,000	2.2	22	5.5	9.4	11.6
1912	300,000	2.5	10	2.5	9.2	11.7

for the Prussian Landtag (the largest state legislature)

ELECTION	ANTISEMITES	CONSERVATIVES	TOTAL
	% of votes	% of votes	% of votes
1898	.16	25.0	25.16
1903	.17	19.4	19.57
1908	.36	14.1	14.46
1913	.31	14.7	15.01

only was their electoral base small, it was remarkably narrow: 35 of those 78 seats, or 45 percent of them, were won in the same area that elected Böckel: Electoral Hesse, a small province in the west/center of the country, north of the city of Frankfurt, that Prussia had conquered and annexed in 1867. By the 1880s, the region was economically depressed, and Böckel and his followers thought they knew who was responsible. His party ran on the slogan "*Gegen Junker und Juden*," "Against the Prussian nobles and the Jews." Notice the order. Moreover, of the 44 men who ever held those 78 seats, 1 was a peasant, 2 were aristocrats, and 41 belonged to what Germans call the *Mittelstand*, which means they were mostly artisans and shop owners, people who worked for themselves and were struggling against competition from factories and department stores.

These data suggest that as an electoral phenomenon antisemitism was largely a vehicle of economic protest and not sufficiently popular in its own right to sustain a political movement. So do two other interesting pieces of electoral sociology. First, the only other part of Germany where antisemites did unusually well was the Kingdom of Saxony, along the border with today's Czech Republic, which elected another quarter of those antisemitic Reichstag deputies. But of the six seats they had won in the election of 1893, they lost five even before 1903, when all of them went to the left-wing Social Democrats. Second, notice in figure 2 what happened to the Conservatives after they added an antisemitic plank to their platform at the Tivoli Convention of 1892. At the national level, their vote rose slightly in 1893, but it then declined steadily thereafter, falling by more than one-third by 1912. In voting for the Prussian parliament their support dropped by an even steeper 41 percent. In Imperial Germany, antisemitism was hardly a ticket to electoral success.

Why could German antisemites generate a series of bestselling books, such as Julius Langbehn's *Rembrandt als Erzieher* (Rembrandt as Educator) in 1890 and Houston Stewart Chamberlain's *The Foundations of the Twentieth Century* in 1899, but not a sustained national political movement or any legislative victories? One reason was that the leaders of the antisemitic parties were often incompetent and corrupt, which generated scandals that undercut their popularity. Another was that these leaders had trouble working together, so the history of antisemitism in Imperial Germany is a history of constant mergers and splits and little stability to even the names of the groupings. Wilhelm Marr, the so-called patriarch of German antisemitism, was so disputatious that he ended up quarreling with virtually every other leader of the movement in the 1880s and then repudiating antisemitism altogether. In parting, he mocked the ideology as "a business" that blamed Jews for social problems created by industrialization.

But the more fundamental problem for the antisemitic parties was that the discontent they mobilized was always sectoral; it was generally confined, in the period 1887–1912, to one or two particular parts of the country at a time or to one or two particular social groups. Broadly speaking, when Hesse was hurting, Bavaria or Brandenburg was not suffering as badly or in the same ways; when artisans and farmers were complaining, the fortunes of workers were improving. So long as discontent was not general or other groups offered responses to it that some people found more persuasive, as the Center Party did to devout Catholics, the socialists did to industrial workers, and the Conservative Party did to landowners and pious Lutherans, political antisemitism could not thrive. Intellectual antisemitism, however, was another matter; it had a broader, more constant audience and reflected a persistent unwillingness to see Jews in Germany as Germans.

In Imperial Germany, a peculiarity of the electoral process erected one additional barrier to political antisemitism. The German constitution that governed national elections mandated universal manhood suffrage, but the separate states of Germany had their own electoral systems that often privileged wealth. Two states, Prussia until 1918, which made up over 60 percent of the country, and Saxony from 1896 to 1909, weighted votes in parliamentary and local elections according to the taxes on property and income that men paid. Basically, those who paid the top third of taxes in each election district chose one-third of the electors for a seat, the men who paid the next third chose the second set of electors, and the remaining male taxpayers chose the third set. People too poor to pay direct taxes could not vote at all. This system awarded disproportionate influence to the prosperous. In Essen, Alfred Krupp, a vastly wealthy coal and steel magnate, cast the only vote for the first third of the electors from 1886 to 1894, so he in effect chose them. In Berlin 10 percent of the population chose the first third, and the usual breakdown in election districts was something like 3–10 percent/10–15 percent/75–87 percent. This meant that local and state elections in Prussia and Saxony were decided by the richest quarter or less of the electorate, which consisted of only 15–20 percent of the adult male population. Because Jews were disproportionately well represented in the top two tax groups in most cities, their votes carried extra weight in urban districts and municipal elections. For example, in Frankfurt in 1900, Jews made up 63 percent of the people who chose the first third of the electors. Distributions like this worked against antisemitic candidates and encouraged others to support Jews' rights or at least to pay lip service to them. After the German Empire fell in 1918, the new republican regime made German elections more uniformly democratic, and the electoral prospects of antisemitic candidates actually benefited.

As political antisemitism both ebbed and flowed during the life-span of the German Empire, another contradictory set of trends developed—namely, a transformation of the German Jewish population that made Jews both more like and more unlike the rest of the nation's citizens. On the one hand, Jewish distinctness seemed on the way to disappearing and Jews on the way to fitting into German society in three senses. First, the Jews of Germany constituted a steadily declining share of the population (from 1.25 percent of the national population in 1871 to 0.95 percent in 1910) and, after 1910, when 615,000 Jews lived in Germany, a steadily declining number of people, too. The cause was not conversions to Christianity, as only about 34,000 of these took place from 1800 to 1918. Rising rates of intermarriage also played but a small role, as they began to jump only at the end of the imperial period, when the ratio of mixed to all-Jewish marriages rose from 1:5 in 1901–05 to 2:5 in 1916–20. The main reason was the drop in the Jewish birthrate to just above replacement level. If almost 80,000 Jews had not immigrated to Germany under the empire, the Jewish population would have barely grown at all between 1871 and 1910. Despite an inflow of a roughly comparable number of Jewish immigrants in the years surrounding the end of World War I, the Jewish population in Germany continued to fall; in 1933, it was almost 20 percent smaller than in 1910.

Second, German Jews became increasingly acculturated, demonstrating great enthusiasm for German literature, art, and philosophy and eagerly participating in the German glorification of *Bildung*, or cultivation. One consequence was the steep and rapid decline of Jewish schools and the use of Yiddish, and the nearly total integration of Jews into the German educational system. Third, Jewish religious practices also moved in a somewhat syncretic direction, as Germany became the homeland of Reform Judaism. That movement relaxed observance of many of the 613 laws, abandoned routine rituals and customs that seemed to smack of non-European origins, and introduced new forms of observance, including the seating of men and women together in the synagogue, the use of choirs and music during worship services in German, and sometimes the designation of Sunday rather than Saturday as the Sabbath. Though Jewish synagogue architecture remained quite distinct, favoring Moorish towers and domes, in other ways the observable differences between Christian and Jewish practice clearly diminished.

On the other hand, Jews continued to stand out from other Germans, sometimes increasingly, in four conspicuous ways. First, Jews left the eastern and rural parts of the country—places like Posen,

Prussia, Hesse, and southwestern Germany—and migrated to cities even faster than did non-Jews. Between 1871 and 1910, the percentage of all German citizens living in cities with more than 100,000 residents rose from almost 5 percent to over 21 percent; for Jews in Germany, the corresponding figures were 20 percent to 58 percent. By 1910, almost 28 percent of Germany's Jews lived in Berlin, where they made up about 4 percent of the capital's population; in Frankfurt, their share exceeded 6 percent. Moreover, they tended to cluster in particular neighborhoods in each big city—for example, Mitte, Charlottenburg, and Wilmersdorf in Berlin.

Second, the traditional concentration of Jews' occupations in trade and commerce grew steadily more pronounced, and within those spheres the patterns of Jewish employment were quite distinct. German Jews were three times more likely than all Germans to own their own businesses. Of the roughly one-quarter of Jews categorized as working in manufacturing, more than half were tailors. By the turn of the twentieth century, Jews owned 80 percent of the nation's department stores, 70 percent of its metal wholesalers, and 60–70 percent of the ready-to-wear clothing stores, and had preponderant positions in the advertising and printing industries. Regionally, Jews constituted 75 percent of the livestock dealers in Franconia, Westphalia, and Hesse, and half the grain dealers in Hesse and Baden. Finally, in 1910, when Jews made up less than 1 percent of the national population, they were 15 percent of the lawyers, 6 percent of the doctors and dentists, and 10 percent of the law school students and 14 percent of the medical students. As a result of the declining birthrate, all of these figures trended downward after World War I, as did the margin between the average income of Jews and non-Jews in Germany, but that did little to offset the general identification of Jews with non-manual labor and prosperity.

Third, Jewish immigrants under the empire bulked larger because they concentrated in cities. Jewish immigrants from Poland, who were often far more traditional in dress and religious practice than

German Jews, came to only 13 percent of the Jews in all of Germany in 1910 but to much larger shares of those in certain municipalities: 67 percent of the Jews in Leipzig, for example, 53 percent in Dresden, and 15 percent in greater Berlin. They stood out and created an illusion of a massive influx of alien people. After 1914, only 90,000–100,000 more Jews gained entrance to Germany, but their visibility and even greater concentration in places like Berlin and Leipzig had the same effect and gave rise to a veritable psychosis of "inundation" by Jews that antisemites cultivated.

Finally, German Jews stood somewhat politically apart from their fellow citizens, voting noticeably more frequently for the moderate left than most Germans. In the empire, this meant that they consolidated increasingly behind the Progressives; after World War I, it meant that they voted mostly for the Democratic Party; and as that party declined during the Depression, they gravitated toward the Social Democratic Party (SPD). Amos Elon writes of the Jewish bourgeoisie, "They lived like bankers but voted like hard-pressed workers and leftist intellectuals."

Once again, Germany was the land in the middle, the country in which native-born Jews were less integrated in society than to the west but more so than to the east. Despite a great deal of acculturation, the separateness of Jews from other Germans remained apparent in certain respects. Similarly, despite the electoral and legislative failure of antisemitism, it enjoyed administrative and sociocultural successes. An example was the tight limits on immigration and naturalization that the Reich imposed. Most of the Jews who migrated to the United States from Eastern Europe in the 1890s and early 1900s embarked from the ports of Hamburg and Bremen. To get there, they traveled in trains that were sealed the moment they crossed from Russian Poland into Germany and that arrived at long piers, built out into the harbors alongside ocean liners. Steel doors were locked behind the last car before the passengers could descend and board the ships. The goal was to make sure that no one could alight in Germany along the way. Almost 80,000 Jews from Eastern Europe got into Germany between 1871 and the onset of World War I in 1914, but the Reich labored hard to limit the number and to restrict the immigrants' chances of becoming citizens.

Another manifestation of lingering antisemitism was the way Germany mixed formal legal equality with a great deal of social and professional discrimination. The Antisemites' Petition may have been a political bust, but 41 percent of the students at the University of Berlin signed it, and it led to the founding of the League of German Students (Verein deutscher Studenten), an increasingly popular organization that promoted the exclusion of Jews and the children of converts from Judaism from much of student life. By 1896, the national association of German university fraternities banned the initiation of Jews. In 1910, the Austro-Hungarian army had 2,000 Jewish officers; the French army, 720; and the Italian army, 500. The Prussian army, which made up the great majority of the Reich's forces, had none and refused to let Jews become officers in reserve units, as well. Jews were largely kept out of prestigious teaching positions: Prussia's secondary school faculties included only 12 Jews in 1910. In the same year, only 2 percent of the professors in all of Germany were Jews, almost all of them in medicine and the sciences. Antisemitism became institutionalized in elite and conservative society rather than in laws. As Shulamit Volkov has demonstrated, it became part of the "cultural code" of German conservatives and right-wingers, part and parcel of their self-described responsibility to uphold traditional values against the ideologies of liberalism, materialism, and internationalism.

Nonetheless, on the eve of World War I, the trend of events seemed to favor German Jews. The three-class voting system assured that attempts to exclude Jews from professions at the local level—for example, as teachers in elementary schools—were much less successful than snobbish barriers at the elite governmental level. The Prussian state had taken firm action against the last outbreaks of ritual murder accusations at Xanten in 1891 and Konitz in 1900, even dispatching troops to put down antisemitic riots in the latter case, and the accused Jews had been acquitted. Prominent Jewish industrialists such as Walther Rathenau, the head of the German General Electric corporation, and Alfred Ballin, the chief of the Hamburg-America Line, were becoming part of the kaiser's entourage (though Jewish wives still were not invited to court). The election of 1912 routed the antisemitic parties and sent more Jews to Parliament than in the preceding thirty years. Not only did the number of deputies of Jewish descent reach nineteen, but also some of them belonged to the National Liberal and Progressive parties, which had not even nominated Jews during the previous two decades. Many people, Jews and sympathetic non-Jews alike, confidently likened antisemitism to a *Kinderkrankheit*, a childhood disease that German society was outgrowing.

The force that shattered these expectations was the cataclysm of World War I, and the turning point came in 1916, when the German High Command, desperate to divert blame for the murderous military stalemate, authorized the infamous "Jew count," or *Judenzählung*. The generals hoped to prove the charge made by antisemites in Parliament that Jews were shirking their military duty and thus to provide an excuse for the army's failure to win the war. In fact, the census showed a slight overrepresentation of Jews in the military compared to their share of the national population: 100,000 served in the German army, 80,000 in combat; 35,000 were decorated and 12,000 killed. The disappointed military leaders thereupon concealed the results; declined to contradict partial, leaked figures that appeared in the antisemitic press; and allowed the army's political arm, the Fatherland Party, to revive accusations of Jewish draft dodging. In a sense, this episode was Germany's Dreyfus affair, another instance of an elite institution, again the army, trying to use antisemitism to conceal its own failures by spreading vitriol against Jews. However, unlike in the Dreyfus affair, a countermovement did not arise to expose and discredit the lie in public, so it had even more lasting effects. Not the least of them is a paragraph in *Mein Kampf* in which Hitler claims that Germany would have won World War I with less loss of life if only 12,000 or 15,000 more Jews had faced and succumbed to poison gas at the front.

The toxic effects of this new libel against the Jews—indeed, of the preceding forty years of ceaseless agitation and vilification—became apparent even before World War I ended in Germany's defeat and humiliation. By February 1918, Kaiser Wilhelm II had convinced himself that an international Jewish conspiracy controlled all the forces arrayed against him. Meanwhile, Erich Ludendorff, one of Germany's two principal military commanders, had begun contemplating the expulsion of two million supposedly politically unreliable Jews from the part of Poland he planned to annex upon winning the war. After Germany's collapse in the fall of 1918, those desperate to blame the outcome on anything or anyone other than the nation's leaders or armed forces echoed the charges that provoked the Jew count and scapegoated the Jews, along with liberals and leftists, for undermining the war effort.

The audience for such claims grew wider than ever before because the sense of crisis was no longer sectoral but had become national. The combined effect of the Versailles Treaty terms and of the huge debt the country had run up to fight the war, the difficult process of demobilizing the army and converting to a peacetime economy, and the huge burden of supporting veterans and widows led swiftly to rising unemployment and runaway inflation. By 1923, the German currency was not worth the paper it was printed on, and the nation was in turmoil. The opportunity this presented for political antisemitism in Germany is reflected in figure 3, which shows the vote for openly antisemitic political parties rising from 10.3 percent in 1919 (a little less than where it stood in 1912) to 26 percent in early 1924. At the same time and continuing into the late 1920s, the incidence of violent acts against individual Jews increased, along with

FIGURE 3: ANTISEMITIC VOTING FOR THE REICHSTAG IN POST–WORLD
WAR I GERMANY

ELECTION	NAZI % OF VOTES	NATIONALIST %	COMBINED %
1919	—	10.3	10.3
1920	—	15.1	15.1
1924	6.5	19.5	26.0
1924	3.0	20.5	23.5
1928	2.6	14.2	16.8
1930	18.3	7.0	25.3
1932	37.4	6.2	43.6
1932	33.1	8.9	42.0

that of politically motivated violence in general. Yet figure 3 also
records that the opportunity passed, and the vote for antisemites
fell again, only to surge once more in 1930 after the onset of the
Depression and then to spike in 1932, after the nation's largest banks
had failed and unemployment peaked at 36 percent of the workforce.

HITLER'S OPPORTUNITY

The statistics in figure 3 suggest that antisemitism acquired a
new lease on life in Germany during the 1920s, a development that
raises two challenging questions: How could a political fixation on
rolling back Jewish emancipation go from a prevalent but unsuccessful movement before 1918 to a victorious one in 1933? And how
could such hatred succeed at a time when the relative position and
even the raw number of Jews in Germany were in decline?

The answers to these questions lie primarily in the changed
nature of Germany's problems after 1918: They were no longer episodic and sectoral, they became continuous and national, and they

therefore generated a pervasive sense of crisis that fostered support for extremist positions and simplifying explanations. The remainder of this chapter concentrates on that crisis and on how the Nazi Party and Adolf Hitler became its ultimate beneficiaries.

But the answers do not lie only in the depth and breadth of Germany's crisis. One other, vital impetus to antisemitism's resurgence both there and in many European countries after World War I emerged from that conflict: the linking of Jews to the specter of communist revolution. In 1917, when the Bolsheviks came to power in Russia, a number of Jews were prominent among their leaders. Leon Trotsky is the most famous, but he was not alone, and supporters of the tsar, including thousands who fled the revolution into Central and Western Europe, played up this fact. Jews such as Rosa Luxemburg, Kurt Eisner, and Bela Kun assumed leading roles in the revolutions in Germany and Hungary in 1918–19, and opponents trumpeted this as proof that these regime changes were alien impositions that confirmed the menace Jews embodied. As a result, a new variation crystallized on the old practice of demonizing Jews as agents of destructive change, and a new kind of fear—fear of communism—became available for antisemites to exploit.

Of course, some conservatives long had linked Jews to the political left, but symptomatic of the new virulence and its appeal was the sudden popularity of a failed prewar fabrication, the infamous *Protocols of the Elders of Zion*. Largely unknown outside Russia before World War I, the *Protocols* purported to be the transcripts of meetings among nefarious Jewish leaders intent on fomenting discord within all nations in order to increase Jews' power and wealth. In the aftermath of the Russian Revolution, tsarist loyalists brought the *Protocols* west, and translations into most European languages found a large and credulous audience. The first German edition in 1920 sold 120,000 copies, for instance. In 1921, the *Times* of London conducted a thorough debunking that exposed the *Protocols* as an invention—in fact, a pastiche of plagiarism from two works of fiction of the 1860s,

Hermann Goedsche's German novel *Biarritz* and Maurice Joly's French political satire *Dialogue between Machiavelli and Montesquieu in Hell*. But these disclosures made no difference to the *Protocols'* fervent devotees. Adolf Hitler spoke for them in *Mein Kampf*, insisting that "the moans and screams" about the falseness of the *Protocols* actually constituted "the best proof that they are authentic after all."

The pervasive sense of crisis that afflicted Germany after World War I was both emotional and material. The emotional part was a product of the way the war ended, which Germans found profoundly humiliating and unfair. When they asked for an armistice, overthrew the imperial regime, and drove the kaiser into exile in 1918, Germans thought they would get a negotiated peace from the victorious Allies, and that it would be based on Woodrow Wilson's Fourteen Points, which promised "no annexations, no indemnities." Instead, the Germans got the Versailles Treaty, which the Allies worked out among themselves and presented in 1919 on a "take it or leave it" basis. Not only was this what the Germans called a *Diktat*, a dictated peace, but it stripped the country of 10 percent of its territory and most of its armed forces, stigmatized Germany with a clause that assigned it sole responsibility for the outbreak of the war, and imposed an at first unspecified but ultimately staggering monetary penalty in the form of a bill of reparations for the damages inflicted on France and Belgium. Germans of all political stripes felt, as their expression goes, *belogen und betrogen* (lied to and deceived). But they already had demobilized their army as required by the armistice, so the German government had no choice but to sign a document that its people never viewed as legitimate. This gave rise to a kind of siege mentality among the Germans after 1918, an attitude of "it's us against the cruel and unjust world."

The material part of Germany's postwar crisis was the result of the combined challenges of paying reparations, trying to undermine them at the same time, servicing the huge debt that the nation had run up to fight the war, converting from a war economy to a peacetime one, and supporting large numbers of disabled veterans and widows. The reparations came to either $12.5 billion, which was what the Allies actually expected the Germans to pay, or $35 billion, which was the amount the Allies nominally imposed to please their own electorates, and the payback period was estimated to last from seventeen to thirty-six years. The sums due yearly came to about 5 percent of the average real annual German national income between 1918 and 1931 ($11 billion), which may not sound particularly onerous, but the Reich's debts, mostly to Germany's own citizens who had bought government bonds, came to another $41.5 billion at the end of World War I. Germany's debt burden, in other words, amounted to 38 percent of the country's total national income during these thirteen years. The repayment obligations, when added to recurrent government expenditures, swamped revenues: In 1922, the Reich collected less than one-fifth of its budgeted outlays. The government could not borrow (who would lend to such a debtor?); it feared raising taxes (which might generate a revolution or help one of the country's recurrent putsches to succeed); and it could not earn funds from exports because of foreign tariffs that priced German goods out of other markets.

The government's only recourse was simply to print more money, and the result was runaway inflation. By 1923, the exchange rate had reached 4.2 trillion reichsmark to the dollar, meaning the German currency was worthless, and the nation was in turmoil. During that year, leftists rebelled in Hamburg; Hitler's Nazis staged the unsuccessful Beer Hall Putsch in Munich; the Lithuanians marched into East Prussia and annexed the city of Memel; and the French occupied Germany's industrial heartland, the Ruhr region, in order to force Germany to keep up with reparations payments and meanwhile to collect their equivalent directly. And, in Berlin, one reflection of the tensions was the Scheunenviertel (Barn District) riot in early November, a small-scale pogrom directed at Jewish immigrants from Eastern Europe who had set up shops in the nation's capital.

The Weimar Republic, the democratic regime that replaced the monarchical German Empire, survived this crisis, thanks to a brief period of military dictatorship and an influx of billions of dollars in loans from the United States attracted by fatefully high interest rates. But both before and after 1923, the nation was deeply polarized over who was to blame for its miseries. On the one side were the political left and the supporters of the republic who said that everything was the consequence of the old regime that had plunged the nation into war in 1914 and then led it badly and to defeat. On the other side were the political right and supporters of the old monarchy, many of them still entrenched in the judiciary, civil service, and the military, who said that the root of all evil was a supposed sinister conspiracy of Marxists and Jews that had undermined the war effort from within, overthrown the kaiser in 1918, and introduced an incompetent parliamentary government. For most of the life of the Weimar Republic, the two groups were fairly evenly balanced, but also internally divided. On the left, the communists and socialists fought each other, and on the right the old-line nationalists competed with other groups, including the fledgling National Socialist German Workers' Party (NSDAP), the Nazis. This situation did not make for stable or effective leadership. Twenty-one governments came and went in the short fourteen years of the Republic, and the constant wrangling and instability undermined the popularity of democracy.

Adolf Hitler was the ultimate beneficiary of this stalemated blame game, though he failed in his first bid for power in 1923. What did he offer Germans, and why and how did he succeed? The core of Hitler's message was a flattering explanation of what ailed Germans and of why they deserved so much better. Flattering because the central claim was that Germans had not brought their troubles on themselves by following a blundering imperial government or fighting a war they could not win. No, the disasters had been done *to* the Germans, not *by* them. Who were the culprits? Above all, the duplicitous Allies, the delusional Marxists, and the debilitating

Jews. Central to Hitler's narrative were the claims that Germany was a victim and thus entitled to lash back by all means necessary. In other words, "they did evil to us, so we get to pay them back." Hitler believed profoundly and unshakably in this narrative because it performed the same function for his wounded psyche after 1918 that the message did for the people attracted to it. It explained his nation's unjust fate, exonerated him and his compatriots for bringing it on, exposed the villains, and exhorted Germans to fight back. The psychiatrist James Gilligan argues that all violence results from the attempt to replace shame with self-esteem. Whatever the general validity of that remark, it brilliantly captures the motivation behind the violence of Hitler's ideology toward Jews, communists, and foreigners. Shame at the defeat in 1918 generated a furious determination to punish the alleged authors of that defeat so as to expunge it and restore national pride.

The rhetorical centerpieces of this story were the phrases "stab in the back" and the "November criminals." The first asserted that the German army had not lost the war but had been undermined at home by an insidious coalition of Jews and leftists; the second labeled the people who had overthrown the monarchy in November 1918 as traitors. Both claims diverted attention from the German military's and the German people's roles in the defeat and the revolution. After all, the General Staff had begged for the armistice in the fall of 1918 as the only way of preventing the retreating German army from completely breaking up, and many Germans were war-weary and welcomed the kaiser's overthrow. But the Nazis explained these facts away by treating them as creations of the forces that had conspired to undermine the war effort and overthrow the old regime. Both phrases became key components of Hitler's and Nazism's insistence that antisemitism was a defensive, not an offensive, stance. This is a central theme in the history of the Holocaust. The argument that persecution was an act of self-defense was so essential as a justification for what the Nazis wanted to do that it repeatedly appears in ever new forms: They threaten us, so we must strike to protect ourselves.

Hitler tricked his message out with a synthesis of pseudoreligion and pseudoscience that may be aptly dubbed a "theozoology": On the one hand, he posed as an evangelist of the *Volk*, the person who would lead a national revival by making the German people sense its own power and, as the Nazi slogan *"Deutschland Erwache"* said, "Awaken Germany." Hitler presented himself as the one person, singled out by providence and arising from modest origins, who could deliver Germans from their afflictions and, indeed, from division, controversy, and internal conflict altogether. "His speeches," an early biographer observed, "begin always with deep pessimism and end in overjoyed redemption, a triumphant happy ending." At the same time, he claimed to be the eugenicist of the race, the person tough enough to purge the German people of defective and degenerate elements and maximize its purity and strength through selective breeding. Together, evangelism and eugenics promised to create a rejuvenated, unified, and healthy people that would shape its own destiny, and the offer had widespread appeal in a defeated, economically troubled, and politically polarized country that felt battered by the demands of the nations that had triumphed over it.

Hitler based his claim to be able to accomplish all this on the assertion that he alone grasped the fundamental laws and processes that govern history. What were these? Basically they amounted to a kind of bastardized Marxism that substituted race for class. Whereas Karl Marx taught that all history is the struggle among classes to control the means of production and distribute wealth in the victorious class's favor, a process he called dialectical materialism, Hitler taught that all history is the struggle among races to control space or territory from which to generate food and wealth that will support further expansion. In 1949, the first postwar president of West Germany, Theodor Heuss, aptly described this doctrine as "biological materialism" because it so perfectly parallels Marxian notions of class struggle. In a nutshell, Nazism is an ideology of feed and breed or race and space that posits a permanent struggle to the death among ethnic groups. Hitler insisted that perpetual struggle is "the law of nature," but a more fitting term would be "the law of the jungle."

Because struggle is perpetual, Hitler insisted that Germans lived in a permanent state of emergency. Although they deserved to succeed by virtue of the cultural superiority he claimed they possessed, they were not necessarily destined to triumph, as Marx had claimed that the proletariat is or as Christ promised Christians in the Sermon on the Mount by predicting that the meek will inherit the earth. The only assurances of success were fertility, military strength, and racial purity. The state's job is to promote these and to destroy anything that works against them. Morality is defined not by principles or commandments but by service to these goals. What promotes them is good and praiseworthy, what impedes them is evil and traitorous. In other words, Nazism combined arrogance about Germany with anxiety about its future, and the combination translated into virtually unlimited aggressiveness.

Given these premises, Nazi ideology was thoroughly and unabashedly self-centered. Hitler openly and repeatedly proclaimed: "We know only one people for whom we fight, and that is our own. Perhaps we are inhumane! But if we save Germany, we have accomplished the greatest deed in the world. Perhaps we perpetrate injustice! But if we save Germany, we have abolished the greatest injustice of the world. Perhaps we are immoral! But if our people is saved, we have paved the way again for morality." This absolute ethical solipsism is a—perhaps *the*—central article of faith of Nazism. That the philosopher Hannah Arendt, herself a refugee from Nazi Germany, believed she had discovered the distinguishing attribute of Adolf Eichmann, the quintessential Nazi "desk murderer," in his supposed "thoughtlessness," which she defined as his inability to see the world through the eyes of others, always has struck me as puzzling. His supposed inability was, in fact, a refusal, and it was not a characteristic feature of the task-fulfilling automaton that she saw Eichmann as, but rather the cultivated trait of a fervent adherent to Nazism. To subscribe to Hitler's ideology was to affirm that only the views and only the fates of Germans mattered; swearing never to put oneself in the place of non-Germans was part and parcel of being a National Socialist.

In this thought system, the greatest enemy of the Germans is *der Jude* ("the Jew") and *das Judentum* (Jewry), generally referred to with these singular nouns in order to deny any variation among Jews and to assert their homogeneity. That people is supposedly like no other in that it has no country of its own, but instead lives as a parasite within other societies. And, like a parasite, "the Jew" allegedly drains the strength of the host. Jews, said Hitler, unalterably seek to undermine Germans' fertility, military strength, and purity in order to make them too weak to cast Jews off and out. Thus, Jews were behind prostitution and venereal disease, delusional notions like international law and human rights, and softhearted ideas about the equality and brotherhood of peoples. Like Nietzsche, Hitler thought Jews had introduced the debilitating language of morality, ethics, compassion, and empathy into the world. Their idea of conscience was, he insisted, choosing his simile deliberately, "a blemish like circumcision"—a supposedly unnatural alteration of how human beings are created.

Logically, then, "the Jew" must be contained and ultimately "removed" from the German sphere if Germany is to succeed in the struggle for "living space" (*Lebensraum*) and survival. Hitler therefore promised, in *Mein Kampf,* to roll back emancipation and drive Jews into their own world or abroad by expelling them first from German political life, then from the nation's cultural life, and finally from its economic life. Most of the Nazi Party's public statements and private planning documents prior to 1933 followed this three-stage format. The Party platform, the Twenty-five Point Program of 1920, for instance, contained Point 4, calling for the denial of citizenship to Jews and their descendants; Point 5, demanding their classification as "resident aliens"; Point 6, excluding them from public office; Point 8, blocking further immigration by Jews and expelling all who had entered the country since the beginning of World War I; and Point 23, barring them from owning newspapers. These were all political and cultural restrictions. The programs laid down by the Legal and Domestic Policy sections in the Party headquarters in Munich in 1931 included these intentions, as well as removing Jews from the civil service and banning intermarriage with non-Jews. In June 1932, Hermann Göring of the NSDAP made a speech envisioning these actions plus an exclusion of Jews from all prominent positions in the press, theaters, film, universities, and schools, all of which are cultural institutions. But he also said that in a future Nazi state every Jewish business person who stayed as an alien "will remain able to operate his business undisturbed and under the protection of the law." So far as the Party let on prior to 1933, the goal was separation of Jews from non-Jews, reduction of Jews' capacity to influence non-Jews, expulsion of immigrant and naturalized Jews, and making the life of the rest so difficult that they gradually would leave.

Although Nazi leaders did not talk openly of murder, let alone en masse, they made plenty of threats of violence and organized occasional local assaults on Jews, such as the bloody riot of 1932 on Berlin's elegant boulevard, the Kurfürstendamm. And the storm troopers (SA) sang a marching tune with the words "when Jewish blood spurts from the knife." Moreover, Nazi antisemitism always was implicitly murderous because of the metaphors it used: Jews were likened to vermin, parasites, germs, and cancer and called carriers of "racial tuberculosis." These are things to kill or cut away, and Hitler dubbed himself more than once the Robert Koch of politics, referring to the famous bacteriologist who discovered the bacilli that cause anthrax and tuberculosis and thus greatly reduced their incidence. Above all, Hitler was always more dedicated to the goal than to any particular means; it was fixed, they were changeable. At the core of the Nazi vision was an unwavering dream of a Jew-free environment, since that was a precondition of German strength and happiness. This is extremely important because, as will become apparent, the combination of the appeal of that dream and its frustration by events drove the Nazis to consider ever more radical means of pursuing Hitler's goal.

In sum: Nazi ideology was a witches' brew of self-pity, entitlement, and aggression. It was also a form of magical thinking that promised to end all of Germans' postwar sufferings, the products of defeat and deceit, by banishing their supposed ultimate cause, the Jews and their agents.

Yet the centrality of the so-called Jewish problem was much more important and obvious to Hitler than to the average German voter. We have no reason to think that the antisemitic nucleus of his ideology propelled Hitler's rise to power. It played an important role in attracting many of the core believers to the Nazi Party, but not the mass of the Nazi electorate. Hitler was a product of crisis and opportunity, and Germans seem to have been drawn to him out of desperation and a sense that only the Nazis were energetic and organized enough to deal with the nation's woes. In 1928, before the Great Depression struck, the NSDAP received only 2.6 percent of the votes in the national parliamentary election, which was less than half the Party's share in the first of two rounds of voting four years earlier. Clearly, antisemitism alone had, as before, little political traction. As always, it could gain mass support only in tandem with a crisis that antisemites could exploit.

After 1930, by which time Germany's economic difficulties had intensified and the Nazis' share of the national vote had jumped to over 18 percent, Hitler and the Nazis actually steadily downplayed antisemitism as a campaign issue, knowing that it already had attracted as many followers as it could. Instead, the Nazis concentrated on attacking what they called "the System," by which they meant parliamentary democracy and free market capitalism, both of which they wanted to replace with more authoritarian political and economic arrangements. The platform they ran on was summarized succinctly by Gregor Strasser, the day-to-day director of Party operations in the early 1930s, when he defined National Socialism as "the opposite of what exists today." And their method in state and national parliaments, as well as in municipal councils, was to disrupt democratic government, make it dysfunctional, and thus "prove" its ineffectiveness in meeting Germans' needs. In a fundamental sense, this highly partisan political force ran against politics, with all its messy compromises, disagreements, and imperfections, and promised to replace it with order and strength. National Socialism promised Germans both radical change and reassuring return to old certainties, and the mix appealed to many people in the atmosphere of anxiety that the Depression spread. In short, dissatisfaction with the nation's political and economic condition, along with fear of communism, the votes for which also were rising, clearly had more to do with Hitler's ascent than hatred of Jews.

Yet, as before 1918, antisemitism continued to have social traction. Various forms of discrimination escalated in the 1920s, including physical attacks on German Jews. In part, these developments were continuations of the earlier backlash against emancipation, since the Weimar Republic had removed the last forms of professional discrimination against Jews. Many of them became professors, judges, and civil servants during the 1920s; a few even became military officers and diplomats. Ironically, even as German Jews' birthrates continued to fall and their rates of intermarriage rose, Jews seemed to loom ever larger in public perception. The 100,000 or so Jews from Eastern Europe who managed to get into Germany during the years of weak border enforcement between 1916 and 1920 became the subject of paranoid fears of "overforeignization" (*Überfremdung*), particularly because of their concentration in Berlin, and the prominence of Jews in the arts became an excuse to blame them for the alleged "corruption" of German culture during the Roaring Twenties. The nation's moralists had a field day with the fact that the leading proponent of sex education and research and of gay rights, Magnus Hirschfeld, was a Jew, as was the owner of Germany's preeminent manufacturer of condoms, Julius Fromm, an immigrant from Poland who had changed his first name from Israel. At a time when Jews were actually a declining presence in German life, whether measured by their total number, their share of the population, their representation in the professions and among university students, and their incidence among the very wealthy and in corporate boardrooms, Jews remained the subject of a persistent fixation on the part of many other Germans who were dissatisfied with the nation's condition.

This fixation eased the Nazi Party's electoral ascent in 1930–32 but did not propel it. The real driving force of Hitler's rise was the widespread and increasingly desperate desire in Germany for deliverance from the Depression and its unsettling effects. The nation's catastrophic economic situation increased receptivity to the Nazi movement and reduced antisemitism as a disqualifier for office. The context of Hitler's rise between 1928 and 1932 was unemployment that exceeded one-third of the workforce, a drop in industrial production by 42 percent, the collapse of the value of stock market shares by 60 percent, a decline in farm prices by 38 percent, a fall in total national income by 41 percent, and a reduction in real wages for people who still had jobs by 15 percent. The parliamentary system seemed incapable of devising policies that would reverse the crisis, and in fact the national legislature was stalemated after 1930 and unable to form a coalition that commanded a majority of the votes in Parliament. The president therefore exercised his power under Article 48 of the Constitution to appoint the prime minister and cabinet and rule by decree. These governments chosen by President Paul von Hindenburg adopted first a policy of deflation, which is to say cutting government expenditures—what we nowadays call austerity—and that only worsened the crisis. The cabinets that followed Heinrich Brüning's then switched in 1932 to a version of supply-side economics, by reducing the tax burden on firms, and that had only slightly positive effects.

But why were the Nazis the principal beneficiaries of the crisis? Why did they alone seem to capitalize on it? Actually, they were not alone; the communists also gained greatly in strength during the death rattle of the Weimar Republic, though not nearly as much as the Nazis did. But this fact actually worked in the Nazis' favor; it seemed to confirm what they constantly reiterated: Germans' choice came down to us or them, brown or red, and no middle ground remained. When the nation's options were reduced to these, the Nazis were bound to benefit. This is why they actively sought to generate street fights with leftist groups; every such battle strengthened the Nazi claim that the nation was on the verge of civil war, and that citizens therefore had to choose up sides between Hitler and the Commies (*die Kozis*).

In addition, the competing political parties all seemed tired and unwilling to reach beyond their natural bases; for the Social Democrats these were unionized workers; for the Center Party, Catholics; for the People's Party, business leaders; for the Democrats, educated professionals; for the Nationalists, primarily aristocrats and farmers; and for the communists, the unskilled and largely nonunionized parts of the labor force. None of these parties had any imaginative or creative response to the Depression beyond waiting it out or, in the case of the communists, nationalizing everything. Even the Social Democrats in the summer of 1932 voted down the so-called WTB-Plan, named for the first initials of the last names of its authors, a massive government spending program that represented the only potentially successful way to jump-start the economy. The Nazis were fortunate in their opponents.

The way the Nazis campaigned—relentlessly and energetically—exploited the contrast between those groups and Hitler's party. Nazism described itself as a movement, a *Bewegung*, and it was indeed a kind of political perpetual motion machine that never shut down.

Nazis did not campaign just during elections but constantly. In the little north-central German town of Northeim, whose 10,000 citizens did not have a lot of entertainment options, the Nazi Party held an average of three meetings per month between 1930 and 1933. And the gatherings had the format and impact of religious revival meetings, with plenty of military music, well-trained speakers brought in from outside the town, and pageantry. Often the speakers were former war heroes or, in Protestant areas, Lutheran pastors who railed against "the Godless left." Always there was emphasis on the youthful nature of the Party, its disproportionate appeal to the young—over 40 percent of Nazi Party members prior to 1933 were thirty years old or younger—in order to demonstrate that Nazism represented Germany's future. Moreover, the Party did not just campaign via meetings, rallies, and street fights. Its brown-shirted members were constantly visible taking up collections for the destitute or opening soup kitchens for the unemployed, thus giving the impression that they had the *will*, a very important word in the history of Nazism, to fix things. All of this made a huge political impact in places like Northeim, which became a bedrock of Nazi support. Long before Adolf Hitler visited the town for the first time in mid-1932, almost two-thirds of its citizens were voting for the Nazi Party.

Related to this was a special feature of Nazi campaigning, the Party's propaganda, which was carefully tailored to disparate audiences. In working-class districts, the Party played up its populist streak, attacked the selfishness of aristocrats and big business, and posed as the defender of the little guy. In traditional areas like Northeim, the Party berated the unions, spoke up for family values, and emphasized patriotism. Nazism was, in other words, not quite all things to all people but agile in adjusting to its immediate surroundings.

The contrast between the lethargy and stasis of the old parties and the dynamism and youthfulness of the Nazis opened the way for them to offer Germans something distinct and appealing: unity.

Alone among the parties, the Nazis could claim to draw followers from every social class and every part of the nation (other than Jews). Even though German Protestants were more inclined to join than Catholics, rural and small-town residents more than city dwellers, middle-class people more than workers, and men more than women, significant numbers of people in all these groups were members of the Party. It alone could claim to be gathering Germans of all walks of life into a "People's Community" (*Volksgemeinschaft*). Unity is a very seductive word when people are tired of or frustrated with politics, and the Nazis seemed convincing in their pledge to wipe out divisions, if necessary by force.

The promise of Nazism was to restore all that was best in Germany's traditions yet also to revolutionize the country at the same time. Perhaps the best way to grasp how this worked is to look at what the Party held out to women: On the one hand, it promised to "emancipate women from woman's emancipation"—that is, to restore their primary field of activity as the home and childbearing; on the other hand, it enlisted women in all sorts of paramilitary, athletic, and productive activity from which they had been largely excluded previously and told them they could be just as important as men in building the People's Community, only in different roles.

These circumstances explain why the Nazis became the largest political party in Germany by 1932, but they were not enough to propel Hitler to a majority in Parliament. At the end of 1932, German politics was deadlocked. Between the parliamentary elections in July of that year and those in November, Hitler had lost 2 million votes, 4 percent of the total cast. His electoral march seemed to have crested, and the Party faced a severe financial crisis because the membership dues and fees on which it depended had fallen off sharply. Early in the new year, the humor magazine *Simplicissimus* ran a poem with the final line, "This 'Führer's' time is up," and the more sober *Frankfurter Zeitung* congratulated Germans on having survived the Nazi onslaught. Elections had carried Hitler to the threshold of power but not across it. For that, he needed the help of an elite conservative group around Franz von Papen, a former chancellor. The conspirators wanted to engineer and serve in a cabinet backed by Hitler's large block of votes in Parliament and expected to be able to control Hitler because the Nazi leader had little formal education and had never held major office. Article 48 left the choice of chancellor to President von Hindenburg, and a clique of aristocrats and landowners went to work on him in January 1933. Led by Papen, they persuaded the aged president to offer the prime minister's position to Hitler.

The Jews of Germany were almost powerless to affect the course of events. Far from being the fantastically controlling wire-pullers of Hitler's feverish imagination, they were too few and isolated and their resources too limited to make any difference. Their fate depended on a German population that contained a minority deeply hostile to them and a vast majority that was indifferent or unsympathetic to them.

Indifference and lack of sympathy were the principal effects of the combination of many decades of vocal German antisemitism and a decade and a half of intense German crisis. Both processes reduced the number of vigorous antiantisemites, the people who were willing to defend Jews or who thought that Nazi threats to Jews made Nazis unacceptable as leaders. If the Nazis' antisemitism was not a major contributor to their victory, neither was it a significant barrier to it. Even sympathetic non-Jews were inclined to understate the menace the Nazis represented by quoting the old German maxim, "Nothing is eaten as hot as it is cooked."

Still, probably 55 percent of the Germans had never voted for Hitler or the Nazis by the time he came to power. A majority had remained loyal to their traditional political allegiances: the Center Party for the Catholics, the socialists and communists on the left for most workers. As a result, William Sheridan Allen has ventured the observation that more Germans "were drawn to antisemitism because they were drawn to Nazism, not the other way around." He probably is correct, and the observation is a reminder that the key to understanding what happened in Germany after 1933 is not so much events and attitudes that predated that turning point but ones that developed after it. The short answer to the question "why the Germans?" is "because Hitler came to power," but it is too short an answer.

CHAPTER 3

ESCALATION:
Why Murder?

HITLER AND THE NAZI PARTY came to power having declared their intention to strip Germany's Jews of citizenship and the right to hold office, to exclude them from the civil service, journalism, education, and the arts, and to ban intermarriage with non-Jews. The new masters of the nation expected these measures would reduce not only Jews' influence over the rest of the population but also their very numbers in Germany, and the regime planned to accelerate the latter process by barring Jewish immigration and expelling all Jews who had entered the country since the outbreak of World War I. In short, the Nazis set out to degrade, segregate, and diminish Germany's Jews but not yet to kill them, let alone all the Jews of Europe. Although Nazi rhetoric toward Jews regularly employed implicitly murderous metaphors, likening Jews to pests or diseases to eradicate, official policy initially concentrated on harassment, intimidation, isolation, and dispossession but generally stopped short of organized and widespread physical violence. The individual Jews subjected to brutality during the formative months of the Nazi dictatorship were usually officeholders or politicians, executives of firms that attracted the Nazi Party's attention for various reasons, or people who dared to object to Nazi actions, and those did not yet include large-scale destruction of property and roundups of Jews, let alone mass murder. Why not? And why did the situation escalate thereafter?

In answering these questions, much depends on whether the intervals January 1933–November 1938 and January 1933–June/October 1941 seem like short or long times. Does the first interval, the time between Hitler's appointment as chancellor and the onset of systematic assaults upon and arrests of Jews during the Crystal Night pogrom, amount to "merely" or "more than" five and a half years? Does the second interval, the time between Hitler's appointment and the beginnings of mass murder of the Jews, come to "merely" or "more than" eight and a half years? If the answer is "merely," the implication is that the Nazi leaders moved fast and probably knew what they were up to rather quickly. If the answer is "more than," that suggests that the regime actually proceeded gradually and may have changed its objectives along the way. Either way, an important question arises about each of the turning points of 1938 and 1941, a question that a good historian has to ask about every significant event she or he studies: Why now?

My answer to that question is that the Nazi regime engaged in a three-stage discovery or learning process between 1933 and 1941. In the first phase, which lasted for just over five years from the time Hitler came to power until the annexation of Austria in March 1938, the so-called Third Reich learned what it could do, namely persecute the German Jews without encountering serious resistance from Germany's other inhabitants or from other countries. In the second phase, which lasted for a bit more than three years from the takeover in Austria until the invasion of the Soviet Union in June 1941, Nazi Germany learned what it nonetheless could not achieve—namely, the complete "removal" or expulsion of Jews from its territory. In the third phase, which lasted only five months from the attack on the Soviets to the fall of 1941, Hitler and his most important advisor and executor in this matter, Heinrich Himmler, recognized that they possessed not only the motive but also the means and the opportunity to murder the Jews in not only the newly occupied territories of Serbia and the Soviet Union under cover of war, but also in all of Europe.

FROM ARYANIZATION TO ATROCITY

The first phase of the Nazi assault on the German Jews proceeded under the euphemistic watchword of "Aryanization" (*Arisierung*), which referred to the process of transferring Jews' jobs and property in Germany into the hands of non-Jews. Since Nazi ideology depicted Jews as parasites who had acquired what they had by draining it from the gentile majority of the population, the Party faithful regarded this process as simple payback for decades of deception and theft and thirsted to begin the repossession immediately after Hitler took office. But the Nazi leaders were more cautious.

Hitler and his principal advisors could not yet be sure in 1933 of how much persecution domestic or foreign opinion would accept, and they had other issues on their minds. After all, over half of the German population had never voted for Hitler, Nazis had only three of twelve seats in the cabinet President von Hindenburg appointed, and the authority to rule by decree was initially the president's, not Hitler's. Hitler knew that even many German antisemites were not as "scientific," by which he meant categorical, in their hatred as he was. He frequently complained that the problem with most Germans is that each had a "good Jew," a friend or acquaintance who did not conform to antisemitic stereotypes and who therefore should be treated as an exception to the general condemnation. The Nazi Führer knew he would need time to win over most of the population to his conviction that persecuting all Jews was a necessary act of self-defense and indispensable to national survival. Moreover, the new regime needed stability and an appearance of moderation while generating a recovery from the Depression that would secure Hitler's hold on power. Finally, the Reich had to lull Britain and France into tolerating the military buildup that was a prerequisite for the conquest of "living space" for Germany in Eastern Europe. Hitler the fanatic was obsessed with Jews, but Hitler the politician and expansionist dared not let the obsession show too much or too early.

Caught between the ideological fervor of its followers and the practical requirements of economic and foreign policy, the Nazi regime devised a two-tier approach to the so-called Jewish question. At the national, official, and public level, a stop-and-go policy allowed the regime to feel its way forward from 1933 to 1937 and to test the limits of public acceptance, both domestic and foreign. Overt displays of organized antisemitism were confined to the boycott of Jewish stores and businesses on April 1, 1933, which the regime depicted as merely a reprisal to a supposed wave of "atrocity propaganda" that Jews had instigated abroad. Otherwise, the Nazis generally contented themselves at the national level with a few well-spaced decrees that enacted the sorts of measures the Party long had advocated. Conspicuous outbreaks of overt violence against Jews, such as two more nasty rampages on Berlin's Kurfürstendamm, in March 1933 and July 1935, were exceptional.

In 1933, the regime focused its efforts on driving Jews from political and cultural life. That goal led to four laws that: (1) purged Jews from the German civil service, including the law courts and hospitals, since these were state institutions in Germany, unless a Jew had held his position since before World War I, served in the army during that conflict, or had a father or son who died while doing so (these were the so-called Hindenburg exceptions, adopted in order to placate the field marshal-turned-president); (2) allowed the government to denaturalize people who had become citizens since that war began; (3) excluded Jews from cultural institutions, such as theaters, orchestras, and newspapers; and (4) imposed a *numerus clausus* restricting Jews' share of students in German secondary schools and universities to 1.5 percent. In the economy, on the other hand, the Nazis treaded somewhat carefully, harassing individual Jewish executives and demanding their removal in many cases, but not actively trying to drive out Jewish owners except in sectors that were particularly important to the Party rank-and-file, notably department stores and breweries. The one major legislative initiative in this sphere in 1933 was a prohibition on Jews owning farmland, a particularly sensitive issue for a Nazi Party that proclaimed the twin pillars of Germandom to be *Blut und Boden*, Blood and Soil.

The year 1934 brought a legislative lull, as the Third Reich decreed only one major antisemitic measure, a law that increased the government's ability to deport people it denaturalized. Then, in 1935, the regime closed the ranks of the German military to Jews, forbade them to display German flags on national holidays, and completed the agenda laid down before 1933 by stripping Jews of most citizenship rights and reducing them to resident "subjects" of Germany, banning new intermarriage and all extramarital sexual relations between Jews and non-Jews, terminating the Hindenburg exceptions, now that the aged president had died, and dismissing the last Jews from the civil service. Nineteen thirty-six saw another lull, as the regime downplayed its antisemitism in the run-up to the Summer Olympics in Berlin, lest other nations decline to participate, and little happened at the national level in 1937, either, aside from a prohibition on granting doctoral degrees to Jews.

This staccato pattern of increasing persecution at the national level from 1933 to 1937 belied, however, a continuous "squeezing" of Jews by Nazi activists at the local or street level, usually out of ear- or eyeshot of foreign reporters. Even in big cities, but especially in small towns, pressure was brought to bear on Jews' jobs and businesses in a host of ways. While the brown-shirted storm troopers of the SA threatened or inflicted harm on Jews' property or children, Nazi officeholders canceled contracts or refused to entertain bids from firms owned or led by Jews, welfare agencies prohibited the use of payments or vouchers at Jewish-owned shops, local leaders forbade their employees to buy at such establishments or to patronize Jewish professionals and publicly posted lists and/or pictures of people who did so, Jews' businesses became identifiable by the absence of "German firm" (*Deutsches Geschäft*) window signs that now proliferated among competitors, municipal councils banned Jews from having stands at public market halls or using public swimming pools, local and regional savings banks and credit unions stopped making loans to Jews or their businesses, branches of the Nazi labor union (the NSBO) insisted on dismissals of managers, tax authorities seized ledger books and charged Jews with tax evasion or illegal transfers of money abroad, and in many places, Nazi stalwarts intimidated non-Jewish shopkeepers, especially sellers of foodstuffs, into refusing to accept Jewish customers, thus forcing them either to move or to shop far from home where they would not be recognized. All the while, the Nazi-controlled press kept up a barrage of allegations regarding supposed Jewish criminality and deceitfulness.

Discriminatory actions of these sorts gave the Party's radical antisemites satisfaction and habituated Germans to Jews' suffering. As the forms of exclusion and persecution multiplied, the Nazi regime also learned that almost no non-Jew would stick up for Germany's Jews; instead, most people and institutions hastened to adapt to the way the wind was blowing. Across the country in 1933, clubs, singing groups, bowling leagues, and similar organizations began restricting membership to so-called Aryans and thus inflicting on Jews what Marion Kaplan has called "social death." Jews found themselves increasingly abandoned and alone.

This popular acceptance, even adoption and internalization, of Nazi antisemitism was not the only success of the two-tier policy between 1933 and 1937. Another was the regime's dispelling or deflecting of international opposition. Despite some vocal criticism overseas, notably at large rallies in New York City, and attempts to boycott the sale of German goods abroad, the persecution of the Jews did little to dampen the urge in Britain and France to avoid war by appeasing Hitler or to undermine the resurgence of the German economy that increased his popularity at home.

Yet from the Nazis' point of view, their success was incomplete and the Jewish problem only half solved by late 1937. On the one hand, they had achieved the isolation of Jews from the rest of the population and gone a long way toward impoverishing them. Since 1933, up to 40 percent of the indeterminate number of businesses that Jews owned in Germany and between 40 percent and 50 percent of their wealth had become the property of someone else or the German state. In addition, most of the Jews still in Germany had been relegated to a destitute economic ghetto, as they scraped together meager livings working for themselves or each other.

On the other hand, the Jewish population in Germany had fallen by only about 35 percent, and the slow pace was an increasing irritant to Hitler. The Führer held the Jews responsible for Germany's defeat in World War I; he did not intend to let them undermine the nation if World War II occurred, and as the 1930s passed, he saw that conflict coming ever closer. Already in mid-1936, he had written a memorandum that laid the basis for an economic Four Year Plan. The document called for an economy impervious to blockade and an army capable of war within four years and included a passage demanding "A law making the whole of Jewry liable for all damage inflicted upon the German economy by individual specimens of this community of criminals." That Hitler inserted a provision about Jews in a long discussion of military and economic preparations shows how seriously he took the stab-in-the-back legend from World War I and how determined he was to hold the Jewish community collectively liable for perceived acts of sabotage.

On November 5, 1937, the Führer presided over a meeting of his foreign and war ministers and his principal military commanders and gave a speech, summarized in a memorandum by his adjutant Colonel Friedrich Hossbach, that Hitler described to them as "in the event of his death, his last will and testament." The gist was that Germany had to fight for living space by 1943–45 at the latest, when the Reich's window of opportunity would close. By then, the greater resources of the British and French empires would have enabled them to catch up with the momentary advantage in armaments that Germany had achieved by breakneck spending since 1933. Meanwhile, however, opportunities to annex Austria and wipe out Czechoslovakia might arise with surprising speed, and the Nazi regime would have to seize them, even at the risk of conflict coming earlier. Hitler said nothing about Jews at this meeting, but its aftermath had a great deal to do with Jews.

Clearly, Hitler's remarks alarmed the people assembled at the conference, as well as a few people outside it. Economics Minister Hjalmar Schacht, who was not there, already had cautioned Hitler that the pace of German rearmament had to slow down lest inflation get out of hand. Now, War Minister Werner von Blomberg, Commander in Chief of the Army Werner von Fritsch, and Foreign Minister Constantin von Neurath warned against precipitous action because they feared the army was unready and the British and French too strong. In the ensuing months, Hitler fired all of these men, Schacht promptly and premeditatedly in November, the others opportunistically the following February when a series of perceived sexual scandals created room for political intrigue.

Moreover, the following months saw the enactment by Acting Economics Minister Hermann Göring of a series of measures designed to speed up the process of driving Jews out of the German economy and then out of the country altogether. The fact that the regime went over to a program of forced, accelerated Aryanization at this juncture was not coincidental. The move reflected Hitler's conviction that the Jews were disloyal and sure to be saboteurs and fifth columnists when a conflict came. Nazi planners knew that at the current rate of attrition through emigration and death, the German Jewish population would disappear in fifteen to twenty years, but that was well beyond Hitler's time horizon for war. More pressure had to be put on Jews to leave, lest they once more have the supposed opportunity to stab the nation in the back.

A crushing avalanche of new decrees designed to pauperize the Jews of Germany and convince them that they had no future in the country began with the definition of Jewish firms as ones with even a single senior Jewish executive or more than 25 percent of their stock in the hands of Jews. Such enterprises became immediately ineligible to receive government contracts, foreign currency to pay for necessary imports, and rationed raw materials, without which those enterprises could not operate. In March 1938, Jewish communities lost their legal status and the right to own property, which opened the way to the confiscation of their synagogue and school sites. In April, all Jewish-owned enterprises were required to register and all Jews were ordered to fill out an itemized census of their property and its value, down to the last teaspoon. To make Jews instantly recognizable, they had to add uniform middle names—Israel for men, Sarah for women—to all their identity papers in August, and in October to have a large red letter *J* stamped onto the front page of their passports. In July, Jews were forbidden to work as traveling salespeople, which cost 30,000 their jobs; in September, Jewish doctors were forbidden to treat non-Jews; and in November, Jewish lawyers were demoted to legal counselors whose sole permitted task was to help other Jews wind up their businesses and dispose of their property. In December, a new law permitted local governments to ban Jews from the public streets on certain days of the week.

As if all this were not enough, now the Nazis decided also to terrorize and deplete the Jewish population. In annexed Austria, unfettered intimidation characterized the German occupation from its earliest days, as Nazis broke into Jews' homes, looting and smashing with impunity. The violence spilled over into Germany during the summer of 1938, producing the destruction of the main synagogue in Munich in June and its counterpart in Nuremberg in August. In both the old and the new parts of the Reich, about 5,000 Jews were carted off to concentration camps on various pretexts, sometimes on none at all. Meanwhile, forced expulsions of foreign Jews occurred, beginning with those who held Soviet citizenship in February and culminating with the deportation of some 18,000 Polish Jews in late October. The Poles had triggered this action by announcing their intention to bar any Polish passport-holder residing abroad from ever reentering the country unless he or she quickly obtained a validation stamp from a Polish consulate by the end of that month. Because the Polish government was trying to shed these citizens, its representatives in Germany dragged their feet in issuing the stamps, obviously trying to run out the clock on the return visits. Because the Nazis wanted Polish Jews in Germany to have somewhere to go, either immediately or eventually, which cancelation of their passports would make more difficult, the Reich decided to round up thousands of the affected Jews and to dump them over the border into Poland. Initially receptive, the Poles soon felt overwhelmed, refused to let further Jews in, and transferred those admitted to miserable refugee camps, where many still languished months later. Among the deportees were the parents of Herschel Grynszpan, a young Jew living illegally with relatives in Paris, and he took his revenge by walking into the German embassy there on November 7, 1938 and shooting the third secretary, a young diplomat named Ernst vom Rath.

Hitler and the Nazi regime seized on vom Rath's death two days later as the pretext for a vicious collective assault on the German Jewish population, once more billed as an act of self-defense against Jewish hostility. This was the so-called *Kristallnacht* (Crystal or Broken Glass Night) pogrom, a wave of destruction and plundering that swept over most remaining Jewish-owned homes and businesses and nearly all of the nation's synagogues. The storm troopers disguised as civilians who spearheaded this operation found a good many fellow citizens, especially teenagers, willing to join in the violence. By the time the mayhem stopped, the perpetrators had killed at least 91 Jews but perhaps many more, driven at least 300 people to commit suicide, and rounded up some 36,000 Jewish men across the country. About 26,000 of them were exposed the following day to public humiliation as they marched to trains and buses destined for the concentration camps at Buchenwald, Dachau, and Sachsenhausen. At least 600 and perhaps up to 1,000 of these men died from brutal treatment in subsequent months at these places, from which a person could obtain release only by signing over virtually everything he owned and promising to emigrate. In addition, in the aftermath the German government seized a fraction of the payments due to the Jews for insured damage and allowed the German insurance companies to renege on paying the rest. Then the Nazi state imposed a collective fine of one billion reichsmark on the Jews, payable in part by the confiscation of all their possessions containing precious metals, except for wedding rings and one table setting per person. And in April 1939, after having stripped nearly all Jews of gainful employment and all unemployed Jews from the welfare rolls, the Nazi state imposed compulsory labor on all Jewish males below the age of sixty-five, tens of thousands of whom now had to clean streets, shovel snow, and work in factories at discriminatory wages.

Even before this cascade of cruelty, few Jewish Germans needed much convincing that they had to leave. By early 1938, more applications for visas to get into other nations were on file at their consulates and embassies in Germany than Jews were left in Germany. But getting out was difficult, especially because the German policy of stripping Jews of all they owned made them unattractive immigrants in the eyes of many foreign governments. Besides, the Depression was not over in most countries, and resistance to immigration fed in many places on fear of competition for jobs. Nonetheless, about 60 percent of the Jews of Germany and 67 percent of those in Austria managed to escape by the time World War II began.

The Nazi regime remained unsatisfied, largely because its foreign policy victories were negating its racial policy successes. As of September 1939, the annexations of Austria in March 1938, of the Sudetenland border region of Czechoslovakia in October after the Munich Conference, and of the remainder of the Czech provinces of Bohemia and Moravia in March 1939 had offset much of the reduction in the Jewish population of Germany proper by that date. On the eve of World War II, the Greater German Reich, including the annexed areas, contained around 350,000 Jews, far too many for the comfort of a Nazi regime that was about to invade Poland, the home of 3.3 million more Jews.

All of this was foreseeable in advance, but the fateful mathematics of German expansionism, the fact that the Reich could not drive out Jews faster than it planned to conquer them, seems to have dawned on German policymakers only during 1938 and contributed heavily to both the accelerated persecution of Jews at the time and to the regime's turn to overt violence. The math also accounts for the emergence in Nazi circles of a new vocabulary about the destiny of the Jews. Given the prospect of not being able to get rid of Jews faster than the Reich added them, officials began to give voice to the previously unthinkable.

The first documented emergence of a new word and a new prediction comes from a report of a Swiss diplomat in Paris of a conversation on November 14, 1938, less than a week after *Kristallnacht*, in which the number two man in the German Foreign Ministry, Ernst von Weizsäcker, said, "The remaining . . . Jews in Germany should immediately be deported somewhere. . . . If . . . no country will take them in, they surely are going sooner or later toward their complete annihilation." Ten days later, on November 24, *Das Schwarze Korps*, the publication of the Nazi Party's elite SS formation, which now also controlled all German police, editorialized as follows: "The German people are not in the least inclined to tolerate in their country hundreds of thousands of . . . impoverished

Jews. . . . In such a situation we would be faced with the hard necessity of exterminating the Jewish underworld . . . by fire and sword.
The result would be the actual and final end of Jewry in Germany,
its complete annihilation." Finally, in January 1939, Hitler made the
new vocabulary his. On the twenty-first, he told the Czech foreign
minister, Frantisek Chvalkovsky, that the Jews of Germany would
be "annihilated" unless other nations cooperated in deporting them.
Nine days later, in a speech to the Reichstag on the sixth anniver-
sary of his appointment as chancellor, he predicted "the annihilation
of the Jewish race in Europe" in the event of a new world war. As yet,
these remarks mentioned annihilation only as something that would
happen under certain conditions, but for the first time the thought
was out in the open. So much so, in fact, that the U.S. consul general in Germany, Raymond Geist, prematurely concluded and told
the State Department on December 6—weeks before Hitler uttered
even the threat—that "[t]he Germans. . . . have embarked on a program of annihilation of the Jews."

On September 1, seven months after Hitler's address to the Reichstag, he launched the Second World War in Europe by invading
Poland. Less than four weeks later, on the day that Warsaw finally
surrendered, the SS created a new subdivision, the Reich Security
Main Office (Reichssicherheitshauptamt, or RSHA), under the direction of Reinhard Heydrich and including a Jews Department (*Juden-
abteilung*) headed by Adolf Eichmann. Initially, the German invaders
shot fewer Jewish Poles than non-Jewish ones; as at home in 1933, the
Nazi rulers were more concerned with punishing potential political opponents and resisters than attacking Jews per se. But sporadic
attacks on Jews occurred and worse followed. The victorious Germans ordered ghettoization and the almost complete abandonment
of Jews' possessions on September 21 as a means of concentrating
Jews along railroad lines for eventual deportation and seizing most
of their property in the meantime. Where were they to go? To what
the Nazis explicitly called, in imitation of the history of the United

States' policies toward Native Americans, a "reservation" (*Reservat*), but where was it to be located? Initially, in an area called Nisko on the San River at the western edge of the Lublin district of the General Government (GG), the rump of Poland that Germany occupied but did not annex. Then, early in 1940, Hitler hoped to talk Stalin into accepting the more than two million Jews still in Greater Germany and occupied Poland, but the effort came to nothing. Finally, after France fell in June, the Germans focused on the French colony of Madagascar, a destination for Jews favored by European antisemites since the late nineteenth century. German planners actually began to work out how many ships would be needed over how long a time to deport the 3.25 million Jews now in Hitler's hands, and the Gestapo compelled several German Jewish leaders to find out whether American Jewish organizations would help to finance the exodus. But the German failure in the aerial Battle of Britain made transportation impossible, so a fourth destination gained prominence as 1940 turned into 1941: Siberia above the Arctic Circle, after victory in the impending invasion of the Soviet Union.

This transition in German policy from encouraging emigration, which remained possible, to planning deportations, marked a major turning point, for it amounted to a first step toward implementing annihilation. To be sure, the regime had not yet decided to kill every Jew, but it had chosen a course that entailed the death of a great many, either in the poorly provisioned ghettos or in the inhospitable designated destinations, for which the Jews would be physically unprepared and materially unequipped. In confirmation of this shift in policy, from September 1939 to June 1941, ghettos and forced labor camps took the lives of more than half a million Polish Jews. Still, as late as May 1940, Heinrich Himmler called "the bolshevist method of the physical destruction of a people . . . un-German and impossible." He was referring in that remark to the treatment of Poles, but events soon made him reconsider whether such inhibitions applied also to Jews.

Several developments in 1940–41 created incentives to find a "total" or "overall solution" (*Gesamtlösung*) to the Jewish question sooner rather than later. While the Nazi Gauleiters, the regional Party bosses, especially Joseph Goebbels in Berlin, clamored to begin deportations of the remaining German Jews to Poland, partly to free up housing for other Germans, partly as an end in itself, a logistical logjam developed in that conquered country. Himmler, freshly appointed as the head of the National Commission for the Strengthening of Germandom (the Reichskommissariat für die Festigung deutschen Volkstums, or RKFDV), had embarked on a massive program of demographic engineering there. It entailed the repatriation to the German-annexed parts of Poland of 500,000 *Volksdeutsche*, people of German descent, from the Soviet Union and the Baltic states, pursuant to the agreement by which Hitler and Stalin had partitioned Eastern Europe in 1939. Simultaneously, at least twice as many Jews and Poles were to be expelled into the non-annexed but German-occupied General Government. But Hans Frank, the Nazi governor there, pushed back, claiming that his fiefdom should not and could not become a "dumping ground" for Jews, since conditions in the ghettos already were awful, and those conditions endangered the health of nearby populations. Himmler's views on the future of the General Government also appear to have evolved during the run-up to the invasion of the USSR. Since the occupied Polish region would no longer be at the periphery, but rather at the center of an expanded German empire, the GG now became in his eyes a potential area for Germanization, instead of the demographic "trash heap" that he had considered it earlier, and that meant the expansion of his aspirations for ethnic cleansing to the whole of Poland.

Meanwhile, the victories in southeast Europe in early 1941, which brought German occupation of Serbia and parts of Greece and cemented the Reich's alliances with Hungary, Romania, and Bulgaria, multiplied the number of Jews within the Nazi ambit, thus increasing the pressure to do something about them on a continent-wide basis. The decision to attack the Soviet Union in 1941 threatened to do the same and to expose German troops to the imagined possibility of Jewish sabotage behind the advancing lines. Finally, that decision, plus Hitler's expectation that America would soon join the alliance against him—the United States had sent troops to Iceland in July 1941, and President Franklin Delano Roosevelt and Prime Minister Winston Churchill just had signed the Atlantic Charter, an implicit alliance, in mid-August—meant that European Jews no longer had any value as hostages whose fate could be used to pressure the Allies or to intimidate other Jews abroad. In the euphoria of the initial German victories in Belarus and Ukraine, any reason for restraint toward the Jews fell away.

In other words, a combination of impatience, frustration, and hubris convinced the Nazi leaders that they had much to gain and nothing to lose by proceeding more radically now against the Jews rather than waiting until the victorious conclusion of the war. As a result, Hermann Göring charged Reinhard Heydrich on July 31, 1941, to prepare "an overall solution of the Jewish question in the German sphere of influence." But by the time he did so, the Germans already had taken the first step toward mass murder. In the course of July, their initial "pacification" efforts in conquered territory developed into a resolve to avoid a repetition of the Polish logjam and the administrative problems that the ghettos presented by bringing death to the Jews in the Soviet Union. The dispensers of this death began as four *Einsatzgruppen* (Operations Groups), comprising fewer than 3,000 men, who were subdivided into eighteen mobile *Kommando* units assigned to advance behind the German troops, foment pogroms, and shoot potential "partisans" and communists. Initially the victims were mostly Jewish men of military age, but the killing spread to women and children in late July 1941, only a month after the invasion began, and two brigades of 10,000 SS men plus 30,000 German Order Police were sent to the East to help do the job. Militias drawn from the local populations, the so-called *Schutzmannschaften*, and security divisions of the regular German army stationed in areas behind the front supplemented these forces.

These disparate killing units slaughtered more than half a million Jews in the last six months of 1941 and perhaps one million by early 1942. Whereas in Poland some Jews had been killed and most ghettoized, in Ukraine, Belarus, and the Baltic states the pattern was reversed: Death became the norm, anything more than brief ghettoization the exception. The murders reached a crescendo between late August and late September, when 24,000 Jews were killed at Kamenets-Podolsk, 28,000 Jews at Vinnytsia, and nearly 34,000 at Babi Yar outside Kiev, in each case over two days. At these places and elsewhere in the occupied Soviet Union, most victims died, in a sense, one by one, by single shots to the back of the head or neck, not by machine-gun fire, because the killers wanted to be as sure as possible that they had not missed or wasted ammunition.

Everywhere the cover for murder was *Partisanenbekämpfung*, combating partisans, even though few were at work in the early months of the war on the Eastern Front. And, everywhere from August on, the Germans claimed that women and children had to die, too, because they served as the eyes and ears of snipers and other guerrillas resisting the German advance. Alongside this military justification stood an ideological one, the Nazi conviction that Jews were the masterminds and wirepullers of Bolshevik rule. General Walter von Reichenau's order to his Sixth Army of October 10, 1941, rolled the legitimations together in the pronouncement that "the soldier must have full understanding for the necessity of harsh but just punishment of the Jewish sub-humans. It has the broader objective of nipping in the bud any uprisings in the Wehrmacht's rear, which experience shows always to have been instigated by Jews." Hitler considered Reichenau's order outstanding and had it distributed to every German unit fighting on the Eastern Front.

The rapid growth in the number of victims is not surprising when one recalls that the Germans entered the USSR with a *Hungerplan* that called for feeding their armies off the land and letting upwards of twenty million Soviet citizens starve to death. In keeping with the plan, the Nazi regime fed and provisioned the prisoners of war from the Red Army so poorly that 58 percent of those captured during the war, more than three million people, died in captivity, more than half of them in the first seven months of the German invasion. Reducing the number of mouths to feed in the conquered East was a consistently high priority for the Germans, and spreading the killing to ever more numerous groups of Jews aligned perfectly with military planning. But the food supply was a reinforcing, not a primary, motive for murder. Events proceeded along parallel lines in German-occupied Serbia during the summer and fall of 1941, with Jews being shot en masse in reprisal for partisan attacks even where provisions were not scarce. The Jews did not have to die because Nazi officials kept finding justifications for murder; the causal process ran the other way around.

By late summer 1941, Nazi policy had evolved from driving Jews from Germany's space to virtually forcing them to leave, to concentrating them for deportation and assuming many deaths along the way, to bringing death to the newly conquered. Only one step remained, bringing the already conquered Jews to death. The first tentative step in that direction occurred in mid-September, perhaps triggered by Stalin's decision to deport the remaining Germans in southern Russia to the country's interior. Hitler now finally agreed to require German Jews to wear a distinguishing Star of David on their clothing, a measure long since enacted in some occupied countries but not yet in Germany itself. Marking the Jews was a preliminary to their deportation, as the Gauleiters had been demanding with increasing insistence, and all that stood in the way of making their departures end in immediate eradication was figuring out how to kill them en masse.

GENTILE AND JEWISH RESPONSES

How was it possible for the Nazis to radicalize their assault on German and later European Jewry without appreciable interference? The question requires breaking down into three more precise subquestions: (1) Why did non-Jewish Germans, most of whom had not accepted antisemitism as a powerful political motive before 1933, act afterward as if it was exactly that? (2) Why did Jews in Germany not organize more effective countermeasures or at least all flee? (3) Why did foreign powers or entities not intervene on humanitarian grounds?

That more than half the Germans had not voted for Hitler by 1933 does not mean that these people rejected antisemitism. Some were faithful Catholics who had voted for the Center Party that was closely associated with the Church but also had absorbed its religiously based hostility toward Jews. Others did not believe that the Jews were the chief cause of the nation's troubles, as the Nazis insisted, but did not particularly like Jews, either. The main problem was that the number of antiantisemites was limited, and most non-Jewish Germans thought the fate of the Jews was secondary to their own concerns. Indifference and self-interest created opportunities for the Nazis to change people's behavior by a combination of carrot and stick, rewards for endorsing the new regime's ideology and punishment for not doing so. The punishment might be, but was not necessarily, violent. It might be only a slowing or blocking of a person's advancement in his or her career. The Nazi regime had numerous mechanisms that promoted conformity and corruption, and one of the most alarming features of the Holocaust is not only the rapidity with which these worked their effects on Germans but also the way in which these effects were replicated in virtually all the Nazi-occupied and -allied lands of Europe later, with disastrous consequences for Jews.

Even among the segments of the German population that were best educated, most cosmopolitan, and most averse to violence, a process that could be called self-coordination (*Selbstgleichschaltung*) set in remarkably rapidly in 1933 and led to a swift abandonment of organized efforts to protect Jews as a group. Several senior German diplomats, for example, considered resigning in early 1933 in protest against Nazi discrimination and brutality, but only one of them, Friedrich von Prittwitz und Gaffron, the German ambassador in Washington, actually did so. A group of leading business executives, including Carl Friedrich von Siemens, of the giant corporation that bore (and still bears) his family name, and Carl Bosch, of IG Farben, the huge chemicals conglomerate, met a few times during the year to draft a document intended to dissuade Hitler from antisemitic actions, but they never actually submitted it. Instead, the typical response of corporate executives was to knuckle under to Party attacks on Jews while seeking, at most, to shield a few valued individuals. Thus, Gustav Krupp von Bohlen und Halbach, the head of the National Association of German Industry, caved in to the demands of storm troopers who occupied his office in Berlin on April 1, 1933, and agreed to dismiss the Jews employed by his organization, along with anyone else the Nazi Party deemed politically unacceptable. Thus, too, Degussa, a firm that refined precious metals, responded to insinuations by Nazi newspapers that it was under Jewish influence by issuing notarized announcements that it had never employed Jews. In this fashion, the firm hoped to divert attention from the facts that several Jews had played a significant role in founding the enterprise seventy years earlier and six Jews still sat on the company's supervisory board in 1933.

Why did prominent, successful, established Germans fail to take a moral stand in 1933? There were many reasons. For one thing, the Nazi regime rapidly acquired a monopoly on political discourse and changed the moral valence of hatred from bad to good. Prior to 1933, antisemitism seemed crude and shameful in many quarters; now it was identified with patriotism everywhere. Conversely, expressing sympathy for Jews was now an unpatriotic act that could attract suspicion or condemnation. Attacking Jews was of far greater importance to the Nazis than defending them was to other Germans, so most such people decided that discretion was the better part of valor and said nothing. Besides, even Germans who found Nazi antisemitism distasteful approved of other aspects of the Party's program—in other words, shared a partial identity of interests with Hitler's movement. Diplomats and military officers, for example, generally longed for the revision of the terms of the Versailles Treaty and the resurgence of the German army, and Hitler promised to deliver these things. Many corporate executives hoped for the suppression of the trade unions and recovery from the Depression, and Hitler embraced these goals, too.

Above all, in the rapidly changing and violent context of early 1933, most upper-class Germans took refuge in a delusional mix of fear for their livelihoods and a misplaced sense of responsibility. As Ernst von Weizsäcker of the Foreign Ministry wrote at the time, "the specialist cannot simply quit the field." Instead, he had to give the regime "all forms of support and experience . . . and help see to it that the . . . current revolution becomes genuinely constructive." Of course, Weizsäcker did not find this particularly difficult because he also deplored what he imagined as the nation's "inundation with Jews" since 1919. But even a somewhat more liberal figure, Fritz Roessler, the head of the supervisory board of Degussa, tried to put the best face on things in 1933 and concluded that people like him "should recognize the good in the movement, ignore the human deficiencies associated with every revolution, and do one's bit so that this wild-grown juice becomes wine."

As in Weizsäcker's and Roessler's cases, a strong sense of duty in 1933 often blinded people in high places to the implications of their choices. In the long run, helping the Nazis "in order to avoid worse," as the phrase of the day went, merely made them stronger and more dangerous. As the pastor of Kurt Gerstein, who later served in the SS and procured some of the Zyklon gas used at Auschwitz, told him in the 1930s, when he decided to join the Nazi Party and try to influence it from within, "you reckon that you can still have a say in things.... [But] he who enters this tumbling avalanche only increases the plunging mass." Very few Germans were this farsighted.

Among younger people still working their way up profession-ally, the way the Nazis mixed intimidation and indoctrination in 1933 comes across very powerfully in Sebastian Haffner's memoir, called in English *Defying Hitler*. That title is melodramatic and sen-sational, but Haffner did flee his homeland in 1938 and make a new career in England as a journalist before returning to Germany after World War II. In his native language, he called his book simply *Geschichte eines Deutschen* (Story of a German). Haffner, whose real name was Raimund Pretzel, was twenty-six years old when Hitler came to power and a law student preparing to take his bar exams. He paints vivid pictures of the marauding storm trooper units that beat up anyone in the streets who failed to raise a hand in the Nazi salute when a swastika flag passed by and of the day in the spring of 1933 when these thugs broke into the law library where he was studying, asked all the patrons, *"Sind Sie arisch?"* ("Are you an Aryan?"), and assaulted those who said no or appeared to be lying. He walked away from that occasion deeply ashamed of himself for having answered the question truthfully with a yes. This was far from the only or even the first such assault on the legal system that spring.

That was the intimidation side of 1933; the indoctrination side came later, when the new regime ordered Haffner and all the other bar candidates to spend the summer at a kind of boot camp for future lawyers, where they were taught the Party's racist ideology and drilled endlessly. Searching for a word to describe what the experience had done to him and his peers, Haffner coined a neologism based on one of the words Party members used to address each other, *Kamerad*, or comrade. He said the camp had *verkameradet* these young men, which means "comraded" or "comradified" them. The militarization of German life by institutions and practices such as this discouraged critical thinking during the 1930s and encouraged group identification, solidarity, and obedience. So did the regime's relentless emphasis on the People's Community (*Volksgemeinschaft*) and insistence that German citizens had moral obligations only to "Us" and no one else. A great, intoxicating glorification of "belonging" began to grip German life. Hans Schemm, the new Bavarian minister of culture, explained the intellectual obligations this imposed in 1933, when he told a group of professors in Munich, "From now on, it is not up to you to decide whether something is true, but whether it is in the interests of the National Socialist Revolution."

These stories illustrate how power magnifies the ideas of those who hold it because of the human tendency to seek safety in conformity. The only antidotes are conviction—loyalty to a strong countervailing ideology—and the freedom to express it. Where these are lacking, as was the case in Germany after 1933, ideologues quickly get the upper hand and call the tune for behavior. A minority of haters, backed by the authority of the state, thus becomes free to drive events forward, to make the lives of any targeted group ever more miserable.

Self-interest dictated to most other Germans that they should ignore what was happening to the Jews or treat it as merely the price of the apparently good things the Nazi regime was bringing. After all, by 1936, the Depression was over and unemployment a thing of the past; the Nazi regime had achieved the fastest economic revival in the world. By the same year, Germany had recovered the Saar region, which France had administered since 1919; had renounced the military limits imposed on the Reich by the Versailles Treaty; and had sent its soldiers back into the Rhineland, the formerly demilitarized western strip of territory that bordered the Netherlands, Belgium, Luxembourg, and France. Within the next two years, Hitler annexed Austria, brought the German speakers of the Sudetenland "home" to the nation of which they had never been a part, and occupied the rest of today's Czech Republic, all without firing a shot or losing a soldier in battle.

Self-interest also encouraged some people to seek to benefit from the persecution, which accounts for the many eager lawyers and brokers who acted as middlemen in the sale of Jews' assets and the numerous willing graspers for their medical and legal practices, their artwork, their houses and apartments, their furniture and carpets, and so on. Many non-Jews concluded that they could not stop the persecution, so they might as well get something out of it. Even Germans who did not exploit the situation in this fashion increasingly looked out for themselves by cutting off contact with Jewish friends and neighbors, thus both increasing their isolation and becoming deaf and blind to their suffering.

Besides, the gradual nature of the Nazi escalation raised the general problem of seeing ahead that affected all parties, including non-Jewish Germans, Jewish Germans, and foreigners. Had people known that cruelty and discrimination would become starvation and slaughter, more might have balked. But even the Nazis did not know this in 1933, so why should anyone else have been sure? Instead of imagining where persecution might lead, Germans got caught up in the completely self-referential intellectual world that the Nazis created, where public information was tightly controlled, foreign publications were banned, the adjective "cosmopolitan" was a preferred term of abuse, and people were constantly reminded to "work towards the Führer," to imagine what Hitler would want them to do and then to do it. The public mind was, in other words, methodically poisoned, and the measuring stick of morality systematically shifted from general ethical principles like the Golden Rule to the specific matter of whether an action strengthened Germany or did not. This warping of people's thinking worked especially powerfully on young people coming of age during the 1930s, who seldom had an independent frame of reference. Teenagers were at the forefront of violent attacks on individual Jews and attempts to humiliate them and those who consorted with them during that decade.

Two caveats about this collective brainwashing need stressing. First, it did not necessarily change what older people thought, but it decisively changed what they would say or do. The Nazis defined public discourse and controlled the social reward system, and that was enough to limit open disagreement or dissent. Second, the corruption of people's sense of decency toward Jews did not happen overnight or without the occasional application of extra pressure. Another story about Degussa illustrates the latter point. The tale concerns the behavior of Ernst Busemann, the head of Degussa's managing board, toward two Jewish families, the Meyers and the Margulieses, who had sold majority interests in their firms to Degussa during the 1920s but retained 26 percent of the stock and management positions in the respective subsidiaries. In November and December of 1937, the NSBO chapter at the first of these subsidiaries wanted it to compete for the honor of being a National Socialist Model Factory. The union therefore petitioned the managing director to make this possible by buying out the Jewish members of the Meyer family and removing them from management. The director dutifully wrote to Busemann and asked what to do. Busemann's reply survives, and it is a remarkable document that begins with fulsome praise for the members of the Meyer family as old friends and upstanding businessmen, then expresses regret that he holds their fate in his hands, and finally delivers the crushing judgment that, nonetheless, "it is pointless to swim against the stream"—the Meyers and their shareholding would have to go. To soften the blow, Busemann contrived a way to pay for their stock in the subsidiary with stock in IG Farben that had the same face value but a considerably higher market worth. In contrast, only a few months later, in April 1938, after the Nazis demanded the expulsion of the Jewish minority owners of the Degussa subsidiary in Austria, Busemann offered the members of the Margulies family only a fraction in cash of what the stock was worth and told them to take it or leave it. Why

the abrupt and extreme change? The political danger of being discovered acting generously or even sympathetically toward Jews had
become much greater in the aftermath of the annexation of Austria
(the *Anschluss*) and Göring's decrees accelerating Aryanization, and
Busemann adjusted his behavior accordingly.

These stories from Haffner's memoir and the history of Degussa
are indicative, but are they representative? What do we know about
what most Germans thought about the persecution of the Jews, and
how do we know it? We actually have quite a few sources, of which
the following four are among the most important: the *Sopade-Berichte*,
periodic reports smuggled out to the Social Democratic Party in
Exile in Prague by leftist opponents of the regime still in Germany;
the *Stimmungsberichte*, or "mood reports," collected by Gestapo
(secret state police) agents among the public and published decades
later as *Meldungen aus dem Reich* (an English translation of passages
concerning Jews comes to 657 pages); numerous diaries kept by non-
Jewish Germans and gleaned effectively by Peter Fritzsche in *Life
and Death in the Third Reich*; and a brilliant, poignant diary kept by
a baptized Jew with a non-Jewish wife, Victor Klemperer, who survived the Nazi regime, which has been published in English in two
volumes under the title *I Will Bear Witness*.

These sources paint a complex, inconsistent picture, in which
acts of kindness mix with extraordinary callousness, but the overall
portrait is of a public split into three groups: people who endorsed
the persecution of the Jews, people who merely accepted it, and people who disliked it but saw little point in protesting, even though
they frequently expressed reservations or felt embarrassed about
specific actions. The Gestapo reports vividly record both the bullying and harassment that Jews experienced on a daily basis and the
distaste that such actions sometimes aroused. In September 1934,
the office in Potsdam regretted to relate that "the Jewish question is
not the main problem of the German public. . . . Utterances on the
Jewish peril are played down, and those engaged in enlightening the

population are depicted to a certain extent as fools." The follow-ing July, the office in Kiel stated, "It is noteworthy that, when-ever there are actions against the Jews, these emanate chiefly from members of the Party and its affiliated organizations, whereas the majority of the population shows little participation." In Octo-ber 1935, the office in Magdeburg had this to say about the public response to the Nuremberg Laws, enacted that year: "all in all, it is accurate to note that the new laws have been received in part with indifference, and in part with very little appreciation and under-standing outside the solid National Socialist-oriented population." Other offices reported precisely the opposite, however, contending that the public welcomed the Nuremberg Laws as finally creating clarity about the position of Jews in Germany.

Insofar as one can generalize about the indications of adult German public opinion prior to *Kristallnacht*, they record general acceptance of antisemitic policies except when they threatened the self-interest of non-Jews. Thus many Germans resented the Par-ty's appeals to stay away from Jewish-owned shops, because they were perceived as often offering better goods at better prices, and many farmers had to be forced to break off their relationships with trusted Jewish livestock dealers. Similarly, but in a more abstract sense, many Germans feared damage to the nation's image abroad from antisemitic actions and from the prominence of virulent anti-semitic publications, notably Julius Streicher's *Der Stürmer*. In the mid-1930s, it was posted conspicuously every day in special glass display cases in many towns and villages, but as time passed, public discomfort led to a decline in that practice. The reaction to *Kristall-nacht* itself reaffirmed this pattern, as numerous people in the street expressed shame and disgust on the morning after, though as much at the wasteful destruction of property and appearance of disorder as at the harm done to Jews. Whatever the mix of attitudes among the non-Jewish population, the decisive point is that violence and viciousness toward Jews increased steadily during the 1930s in Nazi

Germany and in full public view, especially in small cities and the countryside, yet the pattern gave rise to too little rejection or revulsion to make the Nazi regime change course.

Once the war began, hostility toward Jews hardened. Rumors were rife about ghettoization and impending deportation from Germany to Poland, and little dissent emerged in the early years of the fighting. Many Gestapo reports in 1940 stressed the powerful impact on the populace of the propaganda film *Jud Süss*, which clearly strengthened antisemitic feeling. In July 1941, the Gestapo office in Berlin commented on the public response to the first round of newsreels from the Eastern Front in these words, "The images of the arrest of the Jews . . . have met with enthusiastic approval, and people say that the Jews here [that is, in Germany] are being treated with far too much leniency. The series of pictures on the forced deployment of the Jews in clearing operations were greeted everywhere with great delight." And, in September, local offices from all around the country chorused that the order for German Jews to start wearing identifying Stars of David on their clothing had been greeted with "genuine satisfaction" and "gratification." Nonetheless, a month later, Goebbels lamented in his diary, "our intellectuals and high society have once again suddenly discovered their humane feelings for the poor Jews." He therefore made sure that an announcement of new punishments for "Jew-friendly behavior" accompanied the next set of monthly ration books delivered to every German home.

Despite such reminders, the Nazi regime felt the need to take additional precautions against sympathy arising toward German Jews after their deportation began. In Berlin during October 1941, the first contingents of people being sent "to the east" reported to the Levetzowstrasse synagogue in the Moabit neighborhood near the center of the city and then had to walk six kilometers in broad daylight to the loading point at the Grunewald freight railroad station on the far west side of town. When the shipments resumed in mid-1942, the authorities decided to expose fewer witnesses to the spectacle by conducting the marches in the middle of the night. Similarly, later that year, when Berlin Jews began being shipped from another, even more centrally located collection point in the Grosse Hamburgerstrasse to the ghetto camp at Theresienstadt in Bohemia, they made the first legs of the journey before dawn via streetcar to trains that left from the not yet bustling Anhalter railroad station.

The use of Theresienstadt (Terezin in Czech) as a destination for elderly and decorated German Jews also attested to the Nazi regime's residual desire to disguise what was happening. A formerly Austrian garrison town in Bohemia that had been turned into a holding pen for Czech Jews in November 1941, the site became after mid-1942 a supposed refuge for German Jews unable to perform the "work in the east" to which most deportees allegedly were being sent. In reality, this "old people's ghetto" proved to be a mere way station on the road to death for most of the 58,000 Jews from Greater Germany ever confined there. About 41 percent of them were sent on to death camps; a slightly larger share died on the site from cold, hunger, and disease; and only about 7,000 remained at liberation in 1945. Meanwhile, however, Nazi propaganda highlighted the mythical comforts of the installation in order, first, to mislead Germans about the regime's intentions, and then, in 1944, to delude the gullible representatives of the International Red Cross whom the Reich allowed to tour the temporarily prettified grounds.

At least with regard to two categories of German Jews, those descended from or in marriages to non-Jewish Germans, the regime was for a time also cautious. It introduced restrictions on them more slowly than on "full Jews" (*Volljuden*) or people the Nazis counted as such because of their marital status or religious affiliation (*Geltungsjuden*) and deferred expulsion, lest numerous non-Jewish German relatives protest. Still, essentially the same long discovery process that had occurred in making policy toward German Jews took place, only at a slower pace, toward those Germans who had one Jewish grandparent (second-degree *Mischlinge*; 40,000 people in 1939) or two but no other connection to Jews or Judaism (first-degree *Mischlinge*; 64,000 in 1939). Thus *Mischlinge*, unlike Jews, had neither lost German citizenship nor been forbidden to have sexual relations with so-called Aryans under the Nuremberg Laws, though future marriages between Aryans and *Mischlinge* were banned. *Mischlinge* were barred from military service later than Jews and exempted from concentration in so-called Jew Houses and from deportation to ghettos or death camps until 1943. Thereafter the regime cracked down, exhibiting increased confidence or fanaticism in sweeping potential objections aside and encountering, in fact, very few. Roundups for incarceration in forced labor camps began in the spring of 1944, followed in early 1945 by the planned deportation to Theresienstadt of all remaining *Mischlinge* and all of the approximately 21,500 German and Austrian Jews who still clung to precarious existence as part of mixed marriages. Victor Klemperer, the now famous diarist, escaped deportation in early 1945 only because the firebombing of Dresden, where he lived, occurred just before his scheduled departure, and the resulting chaos enabled him to conceal his identity as he and his wife fled the city. Many other prospective deportees were not so lucky. Although shipments from Berlin were impeded by the last Soviet offensive, trains from places like Frankfurt and Leipzig arrived at Theresienstadt, and some of those aboard did not survive the few remaining months of the war; many barely did so. Had the Third Reich endured or even lasted a little longer, most of the first-degree *Mischlinge* and the Jewish spouses of non-Jews appear to have been destined for death and most of the second-degree *Mischlinge* for sterilization.

As Germans grew steadily more hard-hearted toward Jews and steadily more receptive to Nazi propaganda about them after 1933, why did the Jewish community in Germany not defend itself better or at least get entirely out of harm's way? In a sense, the question, like the one often raised about Jewish behavior in the ghettos of Poland examined later in this book, is terribly naïve and cruel. Jews were up against a Nazi movement that was both ruthless and shameless in what it would say about and do to them. They constituted a tiny share of the German population to begin with in 1933 and became ever fewer as time passed. They shared with everyone else an inability to see what was coming, all the more so as it involved behavior unprecedented on the part of a civilized country.

Above all, Germany's Jews, like those of occupied Europe later, were not monolithic and conspiratorially united, as the Nazis claimed, but divided among themselves about what the Nazi onslaught signified and therefore how to respond to it. About two-thirds of them were liberal, acculturated, often somewhat secular or entirely non-observant Jews, either members of or in sympathy with the Centralverein deutscher Staatsbürger jüdischen Glaubens, the Central Association of German Citizens of the Jewish Faith, a name that signified their desire to be integrated into the German nation and to have the same rights as all other German citizens. For this group, the Nazi attack was difficult to comprehend and especially painful to experience because it seemed such an unwarranted rejection of their loyalty to Germany.

The other two principal groups, the Orthodox, who accounted for perhaps 20 percent of Jews in Germany in 1933, and the Zionists, who then constituted 5–10 percent, were not so hurt by the Nazis' hostility, because they expected it. To the Orthodox, it was the work of an inscrutable God but probably a punishment for the apostasy of so many German Jews. The answer was to pray harder. To the Zionists, advocates of settling and founding a Jewish state in Palestine, endemic hostility of gentiles toward Jews was the assumption on which their movement rested. The Zionist answer to German persecution was to work with the Nazis on the basis of a common conviction that Jews and Germans constituted separate nationalities in order to achieve one partially shared objective: emigration of Jews from Germany. Partially shared, not identical—because the Nazis wanted to drive all Jews out of Germany; but the Zionists knew that the *Yishuv*, the Jewish settler community in Palestine, could afford to take only some Jews in, preferably young and fit ones who could speak Hebrew and were willing to do hard physical work on collective farms, the *kibbutzim*. Moreover, even while the Nazis promoted the Zionist goal of Jewish immigration to Palestine, they opposed the Zionist objective of founding a Jewish state there.

This overlapping interest in emigration resulted in the controversial *Ha'avara*, or Transfer Agreement, of August 1933. It created a modest escape route for German Jews during the 1930s, eventually financing the emigration to Palestine of about 20,000 of the 52,000 German Jews who got there by 1939, and contributed to the increasing popularity of Zionism among German Jews during the 1930s. But the Transfer Agreement was morally questionable, hotly debated at the time, and consequently not generally imitated by or for Jewish communities elsewhere. Basically, the agreement set up a system by which Jews seeking to leave Germany for Palestine had their possessions in Germany appraised and then handed them over to the German state. Germany thereupon paid some individual émigrés whose wealth exceeded a certain minimum in reichsmark at least 1,000 Palestinian pounds sterling, the threshold level of cash assets for unrestricted entrance to Palestine. The Reich then was supposed to pay the remainder of all admitted German Jewish emigrants' wealth to the Jewish Agency in Palestine in the form of German goods that the agency could sell for the benefit of these or other new settlers. The *Yishuv* got people out, and Germany got most of the Jews' property, along with increased production for export that buoyed employment at home and thus strengthened the Nazi regime. For a while, this system seemed to offer something to both Zionists and Nazis, but its economic value to Germany declined rapidly. Beginning in 1935, the Nazi regime steadily raised the reichsmark minimum for issuing Palestinian currency and reduced the range of goods available for resale. In the end, exiting German Jews got to retain less than 1.5 percent of their property via the agreement, and it remained operative until World War II began only because Hitler did not wish to abandon any device that might encourage Jews to leave Germany.

As to other forms of emigration, German Jewish leaders at first hesitated. The Central Association discouraged emigration in 1933–35 because leaving amounted to surrendering claims to Germanness and abandoning those Jews who could not get out. But after the enactment of the Nuremberg Laws, the Central Association changed its attitude and began to encourage emigration. The organization remained a proponent of the diaspora over a Jewish state but conceded that German Jewry had no long-term future by renaming itself in 1936. Dropping the reference to German citizenship, the group became simply the Jüdischer Centralverein, the Jewish Central Association. By 1937, as noted above, most German Jews had begun seeking an exit, even though they had limited prospects. But some people had better chances of being accepted elsewhere than others. Broadly speaking, age worked against a person, youth worked for him or her: 84 percent of German Jews under the age of twenty-four in 1933 got out alive, compared to 60 percent of the total population; by 1939, one-third of the remaining Jews in Germany were sixty or more years old, and just more than half were over fifty. A person possessing the few skills needed elsewhere had a better chance than someone whose abilities threatened to compete with residents of other countries. This often meant that people with artisanal or agricultural training had better prospects than professionals. Wealth sometimes enabled people to leave early because other countries were more open to persons bringing money, and in the early years of Nazi rule, Jews could take a larger share of their assets with them than later was allowed. But wealth also tempted people to remain, since the Nazis generally targeted large firms and their owners last, and then such people generally lost almost everything. Men had better chances of going abroad than women,

but the fact that women made up 60 percent of the remaining German Jewish population in 1939 almost certainly reflected something
else—namely, that they more often assumed caretaker responsibilities for aged parents or disabled or handicapped relatives than did
men, given the prevailing gender roles of the day. A good many of
the Jews still in Germany in 1939 simply could not leave someone
behind who depended on them.

The legend that German Jews faced the persecution passively
or incredulously is just that, a legend. They fought back the only
way they collectively could: by equipping as many people as possible
with skills that would help them get out and by mutually sustaining
all those who remained. Already in 1933, they organized a Central
Welfare Office of German Jews and a national organization, the
Reichsvertretung der deutschen Juden, the National Representation of German Jews. These groups collected and disbursed funds
for labor offices, cars for traveling salesmen, legal aid clinics, and
the like. From 1933 to 1937, such welfare offices at the national and
local levels spent 26.3 million reichsmark from their own resources,
plus 7.5 million donated from abroad. Special groups for doctors,
lawyers, and artists came into being and worked to find new positions for unemployed colleagues abroad or at Jewish institutions
within the country. Some 140 retraining institutes were established,
through which 30,000 people passed by 1938, two-thirds of them
younger than twenty. As the government cut Jews off from the state
welfare system, they depended increasingly for support on contri-
butions from the shrinking population of Jews who still had work.
Already in 1935, one-third of the Jews in Germany relied on such
help, and Jewish soup kitchens across the country dispensed 2.5 million meals. But in subsequent years, both the number of people and
the percentage of the population that the community could sustain
dropped along with the size of the remaining population. Jewish
self-help was fighting a losing battle, but it was an effort that did
credit to the people who undertook it.

In 1939, the Nazi regime dissolved the Reichsvertretung and all other Jewish communal organizations and replaced them with a new entity that enrolled all remaining Jews in Germany. This was called the Reichsvereinigung der Juden in Deutschland, the National Union of Jews in Germany. Its leaders continued the heroic struggle to sustain Germany's remaining and increasingly aged and impoverished Jewish population, but the effort proved hopeless as the persecution escalated toward murder. By the time deportations began in October 1941, most of the remaining Jews in Germany were in a beleaguered and wretched state. Crammed at least two people to a room into Jew Houses with communal kitchens and baths and scattered around the worst neighborhoods of the big cities, deprived of their radios and even their pets, allowed fewer ration coupons for food and other goods than those allotted to non-Jewish Germans, and permitted to shop only in the final hours of specified days, by which time stores often had sold out, many Jews were on the edge of starvation and despair. Their leaders in the National Union were subordinated directly to the RSHA and sought to protect themselves, as did their counterparts in occupied Europe, by carrying out the SS's instructions. The Reichsvereinigung thus degenerated into an instrument by which the Nazi regime kept track of all Jews left in Germany, plundered what was left of their possessions, and then managed many aspects of the deportations, including identifying eligible Jews according to selection criteria set by the Reich Security Main Office. In 1942–43, the National Union even sent its own personnel, called *Ordner*, or auxiliaries, to collect the people assigned to each transport if they did not comply with a summons to report on the preceding day. In Vienna the name given to these Jewish helpers of the SS was more descriptive; they were called "lifters" (*Ausheber*).

As was the case in the ghettos further east, such submissiveness resulted from desires for both self-preservation and amelioration. Cooperation with the SS seemed the only available way for Jewish leaders to stay alive and to alleviate the plight of deportees by

providing food and blankets to them at the collection and departure points. But behind the actions of the Reichsvereinigung was
something else that also operated farther east: direct intimidation.
The Nazis took fierce reprisals against recalcitrance or resistance.
Emblematic of the viciousness were the actions that followed an
attempt in May 1942 by a group around a Jew named Herbert Baum
to burn down a propaganda exhibition against the Soviet Union in
Berlin. The Gestapo caught thirty-three conspirators almost immediately and executed not only those people but another 250 Jewish
men, who were rounded up and sent to Sachsenhausen, just outside
the city. Another 250 Jewish males then also disappeared into that
camp, the families of all 500 men immediately were deported "to
the east," and Goebbels stepped up the timetable for making Berlin
"Jew-free."

How did Hitler manage to ratchet up the persecution of Germany's Jews during the 1930s without provoking foreign interference
or even intervention? He did this, in part, by phasing in restrictions
and even occasionally holding out the prospect that some Jews could
remain in Germany—or at least in Theresienstadt—in the long
run. Nazi leaders kept people guessing about their intentions and
said just enough contradictory things to make at least some outsiders believe that the worst would not happen. That some outsiders
wanted to believe this is the second key piece of an explanation. In
Britain and France, the two nations best positioned to alter Hitler's
behavior before German rearmament had reached dangerous pro-
portions, homegrown antisemitism combined with wishful thinking
to argue for noninterference in Germany's internal affairs, however
barbaric they might seem. That wishful thinking propelled the policy of appeasement, which amounted to the belief that protecting
the rights of others, whether German Jews or the Czechs at the time
of the Munich Conference, was not worth the risk of another world
war and the terrible carnage that Britain and France had experienced. Until *Kristallnacht* and sometimes beyond, many appeasers

actually were inclined to blame Jews for poisoning relations with Germany rather than to blame Germany for persecuting Jews.

Hitler played brilliantly throughout the 1930s on fear of war in the Allied nations, and he invited them repeatedly to buy him off with concessions that he later announced were insufficient. This tactic worked so well for him until he occupied the Czech provinces in March 1939, only six months after he promised to leave them independent at the Munich Conference, that the Allies recurrently declined to let the fate of Germany's Jews upset the quest for peace. Hitler and his propaganda agencies also played shrewdly on the antisemitism present in Britain, France, and also the United States. He blackmailed these countries into reticence or silence by the simple trick of claiming that they were tools of the Jews and then citing any protest on their behalf by these countries as proof of his charge. Fearing to seem to confirm his propaganda and thus to arouse domestic antisemites, the Allied governments generally fell into a Nazi trap and pulled their punches, at least until *Kristallnacht*. Even after the pogrom—in fact, less than a month later, on December 6, 1938—France signed a new treaty with Germany reaffirming the integrity of the border between the two countries. Meanwhile, Joseph Lyons, the prime minister of Australia and a vigorous proponent of appeasement, resolutely refused to condemn the atrocities in Germany, lest doing so interfere with his efforts to head off war. Only one nation, the United States, exercised the usual diplomatic form of expressing revulsion at the Nazi rampage by calling America's ambassador home "for consultations."

The Nazi regime was adept before the war at constructing choices that looked bleak either way for both Germany's Jews and the Allied states. German Jews rapidly recognized that they faced a constant choice between complying with Nazi actions and making them worse. They opted to do the best they could under barbaric circumstances and to play for time. The Allies constantly had to choose, at least after 1936, between accepting both Nazi territorial demands and Nazi mistreatment of German Jews or a bloody war that Britain and France expected would weaken their holds on their empires and, as Neville Chamberlain explicitly predicted, put them hopelessly in debt to the United States. Even if they won, the Allies stood to lose, and after 1945, they did, as Chamberlain's fears came true. Britain, after all, suffered under food rationing into the early 1950s because the war did such damage to its economy, and the British, French, Dutch, and Belgian empires melted away following the war.

As the persecution of the Jews escalated, the Nazi regime presented another group with unpalatable alternatives, namely the owners of foreign direct investment in Nazi Germany. Ford, General Motors, IBM, Standard Oil, and many other American corporations all possessed significant German subsidiaries during the 1930s, as did several large Dutch, Swedish, and Swiss enterprises. Recent books have criticized the American firms for not divesting their holdings in protest against mounting Nazi discrimination and brutality and, instead, letting their offshoots in Germany become complicit in German rearmament and in some cases in the persecution of the Jews. Some authors have spoken of a "strategic alliance" between American corporations and Hitler, of corporate "collaboration" and "pacts" with the Nazis.

Such overblown charges overlook a number of aspects of the situation the parent companies confronted. Divestment for political or moral reasons was a virtually unknown practice in the 1930s, which is the principal reason why almost no major corporation with holdings in Germany, regardless of the country in which its headquarters stood, suspended operations or sold out and withdrew. The exceptions were a few of the Hollywood film distribution companies, notably Warner Bros., which closed its German sales operations in 1933, and United Artists, Universal, RKO, and Columbia Pictures, which followed suit fairly quickly. But only Warner's gave up completely on the German market. The other four companies preserved special arrangements with German partners, and MGM,

Paramount, and Twentieth Century-Fox kept trying to get their films introduced into German theaters and making the compromises that seemed necessary to that objective right up until World War II began. And these were not manufacturing firms with major fixed investments. Though businessmen like to say that "all past costs are sunk," meaning that the chief criterion for continuing an enterprise is its future returns, not the capital previously committed to it, few firms in this or any other era have found acting on that maxim palatable, especially when the asset in question is even only slightly profitable. The prevailing tendencies among businessmen were to retain what they had in the hope that political conditions would improve in the future and meanwhile to try to extract the returns that had been the goal of the original investment.

Moreover, financial controls established by the Nazi regime blocked the repatriation of income earned in Germany. Both while a company continued and in the event of its sale, all net proceeds had to be reinvested in the Reich or converted into government bonds. This reinforced the reluctance to divest, since the only comparably profitable investments were likely to be at least as implicated in German government policies as the ones the parent companies already possessed. In the event of divestment, then, the foreign investor faced not quite a total loss, but declining control over assets without appreciable moral gain. Finally, most foreign-owned companies in Germany spent the 1930s fighting and largely losing a rearguard action precisely against this declining control. In almost every case, managers from the owning country gave way to Germans, who took pains to position the subsidiaries as German firms in order to hold onto business and who acted increasingly independently of their home offices, not least because Nazi mandates regarding economic secrecy restricted what the local managers even could report about their activities. As a result, headquarters in Detroit in the case of the car companies and New York in the case of IBM had little influence over day-to-day operating decisions in their German affiliates after

1938 or 1939 at the latest; the same was true of Lever Brothers of the Netherlands, one of the largest foreign investors in Nazi Germany. For all of these reasons, as well as the general difficulty of seeing ahead, the Nazi persecution of the Jews did not encounter the sort of economic pressures successfully brought to bear some fifty years later on the apartheid regime in South Africa.

In any case, IBM's rebellious subsidiary, the *Deutsche Hollerith Maschinen Gesellschaft*, managed by the spiteful German who formerly owned it, did not play the roles in identifying and later rounding up the German Jews or in managing slave labor that the parent firm's critics have maintained. From 1933 to 1943, the Gestapo used the card files efficiently compiled and regularly updated by the Reichsvertretung and its successor to keep tabs on the nation's Jews and their residences. The SS experimented briefly in 1944 with using Hollerith cards and tabulators to steer the deployment of camp inmates to work sites but soon gave up on the idea. GM's Opel division became complicit, in that it began building thousands of trucks for the German army and then aircraft engines for the Luftwaffe well before the United States and Germany went to war in 1941 and the company's plants were placed under a German trustee. But this acceptance of government contracts began only after the Nazi regime threatened to expropriate the firm. In 1939–41, Ford-Werke in Cologne produced fewer trucks for the Wehrmacht than Opel, but some were used in the invasions of Austria and Bohemia-Moravia, and the local management gave in, not to threats but to desperation to offset declining sales of civilian vehicles.

After World War II ended, the economic appeasers who clung to their foreign investments in Germany could claim, like the political appeasers but with more positive results, that events had vindicated their course. The parent companies recovered their assets west of the iron curtain and even such profits as these had accumulated. Perhaps alone among all the groups confronted with poor options by the Nazi regime during the 1930s, the American owners ultimately found playing for time a successful strategy.

In sum, the years 1933–41 taught Hitler and his followers that neither Germans nor foreigners were inclined to interfere with Nazi actions toward Jews. In the context of the regime's inability to expel them faster than it conquered them, such passivity added impetus to ever more radical persecution.

CHAPTER 4

ANNIHILATION:
Why This Swift
and Sweeping?

ONE OFTEN AND surprisingly overlooked feature of the Holocaust is its combination of shocking temporal and spatial compression with sweeping extent. Although the Nazis kept killing Jews until the Third Reich crumbled, and although it rounded them up all over Europe to kill them, several striking fractions give a sense of how concentrated the time and place of the massacre was, as well as how encompassing. Three-quarters of the nearly six million victims were killed within only twenty months, from June 1941 to February 1943, and half of the total victims died within only the last eleven months of that time frame. Moreover, three-quarters of those killed lived before the war in only three countries: Poland, Lithuania, and the USSR (mostly in the northeast quadrant of the European continent, demarcated on figure 4 by dotted horizontal and vertical lines going east and north from Vienna), and probably nine-tenths of the victims died in those places, since that is where the *Einsatzgruppen*, the Order Police, the Reserve Police Battalions, and the great bulk of the Wehrmacht operated and where Germans placed the death camps. Altogether, at least three-quarters of the Jews who ever came within reach of Nazi Germany and its allies were killed, constituting in the end two-thirds of the Jews of Europe (six million out of nine million when World War II began; the oft-quoted total of eleven million given in the minutes of the Wannsee Conference was an exaggeration or included converts as well as their children and grandchildren). For Jewish children sixteen or younger, the mortality rate was almost nine-tenths.

Why was the Holocaust so concentrated in these ways? How could the Nazis come so close to killing all the European Jews—and do so at the average rate of 225,000 people per month, from mid-1941 to early 1943, and 325,000 per month (more than 10,000 *per day*), at the frenetic peak of the Holocaust in 1942–43?

FIGURE 4: THE GEOGRAPHICAL COMPRESSION OF THE HOLOCAUST

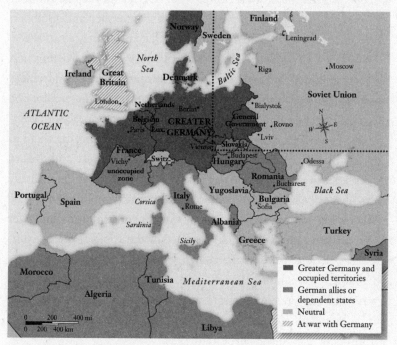

FROM BULLETS TO GAS

In a sense, the heart of the answer to these questions is technical. By 1941, the Nazis had a motive to kill the Jews of Europe—namely, the deep-seated ideological conviction that they were implacable enemies—and an opportunity to do so—the chance to slaughter under the guise of military action. The expansion of the conflict added new rationales to remove Jews from German territory, such as the desire to resettle the *Volksdeutsche* and the need to conserve scarce food supplies, and removed restraints on Nazi action, since a regime already or about to be at war with the whole world had little left to lose. Considerations like these led the Third Reich to decide on a policy of mass murder in the occupied Soviet Union, but there alone, at first.

What seemed to be missing before Nazi Germany took the final, fateful step toward total annihilation of the Jewish population in Europe was the means to accomplish it. But during the late summer and early fall of 1941, in the months of September and October, Hitler and Himmler came to recognize that they already had these. The war had spawned possibilities for carrying out mass killing, and all that remained lacking were installations at which to apply these possibilities. The Nazi leaders knew that they could not employ the methods being used in the lands conquered from the USSR in Central or Western Europe. Simply shooting Jews and burying them in pits was likely to arouse revulsion and opposition there and thus to increase resistance to German rule, which would raise the military costs of maintaining it. Besides, Himmler quickly came to fear the effect on his men of having to shoot women and children hour after hour, day after day. Indeed, at least one of the *Einsatzgruppen* commanders, Erich von dem Bach-Zelewski, later suffered a nervous breakdown, though only briefly. What the Nazi regime needed was a way of killing people that was inconspicuous or, as the SS planners put it, "noiseless" (*geräuschlos*), and that was more, again as they put it, "humane" . . . to the perpetrators.

This is the context in which to interpret the letter of July 31, 1941, that Göring sent to Heydrich, authorizing him to find "an overall solution to the Jewish question in the German sphere." Heydrich already had authority over "emigration and evacuation," as the letter noted. He had no need for new authority unless he was being given a new assignment, and this document extended his competence to the entire "German sphere" and asked him to identify a "total solution," implicitly in addition to the partial solution already being enacted in Russia. In other words, this letter is the surest sign that the Nazi state already was looking for a comprehensive method to apply continent-wide, and Heydrich's task was to find it.

In fact, the regime had possessed such a method since early in 1940. Beginning in 1938 with a single case, Hitler had authorized subordinates in his personal Chancellery to grant parental petitions to kill German children born mentally handicapped, and his regime followed this up in August 1939 with a decree requiring hospitals to report all births of deformed, paralyzed, or mentally deficient children to Berlin. During the same summer, he directed his staff to consult with medical doctors and professors from some of Germany's leading universities to devise a procedure for extending euthanasia to adults in the event of war, when Germany would need to free up hospital beds for military casualties. None of the experts balked at participating, but the matter was legally murky, since Hitler declined to issue a law justifying the killing, lest Germany's enemies use that as propaganda against the Reich. So the Chancellery officials felt the need for a way to assure the people involved of immunity from criminal liability and therefore asked Hitler for some form of written authorization. The result was a letter, signed by the Nazi Führer on his personal, not his official, stationery and backdated to the opening day of World War II, directing the leader of his personal medical staff, Karl Brandt, and the head of the personal Chancellery, Philipp Bouhler, to expand the practice of granting a "mercy death" to irreversibly disabled people in state institutions. This written instruction, unlike any document ever discovered about the Holocaust, connects Hitler directly and in writing to a murder operation, the so-called Euthanasia Action. Known bureaucratically as T4, an abbreviation of the street address of its main office after April 1940, at Tiergartenstrasse Nr. 4, in the center of Berlin, this heavily camouflaged program proceeded under the day-to-day direction of Viktor Brack, one of Bouhler's aides. Though the Euthanasia Action continued for the duration of the Third Reich, the operation had two distinct phases, the first of which, from October 1939 to August 1941, was a direct forerunner of the Holocaust, the second, from 1942 to 1945, an extension of it.

The Nazi regime had prepared the German public for such an action by a propaganda campaign in the 1930s that stressed the drain that handicapped people, described as "useless eaters" and "life unworthy of life," represented for the national economy and food supply. But Hitler favored the program, the evidence indicates, not so much for practical as for ideological reasons. He wanted to cancel out the "negative selection" that wartime casualties would mean for the Aryan race by accompanying the inevitable attrition of young, vital, and fit Germans with the compulsory reduction of the number of those who were genetically deficient. With the onset of war, he expected potential religious objections to decline or fall away.

The children who became the first victims of T4 perished from overdoses of medicines that induced illnesses or physical conditions on which deaths could be blamed. As the program expanded, starvation and direct injection into the heart of poisonous substances, usually phenol, became supplementary murder methods. Usually doctors did the killing in this initial phase. The general procedure was to move the institutional inhabitants whom physicians selected for death to one of six designated sanatoria spread around the country—no more than four of which were operational at the same time—and then to carry out the executions there. By January 1940, the MDs in charge of the program had decided that establishing

small gas chambers at the institutions would be more efficient—
that is, would allow them to kill more people in less time and with
fewer personnel than the injection method. They soon rigged up
rooms that resembled shower facilities with piping that carried
carbon monoxide (CO) instead of water into the chambers. An
institute within the Reich Security Main Office bought the carbon monoxide in large metal flasks from the BASF division of the
IG Farben conglomerate and supplied them to the sanatoria, where
they merely had to be hooked up to the pipes. The gassing method
was not Hitler's idea but adopted upon the recommendation of an
advisory group of pharmacologists. In fact Brandt, the Führer's physician, initially opposed using gas and argued for death by "medical
means." This information undermines the causal connection drawn,
in the filmed German dramatization of the Wannsee Conference
(1984) and the televised and star-studded Anglo-American version
(2001), between the use of gas chambers and Hitler's remark, in *Mein
Kampf*, that more Jews should have been exposed as soldiers in World
War I to poison gas.

In the annexed parts of Poland, an SS man named Herbert
Lange soon modified the killing process in a consequential way. His
assignment was to empty formerly Polish mental institutions and
sanatoria, and he had no interest in going to the trouble of shipping
the condemned residents to the six killing facilities in Germany.
So he retrofitted a large moving van, disguised as a Kaiser's Coffee
delivery truck, with space near the driver for the flasks of CO, which
were connected by tubes to the rear compartment of the vehicle. He
used this during 1940 to pick up the targeted people and kill them
as the truck drove away toward mass gravesites in concealed forest
areas or toward local crematoria that burned the bodies.

In April 1941, a new operation with the code number 14f13
extended the T4 program to inmates of Germany's concentration
camps judged unable to work. This extension caused the construction of relatively small gas chambers at Dachau, Sachsenhausen,

Mauthausen, and several other sites. But most of these installations gassed people only infrequently until the frenetic final months of the war, when overcrowding, epidemics, and food shortages led to increased utilization. Until early 1945, for example, the Dachau camp appears to have used its gas chamber primarily to fumigate clothing. Most of the 20,000 camp inmates who perished in Action 14f13 were transported to die at Sonnenstein, Bernburg, and Hartheim, three of the sanatoria where T4 executions were carried out.

The continued operation of T4, combined with the new 14f13 program, created a supply and a secrecy problem for the Nazi state. BASF could barely keep up with the demand for bottled CO as of 1941, and applying it on a large scale in occupied Poland or further east raised transportation issues. Persuading BASF to increase production would require giving it some assurance that demand was likely to continue, and that might lead to awkward questions about what the product was being used for. These concerns prompted the SS and the T4 operation to explore jointly whether carbon monoxide produced from stationary internal combustion engines could kill patients as efficiently as, and perhaps more cheaply than, bottled carbon monoxide. Tests on mental patients in the conquered Belarusian cities of Minsk and Mogilev in September gave an affirmative answer.

The transfer of the euthanasia killing system to the murder of the Jews already was being prepared at about the same time as these tests. By early 1941, rumors about the euthanasia program had spread across Germany, and many of the relatives of the victims had grown suspicious of the standardized postcards that notified survivors of the deaths. The usual cause was given as pneumonia or appendicitis, even when the victims no longer had appendixes, and the notifications invariably included the statement that the body had been cremated to avoid the danger of an epidemic. A number of Protestant leaders began to speak up, and then so did Clemens Graf von Galen, the Catholic Bishop of Münster. Because mercy killing violates Catholic teaching that only God may give and take life, Galen issued pastoral letters and delivered sermons denouncing the practice, something he never did with regard to the deportation of the Jews, whom he regarded in the typically Catholic fashion of the time as dangerous agents of modernity and Bolshevism. Fearful that Galen's protest would arouse public opinion and harm the war effort, Hitler formally put an end to the first phase of the T4 Action on August 24, 1941. By then it had taken the lives of between 71,000 and 80,000 people. Murders of disabled and handicapped people resumed a few months later but now in more widely dispersed locations and on a slower, better concealed basis until the end of the war. The killers usually reverted to their original methods of injection or overdosing, but gassings did not entirely cease; indeed, camp inmates, some Gypsies, some half-Jewish children, select groups of forced laborers, and even some Germans driven mad in bombing raids subsequently died that way in several sanatoria. In this second and longer phase of the T4 operation, nearly as many people perished as during the first.

Less than three weeks after Hitler acted, Himmler approved the transfer to the command of SS Police Leader Odilo Globocnik, in Lublin, of many of the operational T4 personnel, eventually some 121 men who had been responsible for bringing handicapped victims to their places of execution and for disposing of the bodies. Most of these men did not begin applying their murderous technical expertise in the conquered areas of Eastern Europe until early 1942, following brief service in hospitals on the Eastern Front, but already by October 25, 1941, officials in the Ministry for the Occupied Eastern Territories were discussing setting up "gassing devices" in Riga and Minsk and murdering in them deported German Jews found incapable of work. Around the end of the same month, construction work began on the Belzec death camp, in a village southeast of Lublin that already was the center of a complex of forced labor camps populated mostly by Jews. The new camp's first commander was Christian Wirth, a veteran of not only the T4 Action but of its first gassing, at Brandenburg in 1940, who came under Globocnik's authority on October 14. Also in October 1941, Herbert Lange, the inventor of the gas vans, identified the derelict manor house that soon became the center of the Chelmno death camp, thirty miles northwest of Lodz, in the so-called Warthegau, part of the land annexed from Poland.

At just about the same time, the mechanics of the Security Police motor pool in Berlin, working under the direction of Walter Rauff, solved the carbon monoxide supply problem. They demonstrated the ease with which a T joint could connect the exhaust pipes under a van to its rear compartment and thus replace bottled CO with that produced by the vehicle's motor. In early November, the SS tested the process on forty Soviet prisoners of war at Sachsenhausen; all of them died within half an hour. The motor pool then ordered from a local supplier thirty converted trucks with rear compartments measuring about sixteen feet long by six and a half feet wide, plus a few smaller versions. Some of these were intended for and briefly used by the *Einsatzgruppen* in Belarus and Ukraine, but that practice proved short-lived because the generally poor roads there led to frequent breakdowns and because the German personnel actually preferred shooting people to the gut-wrenching process of unloading the gassed bodies from the vans.

While Himmler, Heydrich, and their henchmen were discovering that T4 had provided them with one means of disposing of Europe's Jews, a group of SS men recognized that Germany's chemical industry had supplied them with another. The setting was Auschwitz, where a concentration camp for Polish political prisoners had existed since May 1940 on the site of a former Polish military base. In August 1941, anticipating the arrival of increasing numbers of Soviet prisoners of war, Commandant Rudolf Höss apparently told one of his subordinates, Karl Fritzsch, to explore means of killing sick or weak prisoners in bulk. Fritzsch hit on the idea of applying Zyklon, a powerful vaporizing pesticide that the camp normally used to fumigate barracks, as a potential poison. He knew that it was lethal to humans—in fact, seventy milligrams, or 1/3000th of an ounce, which is to say a whiff, will kill a 150-pound person within two minutes—and he already had a substantial quantity of the stuff on hand. Although this product is generally referred to as Zyklon B, the label usually said only Zyklon. The "B" sometimes appeared on sales invoices, but the designation was mostly internal to the manufacturers, since it merely distinguished the product's chemical formula from an earlier, very short-lived one.

In the early days of September 1941, Fritzsch tested the efficacy of Zyklon on two groups of Soviet prisoners of war locked into the basement of one of the original stone barracks at Auschwitz. He learned that Zyklon killed reliably, but for maximum effectiveness, the product needed a more open space than the subdivided barracks basement. Quickly thereafter, he and Höss discerned two more things: The substance was evidently plentiful and rather cheap in relation to the damage it could do. At 5 reichsmark per kilogram (that is, per 2.2 lbs.) and an overdosage of 5–7 kilograms for each group of 1,500 victims, the usual practice according to the postwar testimony of Commandant Höss, the average cost of murder per head ultimately came out to about two German pfennig (pennies) a person, which is to say less than one U.S. cent in 1942.

Thus by late October, the SS leaders knew that they had not one but two effective ways of killing large numbers of people, and this knowledge set in motion a series of pivotal events that mark the onset of what the Nazi regime called the Final Solution of the Jewish Question (*die Endlösung der Judenfrage*). First, on October 23, 1941, Himmler issued an instruction to the Gestapo and the SS that forbade further emigration of Jews from the European continent. This document clearly signaled the end of the policy of driving Jews away, either now or later, and suggested that the Nazis had found a new approach to the Jewish problem.

Second, in November, the regime expanded upon the initial deportation of about 20,000 German Jews to Lodz in mid-October by beginning to ship even more German Jews to the Baltic states and Belarus, where some of them were shot upon arrival, and subjected virtually all the Jews already in concentration camps to the 14f13 murder program. Then, on the twenty-ninth, Reinhard Heydrich issued invitations for various ministerial representatives to gather at a villa along the Wannsee, a lake on the western edge of Berlin, to discuss the final solution. He enclosed with the invitations copies of Göring's letter to him of July 31. Originally scheduled for December 9, the meeting did not take place then because of two surprising events that threw the German capital into confusion, the Soviet counterattack around Moscow on December 5 and the Japanese bombing of Pearl Harbor two days later. Beyond the addition of two officials of the General Government to the initial invitation list, no evidence suggests that the agenda for that meeting changed between its canceled and actual occurrence, on January 20, 1942, when Heydrich laid out a plan "to comb Europe from west to east" of Jews, deport them to Poland, put them to work at hard labor, and subject those who survived this ordeal to "special handling" (*Sonderbehandlung*). The SS leadership probably already envisioned all or most of this when the first round of invitations went out. Eleven days earlier, on November 18, Alfred Rosenberg, the Minister for the Occupied Eastern Territories, had briefed trusted German reporters on deep background and spoken of the "biological eradication of the entire Jewry of Europe."

Third, on December 12, 1941, the day after Hitler declared war on the United States in solidarity with his Japanese ally, he met with the Nazi Party Gauleiters at his private apartment in Berlin and informed them that the Jews would have to pay "with their lives" for the war they had inflicted on Germany—indeed, that they already were doing so. As historian Peter Fritzsche has remarked, "this is as close to a Hitler order as historians will get," meaning the closest counterpart to the euthanasia letter he signed that we are likely to find to connect Hitler personally with the command to kill the Jews.

To sum up what we know about the decision-making process that produced the Holocaust: By August 1941, the Germans were engaged in slaughtering the Jews of the Soviet Union, including women and children. By October, the Nazi leaders knew they had the means to kill people en masse in gas chambers, began constructing sites to do so, and tried to close the escape hatches from Europe. By November, the key figures were ready to bring the German press on board by leaking what was coming and to inform—and implicate—the bureaucracy while seeking its cooperation at the Wannsee Conference. And, in December, Hitler let the Gauleiters in on the change in policy. The Final Solution, the annihilation of the Jews of Europe, was in motion.

Implementation became the next order of business. As it happened, Europe was not combed from west to east, as Heydrich predicted at Wannsee, but almost in the reverse direction. Nazi ideology designated Eastern Europe as the destined living space for an ever growing German *Volk*. Propelled by this expansionist vision, murder gathered mass and momentum faster there than elsewhere because a majority of the continent's Jews still lived in or around the old Pale of Settlement, and it was the conquered region where Germany had least reason to worry that killing Jews would arouse objections from other inhabitants. Accordingly, the six death camps set up in 1941–42 were all within prewar Poland, and each initially concentrated on killing the Jews who lived in its vicinity. Nor was this the only respect in which developments did not proceed according to plan. As the pioneering scholar of the Holocaust Raul Hilberg emphasized, the Holocaust bore the characteristic features of many Nazi initiatives: little foresight or preparation, rocky coordination of participating agencies, and even haphazard budgeting. Yet the killing of millions of people turned out to require no better.

The six death camps divided into two groups. Group 1, consisting of four camps that employed carbon monoxide gas, like the T4 Action in which all of their initial commanders had participated, predominantly killed Jews from designated portions of Poland's pre-war territory and operated only as long as any of these people were left. The first such camp was Chelmno, and it was the only one to use gas vans exclusively, certainly because Lange, its first commander, was so experienced with them. Chelmno began operations with two converted Dodge trucks on December 8, 1941, and then expanded its fleet and its death toll. Each truck carried fifty to seventy people and made five to ten return trips per day from the camp to body disposal areas in a nearby forest. By December 31, 1942, the operation had killed 145,301 people, according to the SS's tabulation, nearly all of them drawn from the part of western Poland annexed to Germany. Closed in March 1943, Chelmno reopened in 1944 to liquidate about 7,200 inhabitants of the Lodz ghetto, and that brought total documented mortality on the site to 152,000 people. This is surely the minimum figure; itemizations of the transports that went to Chelmno suggest at least 20,000 more victims, and the most recent Polish research indicates that the number may have reached 225,000.

The other death camps that used carbon monoxide became operational in 1942 and used stationary gas chambers, initially rather jerry-rigged edifices made airtight by a layer of sand between the inner and outer wooden walls and an external coating of tar paper. Soon, brick or concrete buildings replaced these, but the new structures were still very simple, easy to put up and easy, later, to take down. Like Chelmno, the three sites were chosen for their remoteness, but unlike it, all were located on branch rail lines on the eastern edge of the General Government. In order of foundation and coincidentally from south to north, these were Belzec, which began gassings in March 1942; Sobibor, which came on line in May of that year; and Treblinka, which followed in July. All were conceived as the instruments of Operation Reinhard, the name the Nazis gave at mid-year, following the assassination of Reinhard Heydrich in Prague, to the annihilation of the Polish Jews. All three camps used captured Soviet tank engines to generate the carbon monoxide, and all usually operated with stunning efficiency under the initial direction of veterans of the T4 operation.

Belzec killed at least 434,000 people, but perhaps as many as 600,000, in the only ten months that it was open, an average of up to 2,000 people per day, more than two-thirds of them from southern and southeastern Poland and the rest Jews from other parts of Europe who had been deposited in ghettos in and around Lublin. Sobibor consumed between 167,000 and 200,000 people during its seventeen-month life span, most of them from Poland, but some from prewar Czechoslovakia, many from France and the Netherlands, and a few from Greater Germany, Belarus, and Lithuania. Treblinka, the last to close, wiped out up to 925,000 people in the eighteen months before Operation Reinhard ended in November 1943, which made it almost as lethal as Belzec on a daily basis. However, at the time of its peak murderousness, from July 22 to August 27, 1942, Treblinka killed 280,000 people, an average of 56,000 per week, or 8,000 per day. During one of those five weeks, the daily average reached 10,000. Nearly all of Treblinka's victims came from central and northern Poland, but about 32,000 Czech, Greek, and Macedonian Jews also died there. All three Reinhard camps were in operation simultaneously for only four out of the six months from July to December 1942, yet in that half-year the three sites killed more than one million Jews, which is more Jews and nearly as many people all told as Auschwitz-Birkenau wiped out in four years. Altogether, these three places devoured between 1.5 and 1.8 million human beings. Including Chelmno, the four CO camps killed up to 2 million people. Fewer than 400 Jews ever emerged alive from all four sites, and of these only somewhere between 90 and 150 outlived World War II.

The second group of death camps consisted of only two installations: Auschwitz-Birkenau and Majdanek, which were different from Group 1 in three respects: (1) they primarily used Zyklon, not CO, to kill people (though Majdanek also sometimes employed bottled CO and had a gas van); (2) they were dual-purpose camps—both death and slave labor camps—and thus had larger ongoing inmate populations; and (3) they were not closed until the Soviet armies approached, and thus they were the principal destinations, Auschwitz especially, for Jews from outside of Poland, and the only death camps still open in 1944. Their importance as labor reservoirs began as part of the plans for an SS agricultural research center at Auschwitz and a complex of SS-owned factories at Majdanek, but then greatly expanded because they stood at or near the ends of the Polish part of Durchgangstrasse IV, the long highway that the Nazis were building from Silesia to the Caucasus as the lifeline of their power in conquered Ukraine. The need for labor for this project inspired the addition of Birkenau to Auschwitz in October 1941 and of Majdanek to a nearby preexisting labor camp in Lublin. Both were built for Soviet prisoners of war as the prospective workforce but later populated primarily by Jews—in Auschwitz's case throughout its existence, in Majdanek's only until November 1943, when nearly all of the remaining Jews were shot to death, not gassed.

Over time, other labor needs arose to sustain the importance of each camp. Auschwitz became the geographical center of frantic industrial development because it was near coal and water supplies and out of reach of Allied bombers based in Britain. The biggest plant located in the region was the IG Farben installation three miles east at Monowitz, where at least 27,000 prisoners died while constructing a factory for synthetic fuel and rubber and operating the firm's coal mines in the area. But tens of thousands of other inmates labored at more than forty branch camps in the region, including the giant synthetic fuel factories at Blechhammer and Heydebreck and numerous mines. Majdanek became the hub of the SS's plans to process and recycle the goods collected from the people killed at Reinhard camps, especially the hundreds of thousands of leather shoes that one can still see filling warehouse barracks on the site.

Both Auschwitz and Majdanek had another distinguishing feature: gas chambers built to last. The three at Majdanek were relatively small, solid stone structures, and they are still there. Auschwitz initially turned a small munitions magazine at the edge of the main, original camp into a crematorium that also could be used for gassings, then converted two peasant cottages on the plain near Birkenau into gas chambers, and finally constructed and opened in 1943 four large brick buildings in the Birkenau or Auschwitz II camp that contained both gas chambers and crematoria to dispose of the bodies at the rate of 4,000 to 8,000 per day. The first, small chamber at the main camp remains today; the cottages are gone, and only ruins of the brick buildings survive. Since the chambers could kill faster than the crematoria could incinerate, bodies sometimes also burned on open-air pyres. If the Nazis had been able to ship all the remaining Jews in Europe to Auschwitz in 1945–46—that is, if the war had gone on and the impediments to rounding up the remaining Jews been pushed aside—Auschwitz could have killed them all by early in the latter year. As it was, some 1.3 million people arrived at the camp between its opening in May 1940 and its evacuation in January 1945, of whom approximately 1.1 million died—there or in one of the subcamps. Perhaps half of the survivors died at other installations before World War II ended, and only 100,000 emerged alive from the conflict. Majdanek was far less lethal, especially for Jews, and recent research findings have driven down the probable number of Jews killed there from some 145,000 to about 59,000, perhaps one-third of whom were gassed.

The death camps were distinct from three other principal kinds of Nazi camps:

(1) The main SS concentration camps, such as Dachau and Buchenwald in Germany and places like Natzweiler in Alsace-Lorraine and Stutthof along the Baltic coast and their more than 1,100 satellite installations. These were

murderous places, especially in the last year of the war, but they were not "factories of death," and their populations did not consist primarily of Jews. A partial exception in the former regard was Mauthausen, founded in 1938 near the city of Linz, Austria, and the subcamps it spawned at nearby military production installations. Reserved for "incorrigible . . . and barely educable" political opponents and criminals, this harshest of the concentration camps killed 52 percent of its almost 16,000 inmates in 1941 and almost 10 percent of its constantly replenished prisoner population every month between mid-1941 and April 1943. By the time American troops liberated the camp, more than half of the almost 200,000 people ever held there had perished, some of them in a gas chamber on the premises that used Zyklon, some in gas vans, and others at the nearby Hartheim sanatorium. About 25 percent of the victims were Jews.

(2) So-called transit camps, where particular groups of people were collected, generally in order to be exchanged later with the Allies. The best known of these was Bergen-Belsen, in northern Germany. These were relatively benign places until the German supply system collapsed toward the end of the war, at which point they became murderous centers of infection and starvation.

(3) Labor camps, of which tens of thousands came into existence by the end of the war. Here, the inmates could be and were treated viciously, but the goal of production exerted some, though limited, protection against large-scale killing. But one must draw a distinction within that distinction. Labor camps in the East were far worse than those even in the General Government, let alone Germany. The ones established for Jews along Durchgangstrasse IV were little more than delayed murder stations, and the same was true

of Janowska, a camp in Lviv that began as a labor site in late
1942 but turned into such a voracious venue for the mass
shooting of Jews that it may have taken more of their lives,
all told, than Majdanek, without possessing a gas chamber.

One of the most chilling aspects of the history of the Holocaust is
that so much carnage could occur without any serious ill effect on the
German war effort, in fact with little diversion of manpower, matériel,
and money. Aside from the loss to Germany and the gain to Britain
and the United States of the Jewish scientists and other loyal citizens
driven to flee during the 1930s, the Reich hardly had to pay a price for
all the pain and suffering it dispensed. Yes, it came to miss the labor
of most of the last remaining Polish Jews, some 300,000 of whom the
SS massacred in 1943, but otherwise the balance sheet of murder was
strikingly favorable to Germany, at least in the short run, which was
the only time horizon that mattered to the Nazi regime.

In the first place, the camps took in enormous plunder as well
as payments for the laborers that they leased to industries and government offices. Although enslaved camp inmates were not paid,
they were paid for. In part as a result, Auschwitz, the biggest labor
vendor, made a profit of 100 percent in this fashion from 1941 to
1945. It took in sixty million reichsmark in fees for workers, whereas
it spent only thirty million, all told, to feed and house them. Globocnik's office in Lublin calculated that its net loot from Operation
Reinhard, after deducting all the personnel and other costs associated with the deportations and murder, came to almost 179 million
reichsmark, conservatively estimated, including more than 80 million reichsmark in cash, 52 million reichsmark in jewelry and precious metals, and 46 million in recyclable clothing. Because the T4
people at those camps sent additional amounts directly to the Führer's Chancellery and to the Reichsbank, the overall income clearly
was much more. We do not know how much plunder Chelmno collected because that booty was shipped to the Lodz ghetto admin-

istration and mixed in with its other extortions from Jews. But one document from May 1942, a year before Chelmno suspended operation, speaks of needing 900 trucks to transport clothing the camp delivered for reuse.

In the second place, the Germans did not pay for transporting the Jews to the camps; they made Jewish community administrations do this, just as they usually made them, at least in Western Europe, Germany itself, and the Polish ghettos, do the dirty work of identifying potential deportees or even drawing up lists of them whenever the Nazis dictated a certain number or category to be shipped out. Even the offices from which the killing orders came had been Jewish-owned property, now repurposed for murder. SS-Obersturmbannführer Adolf Eichmann coordinated deportations from the former premises of the Jewish Brethren Society, a charitable organization, in Berlin's Kurfürstenstrasse 116; the euthanasia program's headquarters at Tiergartenstrasse 4 had belonged to relatives of Max Liebermann, a famous Jewish German painter. Meanwhile, the Reich raked in enormous sums in confiscated bank accounts, jewelry, art works, and other fungible forms of property from Jews in all the occupied countries. As a result, the Holocaust as a whole was not only a self-financing but also, like Auschwitz standing alone, a profit-making enterprise. Consider the example of the Netherlands. Here, Nazi Germany reaped more than one billion guilders from the sale of property stolen from Jews, most of which went directly into the occupation administration's coffers or into the accounts of front organizations that bought German and Dutch government bonds and thus helped support the German war effort. A tiny share of the income—25 million guilders, or less than 2.5 percent of the total—was expended to expand and maintain the two Dutch transit camps at Vught and Westerbork and to pay for the roundups and deportations. About 75 percent of the Dutch Jews were killed, some 105,000 people, at a cost that came to a small fraction of what the German state seized from them.

In the third place, the costs of murder that Jews did not pay were quite low. Aside from Auschwitz from 1943 on, the death camps were remarkably low-tech, non–capital intensive entities. Chelmno consisted of a rundown manor house surrounded by a wooden fence. Jews came in the main gate on trucks, descended from these on one side of the house, lost what was left of their possessions as they passed through its basement, and walked into vans at the back entrance. After Jewish prisoners closed and barred the doors, the vehicles either idled or drove until the people inside died of the exhaust fumes, and then delivered the bodies to a forest clearing, where other Jewish prisoners burned the corpses in pits. Even at Auschwitz, the first gas chamber was a preexisting building, and much of the construction material for the barracks and fencing was obtained from IG Farben in a barter agreement of steel, bricks, and barbed wire for workers and gravel. So improvised were the first two gas chambers at Birkenau, the converted peasant cottages, that they lacked mechanical ventilation and thus could not function in rapid succession. Treblinka and the other Reinhard camps were Potemkin villages of building facades, plus a few workshops, around square reception areas where the arriving victims disembarked and undressed. The rear side of the square led to a "tube" (*Schlauch*), a narrow passageway framed by wooden sawhorses, covered in barbed wire and pine boughs, and into the gas chambers. None of this cost much to erect.

Moreover, the operating costs of these sites were low. Gasoline to generate carbon monoxide was inexpensive and not in short supply until after Operation Reinhard ended, and the motors used came from captured Soviet tanks. The nearly 32 metric tons of Zyklon sold to Auschwitz and Majdanek in 1942–44 cost just under 160,000 reichsmark, or about 64,000 U.S. dollars at the time. Only about one-fifth of this Zyklon actually was used for gassing—the rest went to fumigating barracks and the like or simply spoiled on the shelves—so the quantity needed for murder was even less expensive, probably costing only about 30,000 reichsmark, or U.S. $12,000 at the time.

Nor was it expensive to staff the places. Auschwitz was the only camp with a large, nearly all German guard force. Its average size during the life of the camp was about 2,500, and some 7,000 Germans served there from 1940 to 1945, which is about one-third as many men as the German armed forces shot for desertion during World War II. But Belzec and Sobibor needed only about twenty Germans at any one time, as did Treblinka initially, though its German staff rose in 1943 into the thirties. The rest of the guards, 90–130 men at each site, were Eastern European *Hiwis* (an abbreviation of *Hilfswillige*, which means "volunteer helpers"), usually recruited from starved Soviet prisoner-of-war camps, and offered uniforms, room and board, low pay, and the chance to pillage the Jews in return for serving as support troops for the Germans. A special camp at Trawniki in Poland trained 4,750 of these people by the time it closed in September 1943. The Germans at the death camps earned substantially more, in fact something like ten times their nominal monthly pay of fifty-eight reichsmark, thanks to a special daily allowance of eighteen marks, a loyalty bonus, and a "Jew murder supplement" paid from the budget of the T4 program. Even so, that program also operated in the black thanks to the proceeds on the dental gold extracted from victims' mouths and the practice of routinely waiting for about ten days after an execution before entering the death notice in the records, meanwhile assessing per diem charges to the person, agency, or insurance company responsible for maintaining the now deceased disabled person.

Finally, legend has it that the deportation trains to the camps must have impeded the German war effort. Nothing could be further from the truth. Very few deportation trains were in transit at any one time, and they had the lowest priority on German railroads, which means they were never allowed to obstruct or delay troop movements or supply trains. That is one reason why the trips from

Western Europe to the death camps, and even the ones in the early stages of the deportations from Warsaw to Treblinka in 1942 that traveled only sixty miles, often took as long as three or four days and arrived carrying numerous suffocated, starved, parched, and in winter frozen corpses. Boxcars usually were used in the East, and either closed cargo wagons or third-class passenger cars from Western Europe, but in both cases, the transports nearly always consisted of dilapidated equipment. Even the locomotives were relics. Loading each transport of 1,000 people or more generally required only ninety Germans, and the guard personnel en route usually consisted of only fifteen, since sealed boxcars required little supervision. Indeed, the Germans preferred them in part for that reason.

All told, the Germans used about 2,000 trains to move three million people to camps over thirty-three months in 1942–44, which works out to sixty trains per month or two departing per day, on average. In contrast, the German Reichsbahn carried 6.6 *billion* passengers in 1942–43 and ran 30,000 trains *per day* in 1941 and 1942 and about 23,000 per day in 1944. In that final year, the Nazi regime needed only 147 trains over eight weeks, an average of fewer than three per day and never more than six, to deport almost 440,000 Hungarian Jews. Allocating even that many trains in a short time for a murder operation was unprecedented, and it happened only because the deportations had a subsidiary purpose directly tied to the war effort. Auschwitz was supposed to extract 100,000 able-bodied workers from the deportees, 10–15 percent of the initially anticipated total, and ship them immediately on to the Reich, where they were to labor on the massive effort to put Germany's war production plants underground. Even so, at the height of the deportations from Hungary, those trains constituted no more than 1–2 percent of the daily railroad traffic in that country. They employed an infinitesimal one-fifteenth of 1 percent of the functioning locomotives and one-tenth of 1 percent of the operating rolling stock under the jurisdiction of the German Armaments Ministry at the time. Clearly, the shares of

German railroad equipment and activity devoted to the Holocaust were tiny, both in total and at any particular time.

As sometimes happens in historical writing, the most conclusive demonstration that the deportations had no significant impact on the German war effort is a book that purports to prove the opposite, Yaron Pasher's *Holocaust vs. Wehrmacht* (2014). Pasher examines four German military defeats, each of which occurred at approximately the same time as a wave of deportations: the failure to take Moscow in 1941 as the first transports of Jews were leaving Germany; the failure to relieve Stalingrad in 1942–43 during Operation Reinhard; the debacle of the Battle of Kursk in the summer of 1943 shortly after the suppression of the Warsaw Ghetto Uprising; and the successful Allied invasion of and breakout from Normandy in June to August 1944, which partially overlapped with the massive deportations from Hungary. At each juncture, Pasher asserts that the primary reason more troops and supplies did not arrive at the German front lines was a shortage of trains to carry what was needed, that shortage having been caused by the use of rolling stock to deport Jews. In the process, he makes statistical calculations that count, for example, each journey by the same one or two slow and rickety trains with sixty boxcars going back and forth between Bialystok and Treblinka and between Theresienstadt and Auschwitz every two to three days in early 1943 as potentially the trip of a fully loaded and speedy supply train to a battlefront. His estimates, in each instance, of what the trains that carried Jews instead could have brought to the German armies still fall drastically short of his own understated tallies of what the Reich's soldiers lacked in men and matériel compared to their adversaries. In all four cases, Germany's defeat was massively overdetermined. For that reason, repeatedly asserting, as Pasher does, that "every train counted" is not nearly the same thing as showing that every train mattered.

So how could the Nazis achieve such an extensive massacre in so short a time? The first piece of the answer is: because they perfected a low-cost, low-overhead, low-tech, and self-financing process of killing with great speed. We turn now to a second component of the answer: because the Nazi movement and state generated and unleashed remarkably dedicated killers.

PERPETRATORS: THE "GENERATION WITHOUT LIMITS"

The Holocaust involved tens of thousands of people who participated in it directly—the SS guards, the *Einsatzgruppen*, the Order Police, the regular military units that often helped with rounding up Jews and killing them, and the thousands of bureaucrats and officials who planned the murders and made the death-dispensing system function—as well as hundreds of thousands of German civilians who facilitated the persecution at some remove from the process. How can we explain their behavior? How could they do these things?

Broadly speaking, two schools of thought dominate attempts to answer these questions, the volitional and the situational schools, and each gets deployed to account for behavior at two different levels, subordinate and senior. The volitional school holds that people persecuted and killed because they chose to; the situational school argues that they acted in response to their immediate context, not their convictions. Recently, a number of German-educated authors have laid the basis for a powerful and persuasive synthesis of the two points of view.

With regard to the subordinates who actually did the killing in the shooting units and gassing installations, the classic formulations of the volitional and situational points of view are, respectively, Daniel Goldhagen's *Hitler's Willing Executioners* (1996), a bestseller that the public loved and most historians panned, and Christopher Browning's *Ordinary Men* (1992), which won academic acclaim as well as a popular audience. Goldhagen insists that Germans killed Jews because they wanted to; they wanted to because they universally hated Jews; and they hated Jews because Germans always had—their nation's culture had been thoroughly and pervasively antisemitic for hundreds of years. On the basis of postwar trial testimony by the former shooters of Reserve Police Battalion 101, Browning maintains that antisemitic convictions had little to do with the readiness of Germans to commit murder; rather, they acted out of loyalty to one another. Their sense of group solidarity made them unwilling to let one another down by showing weakness. In making his case, Browning draws heavily on two sets of social psychology experiments. The first, conducted by Stanley Milgram in New Haven in 1961, led volunteers to believe that they were administering electric shocks upon orders from a supposed scientist. The second, Philip Zimbardo's at Stanford in 1971, simulated relations between prison guards and inmates. Each experiment highlighted human tendencies to defer to or to abuse authority.

Both Goldhagen's and Browning's analyses have drawbacks: Goldhagen's picture is static; it contains no change over time; the attitudes of Germans in 1642 are identical to the attitudes of Germans in 1942 and just as uniform, which is implausible. Moreover, Goldhagen makes no allowance for the stark fact that power magnifies the ideas of those who hold it. Thus he underplays the decisive importance, with regard to German behavior, of the period after Hitler came to power. Browning, on the other hand, relies a good deal on his protagonists' descriptions of their motives, which he acknowledges is a risky practice. Not for nothing do lawyers say that "no one can be a witness in his or her own cause." In this instance, as is usually the case in court proceedings, some of the protagonists had a reason to lie. They gave their testimony in a potential West German murder investigation. Under German law, a murder conviction required proof that a person acted with a "base motive," such as greed or hatred, or exhibited sadistic zeal. That made former shooters reluctant to admit to antisemitism or to ascribe it to a comrade, even though anyone indicted was likely, given German legal practice at the time, to be charged as an accessory to murder, which entailed less severe punishment.

Although Browning has the better of the argument with regard to the men of Police Battalion 101, and his findings have chilling implications regarding the general susceptibility of men in certain situations to inflict hideous violence, two sorts of considerations, one theoretical and one empirical, suggest that more remains to be said about why most German killers acted as they did in 1941–45. In the first (theoretical) place, Goldhagen and Browning probably tried to be too precise in capturing motives that may have been diverse, mixed, and variable over time. Moreover, given the assignments doled out to the shooting units and the ideological environment in which they lived, many shooters may have embraced antisemitism at the time as a conveniently available form of legitimizing what they had been ordered to do. In other words, they did not kill because they hated their victims, but they decided to hate them because they thought they had to kill them. Psychologists call this sort of mental mechanism, in which beliefs conform to behavior rather than the other way around, a response to "cognitive dissonance," and it may have been just as important as animosity or sadism in explaining why so many Germans showed or expressed pleasure in torturing and killing Jews. Hatred and even glee became ways to ease the task at hand, and we know that it was not easy, at least not initially. Himmler called what he thought the SS had to do "a repulsive duty" and "a horrible task." The *Einsatzgruppen* and the foreign auxiliary units often had to get drunk to carry out the slaughter. German women serving as nurses and soldiers' aides on the Eastern Front reported repeatedly that men who returned from massacres "all had an intense need to talk" about what they had done.

In the second (empirical) place, Edward Westermann has demonstrated conclusively that Police Battalion 101 was not typical of the police units sent east to kill Jews. Some 80 percent of these personnel were not reservists at all, as the men in Police Battalion

101 were, and most units did not consist, as it did, of middle-aged men who had matured before Hitler came to power. On the contrary, the battalions generally comprised young, heavily indoctrinated career policemen who saw themselves as "political soldiers" in service to Nazi racial ideology. They were not workaday civilians placed in unfamiliar and extreme circumstances or typical Germans of an earlier era but rather military creations of the Nazi regime, schooled in the need for racial purification. Although Browning's work shows that even "ordinary men" were prepared to kill in the German-occupied east, most of the killers there in the early 1940s were not ordinary men.

Like Omer Bartov, who wrote *The Eastern Front, 1941–45*, Westermann stresses the role of ideological indoctrination in shaping the behavior of the police shooters, but unlike Bartov, Westermann thinks these units did not need to experience the increasing barbarization of warfare over time in order to become hardened killers. They were ready to act as such from the first day of their arrival in the east. Waitman Beorn's *Marching into Darkness* (2014) reaches a similar conclusion about the regular German army units that began massacring Jews in Belarus in the fall of 1941, well before encountering serious resistance or partisan activity. His close examination of several mass shootings reveals that relentless propaganda about the Jewish-Bolshevik menace disposed most of these men to slaughter virtually from the beginning of the invasion of the USSR.

Among the most insightful works on this topic are studies by the German scholars Harald Welzer (*Täter*, 2005), Felix Römer (*Kameraden*, 2012), and Thomas Kühne (*Belonging and Genocide*, 2010). (Thomas Kühne now teaches in the United States.) Using somewhat different sources and analytical approaches, these scholars agree in highlighting the Hitler regime's success in developing, among Germans, "a Nazi self" with an inverted value system that offered a host of justifications for cruelty. The Third Reich redefined morality and turned humiliation, persecution, and murder into virtues.

Overcoming scruples against inflicting pain became a sign of moral progress, not of indecency. If a person had difficulty doing this, so much the better, since that engendered more self-pity than pity for the victims, and thus made Germans more willing to lash out at the people whose existence was causing such discomfort. Kühne provides some memorable phrases to describe what happened: He says that the Nazis created a "dichotomist ethics" of Us vs. Them and a "moral grammar of comradeship" that glorified acts of solidarity and shamed ones born of individualism. He reminds us of Browning's observation that even the members of Police Battalion 101 who said that they could not shoot did not raise moral objections; instead, they just said that they were "too weak" to do what was asked. The same pattern held for the exceptional regular army personnel who asked to be excused from killings, according to Beorn. As he writes, "By claiming weakness or sentimentality as their reason for non-participation, soldiers . . . avoided directly challenging the actions of their comrades. This allowed them to remain within the community of their peers." Even when saying no, individual Germans partially affirmed the collective purpose. And most Germans ordered to kill did not say no. Römer's study, which is based on the bugged conversations of some 3,000 German prisoners of war who passed through Fort Hunt outside of Washington, DC, concludes that even when they professed to believe that "extreme violence against defenseless civilians, women, and children . . . cross[ed] a line, they were always capable of such violence, the minute group pressure or the circumstances demanded it." That reflexive readiness owed a good deal to the pervasiveness among admired and veteran junior and noncommissioned officers of a "particular military mentality" that, in turn, reflected what Welzer calls a "particular National Socialist morality."

Welzer's, Römer's, Kühne's, and Beorn's findings demonstrate that the situational can become volitional; beliefs adjust to circumstances, and power magnifies the ideas of those who wield it.

Ordinary Germans could and did *become* willing executors of Nazi persecution and even in many cases willing executioners. In a book called *Experten der Vernichtung* (Experts of Annihilation, 2013), Sara Berger has reached a similar conclusion regarding the T4 participants who went on to staff the Operation Reinhard camps. Having closely studied their records and postwar testimonies, she stresses that they did not become killers on their own initiative, but that they became willing and increasingly identified with the Nazi regime's justifications for murder. As a result, none of them exercised their option to transfer back to their previous postings.

The treatment of the two known railroad officials who declined to participate in transports confirms a point established in numerous postwar examinations of the military and SS records and reinforced by Browning's research: Opting out of the killing process went unpunished in Nazi Germany but was nonetheless rare. Richard Neuser, a conductor based in Bialystok, asked to be relieved of having to work on transports to camps, and he was reassigned without penalty. Alfons Glas worked in the main passenger train office at Gedob, the organization that ran the railways in the General Government, and he learned from subordinates in the field enough about what was happening to trains carrying Jews that he asked for a transfer, which he received without any disadvantage to his career. But these were highly exceptional cases. The behavior of German railroad personnel paralleled that of police and other uniformed organizations. The senses of group solidarity and/or professional obligation and/or ideological conviction outweighed any reservations or compunction people might have felt. Similarly, the German postwar trials of Operation Reinhard death camp personnel produced only two documented instances of SS guards who asked to transfer out of direct involvement with the killing process. Both succeeded without adverse consequences.

Oskar Gröning, an SS bookkeeper at Auschwitz who was interviewed by the BBC in 2005, explained his own behavior with reference to compartmentalization and indoctrination. He had volunteered for the SS in 1940 and then worked in a paymaster's office until transferred to Auschwitz in 1942, when he was twenty-one. There he tallied the money taken from the camp's victims. Although upset by instances of brutality that he saw, he generally endorsed the need to wipe out the Jews as Germany's mortal enemies who had defeated it in World War I and would try to do so again. He therefore regarded their murder as necessary. But he felt detached from the killing; his unit carried out the desk job side of life at Auschwitz, not the murders, and he considered the two activities more or less separate. So he stayed until September 1944, when the SS granted his request for transfer and sent him to a Waffen-SS unit that later fought in the Battle of the Bulge.

At the camps, key elements in explaining guard behavior are the small numbers of perpetrators involved, the sorts of people they were, and the ways they delegated the worst of the killing process and thus distanced themselves from it. The small number of perpetrators required made them easy to find. Remember, only twenty Germans and Austrians were at Belzec at any one time; fewer than five hundred ever were at all three camps of Operation Reinhard. Each camp crematorium required only five to twelve German supervisors. Even if we assume that they were all psychopaths, we have to concede that recruiting that few cannot have been difficult. The guard staffs were often very poorly educated; for example, at Auschwitz only 30 percent of the SS men who served in the garrison ever got beyond grade school. Except at Auschwitz, the guard personnel consisted largely of foreign auxiliaries—the *Hiwis*—with a strong interest in satisfying their German masters. Each Operation Reinhard camp had 90 to 130 such men. At Auschwitz, *Volksdeutsche* eager to prove that they were just as tough and German as their native-born comrades made up a large percentage of the garrison.

Moreover, the Germans were adept at insulating themselves from the worst aspects of the killing processes. In the ghettos, they often made the Jewish police forces do the dirty work of rounding up people who did not appear for deportation when scheduled to do so. In the camps, they used other Jewish prisoners in *Sonderkommandos* to empty the gas chambers, burn the bodies, and, in the case of Crematorium III at Birkenau, to hold open the heavy lid of the chute through which an SS man poured the Zyklon pellets. Finally, among the camp guards, as in the shooting squads, a fateful element was self-centeredness, a preoccupation with one's own challenges rather than the pain being inflicted. For the guards, the daily problem was to manage large numbers of prisoners, and brutality was always the easiest method available. The basest elements of people's temperaments were elicited by the nature of the camp system, where the rules encouraged such things as goading prisoners into trying to escape so a guard could shoot them and thus earn an extra day's leave.

So what do all these explanations add up to? Why was there no shortage of Germans ready to participate in the torture and killing of Jews? Above all, because the Nazi regime succeeded in creating a closed mental world, an ideological echo chamber in which leaders constantly harped on the threat the Jews supposedly constituted and the need for Germans to defend themselves against it. The war itself, the air raids on German cities, the snipers at sentries in the occupied east—everything was the work of the Jews. At the same time, the regime degraded the Jews so thoroughly in ghettos, camps, and transports that they came to resemble the vile picture that the regime painted of them as dirty, disease-bearing, self-seeking, and uncivilized creatures, which fostered German contempt for them and readiness to inflict harm. Nazi propaganda and power combined to turn antisemitism into a relentlessly self-fulfilling feedback loop, and rank-and-file Germans behaved accordingly.

Wendy Lower's *Hitler's Furies* (2013) reinforces this line of analysis with evidence concerning a previously largely unstudied group: the half-million German women sent into occupied Eastern Europe as wives, secretaries, nurses, teachers, settlers, Red Cross volunteers, and radio operators, and in many other capacities. Some 300,000 German women served as auxiliaries in Gestapo and police offices and in prisons in the occupied east, another 10,000 in the German civil administration, and 3,500 more as camp guards. Almost all of these women were between the ages of seventeen and thirty. They saw a very great deal of persecution and murder; most of them facilitated it in one respect or another, such as typing up liquidation orders, and some of them perpetrated it, entering ghettos and shooting inhabitants or helping men root Jews out of hiding. As Lower points out, "In favoring perceived duty over morality, men and women were more alike than different." They were also alike in succumbing to the temptations of absolute power that Germans enjoyed in occupied Eastern Europe. One of the killers, Erna Petri, who presided with her husband over a confiscated estate in eastern Poland from 1942 to 1944, summed up many of their intertwined motives when she said after the war, "I did not want to stand behind the SS men. I wanted to show them that I, as a woman, could conduct myself like a man. So I shot four Jews and six Jewish children. I wanted to prove myself to the men. Besides, in those days in this region, everywhere one heard that Jewish persons and children were being shot, which also caused me to kill them."

When all these impulses to conformity failed, when expressions of human sympathy or solidarity somehow asserted themselves among Germans in uniform, the Nazi regime resorted to violent retribution. Opting out of murder qualified as understandable weakness, and a German officer could get away with arguing, as Major Karl Plagge did as head of a repair yard for army vehicles in Vilna, that military needs justified keeping Jewish workers and their families alive for the moment. But overt assistance to Jews constituted sabotage punishable by death. Thus, on April 9, 1942, Anton Schmidt, a forty-two-year-old member of a rear echelon (*Landesschütz*) battalion, wrote a farewell letter to his wife shortly before his execution in Vilna. He told her that, shocked by the massacres there, including the killing of babies by slamming them against tree trunks, he had used his position as leader of a straggler collection point throughout the fall of 1941 to facilitate the escape of more than 100 Jews from the city's ghetto (postwar research established that the real number may have exceeded 300). Exposed in January 1942 and court-martialed, he explained to his wife, "you know how it is with me and my soft heart," adding that "in my room are six men aged 17 to 23 who have the same fate. Condemned for desertion and cowardice in the face of the enemy. Jews too are the enemy—that's just the way it is." Though outcomes of this sort were rare, even their possibility dampened humane inclinations on the part of Germans in the field.

If the most convincing explanations of the readiness of subordinate Germans to behave viciously toward Jews blend situational and volitional elements, that is not the case with regard to the senior figures who designed and gave the orders for the Final Solution. Fifty years ago, Hannah Arendt tried to use the figure of Adolf Eichmann to argue that these people were faceless and, as she put it, "thoughtless" bureaucrats who acted out of personal ambition more than ideological conviction and thus represented what she called "the banality of evil." Almost no historian believes this anymore. As Tom Segev wrote in his study of concentration camp commanders, *Soldiers of Evil* (1987), what characterized them was not banality, "but rather inner identification with evil."

Detailed prosopographical studies (collective biographies) have shown that perpetrators at this level were almost all highly educated, enthusiastic, and conscious proponents of murder and true believers in Nazi ideology. The most powerful such study is a book by Michael Wildt available in English under the title *An Uncompromising Generation* (2009). This is a rather wan translation of the German title, *Generation des Unbedingten*, which means something like the "generation without limits or restraints." Wildt examined the life histories of 221 people who occupied leading positions in the RSHA, the SS office most responsible for carrying out the Holocaust, either during 1939–41, when the organization took shape, or for at least eighteen months in a later period. He found that 60 percent of them were born between 1900 and 1910, and another 17 percent were even younger. That means that most of them were in their thirties or, at most, their early forties during the Holocaust. In this respect, they were like their most prominent leaders. Heinrich Himmler, dubbed the "architect of genocide" by one scholar, was born in 1900, as was Rudolf Höss, the commandant at Auschwitz during most of the camp's existence. Ernst Kaltenbrunner, the head of the Reich Security Main Office from 1943 to 1945, came into the world in 1903; Reinhard Heydrich, Kaltenbrunner's predecessor and the man who launched the Final Solution, in 1904; Adolf Eichmann, who arranged many of the deportation trains, in 1906; and Joseph Mengele, the doctor who sorted arrivals at Auschwitz between life and death and who conducted vicious medical experiments on them, in 1911. Similarly, those 121 T4 personnel who helped staff the Reinhard camps were remarkably young: more than 83 percent of them were born between 1900 and 1914.

The RSHA leaders were usually youthful, upwardly mobile men on the make, eager to prove themselves, to make a mark and a difference. Most were well educated—one-third of them had PhDs, as did all four of the first *Einsatzgruppen* commanders, and many had studied at Germany's best universities, notably Heidelberg, Leipzig, and Tübingen. Most had long records, dating to their student years in the 1920s, of involvement in extreme nationalist, antisemitic, and violent politics, and most had dedicated themselves to remaking the world by avenging the wrongs supposedly done to Germany. Imbued with a romantic view of war and a hunger for action, they were men on a mission who scorned sentimentality. *Gefühlsduselei* was the word they used for all forms of human empathy, and the literal translation into English, which is "spraying of feelings," conveys a sense of the contempt they expressed. They knew exactly what they were doing, and they believed completely in their utterly Germanocentric vision of national redemption through revenge and racial cleansing. Although the T4 personnel generally came from lower down the social scale, they also constituted a highly indoctrinated group.

To this mix of idealism and careerism, the RSHA and T4 people added a hard-hearted form of professionalism, a cold-blooded determination to do their jobs well. The phrase in German for someone who will stop at nothing is *"sie/er geht über Leichen,"* "s/he walks over corpses," and it applies literally as well as figuratively to these men. They found the language of "duty" very convenient; in its name, almost anything was justifiable as long as it served the German *Volk*. Invoking duty not only relieved them of personal responsibility, it made murder into a higher calling. Higher because they also claimed that the Reich's expansion to the east was part of a civilizing process that expanded European culture at the expense of supposedly barbaric Asia. Hitler once called Eastern Europe "our India," and on more than one occasion he likened Germany's eastward expansion to America's westward one. The men atop RSHA believed deeply in this missionary vision, and they expected to have to kill millions of people to realize it.

In short, most German perpetrators of the Holocaust fit a pattern of militarily inspired, nationalist young men who seized on the opportunities for advancement and fulfillment that were created by the enormous increase in the ranks of the SS in the late 1930s, especially as it absorbed the police, and by Germany's expansion. They also hailed disproportionately from areas the Reich had lost after World War I or from border regions, which is to say from environments that heightened senses of national consciousness and competition. Very few of them were new to political violence or mere draftees. As the sociologist Michael Mann has summarized the evidence, "the majority of Nazi genocide . . . was accomplished by ideological, experienced Nazis. . . . The vast majority of those involved in actual killing knew what they were doing, [and] most thought there was a good reason for it."

Zealotry is especially characteristic of the chief perpetrators, namely Himmler, Heydrich, Eichmann, Höss, Kaltenbrunner, and two men not previously mentioned, Oswald Pohl and Hans Kammler, the leaders of the SS Economics and Administration Main Office (WVHA), the organization that ran the Nazi slave labor system. Heinrich Himmler rose to power and exercised it as the embodiment of the SS's motto: "My honor is called loyalty" (*Meine Ehre heißt Treue*). Even though he became a Party member before the Beer Hall Putsch of 1923, having already imbibed the mixture of romanticism about Germany and animosity toward foreigners, Jews, and leftists that characterized the movement, he was initially closer to other early Nazi leaders than to Hitler. But after becoming head of the Führer's personal bodyguard in 1929, Himmler made himself into Hitler's reliably ruthless agent in dealing with people or groups that Nazism defined as enemies. As a result, the main paper trail that connects Hitler to the Holocaust runs through Himmler's appointment books for 1938–42. They reveal how closely radicalizations of Nazi policy toward Jews followed meetings between the two men.

Nearly everyone who ever met Himmler—or who has written about him since—has commented on his unprepossessing appearance and colorless personality. Short, unathletic, and nearsighted, he hardly embodied the Nazi ideal. In fact, a Gauleiter once remarked, "If I looked like him, I would not speak of race at all." Yet beneath the exterior lurked two driving, apparently contradictory characteristics that also have struck most observers: his absorption in a fantasy world—including faith in astrology and herbalism, pleasure in torchlight rituals, the conviction that he was the reincarnation of German Emperor Heinrich I ("the Fowler," who died in 936), and the dream of populating the colonized German East with interlinked settlements of Teutonic warrior-soldiers (*Wehrbauern*)— and his methodical attention to practical bureaucratic details. The combination underpinned his "success" as a mass murderer. He demanded organized, thorough, and "merciless" translation of his

Aryan supremacist dream world into reality, and that demand animated the organizations responsible to him: the SS, the RSHA, the German police, the *Einsatzgruppen*, and all their auxiliaries.

Reinhard Heydrich came to the Nazi Party relatively late for one of its main leaders. He initially pursued a naval career that was cut short by his court-martial for having an affair with a woman other than his fiancée. The woman's family turned out to have powerful connections, but what really led to his dismissal from the navy was the arrogance he displayed before the court. Though he had been active in conservative nationalist groups in the 1920s, the fiancée, whose portentous name was Lina von Osten (Lina from the East), pushed him, beginning in 1931, toward the Nazi Party and membership in the SS. Physically, he was the model SS man: tall, blond, blue-eyed, long and thin in the face, athletic, and graceful. As one of his German biographers noted, "[I]f National Socialism had looked in the mirror, Reinhard Heydrich would have looked back." Emotionally, too, he fit the mold: tough, decisive, hard-driving, persistent, relentless, and risk-taking. His favorite adjective was "*unerhört*," unheard-of or unprecedented, and he strove to make his actions earn that description. Carl Jacob Burckhardt, a Swiss diplomat and historian, said after their first meeting that Heydrich was "a young, evil god of death." At his funeral after his assassination by Czech resistance fighters in 1942, Hitler called him "the man with the iron heart."

Heydrich's manifest conceit and cold-bloodedness increased as time passed, probably in compensation for his late entrance into the Party, his scandalous eviction from the navy, and the persistent rumors, which proved false but led to a humiliating internal Nazi investigation in 1932, that his mother's parentage was Jewish. These impetuses, along with his close personal friendship with Himmler and his considerable organizational talent, turned him into a murderous executor of Nazi ideology. He became the epitome of the Nazi belief that only Germans counted; everyone else was simply outside his moral universe and expendable. Some of his biographers contend that he adopted Nazi ideology merely as a vehicle for his urge to power, but this is too simple. His conviction was genuine, as was his emotional addiction to military life and violence. Also genuine was his belief, typical of Nazi perpetrators, that he was innocent, high-minded, and self-sacrificing in fulfilling the tasks assigned to him. As he reportedly told his wife, "I feel free of all guilt. I make myself available; others pursue egotistical goals."

Adolf Eichmann was in some respects a rather pathetic figure, which did not prevent him from becoming an extraordinarily destructive one. His family moved from an industrial city not far from Düsseldorf to Austria in 1913, when he was seven years old, and he never managed to graduate from either an academic or a vocational high school. Helped by his father's business contacts and by his stepmother's Jewish relatives, he got jobs as a salesman for first an electric company and then an oil firm, but lost the latter post in May 1933 during the Depression. By then, he already had joined the Nazi Party, impelled largely by his Protestant, pro-German family milieu, and this new political affiliation led him to return to Germany after the Austrian government cracked down on the Nazis in mid-1933. There he volunteered for the SD, the Security Service of the SS that Heydrich had started a few years earlier, and received an assignment to keep tabs on Freemasons in Germany. He moved on to the SD's Jewish Department in 1935, and by 1938 was in charge of the agencies in Vienna dedicated to driving the Jews out of the city and confiscating their wealth as they left. Responsibility to handle Jewish affairs within the RSHA followed in 1939, along with the task of arranging the deportations of the Poles and Jews that Himmler wished to push out of the parts of Poland annexed to Germany into the General Government. Later, his portfolio expanded to include transportation to the ghettos and/or death camps of all the Jews of Europe except those already inside the General Government—their removal was the job of another SS officer, Hermann (Hans) Höfle.

When Hannah Arendt described Eichmann as the embodiment of the "banality of evil," the bureaucrat without convictions who saw no difference between shipping cargo and shipping people, she fell for the cover story that he constructed for himself in preparation for, during, and after his trial in Jerusalem in 1961. He knew that his only conceivable defense was to portray himself as a mindless cog in the machine, someone who merely had obeyed irresistible orders. In truth, he had come, during the 1930s, to believe deeply in Germany's need to fight the Jews. That belief hardened, following the conquest of Poland, into a readiness to kill and then into a determination to do so that had become so intense by November 1944 that he circumvented a direct order from Himmler to stop renewed deportations from Hungary. Thanks to the assiduous research of Bettina Stangneth, who examined Eichmann's many recorded utterances to fellow Nazis and their sympathizers while he was hiding in Argentina between 1950 and 1960 and assembled them in *Eichmann Before Jerusalem* (2014), we now know how proud he was of his SS service in retrospect and how thoroughly he rationalized it, not as conscientiously carrying out an allotted task as a dutiful civil servant but as creatively and energetically defending his nation against perfidious attacks by Jews. Antisemitism was a means to his advancement, but it was not only that.

Rudolf Höss was a rather different sort of person and perhaps the one leading perpetrator who most closely resembled Arendt's depiction of a "thoughtless" Nazi desk killer. Höss came from a deeply religious family and felt attracted to military life because it offered a comradely antidote to his lonely upbringing and temperament. After service in World War I as only a teenager, he joined a right-wing paramilitary unit, got caught up in the murder of a comrade, served five years in jail, and emerged in 1928 lost and adrift. Hoping to start a farm, he joined a rather mystical agricultural group called the Artamanen, where he met Heinrich Himmler. In 1934, his invitation drew Höss into the SS and concentration camp work, which offered the attraction of a quasi-military life. Once in, Höss sought to win commendation by accomplishing whatever he was asked to do, without regard to its content. He remained Himmler's man throughout his career, not least because others in the camp system hierarchy disliked Höss intensely.

One of his biographers has called him "a functionary in the true sense," a man so empty that he found meaning only in carrying out directions and serving values that were created for him. He was a monument to what Germans call "the secondary virtues": selflessness, loyalty, diligence, helpfulness, and order, all displayed without reflection on the purposes to which they were being put. In a succession of camp command posts, culminating with Auschwitz, Höss demonstrated neither pleasure nor discomfort in inflicting suffering. Whether his many victims deserved their fate was a subject on which he, in his own devastatingly self-incriminating words, "had never really wasted much thought." Duty was his only concern, and at the end he therefore depicted himself, not the people he killed, as a victim of the fate that had cast him in the role of Auschwitz camp commander. None of these comments means that Höss was a robot. Within given policy parameters, he was inventive and energetic. But he appears to have thought entirely within the box of pleasing his superiors and performing his assigned tasks

Ernst Kaltenbrunner, who imbibed his politics, including intense and vocal antisemitism, from his extremely right-wing father, joined the Nazi Party in 1930, eight years before his native Austria became part of the Reich, and the SS only a year later. He promptly recruited Adolf Eichmann, and then spent the 1930s brawling with political opponents and agitating for the *Anschluss*. In its aftermath, he became the chief of the SS and the police in Vienna from 1938 to 1943, when he moved up to succeed Heydrich as head of the Reich Security Main Office. Kaltenbrunner referred to Himmler as his "*Übervater*"—that is, his ideal and role model. Even after the war, Kaltenbrunner gave vent to his fervent Nazism by attesting that the

Party presented "a world view encompassing life in its entirety," that the idea of race constituted "the divinely inspired building block of mankind," and that the Jews, especially in Eastern Europe, were "really the only stratum that possessed enough intellectuality to provide the enemy with the necessary actors to execute his plans."

The last two figures in this rogues' gallery, Oswald Pohl and Hans Kammler, directed the murderous slave labor system, the former with responsibility for administration and finance, the latter for engineering and construction. Both were veterans of right-wing paramilitary formations, and both had joined the Nazi Party before Hitler became chancellor in 1933. They harbored dreams of an industrial empire that would provide building materials for the massive architectural expressions of the new Germany, furniture and knickknacks for German settlers in the conquered East of the continent, and roads to connect them. All of this was to contribute to the demographic transformation of Europe and the creation of a new state-owned economic sector. Like the other killers described above, Pohl and Kammler were ideologically inspired creators of a Nazi New Order, imbued with a spirit of activism and with "ideals" of racial supremacy. Neither had any hesitation in carrying out Himmler's instruction to work the concentration camp inmates like the Pharaoh's slaves.

Perhaps the most remarkable feature of the mentality of the Nazi perpetrators was their self-delusion, their capacity to distract themselves from what they were doing by calling it something else. Perpetrators never owned up to torturing and slaughtering; they always professed to be serving a sanctified purpose that immunized them from the charge of immorality. The epitome of this stance was Himmler's speech to the assembled SS commanders at Posen in October 1943. He summarized the philosophy of the SS bluntly: "honest, decent, loyal, and comradely must we be to members of our own blood and to nobody else." He congratulated his men for having waded through gore but nonetheless "remained decent." He referred to their deeds as a "never to be written page of glory" in Germany's history. Of course, he was not just saying that the end justified the means, though he was saying that. He was also congratulating his subordinates on being people who could, to use contemporary phraseology, bite the bullet and do what had to be done. He was praising them for understanding that "winning is the only thing." When we put his language into ours, we are reminded of how common such self- and principle-abandoning thinking is in the world. Maybe Stanley Milgram and Philip Zimbardo were right after all in suggesting that "How could people do such things?" is a naïve question.

A nation is not only what it does, Kurt Tucholsky, the great German satirist, wrote in 1934, but also what it puts up with. What of the ordinary Germans who did not carry out the killings directly but witnessed the deportations, sometimes photographed them for local histories, frequently took over the possessions left behind, and heard the rumors that abounded about the fate of not only Germany's Jews but also those in the east? What did they know of the murders, and how did they respond? Awareness of the self-dug graves and shootings by the *Einsatzgruppen*, the Order Police, the foreign auxiliaries, and the German army was widespread, thanks to letters home and troops on furlough. Indeed, such information was sufficiently plentiful as time passed that more and more Germans spoke with open dread of the reprisals or retribution that they expected to experience once the tide of the war turned. A representative expression of this view, as well as of slightly more complete knowledge, is this diary entry by Curt Prüfer, a semiretired diplomat and an antisemite who had purchased property formerly owned by Jews. On November 22, 1942, he wrote the following—mostly in French, as if to conceal what he was saying: "Men, women, and children have been slaughtered in large numbers by poison gas or by machine guns. The hatred that inevitably must arise from that will never be appeased. Today every child knows this in the smallest detail." Already in March of that year, the isolated diarist Victor Klemperer recorded that he had heard of a place called Auschwitz where Jews were worked to death rapidly; by October, he could describe it as a "swift-working slaughterhouse." Meanwhile, in April 1942, he had written that his wife heard an eyewitness report of mass murders of Jews in Kiev, a reference to the killings at Babi Yar seven months earlier. Several months before Germany surrendered, Klemperer, again quoting only what his "Aryan" neighbors had told him, knew even the approximate death toll of the Holocaust. He wrote in his diary for October 24, 1944, "six to seven million Jews . . . have been slaughtered (more exactly: shot and gassed)."

Knowledge of the Holocaust in Germany was extensive because, as Peter Fritzsche shrewdly has noted, "the Nazis wanted to manage, but not entirely conceal, the facts." After all, Goebbels announced in the journal *Das Reich* on November 16, 1941, that "world Jewry . . . is now gradually being engulfed by the same extermination process that it had intended for us." On April 30, 1942, the *Völkischer Beobachter*, the official mouthpiece of the Nazi Party, reported "the rumor" that "it is the task of the Security Police to exterminate the Jews in the occupied territories. The Jews were assembled in the thousands and shot; beforehand they had to dig their own graves." Hitler reminded Germans of his prophecy that a world war would bring about the annihilation of the Jews in no fewer than seven major speeches: on January 30, 1941; on January 30, February 24, October 1, and November 8, 1942; on February 25, 1943; and on January 1, 1945. By one scholar's count, the Führer referred to the wiping out of the Jews in at least a dozen wartime public speeches or pronouncements. If such partial revelations had a purpose, it was to secure loyalty by reminding people of their complicity. Having allowed such brutality, Germans could expect nothing but reprisal, so they had best fight tooth and nail to sustain the Third Reich. For the most part, this strategy succeeded.

Whatever the state of their knowledge, the German public's willingness to help Jews was exceedingly limited. Jews who went underground, who refused to answer the order to appear for deportation and then hid their identities and tried to survive within the Reich, were called U-boats, after the German word for submarines. Perhaps 10,000 people tried this means of outliving and outwitting the Nazis, about half of them in the city of Berlin; both there and nationwide, somewhere between 30 percent and 50 percent of them made it to 1945. The mortality rate was high, and the numbers involved small. But for every person who did survive, the number of non-Jewish Germans who helped at one time or another had to be substantial. Sometimes that help was active, as in the creation of forged identity documents or the offer of a place to live; sometimes it was passive, as when an old acquaintance recognized a U-boat on the street but did not expose the person. Konrad Latte, whose father and mother had converted to Protestantism, spent the months from March 1943 to May 1945 as a U-boat. Before he died in 2005, he named fifty people who protected him in one way or another, only one of whom was ever caught and punished. Arthur Arndt, a Jewish doctor hidden with his wife and two children in Berlin, cited exactly the same number of non-Jews on whom the family's survival had depended. Max Krakauer, still a third successful U-boat, put the number in his case at sixty-six.

Despite such numbers, heroic behavior of this sort was rare. That makes it both admirable and a standing reproach to the general attitude of the German population, which to the very end of the war viewed the persecution of the Jews only through the self-interested lens of the benefit or punishment Germans were likely to receive because of it. Until the fronts began to close in on the Reich in 1944, the benefits greatly outweighed the potential costs, as Germans profited from the Holocaust in ways that ranged from the government revenue obtained from stealing the Jews' precious metals to the individual allocation of the furniture from their apartments to Reich citizens who had been bombed out. In Hamburg alone from 1941 to 1943, the authorities auctioned off some 4,000 shipping containers holding the goods of Jews who had emigrated, and the Nazi state took in 7.2 million reichsmark in proceeds. In 1942–43, forty-five shiploads of goods taken from Dutch Jews went to the same German port city. A German scholar of the subject estimates that between 1941 and 1945 "at least one hundred thousand" inhabitants of the town and its environs bought household property confiscated from Jews. Similarly, the occupation of Europe generated enormous benefits to Germans in the form of food and goods shipped home by far-flung troops, most of it bought by soldiers flush with local currency but some of it stolen. Returns on conquest and murder such as these did much to preserve loyalty to the Nazi regime well into 1945.

How little effective help most Jews could expect from the German public is demonstrated by an event that some commentators cite as evidence for not only the opposite point, but also the potential of popular opposition to alter Nazi racial policy. To be sure, the Rosenstrasse protest of February 27 to March 6, 1943 in Berlin constituted the only outbreak of popular resistance to deportations of Jews in the history of Nazi Germany, but the events were far less consequential than legend has it. The trigger was a push finally to make Germany virtually *judenrein* (cleansed of Jews) by rounding up all remaining Jewish forced laborers at their workplaces and then deporting all except those in mixed marriages to Auschwitz or Theresienstadt. Across Germany, Jewish spouses in those marriages who got caught up in the Gestapo raids were released immediately, and in Berlin more than three-quarters of them were. But the SS detained some 2,000 such men in a Jewish community building on the Rosenstrasse in the middle of the city in order to double-check their marital status against the records deposited there and to identify personnel suitable for future assignment to nearby Jewish institutions as replacements for *Volljuden*, or "full Jews," the regime intended to (and did) deport a few weeks later. As these processes dragged on, several hundred of the worried non-Jewish wives and female in-laws of the detained men gathered around the building seeking information about their relatives, occasionally crying out for their release but mostly, as one participant reported, standing in "silent protest," and in defiance of repeated police efforts to disperse the crowd. Once the releases from the building gathered pace, the assembly dwindled, and the episode came to a close.

The Rosenstrasse protest required considerable courage of the women who carried it out, but two telling aspects of it deserve emphasis. First, it was limited to a few hundred relatives of the rather small number of men affected, not joined by other so-called Aryans, and not accompanied by any popular resistance to the deportation of thousands of other Jews from Berlin and the Reich at this time. Second, the protest accomplished little in protecting men whom the SS intended to use in the near term and dispense with later. With the partial exceptions of the spouses transferred to Jewish community institutions, the Jewish parties to mixed marriages became subject to increasingly severe measures in the ensuing months. Not allowed to return to their factory jobs, they were condemned "to the hardest manual labor," increasingly driven with their non-Jewish spouses into vacated Jew Houses, shipped off to work camps, and finally included in the directive that consigned all part-Jews, or *Mischlinge*, to Theresienstadt in early 1945. The scant remaining statistical evidence suggests that fewer than half the mixed marriages of 1943 still existed when the war ended.

Far from demonstrating what greater popular resistance to Nazi persecution might have accomplished, the Rosenstrasse incident showed that overt protest had little impact on the direction or pace of the regime's relentless course. Ironically, in Nazi Germany the prospect of popular opposition sometimes stayed the regime's hand, as clearly happened in dissuading Hitler and his entourage from promulgating a law automatically dissolving all mixed marriages, but the reality of resistance generally goaded the Reich into more radical action, not only in Germany but also in occupied countries.

As World War II drew toward its close, and the returns on persecution turned adverse for Germans, few of them paused to reflect on the horror they had inflicted. Instead, they devoted most of their attention to the supposed injustice of their own suffering, either at the hands of Allied air raids or as the likely result of the regime's crimes when vengeful enemy troops rolled in. The self-pity and sense of victimization that gave rise to Nazi rule also outlasted it.

ENSLAVEMENT

The most drawn-out and agonizing, though numerically least lethal, form of murder, after gassing and shooting—namely, the system of slave labor—accounted for at least one-half million deaths in the Holocaust. Why and how did the Nazis develop this system? Why did they bother to keep some Jews alive for labor for at least some period of time? Why did they treat such laborers so apparently counterproductively? With regard to these questions, perhaps more misinformation has accumulated than concerning any other aspect of the Holocaust. This is so for an ironic reason: Many of the lawyers who in recent decades worked hard to obtain compensation for former slave laborers sullied a good cause by frequently misrepresenting how the system came into being and how profitable it proved.

Slave and forced labor were two parts of a common system. Forced laborers were non-Jews recruited or rounded up in occupied countries during World War II and brought to work in Germany for nominal wages. They were often, though not always, badly fed, housed, and treated and kept segregated from the German population. Collected and supervised by a Nazi *Gauleiter* named Fritz Sauckel, they made up 15 percent of industrial workers in Germany in 1942, a figure that rose to 30 percent in 1944, but 20–50 percent of the labor force in the largest and most militarily important German firms during that time frame, and more than half the people working in German agriculture. In August 1944, they included almost 1.3 million French people, over 580,000 Italians, almost 2.8 million Soviet citizens, and almost 1.7 million Poles. Their number peaked at 6.8 million at the end of 1944, but altogether 13 million people did forced labor in Germany from 1939 to 1945, 4.6 million of them prisoners of war and 8.4 million of them civilians. This was a staggeringly large system of exploitation.

Slave laborers, who numbered some 1.1 million people during the whole of World War II, of whom about 714,000 were toiling at the beginning of 1945, were inmates of ghettos and concentration camps, mostly but not always Jews. Indeed, the number of non-Jews among them rose during the final year of the war, especially as more and more Eastern European women were put into camps like Ravensbrück and Sachsenhausen and then parceled out to labor sites. The Economics and Administration Main Office of the SS supervised and controlled most slave laborers and leased them to government agencies or private industries for a set price per person per day. In other words, they were not paid, but they were paid for. And, contrary to legend, they were not necessarily cheap. The SS charges in many cases exceeded what a German civilian laborer, especially a construction worker, would have received; even when this was not the case, the productivity of slave laborers often was so limited that it offset their low wages. After all, few slave laborers had done manual labor before, especially on construction projects. All this gave the employers a perverse incentive to economize on food and housing for slave laborers, to drive them excessively hard, and to work them long hours, at least so long as ample numbers were available to replace people who died of maltreatment. In this respect, the term "slave labor" is actually misleading. Slaves are bought, and their owners thus acquire an economic interest in their survival. But camp and ghetto inmates were rented by the day. The renter had little interest in their long-term survival unless they were highly skilled. Meanwhile, the employer could send any flagging workers back to the camp they came from and trade them for fitter workers.

What difference this made is illustrated by the relative fates of the men and women slave laborers used at a plant of a Degussa subsidiary at Gleiwitz in Upper Silesia between 1943 and 1945. Only two females out of 209 in the workforce died, and they committed suicide the day the SS took over supervision of the laborers' barracks in 1944. But a substantial share—probably about one-third—of the more than 1,000 men put to work on the site expired. Why? The men worked on construction and were of no interest to the firm once the plant was finished, but the women were indispensable to its manufacturing, at least as long as the war lasted. The surviving statistics indicate that the company was indifferent to the working conditions and fates of the men but very concerned to retain the women. Food and medical help must have been better for the women than the men, because relative working conditions alone—the men did heavy labor outside, the women worked indoors mostly packaging the output—are not enough to explain the discrepancy in survival rates. One scholar who has examined mortality rates of slave laborers meticulously has concluded that those put to work on construction projects were five to ten times more likely to die than those employed on assembly lines, but at Gleiwitz the men were 150 times more likely to die. This example illustrates a general pattern: Firms could make a difference to the survival chances of their slave laborers, but tried to do so only when self-interest commanded such action.

How and why did these systems come into being? The forced labor system was rooted in the mathematics of the German labor force during World War II: The Reich called up eleven million men for military service, and a larger percentage of German women were employed already in 1939 than was ever the case in Britain or the United States during the war, which meant that relatively few German women were available as replacements. Yet the war created demand for enormous increases in output. Germany therefore faced a choice between farming out production to the occupied countries or importing replacement workers. For the most part, the Reich opted for the latter to guard against sabotage and/or the loss of industrial secrets. The forced labor program that developed drew on two precedents for compulsory work in Nazi Germany: first, the conscription of unemployed Germans and those with jobs in nearby factories into work columns to build new highways (the Autobahnen) and fortifications in the Rhineland (the Westwall) in the 1930s; and second, the use of primarily Polish and French POWs as supplementary workers beginning in 1940.

The slave labor system, however, had its roots in Nazi antisemitism, which contended that Jews avoided manual labor and thus should be forced to do it, and in the economic interests of the SS, which wanted to become financially self-sustaining. The system had two forerunners. First, the Reich inaugurated a compulsory labor program for German Jewish males on Hitler's birthday in April 1939. Cut off from other gainful employment and the German welfare system, Jews were supposed to "earn their keep" in road-building and street-cleaning projects and in private industrial assignments, notably at the large Siemens plant in Berlin. The Nazi regime extended this program to all Jews in Poland in October 1939, and many died when forced to do river dredging and straightening projects and airfield and road construction under brutal overseers. Two of the later death camps, Belzec and Treblinka, began as labor camps for Jews put to work digging tank traps and other fortifications along the nearby border with the Soviet Union following the partition of Poland. Second, in 1936–39, the SS set up a web of its own companies that used camp inmate labor to generate revenue. The holding company was called the German Economic Plants (DWB). One of its subsidiaries was the German Equipment Works (DAW) that made weaponry. Another, the German Earth and Stone company (DEST), made bricks at most camps in Germany and operated an infamous quarry at Mauthausen in Austria that supplied much of the building material for the Nazi Party Grounds in Nuremberg.

Although these were the precedents, they were not the actual triggers for the vast expansion of the slave labor system during World War II. Three developments set that process in motion. First, ghettoization created both labor pools that attracted German firms and an incentive for the Nazi administrators to develop revenue-generating initiatives that would make the ghettos pay. Second, the Reich decided in the Fall of 1940 to build a road in southern Poland that would link the Autobahn from Berlin to Upper Silesia with the highway they envisioned (Durchgangstrasse IV) running across Ukraine all the way to the Black Sea after the invasion of the U.S.S.R. This was the impetus for the formation of the Organisation Schmelt, named after the SS officer who commanded it, which developed the system of wage rates, barracks, underfeeding, and severe treatment that later characterized the slave labor program everywhere. A simultaneous project connecting Berlin to Lodz led to the first use of slave labor by German private industry, in this case the construction firm Philipp Holzmann. The route through southern Poland stimulated the expansion of the Auschwitz and Majdanek camps, which were to be the sources of labor for the construction. When Heydrich referred, at the Wannsee Conference, to the use of able-bodied Jews on road building in the East, Durchgangstrasse IV was the undertaking he had in mind. It ultimately consumed the lives of at least 25,000 Jewish construction workers, who toiled without the assistance of machinery and were brutally mistreated. Third, in early 1941 two of the largest corporations in the Reich, Volkswagen and IG Farben, chose to deviate from industry's earlier refusal to hire camp inmates. Volkswagen agreed to set up a concentration camp on the factory grounds in Wolfsburg, in northwest Germany, ultimately to construct an aluminum foundry, and Farben agreed to build a huge synthetic rubber plant just east of the town of Auschwitz and to lease camp inmates as construction workers.

From these small beginnings, the use of slave labor mushroomed, especially after September 1942, when the SS broadened its usual policy of hiring out inmates only for production in and around concentration camps by agreeing to expand upon the Volkswagen precedent with the establishment of satellite sites near important factories. The most voracious consumers of slave labor became the Eastern Front, for military installations and factory reconstruction; the French Atlantic coast, where inmates built most of the defenses; Upper Silesia, the preferred location of massive new factories for fuel and rubber because Allied bombers could not reach the area from bases in Great Britain; and the Project Giant (*Projekt Riese*) site in the Owl Mountains of Lower Silesia, a warren of underground passages that began as a huge prospective bombproof headquarters for Hitler and then morphed into military production lines. All told, slave labor camps in Nazi-occupied Europe numbered in the tens of thousands, and they extended from the island of Alderney, in the English Channel, to the farthest reaches of German penetration into the Soviet Union.

Despite (or because of) the size of the system, it was never efficient or well managed. Half the inmates of Auschwitz never even got labor assignments. The SS companies were neither profitable nor usually successful in their joint ventures with private enterprises to manufacture military equipment inside camps, though one initiative, involving the construction of fighter planes at Flossenbürg with Messerschmitt, made money and contributed to the German war effort. Until the turn of 1943/44, Jewish slave laborers were generally kept out of Germany proper, and projects were brought to them in occupied or annexed territories—the inmates supplied to Volkswagen in 1941 had included only a few Jewish political prisoners—but the Nazi regime reversed this practice as labor shortages mounted and British and American air raids took a toll on the Reich. This change in German policy had major consequences for the survival chances of people arriving at Auschwitz. Up until late 1943, the camp primarily wanted men to work on construction, so fewer women were selected for admission to the camp than men.

Combined with the fact that women generally outnumbered men on transports into the camp, this meant that the female mortality rate upon arrival was much higher than the male. Beginning in late 1943, however, demand rose for women to work on assembly lines, so the number of them selected caught up with and sometimes exceeded the number of men. This is why the young women from Hungary who arrived at Auschwitz in 1944 had better chances of surviving the camp than almost any other Jewish group.

One can get a sense of the variable horrors of the slave labor system by looking at two examples from occupied Poland of production sites that continued to operate long after most other installations using Jews had been liquidated: Starachowice and Skarzysko-Kamienna. Both lay south of Radom in the middle of the General Government, and both endured because they produced munitions. The two sites also had a common and peculiar feature that proved decisive in the survival of some of their slave laborers: Neither plant was incorporated into the SS camp system under the jurisdiction of the WVHA. Both remained largely governed by pragmatic factory managers who behaved erratically and unpredictably but, on the whole, less ruthlessly than the SS.

Starachowice came into existence as a camp on October 27, 1942, following the liquidation of the surrounding ghettos, during which two-thirds of the inhabitants were sent to death at Treblinka and one-third brought into the new, hastily constructed camp. The installation lasted twenty-one months, until July 28, 1944, and the transport of the workers to Auschwitz. Shifts were either eight or twelve hours long, depending on the strenuousness of the work and not counting marching time to and from the camp to the factory. Output quotas were high, but working conditions depended heavily on the character of the German or Polish foremen, which varied immensely. The predominant recollection of survivors is of the extreme filth that prevailed. One former inmate said that when he got to the Monowitz camp alongside the IG Farben factory near Auschwitz, he found that wretched site much cleaner than what he was used to at Staracho-wice, where he had not showered for months on end.

Skarzysko-Kamienna operated from April 1942 to August 1944 on the site of several former Polish state ammunition plants that a German munitions producer, the Hugo Schneider AG (HASAG), had taken over. Some 25,000 Jews passed through the camp during its life, and about four-fifths of them perished. The inmates worked in two shifts, day and night, without special work clothes or adequate sanitary conditions. In the shell department, women workers were expected to carry 180 nine-pound shells to each polishing machine during each hour in a ten-hour shift—in other words, three per minute. In the antiaircraft department, supervisors whipped work-ers who produced defective pieces. In the mine department, packers had to cram explosives into the shells by hand with no gloves or aprons to protect them. Those who worked with picric acid found that their hands turned black and their hair turned green; those who worked with TNT saw their skin turn reddish-pink. As the TNT was being prepared, women had to stir it while it boiled at a rate of 1,800 stirs per hour and 21,600 stirs in a twelve-hour shift, all while standing. The food was the usual watery soup, ersatz cof-fee, and crusts of bread. The workers wore wooden clogs. The bunk beds had no mattresses or blankets and were lice-infested. Typhus was rampant, and weak prisoners were shot weekly until the spring of 1943, when the Germans began to worry about running out of them. Yet the camp and its factories continued to operate and some Jewish inmates continued to live until the Soviet army appeared on the horizon in late July 1944, when the sick were killed and every-one else shipped out to HASAG plants in Germany. Their survival was highly unusual, and it resulted from the fact that even Himmler could not bring himself to order the deaths of the people who in 1944 produced one-third of the German infantry's ammunition.

Beginning in late 1943 and with gathering speed during 1944, the Germans reversed the policy of keeping Jews out of the Reich and began to bring more and more concentration camp inmates to work in Germany. The model for what could be done became the Dora-Mittelbau site in the Harz Mountains, where V-rockets were to be produced. Sixty thousand prisoners passed through this installation in 1943–45, and more than 40 percent of them had died by the time the war ended. The SS installed an assembly line in two large shafts that had been driven into Kohnstein Mountain since 1937 to create a huge storage installation for aircraft fuel. The shafts were not straight lines, but S-shaped, each about a mile long, about 30 feet wide and 23 feet high, just under 300 feet apart, and connected every 100 feet or so by somewhat smaller cross-shafts, creating a sort of curved ladder design. The original idea was to lay railroad lines down in each shaft, to put the storage tanks in the cross-shafts, then to bring trains into the mountain to fill their barrel cars with fuel, and finally to drive the trains out the other side. This conception lent itself readily to conversion to rocket assembly lines, with weapons moving down the tracks and the 20,000 different components of each, which were stored in the cross shafts, applied in succession. But only one of the shafts actually passed completely through the mountain and out the other side, so the assembly-line plan had to be altered somewhat. Even so, the scale of the underground production facility was vast, coming to more than one million square feet.

The project began in August 1943, with a non-Jewish labor force drawn from Buchenwald concentration camp, and the camp sent an additional 800 workers per week in the first months. Fed a meager and watery diet, they were quartered in the stinking, dusty, lice-ridden, and overcrowded cross-shafts, which were never quiet because the assembly work was continuous in two twelve-hour shifts. The prisoners had no safety gear and little protection against outbreaks of disease. Oxygen in the interior of the shafts was in short supply, cold water accumulated on the floors and chilled the bootless workers, and the interior temperature never rose above 59 degrees Fahrenheit. When production of rockets began in January 1944, the

Dora camp adjacent to the site held more than 10,000 inmates, and about 4,000 of them were working in the shafts. Over the next three months, they turned out about 300 rockets, most of them defective because of design flaws, and the camp acquired a terrible reputation for mortality. By the beginning of April 1944, when most of the production problems were ironed out, 34 percent of the cumulative population to date of just over 17,000—that is, almost 6,000 people—had died, at a rate that had reached 20 to 25 inmates per day. That death rate was the highest of any concentration camp at the time. Another 20,000 prisoners died in the next twelve months, making total mortality among the people who assembled V-1 and V-2 rockets about two-thirds greater than the total number of English and Belgian citizens killed by them.

Dora-Mittelbau was the prototype of what became, in March 1944, the Fighter Staff Program (*Jägerstab-Programm*), a massive effort to bury German arms-producing factories so that Allied bombing could not damage them. Junkers aircraft motor factories and assembly lines were installed in the northern end of the Mittelbau shafts and in other caves in nearby mountains. By September 1944, 12,000 Dora inmates, now including Hungarian Jews, were at work on these sites in central Germany, and tens of thousands of laborers from other camps were carving caves into the steep banks of the Rhine or pouring and camouflaging concrete hangers in open Bavarian fields. As the workforce at Dora grew, the SS created a new concentration camp consisting of some ninety buildings outside the south end of one of the tunnels, where the production of V-1 rockets was concentrated after September 1944.

No one has ever succeeded in precisely tabulating the total number of people killed across Germany in this crazed attempt to protect plants from bombing, or in the slave labor program altogether. One-half million deaths is the best rough estimate. We know that mortality rates fluctuated: They were high in 1942–43, when laborers seemed so numerous as to be expendable; they dropped in 1943–44, and then they surged again during the Fighter Staff Program and the collapse of Germany. The number of former Jewish slave laborers still alive in 1945 may have been as low as 150,000.

This was a state-driven system, not one propelled by private greed, as is often implied. The principal reason private enterprises asked for slave laborers was the absence of alternative ways to meet rising production targets or, late in the war, to salvage their machinery by getting it underground. Of course, if Germany won the war, the companies expected to gain in the form of having new plants that slave laborers had helped construct. But corporate executives generally fixed their eyes on more short-term objectives: doing their national duty, protecting their market or political positions, and continuing to produce. At Auschwitz, IG Farben remained wedded to using and paying for slave labor, even though camp inmates accomplished only about 15 percent of the construction work, primarily as a disguised form of bribing the SS for future favors. Very few companies, in the end, made much money off the system, not least because much of what they built was lost in the war or afterward. For example, IG Farben's plant near Auschwitz and Degussa's at Gleiwitz produced for only a few months before being overrun by the Red Army. The beneficiary of both turned out to be the Polish Communist state, which nationalized the factories after 1945 and operated them until the fall of communism in 1989.

In other words, the use of slave labor by German companies was criminal, but not because it was profitable, which it often was not. The principal profiteer from the slave labor program, as from Aryanization in general, was the German state, which collected fees on the labor, estimated at 600 to 700 million reichsmark in 1943–44 alone, commissioned most of the projects into which that labor went, and consumed most of the products that the labor ultimately generated.

Probably the most murderous phase of the slave labor program was the final one, the interval between January and May of 1945, when the retreat of the German army on all fronts prompted the regime to try to salvage slave labor for the Reich by marching camp inmates back into Germany. This effort to save the laborers turned into a massive destruction process, to which about 35 percent of the people involved succumbed in the last five months of World War II. Often columns of prisoners set out from camps with no clear sense of how to get where they had been told to go, and confusion was compounded by the rapid movement of Soviet or other Allied forces that often blocked previously open escape routes. Most of these evacuation columns carried little food with them and consisted of ill-shod and ill-clad people marching in the dead of winter. Massive casualties resulted, as the guards, terrified of being captured if the columns slowed down, shot anyone who faltered or straggled. In the evacuation of Auschwitz in January 1945, prisoners marched through the snow on either of two routes, both over thirty miles long, until they reached a passable railroad line and were loaded onto open freight cars in subfreezing temperatures. Amazingly, the death toll in this first round of retreat was relatively modest, something like 7,000 out of 56,000. But 15,000 of those survivors went to the Gross-Rosen camp, which was abandoned, in turn, in February, and in that retreat the mortality rate was much higher, amounting to perhaps 50 percent of the 97,000 prisoners marched out.

Among the most horrible of the death marches were those launched from Stutthof and its subcamps on the Baltic coast in January 1945. Almost 69,000 prisoners, most of them Jews and over half of them women, each carrying only eighteen ounces of bread and four ounces of margarine, and many of them barefoot, left the camp in six marching columns on the morning of January 25. The lucky columns were the ones the Soviets caught up with; the others marched westward for hundreds of miles, growing thinner by the day, or suffered a more swiftly murderous fate. In Palmnicken, a village thirty-one miles west of Königsberg where one of the prisoner columns with about 3,000 inmates bivouacked in a factory building for a few nights, the guard force and the local Nazi Party leader decided that they did not want the town to contain inmates when the approaching Russians arrived. So the Germans marched the prisoners, most of them women, some three miles to a row of high bluffs overlooking the Baltic seashore and machine-gunned them into the freezing water below.

These ghastly retreats also had calamitous ripple effects, as the camps that received retreating prisoner groups swiftly became unable to feed or otherwise maintain them. Throughout the concentration camp system, all semblance of sanitation and sustenance collapsed. As a result, the overwhelmed guard staff at Neuengamme, near Hamburg, began killing the sick with poison injections; at least 8,000 died this way from February to April 1945. At Dachau, conditions became so horrendous that 4,000 inmates died of typhus in February of that year. At Buchenwald, the prisoners arriving from elsewhere were stuffed into a sector called the Little Camp; its population rose from 6,000 in January to 17,000 in April, even as some 5,200 inmates of the site died during that time span. At Ravensbrück, Sachsenhausen, and Mauthausen, and possibly at Dachau, the response was to set up gas chambers or to activate the small ones left from the 14f13 operation for sick, infirm, and troublesome prisoners. About 10,000 inmates were asphyxiated at these places from February to April 1945, mostly with Zyklon but some perhaps in gas vans. The last gassing of the Holocaust occurred at Mauthausen on April 29, the day before Hitler killed himself.

By far the worst conditions prevailed at Bergen-Belsen, in northwestern Germany, not far from Hanover. Once a small site that held Jews who were to be exchanged for Germans in Allied hands, the camp ballooned to 15,000 inmates by November 1944, most of them sick prisoners dumped there from other camps. By March 31, 1945, the population had reached 44,060, even though the mortality rate had averaged between 250 and 300 people per day in the preceding four weeks. And this was before six convoys containing

20,000 prisoners arrived from Dora-Mittelbau in early April. As far as historians can reconstruct from the records, approximately 35,000 people died from disease and starvation at Bergen-Belsen in the final months of the war. This was an instance of what one might call unplanned annihilation, though one should add that intention was clearly present, since the humane thing to do was to leave the prisoners in camps for the Allies to capture. The decisions to withdraw them under horrendous conditions and then to try to maintain control of them for as long as possible were, in effect, murderous, and the number of resulting deaths was about as large as in the massacre of Hungarian Jewry in the spring of 1944.

These decisions were Heinrich Himmler's. Hitler had favored slaughtering all the camp inmates and blowing up the sites, but the leaders of the WVHA, the SS economics division, who had been put in charge of jet aircraft as well as V-rocket production, wanted to hold on to the labor supply as long as possible, and Himmler hoped to keep some Jews alive as a bargaining chip with the Allies. Although he vacillated somewhat between preservation and massacre during the final months, evacuation was a way of accomplishing both goals simultaneously, and his instruction of mid-April that "no inmate may fall into the enemy's hands alive" left the final choice up to camp commanders. Not all of them opted to send their inmates meandering around the Reich's shrinking territory, but most did. Thus, Bergen-Belsen fell to the British in mid-April without prisoners having been pulled out. But Buchenwald's 48,000 inmates were sent off in trains and on foot to Dachau and Flossenbürg only a few days after Belsen was captured; at least one-third perished in the following three weeks. At Neuengamme the SS also began dispersing the prisoners, sending 10,000 of them to the port city of Neustadt, where they were loaded onto three vessels anchored in the harbor. When the British bombed the city on May 3, the ships caught fire, and at least 7,000 of the prisoners burned, drowned, or were shot by German guards while trying to swim to shore. At Flossenbürg, evacuations began even as prisoners from Buchenwald were coming in; of almost 46,000 inmates sent mostly southward toward Dachau, at least 7,000 died in the ensuing three weeks. Finally, in late April, the SS emptied Sachsenhausen and Ravensbrück and forced the prisoners to march northwest toward the Baltic coast. American troops liberated approximately 20,000 of them in Schwerin. About 40,000 others endured the last days of the war in an open-air camp in a nearby forest, where thousands died of exposure and starvation.

At the end of April 1945, Bavaria and Austria remained under Nazi control, and they contained two large camp complexes, those of Dachau and Mauthausen, each with numerous subcamps. As the SS abandoned the most distant of Dachau's satellites, the guards simply burned down the barracks, with the sickest and weakest inmates inside. But once the dispersals from the main camp began in late April, the columns had no place to go, and those that set out were intercepted so quickly by American troops that only about 1,500 inmates died en route. Back in the Dachau camp, however, conditions were far worse for those inmates left behind or arriving on trains pouring in from elsewhere, and the last-minute ravages of hunger and disease were considerable. As for Mauthausen, it and its subcamps at Gusen, Ebensee, and Gunskirchen contained some 85,000 prisoners in early 1945, even though the mortality rates on the marches from other camps toward these sites had been devastating. Of 76,000 Jews handed over to Germany by Hungary at the former Austrian border at the turn of 1944/45, for example, at least 45,000 died on the way to Mauthausen in early 1945, often at the hands of civilians along the route or the *Volkssturm* militia units assigned to guard the prisoner columns. Those who reached the camp still faced long odds against survival. About 15,000 Jews were sent from Mauthausen to Gunskirchen in late April 1945; on May 4, the arriving American forces found 5,419 survivors, and of them, a soldier bleakly wrote, "many of the living people look dead. Bones covered in skin with almost no sign of flesh, sunken cheeks and deeply sunken eyes and a glassy expression, the expression of the living dead." One of those people was Theodore Zev Weiss, the man whose name is on the professorship I held at Northwestern for sixteen years. As of this writing, he is eighty-five years old and living in Wilmette, Illinois. Neither he nor any other inmate was supposed to survive. If the GIs had arrived even a week or two later, none would have.

CHAPTER 5

VICTIMS:
Why Didn't More Jews
Fight Back More Often?

WE TURN NOW from the perpetrators of the Holocaust, and the questions of why and how they killed so many, to the victims of the Nazi murder campaign, the surrounding populations, and the international community, and the question of why these groups could or did not do more to stop the carnage. First, the sensitive and controversial matter of the response of the Jews themselves: "Why didn't more Jews fight back more often?" is a common question that succeeding generations have posed from the comfort of living in liberal and law-observing societies. Why did the Warsaw ghetto's inhabitants not rebel against the Germans until April 1943, the inmates of Treblinka and Sobibor until August and October of that year, and the *Sonderkommando* of Jews detailed to operate the crematoria at Auschwitz until the fall of 1944—in each case only after the Germans' intention to kill the last of them became unmistakable?

The question is not quite fair, since flare-ups of armed resistance did occur when the Nazis began deportations from particular places. For example, in Cracow in December 1942, a Jewish group blew up a café favored by German officers in an effort to slow the transports. Two months earlier, an inmate killed a German staff member named Max Bialas at Treblinka. Jews were involved in an attempt to free the roughly 1,000 deportees on the twentieth transport from Belgium to Auschwitz on April 19, 1943, which actually enabled seventeen people to escape from one boxcar, ten of whom were not recaptured. But, as that small number suggests, these incidents had very limited consequences and were easily snuffed out. Perhaps, as various scholars contend, armed Jewish underground movements came into existence in five to seven of the large Polish ghettos, forty-five smaller ones, five death or concentration camps in Poland, and eighteen forced labor sites, but even so, their ultimate effectiveness was slight. On the whole, the Jewish response to the Nazi onslaught was to comply with German demands and orders in hopes of preventing them from getting worse.

COMPLIANCE AND RESISTANCE

Towering figures in the study of the Holocaust, notably Raul Hilberg and Hannah Arendt, have addressed the matter of this Jewish response in highly provocative form. The very first page of Hilberg's monumental *The Destruction of the European Jews*, both when first published in 1961 and again when an expanded third edition appeared forty-two years later, speaks of "the Jewish collapse" in the face of the Nazi assault and calls this "a manifestation of failure." He goes on to argue that the efforts of Jewish communities to sustain themselves, to maintain order, and to placate the Nazis actually helped the Germans to achieve annihilation. Hannah Arendt's famous work of 1963, *Eichmann in Jerusalem*, pushed this point further. She called "the role of the Jewish leaders in the destruction of their own people . . . the darkest chapter of the whole dark story." In

her opinion, "without Jewish help in administration and police work
. . . there would have been either complete chaos or an impossibly
severe drain on German manpower."

The charge by both Hilberg and Arendt has two parts. The first is
that Jews did not resist because the only meaningful resistance would
have been armed action, in which relatively few Jews engaged. The
second is that Jews actually made things worse by trying to survive
in ways other than fighting. The Israeli historian Yehuda Bauer has
rejected both arguments emphatically. He defines Jewish resistance
as any undertaking designed to frustrate the Germans' purpose of
harming or killing the Jewish people. He invokes the Hebrew word
amidah to describe the many forms this unarmed resistance could
take, from smuggling food to organizing schools and cultural events,
and he insists that all of these actions were the best Jews could do
with a hopeless situation, a testament to their dignity and will to live
against enormous odds. Bauer is determined to avoid blaming the
victims for their fates, and if that means he sometimes stretches the
definition of resistance to include ordinary acts of self-preservation,
his position is nonetheless preferable to Hilberg's and Arendt's. Their
harsh accusations have not stood up to historical analysis over the
past forty years. Above all, they underestimate the forms of resistance that Jews participated in, and they overestimate the possibilities of armed resistance or even noncooperation that were available to
Jews, either upon initial contact with the Nazis or later.

With regard to the underestimation, Hilberg is probably right
that the Germans lost no more than a few hundred men, dead and
wounded, in the course of the destruction process, and that one cannot identify many incidents in which Jewish resistance appreciably
slowed or impeded the killing machinery. Still, up to 25,000 Jewish fighters operated in Lithuania, Belarus, and the occupied Soviet
Union, and several thousand more in the mountains of Greece and
Yugoslavia. Diverse estimates describe the share of Jews among
French resistance fighters as declining from 40 percent early in the

occupation to 15–20 percent later, partly as a result of attrition, partly because more non-Jews began to take up arms. At either figure, the overrepresentation of Jews in comparison to their proportion of the French population (less than 1 percent) is striking. Jews in Charles de Gaulle's Free French Forces were six times more numerous than predicted by that figure. These are not huge numbers, but they are not nothing, either. Even so, Benjamin Ginsberg, the author of *How the Jews Defeated Hitler: Exploding the Myth of Jewish Passivity in the Face of Nazism*, apparently knows that such statistics are not enough to make his case. He includes Jews in the American, British, and Soviet armies and intelligence services among his Jewish resisters, which is rather like moving the goalposts, since these people were not subject to anything like the same constraints, were not generally acting as Jews but rather as parts of national war efforts, and were not necessarily volunteers.

To understand the degree of overestimation, one has to begin by looking at how the Germans proceeded against the Jews in occupied Eastern Europe, where the bulk of the killing occurred. In the first place, the Nazis applied in remarkably short order all the lessons they had learned from the persecution of the German and Austrian Jews in prior years. Even before the conquest of Poland was complete, on September 21, 1939, Chief of the German Security Police Reinhard Heydrich directed his subordinate offices in occupied Poland to enforce "the concentration of the Jews from the countryside into the larger cities. . . . which either are railroad junctions or at least lie on railroad lines." So far as possible, responsibility for the implementation of not only this policy but also all subsequent German orders regarding the new areas of residence was to be imposed upon Jewish Councils of Elders (*Judenräte der Ältesten*), modeled on the body that the Nazis had created in Vienna in 1938 and composed of community leaders. Six days later, as we have seen, Heinrich Himmler, acting as head of the SS and of the German police, created the Reich Security Main Office under Heydrich and entrusted him with overall responsibility for the Jewish question. Within this organization, Adolf Eichmann, who recently had supervised the fleecing and expatriation of thousands of Austrian Jews, assumed control of the "Jews Department" that was to handle the logistics of the incipient ghettoization.

In short, less than one month after invading Poland and adding approximately two million Jews to its realm, the Nazi regime had devised a system of segregating these people from the surrounding population, positioning them for swift roundup later, stripping them of all their immovable and most of their movable property in the process, and turning the leaders of their communities into the executors of German policy.

This last feature of German policy, the assignment of responsibility for carrying out German instructions to Jewish Councils, was a diabolically effective means of minimizing the resources Germany would have to use to police the Jews and making them complicit in their own persecution. In effect, the Nazis applied the tried-and-true colonial practice of indirect rule through favored natives who got privileges or exemptions from punishments in exchange for helping to control everyone else. This tactic of dividing and conquering turned out to be almost impossible to resist, because it was coupled with force. When the first Jewish Councils were appointed in towns and villages, often before ghettoization had begun, those who declined to carry out distasteful or cruel German orders were simply shot on the spot; sometimes the first round of council members was shot for no reason other than to intimidate the members of the second round. In Lodz, for instance, twenty-two of the first thirty council members were killed to set an example. Serving on the councils and executing German orders were the first iterations of the "choiceless choices" (Lawrence Langer) with which the German occupation repeatedly confronted Jews. The appointees could refuse and die now or consent and perhaps die later or not at all. Almost everywhere, the designated members of the councils, like the inhabitants of the ghettos as a whole, chose the latter and played for time.

Although the Germans conceived of the ghettoization program rapidly, they translated it into practice in Poland unevenly and halt-ingly. Events moved fastest in the regions annexed to the Reich, namely eastern Upper Silesia, West Prussia, and the Warthegau. The last-named included the city of Lodz, which became, on May 1, 1940, the site of the first large-scale ghetto to be sealed off from the outer world. Initially with 163,177 residents crammed into 2.4 square miles of a slum district that mostly lacked indoor plumbing and sewers, the Lodz ghetto became, under Hans Biebow, its German administra-tor, and Chaim Rumkowski, its Eldest of the Jews, the most self-sustaining and the longest-lasting of the Jewish population centers, even though it was now officially within Germany. In contrast, War-saw's ghetto in the General Government was not closed off until November 1940, and its staggering congestion—by March 1941, more than 460,000 Jews were confined to less than one square mile—made it less manageable and more lethal. Further to the east, in Lublin, the gates did not shut on some 40,000 Jews until April 1941, and the permeability of the ghetto boundaries remained much greater. This was also the case at many of the smaller sites and even at Czestochowa, the second largest ghetto in the General Government. In fact, in the many villages of the largely rural Lublin district of the GG, a majority of the Jews were still in their own homes in 1942.

The variability of ghettoization had a number of causes. The cha-otic and contradictory nature of German population policy in Poland slowed implementation, as did shortages of personnel and transpor-tation. German administrators squabbled about whether and how ghetto inmates were to be kept alive and thus about how much trade they could do with their environs and with the occupying regime. Among the SS men put in charge of the ghettos, the group scholars call "attritionists" thought that the inhabitants should just be allowed to die off, whereas the so-called productionists encouraged economic activities by which the ghettos could earn their keep. Above all, no German planner seemed to know how long the ghettos were to last and where the denizens someday were to be sent. Nazi leaders spoke consistently of eventually consigning the Jews to a "reservation" but kept changing its location. With each change of venue came a deferral of deportation and thus, among the German occupiers, a declining sense of urgency about completing the ghetto system—but also declining patience with its existence.

Among the Jewish inhabitants, the result was the opposite: The longer the ghettos lasted, the more the illusion of their permanence developed, and people settled into the hope that they could create sustaining institutions that could preserve at least some share of the population. By early January 1942, before the liquidations began, the populations of the Lodz and Warsaw ghettos were about the same size as when their gates closed in May and November of 1940, respectively. As figure 5 indicates regarding Lodz, new arrivals had offset thousands of deaths from starvation and cold, especially from the three predominant diseases in the ghettos: tuberculosis stoked by hunger and dank conditions; typhoid caused by contaminated food or water; and typhus or spotted fever, spread by the ubiquitous lice. Although conditions were wretched, the possibility of sustenance seemed real, at least for those who had money, jobs, or positions in the ghetto administration. Such prospects became weapons in the hands of the Germans, however. Subjected to ever-mounting scarcity, Jews were pitted against each other in the struggle for food, clothing, shelter, and sheer survival, and their ability to sustain one another both materially and morally eroded steadily. On May 30, 1942, Dawid Sierakowiak, an eighteen-year-old boy trapped in the Lodz ghetto, recorded one of the more extreme consequences in his diary, as he told of how his own father seized and ate both Dawid's and his mother's bread rations, and then devoured all of the family's small allotment of meat and whey. If even family ties snapped, imagine what happened to solidarity among unrelated people.

FIGURE 5: THE FATE OF A GHETTO: LODZ, 1940–44

DATE	POPULATION	DEVELOPMENTS
May 1, 1940	163,177	Ghetto sealed; in an area of only 2.4 square miles, the Jewish population exceeded that of either Bohemia-Moravia or the Netherlands when World War II began.
March 31, 1941	150,436	
May 1, 1941	148,547	On October 9, the daily mortality rate dropped to its lowest point to date: 11. From 16 October to 3 November, 21 transports arrived, bringing 19,883 Jews from Germany, Austria, and Bohemia.
January 1, 1942	162,681	"Resettlement" began on 16 January; 55,000 people deported by the end of May.
June 1, 1942	104,469	More than 15,000 people sent to Chelmno in the second large round up, September 1942.
January 19, 1943	87,164	
July 1, 1943	84,495	
February 8, 1944	79,777	
July 1, 1944	73,217	Liquidation of the ghetto began on 23 June.
January 19, 1945	877	

Approximately 45,000–50,000 of the people who entered the ghetto died of starvation, disease, brutality, or some combination of those causes in a period of forty months. At least 140,000 were massacred, mostly at Chelmno but in the final stage also at Auschwitz, during the nine months when deportations took place (January to May and September 1942, and June to August, 1944).

Internal disunity among Jews aggravated the situation. They were even more divided in the ghettos than were the Jews in Germany during the 1930s, though along somewhat different lines. The major cleavages ran between (1) the secular, socialist, nonseparatist, primarily urban populations associated with the Bund (Alliance) Party; (2) the Zionist groups, which splintered among religious, secular, general, revisionist, and Marxist factions; (3) the traditionalist Orthodox groups; (4) the ecstatic Hasidim; and (5) a smattering of communists. All of these strains of opinion had their own institutions, networks, and longstanding difficulties in communicating with each other, and their differences did not disappear in the crucible of Nazi persecution. Indeed, as ghetto communities tried to decide on the proper response to the German onslaught, groups took divergent positions. Unlike Zionists, Bund members generally rejected service in the ghetto administrations, but also discouraged attempts at overt or armed resistance, unless these occurred in partnership with gentile groups outside the ghettos. Generational differences overlaid the political and religious ones, with the various forms of Zionism, especially the more militant ones, gathering a growing following among younger ghetto inhabitants.

Finally, class and regional conflicts arose: Working-class Jews tended to resent the dominance of middle-class and elite professionals in certain councils; people who had been sent to ghettos from elsewhere sometimes felt disadvantaged by the original residents, especially in obtaining favorable work assignments. Professionals felt a loss of status unless they could obtain positions in the ghetto administrations, while a frequently ostentatious clique of nouveau riche smugglers and traders sprang up and aroused envy. Even before the deportations began, gradations in wealth and status frequently made the difference between survival and starvation. According to Mordechai Lensky, a physician who survived the Warsaw ghetto by escaping in the nick of time with his family to the "Aryan side" of the city, "When deportations started in July 1942 . . . the community's social structure disintegrated [and] the upper economic and social classes sacrificed the lower classes to save themselves."

Internal competition to survive was perhaps the strongest impediment to organized resistance within the ghettos, but it was not the only one. Just as the Germans staggered or spaced out the formation of ghettos and thus prevented Polish Jews from grasping exactly what was happening to them in 1940, so were the liquidations of the ghettos done in such a fashion during 1942–43 that word of them spread slowly, and Jews could not immediately recognize that wholesale massacre was unfolding. Deportations from Lodz and Lublin, at opposite corners of German-dominated Poland, began in early 1942, but Warsaw's turn did not come until the summer of that year, and Bialystok's not until February 1943. There followed the liquidation of Cracow's ghetto in March, Lviv's in June, Minsk's and Vilna's in September, Riga's in November 1943, and finally the ghettos of Kovno and Lodz in the summer of 1944. Even when inhabitants of one place got wind of murderous events in another, people could cling to the hope that their fate would be different and continue to play for time. The same delusion operated even within ghettos once the liquidations began, because they were carried out in phases, as figure 5 (above) shows in the case of Lodz.

The urge to grasp at straws of hope was powerful within the ghettos because mass murder seemed not just unimaginable but downright irrational. Why would the Germans kill people who could be useful, especially in those ghettos that set up productive workshops and factories? This conviction that the Germans would not act against their own interests has much to do with the remarkable refusal of ghetto residents in both Lodz and Bialystok to believe that deportees were being killed, even after the trains that took them away returned to the ghettos with the clothing and personal identification cards of inhabitants who had left only recently. Calel Perechodnik, who served for a time as a Jewish ghetto policeman and later briefly as a resistance fighter, left behind at his death in

1944 a remarkable testament that includes this vivid passage conveying the extent of Jews' denial in his little town in central Poland at the beginning of 1942:

> They say . . . that in Slonim they gathered in the town square fourteen thousand people—women, children, men—and all were machine-gunned.
>
> I ask you . . . is it possible to believe such a thing? To shoot without reason women, innocent children just like that in full daylight? After all, even the worst female criminal cannot be sentenced to death if she is pregnant—and here they apparently killed small children. Where can you find people, fathers of families, who would have the courage to aim their machine guns at helpless, small children? Where is the opinion of the cultured world? . , . How can the world remain silent? It is probably not true.
>
> Following this news comes another one, even more monstrous: In Wilno [Vilna], they killed sixty thousand people; in Baranowicze, twenty thousand. People stop understanding this; in truth, they believe it, but they can't visualize that one day someone can come to murder my two-year-old daughter, who scarcely can talk yet, only because she was born to a Jewish mother and Jewish father.
>
> Finally, we hit on an explanation. Those Jews were killed because they were Soviet citizens and probably because they fought against the Germans. But we are citizens of the *General Gouvernement*; such a thing cannot happen here. Moreover, there is martial law there, whereas here we have a civil administration.

In the space of these four paragraphs, disbelief turns into discounting, as people desperately sought and found ways to immunize themselves to the rumors that flew.

What else stood in the way of organized resistance to the deportations, once they began? First, the Nazis went to great lengths to camouflage what they were doing. Sometimes they exempted the ill and hospitalized ghetto residents from deportations in order to imply that the people being shipped out really were going to work camps further east; sometimes they made a great show of exchanging local or ghetto currency for other forms of money before people got on the trains; and sometimes the Germans even sent postcards back to the points of departure, supposedly from recent deportees, to reassure those left behind about the destinations. This was a particularly common practice with regard to deportees from Western Europe; most of the cards were postmarked from Leipzig in Germany, but some even came from Auschwitz and Birkenau.

Second, the Nazis mixed the carrot and the stick, bait and threats, to assure compliance with deportation orders. Soup, bread, and jam were offered at assembly points and prospective deportees were told they could have certain privileges with regard to baggage and rations if they showed up when ordered to, but that these would be taken away if they failed to appear. Conversely, Adam Czerniakow, the Jewish Council head in Warsaw, was told that his wife would be shot if he impeded deportations in any way; Joseph Parnes, a Jewish leader in Lviv, was killed when he declined to designate people for deportation to a labor camp. In Amsterdam, the Nazis told the Jewish Council that failure to cooperate in the deportations "for labor in the East" would result in shipment to concentrations camps such as Mauthausen instead, which initially sounded much worse.

Third, the delegation of the dirty work to the Jewish Councils gave them an illusion of some control over what was happening and saddled them with responsibility to minimize the damage. In most ghettos, just as was the practice in Amsterdam and the Westerbork transit camp, the Nazis simply told the Jewish Council how many people to assemble for deportation on a given day and left the choice of the people, until the very end of most liquidations, to the council. In Warsaw, the SS demanded delivery of the first 6,000 people on July 22, 1942, and the same number by 4:00 every subsequent afternoon until further notice. We know in what sort of position this put the Jewish authorities in the Lodz ghetto because of a remarkable record of a visit by a German named Friedrich Hielscher in the spring of 1942. He talked with the head of the Jewish police, Leon Rosenblatt, who admitted to knowing that the deportees were being sent to be gassed and then spoke as follows:

> I have to choose people for this. If not, I will be shot. That for me would be a simple solution. What will they do then? The SS already told me. Then *they* will choose. That is, the strong ones, the pregnant women, the Rabbis, the learned ones, the professors, the poets—they will be the first for the oven. But if I stay where I am, I can take the volunteers. Often they demand to be taken, and sometimes I have as many as I have to deliver, and sometimes they are few, and then I take the dying that Jewish doctors tell me about, and if these do not suffice, I take the seriously ill. If these, too, are not enough, what shall I do? I can take the criminals. . . . Who will be the judge? I asked the heads of the community, the Rabbis, the learned people; all of them said: You did the right thing by staying at your post. . . . Tell me—should I remain at my post, or should I prefer to be killed?

The same logic of "better us than them" propelled the conduct of Abraham Asscher and David Cohen, the co-chairs of the Jewish Council in Amsterdam, when confronted in May 1943 with a German request for a list of 7,000 council employees (about 40 percent of the total) who were to be deported next. Ignoring the pleas of colleagues to destroy their central card registry of all remaining Jews rather than comply, the council leaders and some staff members worked frantically for two straight days and nights to designate and provide the names.

Rosenblatt, Asscher, and Cohen may have thought that they were adhering to Jewish religious law, but they were not. According to David Daube's careful examination of pertinent passages of the Talmud, handing over a person specifically demanded by name by an oppressive power is permissible as compliance with a threatening order, but handing over "simply any odd person for execution" is not because that involves choosing the victim and thus amounts to taking on personal guilt.

The most extreme example of the excruciating position in which German procedures put the councils occurred on September 4, 1942, when Chaim Rumkowski addressed the assembled ghetto population in Lodz:

> A severe blow has befallen the ghetto. They are asking from it the best it possesses—the children and old people. . . . I never imagined that my own hands would have to deliver the sacrifice to the altar. In my old age, I must stretch out my hands and beg: Brothers and sisters, give them to me! Fathers and mothers, give me your children! . . . Yesterday during the day, I was given a command to send twenty-odd thousand Jews out from the ghetto; if not—"We will do it." And the question arose: "Should we take it over and do it ourselves, or leave it for others to carry out?" But being dominated not by the thought "How many will be lost," but by the thought "How many can be saved," we, i.e., I and my closest co-workers, came to the conclusion that as difficult as this will be for us, we must take into our own hands the carrying out of the decree. I have to carry out this difficult and bloody operation. I must cut off limbs in order to save the body! I must take the children because, if not, others could also, God forbid, be taken. . . . One needs

> the heart of a bandit in order to ask for what I am asking
> of you. But put yourself in my position and think logically,
> and you yourself will come to the conclusion that you can-
> not act differently because the number of the portion that
> can be saved is much larger than the part that must be
> surrendered.

This passage illustrates how perfectly and diabolically the system of divide and conquer worked, and so do the lists of people excepted from the initial deportation orders and from all others prior to the very end. Most of these were people performing valuable labor functions for the Germans, but two other groups were conspicuous among those exempted: people who worked for the Jewish Councils in the administration of the ghettos, of whom there were almost 13,000 in Lodz and 6,000 in Warsaw, and members of the Jewish Order Service, the police force in the ghettos, who totaled 800 men in Lodz and 2,000 in Warsaw. Some of the police were recruits from the prewar Jewish communities of these cities, but most had arrived from elsewhere and thus had few local ties to inhibit them. Joseph Szerynski, the head of the Jewish police in Warsaw, had converted to Catholicism, did not consider himself a Jew, and had no bonds with the local community. He and his men were so hated that the underground in the ghetto wounded him badly in an attempted assassination and succeeded in killing his successor. Paid little or nothing, ghetto policemen became increasingly corrupt and extortionist, demanding bribes to keep people off the lists for forced labor or deportation or routinely seizing attractive possessions. When the final stages of a liquidation arrived, and the Germans began instructing the councils not to select the deportees by name but rather to round them up from particular portions of a ghetto that were being cleared, these police did the footwork in most cases. They did so on the calculation that they and their families would remain alive as long as they were useful, and the Germans sometimes deceptively promised that they would survive even longer. The same motives account for the cooperation of the Jewish *Ordedienst* from the Westerbork camp in rounding up Jews in Apeldoorn and Amsterdam in 1943 and in loading and sealing the deportation trains from Holland in 1942–44. And the *Ordedienst* men shared the distancing social profile of their counterparts in the Polish ghettos: About half of them, including their commander, were not Dutch Jews but German or Austrian Jewish refugees in the Netherlands.

A fourth impediment to resistance was the weakened condition of the ghetto inhabitants, which is something that cinematic depictions of the Holocaust generally cannot convey. Usually, as in Lodz and Kovno, the Germans sited the ghettos in the most miserable parts of a city, without sewers or much running water. Daily food intake for most ghetto inhabitants, aside from the privileged ones who worked in the administration or war production, hovered between 400 to 1,000 calories per day; in the largest ghettos, it usually averaged far less; in Warsaw in 1941, the daily allocation per person was between 180 and 220 calories. In Perechodnik's ghetto at Otwock, most of the 14,000 Jews barely subsisted in early 1941 on a weekly ration of 1.5 pounds of bread per person; there was no allotment of meat, eggs, or vegetables. Hunger, rampant disease, cold, filth, overcrowding, and enervation all took terrible tolls and undermined any desire to fight back. By July 1941, 5,550 people were dying in the Warsaw ghetto per month, almost 200 per day. One hundred thousand Jews died in the ghetto between its inception and the onset of the great deportations in mid-1942. The Germans designed the ghettos to confirm the picture of Jewish degradation, dirtiness, and disease that Nazi ideology posited; they were in this sense the fulfillment of an ideological prophecy, and cramming people together was part of the plan. In Warsaw, for instance, the ghetto inhabitants outnumbered the available rooms 7 to 1, and the population density worked out to 200,000 people per square kilometer in April 1941; in Kovno, 30,000 people lived where 7,000 had previously, in Vilna, 29,000 where 4,000 had. Under such conditions, people often lost the ability to think ahead, and those ghetto inhabitants who still could do so generally calculated that endurance was preferable to resistance or flight because of concern about family members and dependents who would be put at risk. Fleeing from the ghettos was also not an appealing prospect for most people because the topography of Poland was not conducive to hiding, and neither were the prevailing attitudes among the surrounding non-Jewish population.

Fifth and finally, the viciousness of the reprisals the Germans took was a powerful deterrent to resistance. These occurred not only in the form of individual beatings and shootings but also at the collective level. After all, putting aside the heroism of the people who launched the Warsaw Ghetto Uprising, the military balance sheet of trying to fight the Germans was catastrophic. In the course of suppressing the uprising, the Germans and their auxiliaries suffered somewhere between 110 casualties (seventeen dead and ninety-three wounded, according to the official figures) and three times that many (according to the resisters). Either way, the figure is tiny compared to the 56,065 people the Germans captured or killed. A few weeks later, the poorly prepared, more spontaneous resistance against the German drive to empty the Bialystok ghetto resulted in exactly nine German soldiers wounded, compared to the deaths of about 30,000 Jews either in the fighting or as a result of deportation to Auschwitz and Majdanek. Also in August 1943, the attempted breakout at Treblinka enabled only fifty to seventy inmates to survive the war. The camp uprising at Sobibor that October led to the deaths of only eleven or twelve SS men and two *Hiwis* and the survival of only forty-seven inmates out of the 650 or so present when the fighting began. Moreover, the price of these events was Operation Harvest Festival in the fall of 1943, when Himmler ordered the liquidation of nearly all the remaining Polish work camps and ghettos in reprisal for these acts of Jewish resistance and as a sure method of preventing more of them. The shooting on November

3–4, 1943, of 42,000 Jews in the Lublin district, most of them at Majdanek and nearby Poniatowa, constitutes the largest single massacre of the Holocaust. At Poniatowa, one men's barracks tried to resist; the Germans locked the doors from outside and set it on fire, incinerating everyone inside. The only known survivors of those two days of killing were three women who had been left for dead in a mass grave. Only lightly wounded, they crawled away under cover of darkness, received succor from a Polish woman, and lived to see the end of the war.

Given all these circumstances, about the only effective form of resistance the Jews in ghettos could exercise in the short run was to defeat the Nazi effort to starve them to death. The principal way of doing this was through smuggling, and both the Warsaw ghetto administration and individual informal networks developed that into a fine art, which undoubtedly prolonged the lives of many people. Smuggling could not stop deportations once they began, though it sometimes became a means of helping individuals escape the trains. Otherwise, the only other form of resistance that offered a prospect of success was itself an expression of hopelessness. This was the attempt in almost all ghettos to leave a record of the Nazi crimes and a proof that the Jews had existed and struggled to survive. Both at Warsaw and Lodz, networks of people collected and hid extensive archival records and compiled a chronicle of the major events in the ghetto's history. Emanuel Ringelblum, a historian, and an organization called Oyneg Shabes, independent of the ghetto administration, did this work in Warsaw and buried the resulting documents under basements in the ghetto, where most of them were recovered after the war. At Lodz, the chronicle was the work of historians in an official ghetto archive that the Jewish Council established, and about two-thirds of these records were unearthed under various ghetto buildings after 1945. Along with a number of surviving individual diaries, these are our primary sources of information on the internal conditions of the ghettos during the Holocaust.

Perhaps the most conclusive demonstration of Jews' limited ability to affect their own fates, whether they chose to resist or not, is that several Jewish ghetto administrations adopted different survival strategies, different mixes of compliance and resistance, but regardless of what they chose, they ultimately came to the same end. In Warsaw, Adam Czerniakow, the head of the Jewish Council, followed a strategy of placating the Germans until he realized that they intended to kill all the ghetto inhabitants, so he committed suicide in July 1942 rather than cooperate further. His act did nothing to head off the massacres of most of Warsaw's Jews that summer and of the last remnant in May and June of 1943. In Vilna, Jacob Gens, the head of the Jewish Council, tried to walk both sides of the street, providing the Germans labor and cooperation but also aiding the resistance in and around the city. The Nazis nevertheless liquidated the Vilna ghetto without interference from that resistance in September 1943. In Minsk, the two ghetto leaders Eliyahu Mushkin and Moshe Yaffe did not defy the Germans, but they were among the Jewish Council leaders who were most supportive of armed resistance, perhaps because some 10,000 Jews were actively fighting back in the nearby forests of Belarus. Still, that availed them little as the ghetto's population dropped from 100,000, in October 1941, to 12,000, in August 1942. By then both men were dead, too, and what was left of the ghetto was liquidated in October 1943. Finally, Chaim Rumkowski, the Jewish Council leader in Lodz, was the most persistent proponent of satisfying the Germans' every whim as the only way to survive. The strategy probably helped his ghetto endure longer than any other one, but it did not prevent the liquidation of its last 70,000 inhabitants in August 1944. In short, whatever the Jewish leaders did—kill themselves, aid the resistance, appease the Nazis—the outcome was the same. Historian David Silberklang's judgment, on the basis of studying hundreds of ghettos in the Lublin district of the General Government, holds throughout Eastern Europe and probably throughout the continent as a whole:

"No Jewish action caused any significant difference for large groups of people in terms of survival, though certain actions could make a difference for individuals."

The Jews had almost no control over their collective fate. Individuals could flee to the forests in some cases and try to survive, but whole communities could not. Neither could they devise a strategy that could accomplish anything more than to delay their deaths. It is unfair and inaccurate to hold the Jewish victims responsible for what happened to them. Whether they lived or died depended on two things alone: the actions of the Nazi regime and the progress of the Allied armies.

Two incidents—one of resistance and one of compliance—demonstrate this emphatically. The first, already discussed, is the Warsaw Ghetto Uprising of 1943, which failed utterly because it could not withstand the armed might the Nazis could bring to bear. The second illustration of the dependence of the Jews on the progress of the Allies is the fate of the Lodz ghetto. When its liquidation began, Soviet forces stood only seventy-five miles away to the east, where they had stopped their offensive at Warsaw in order to regroup and resupply their forces and to allow the Nazis to crush a rising that Polish nationalists launched in the city as the Red Army approached. Stalin planned to install a communist government in Poland after the war, and he thought that the suppression of this rising by the Germans would make that goal easier to achieve. Had he not made this cynical calculation and instead quickly resumed his military advance, the Germans probably would not have had time to liquidate the remaining Jewish population in Lodz, and Rumkowski's gamble of exchanging Jewish compliance with Nazi wishes for long-term survival might have paid off. Of course, the Nazis might have marched the survivors west, and many would have died in the process, which is what happened in July 1944 to the inhabitants of Kovno, the only other remaining ghetto of significant size. But the number of people to emerge from the Lodz ghetto alive at the end of the war probably would have been larger than turned out to be the case. Throughout the Holocaust, the Jews were at the mercy of the decisions of others.

Leo Baeck, the rabbi and leader of the German Jews who ultimately survived the war in Theresienstadt, knew this, and his knowledge informed his most controversial decision. Even after he learned that most Jews were being gassed or shot, he refused to admit what he knew to the people around him and persisted in concealing their likely fates. Why? Because he believed that "living in the expectation of death . . . would . . . be . . . harder" than living with an illusion. His position may have been highly humane, but it was also debilitating. As the late dates of the ghetto and camp uprisings show, hope of surviving was the enemy of fighting back. So long as hope remained, people generally chose not to charge the German guns and urged their fellow Jews not to do so lest that provoke reprisals. Everywhere, Jews took arms only when they knew the alternative already was certain death.

In May and June of 1944, Hungary's Jewish leaders, principally Samu Stern, the head of the national Jewish Council that had come into existence when Germans occupied the country that March, similarly learned of what was happening at Auschwitz and chose to keep the information to themselves as the deportations from the Hungarian countryside began. Stern believed he was "running a race against time," in which his job was to keep at least some Jews alive until the progress of Germany's enemies cut off the transports. For Jews to survive that long, he insisted they had to obey the authorities, and to make sure that Jews did, he withheld from them his knowledge of the fate that awaited those who boarded the trains. The result was the almost complete and almost completely unresisted annihilation of Hungarian Jewry, as the Nazis deported faster than the Russians advanced.

In assessing Jewish resistance to the Holocaust, some comparisons are instructive. Did any other persecuted group act more forcefully as the Holocaust proceeded? Consider the behavior of the 5.7 million captured Soviet prisoners of war, 3.3 million of whom died in German captivity, a mortality rate of 58 percent. Confined to prison camps or labor brigades, the survivors staged no important uprising until the very end of the war, even though they, unlike the Jews in the ghettos and occupied states, consisted almost entirely of young men with military training. Or consider the behavior of the occupied European peoples, among whom resistance movements generally became significant only after Stalingrad, by which time most of the European Jews already were dead. Even in 1943–44, according to the most authoritative estimate, only 2 percent of the French population consisted of active resisters. Finally, in assessing the conduct of the Jewish Councils, bear in mind that the Dutch civil servants who remained at the head of ministries in the Netherlands protested the deportations and threatened to resign if they continued but never could summon up the courage actually to do so. Instead, Dutch police, along with Dutch transport and railway workers, frequently helped the Germans carry out their plans.

Where resistance movements flourished, they generally had four advantages: favorable topography in mountainous and/or heavily forested places like Yugoslavia and central France; sympathetic local populations; trained military veterans of the sort that the Germans usually killed upon arrival in the East; and equipment supplied by the Allies. The Jews of the ghettos, especially those in Poland and Ukraine, lacked all of these things.

In sum, why didn't more of them fight back more often? Because the odds were stacked against them, because they could not see or could not bear to see what was going to happen to them, because the slimmest chance that some might survive tempted them to avoid committing suicide by fighting back, and because they clung to life as best they could in ever more adverse circumstances. We have no right to expect or demand that they should have behaved more forcefully or heroically. They were, in the end, subjected to excruciating torture and confronted with "choiceless choices" in which all alternative courses of action seemed to present more danger than relief.

Let me drive home this point about our obligation to withhold judgment with reference to a pair of iconic photographs that are reproduced in figure 6, the first of the little boy wearing a cloth cap and holding his hands up after being captured in the Warsaw ghetto, and the second of a group of Warsaw ghetto inhabitants being marched away by the Germans, with a young girl in the front row on the right. German photographers took both pictures, and they surfaced after the war in a few extant copies of an album made to commemorate the suppression of the uprising and later published under the title *The Stroop Report*, using the last name of the German commander of that operation. Often overlooked because of the poignancy of these pictures is the most remarkable feature about them: that each shows the presence of a child under the age of ten as the ghetto was being liquidated. In fact, the first picture shows three or four more young children in the background. Yet the population of the ghetto had fallen from almost 460,000 at its peak in March 1941 to about 53,000 just before the Ghetto Uprising broke out in the spring of 1943; the corresponding figures for young children are from approximately 51,000 to fewer than 500, 255 boys and 243 girls. Moreover, the uprising occurred seven months after Rumkowski told the Jews of Lodz that they had to give up their children under the age of ten. The only children spared in Lodz were those of the Jewish policemen and firemen who helped round up all the others and those of the Jewish ghetto administrators. Almost certainly, the same was true in Warsaw, and the children you see in those two photographs are the offspring of people in or well connected to the Jewish Warsaw ghetto administration, people with enough clout there to shield their children from deportation, people who at the same time had benefited from the German exemptions and perhaps had helped organize the deportation of others, people who probably had argued against resistance so long as their positions gave them a

FIGURE 6: Two Photos from *The Stroop Report*

Credit: United States Holocaust Memorial Museum

chance of survival. We actually know who the girl was, unlike the boy in the first photo. Her last name was Neyer, and she is walking beside (from left to right) her mother, Yehudit, her paternal grand-mother, and her father, Avraham, who was a member of the Bund Party and the only person in this family who survived the war. Now that you have the backstory of these children and what their parents may or may not have done, do you feel any less sympathy for any of them than you did when you first saw their images? I hope not.

Immediately after the Holocaust, its survivors had trouble understanding this point, not least because their pain was so fresh and their desire to imagine different outcomes so intense. Ad hoc Jewish Courts of Honor sprang up to unmask and punish alleged Jewish "collaborators," especially former so-called *Kapos* (who led work details) and members of Jewish councils or police forces. One such body in Italy convicted two former Jewish Council members in Lviv and Bedzin and banned them from "any position in the public life of the Jews"; a similar court in the American occupation zone of Germany handed down an identical judgment and penalty for a former Jewish Council member in Upper Silesia. In Amster-dam, another such court reached the same decision and imposed the same punishment in 1947 on the former co-chairs of the Jew-ish Council there, Abraham Asscher, who had survived Bergen-Belsen, and David Cohen, who outlived Theresienstadt. But a vote of the Permanent Committee of the Netherlands Israelite Church Organization vacated that decision three years later. Asscher died shortly thereafter, completely alienated from the Jewish community. Cohen continued defending his conduct until his demise in 1967, never abandoning the implausible claim that he first learned of the death camps after he got to Theresienstadt and thus did not know until then that the people on the deportation lists he compiled were almost certain to die.

The case of Rezso or Rudolf Kastner in postwar Israel was even more divisive, and its outcome more violent. A Zionist official in wartime Budapest who had helped Jews from elsewhere find refuge in Hungary, he knew by May 1944 that the Jews about to be deported from that country were likely to die, but he undertook no effort to warn them and instead began negotiating with Eichmann to let a limited number of them escape in return for cash payments. He thus managed to save 1,625 people, including several hundred from his hometown, his mother, wife, and siblings, and many dedicated Zionists. Because he was a parliamentary candidate of the governing Labor Party in Israel and the press spokesman for a government ministry, his conduct became an issue in Israeli partisan and identity politics. In 1952, an elderly journalist named Malchiel Gruenwald published a pamphlet attacking Kastner as a collaborator with the Nazis who had saved some of his family and friends in return for allowing the Hungarian Jews to cling to a false sense of security as they boarded the trains going northward. The Israeli attorney general insisted on suing Gruenwald for libel on Kastner's behalf, only to have the presiding judge conclude that Kastner had "sold his soul to the devil . . . by deliberately avoiding his duty . . . to reveal to the Jews the fate awaiting them." The Israeli Supreme Court overruled that verdict by a vote of 4–1 in January 1958, on the grounds that Kastner's "thoughts were directed to good and not to evil, to rescue and not to extermination." But the vindication was no help to Kastner, who had been assassinated ten months earlier.

The few surviving Jewish ghetto or council leaders who fell into the hands of the Soviet Union also faced summary justice. Moshe Kopelman, the Kovno ghetto Jewish police chief from 1941 to 1943, managed to escape as the ghetto was liquidated in July 1944. Captured two months later by the Red Army, he was tried for collaboration and sentenced to fifteen years of hard labor despite a plea for clemency from more than seventy other Kovno survivors. Almost exactly a year later, he died in a Siberian camp. The Soviets condemned Walter Lustig, the last leader of the remnant Reichsvereinigung in Berlin, as a collaborator and executed him in December 1945.

Although such sentences came readily to Soviet judges, David Ben-Gurion, the first prime minister of Israel, struck a wiser note in two letters he wrote, one right after the final court verdict on Kastner, one almost five years later. He said, "I would not take it upon myself to judge any Jew who was there. The Jews who lived in safety during the time of Hitler cannot judge their brothers who were burned and slaughtered or those who were saved. . . . The tragedy is deeper than the abyss, and the members of our generation who did not taste that hell would do best (in my modest opinion) to remain sorrowfully and humbly silent." As time passed, most Israelis came to accept Ben-Gurion's point. Although the Knesset, Israel's parliament, had enacted the Nazis and Nazi Collaborators (Punishment) Law in 1950, the last prosecution of a Jew for violating it occurred in 1972.

THE WORLD OF THE CAMPS

One cannot write about the Holocaust or about compliance and resistance without discussing the concentration camp system, but it is a confusing, dismal, and often inaccessible subject. It is probably also the aspect of the Holocaust about which people have the most misleading images in their heads, not least because most films dare not represent a reality that was so repellent, so the great majority are distortions. Probably the greatest offender of this sort is the Oscar winner *Life Is Beautiful*, but even *Schindler's List* misrepresented the Plaszow camp for artistically symbolic reasons (in reality, Commandant Göth's villa was somewhat below, not above, most of the camp site, and he aimed his rifle up, not down, at the prisoners).

A great many types of camps existed, and a few, especially Auschwitz and Majdanek, combined all the different sorts. Indeed, the sheer number of camps is staggering. It used to be said that more than 1,000 of them dotted the German landscape by 1945. But if one includes all the sites identified by the United States Holocaust Memorial

Museum, which is publishing a massive, multivolume encyclopedia of camps and ghettos, the number of camps established at one time or another in Germany and occupied Europe runs to about 40,000. They were, in short, neither rare nor invisible, but in fact constant, frequent presences across the continent and within the Reich. And they were not completely closed off from their surrounding areas but penetrable in many cases, and even sometimes visited and inspected by local dignitaries.

At the core of the system were camps established for political prisoners, people who were regarded as threatening or disloyal to the Nazi regime, at first in Germany (for example, Dachau, Buchenwald, Sachsenhausen, Gross-Rosen, Flossenbürg, and Ravensbrück) and then in the annexed and occupied regions (for example, Mauthausen in Austria, Westerbork in the Netherlands, Natzweiler in Alsace, Theresienstadt in Bohemia, Stutthof in northern Poland). Such installations and their satellites held fewer than 22,000 people when the war began in 1939 but then metastasized during the war until their population peaked at more than 714,000 in January 1945 (of this figure, 28 percent were women). Not including Jews, about 1.65 million people passed through the camp system between 1933 and 1945; about one million died. For Jews, the survival rate was far worse; at most, about 150,000 Jewish veterans of these core camps, probably fewer, emerged alive at the end of the war out of the nearly four million Jews sent there. From the camps dedicated solely to murder, the "death factories," survival rates were infinitesimal: perhaps seven people sent to Chelmno and only two sent to Belzec—all of them men—were still alive when World War II ended.

Within the camps, a highly stratified system of indirect rule developed in which the Nazi officers were a feared but usually distant presence, and they delegated the management of the prisoners to privileged figures among them. These prisoner functionaries often occupy much more vivid—and hated—places in the memories of survivors than the SS personnel. *Kapos* led work details, and a Block

Senior or Elder ruled over each barracks. The SS usually selected these people from among the inmates incarcerated for political or criminal offenses. In fact, a hierarchy of prisoner categories developed in the camps, with each group clearly designated by the color of the triangles sewn onto their uniforms or clothing, next to each prisoner's identification number. Political prisoners wore a red triangle, criminals green, so-called asocials black, homosexuals pink, Jehovah's Witnesses purple, Sinti and Roma brown, and Jews yellow, sometimes by itself, sometimes in combination with a triangle of another color.

In the context of scarce food and grueling work, competition for favors was rife and corruption endemic. The reds, greens, and blacks fought a constant struggle to control the most important trustee assignments—not only as *Kapos* and block elders but also as clerical personnel in central offices, where a prisoner could gather important intelligence, and as workers in the kitchens, where an inmate could obtain extra food. Generally, when the reds were in charge, conditions improved, especially for fellow prisoners of the same political persuasion. Hermann Langbein, a political prisoner at Dachau, Auschwitz, and Neuengamme, has left a vivid account of the jockeying for position and its consequences in *People in Auschwitz*. But no matter who the trustees were, they were almost never Jews, who were at the bottom of the social pyramid, along with gays. Here, as in the ghettos, the lowest instincts of self-preservation were encouraged by the system of constant fear and deprivation, and survival seemed often to require sacrificing others.

This is probably where this book should address the matter of "other victims" of the Holocaust, even though doing so involves a partial digression from the central theme of this chapter. Up until now we have talked exclusively about Jews and the people with disabilities targeted by the T4 campaign as victims of the Holocaust, even though most museums and memorials in the United States also refer to the other groups that had their own camp triangle colors, especially the Jehovah's Witnesses (called by the Germans *Bibelforscher*, Bible researchers), Sinti and Roma people (colloquially referred to as Gypsies), and gays. Although it is true that Nazism attacked these groups, it did not do so for the same reason it attacked Jews or with the same intensity or to the same extent. The Nazis did not consider any of these groups nearly as threatening to German power as Jews supposedly were and thus did not set out to kill every one of them. The Nazis also thought that the offenses of these groups were ones of behavior, not essence, so if they changed the offending behavior, they often were spared, whereas people of Jewish descent had no such option. Thus the Third Reich attacked Jehovah's Witnesses because they were pacifists; if they recanted and agreed to serve in the army, they were welcomed, though few, if any, took advantage of this opportunity.

Most Sinti and Roma were racially impure in German eyes, but not all of them, so some were killed and some allowed to live. The Nazi regime even allowed some German Gypsies to remain in the German army into 1943; ultimately the Reich appears to have deported and killed about two-thirds of them and left one-third of them alone. In most of the occupied countries, the Gypsies rounded up were the itinerate ones; people with stable and continuous residences were not molested. Deportation rates of Sinti and Roma from Western Europe were thus not very high. Further east, inconsistency prevailed, but the proportion of the Gypsy population murdered was much lower than that of the Jewish population. Some 5,000–7,000 out of almost 12,000 Gypsies identified in the German-controlled Protectorate of Bohemia and Moravia by 1943 were put in camps and killed; in occupied and annexed Poland, the death rate appears to have been 8,000 out of 28,000; in occupied Serbia, 20,000 of 150,000; in Hungary, perhaps 30,000 out of 300,000. The most murderous place was the occupied Soviet Union, but even here policy varied by both time and place. Nearly all Gypsies died in the Crimea, but sedentary ones tended to survive further north, and Muslim Gypsies sometimes were treated differently than others, as was the case in Croatia. Two-thirds of Lithuania's Gypsies survived the German occupation, but virtually none of Latvia's or Estonia's did. As an indication of the arbitrary and capricious nature of Nazi policy toward Gypsies, consider the example of the six Roma deported from the border region between the Warthegau and the General Government in 1940 and sent to a labor camp at Belzec. Instead of being put to work and later gassed at the death camp that arose next door the following year, these Gypsies were released with a warning that they would be arrested again if ever found within Germany's borders without official permission. They lived not only to return to Germany after the war but also to petition a state government for restitution of lost property. Overall, then, the Nazis murdered Gypsies, including 20,000 of them sent to Auschwitz, but not systematically. Estimates of the death toll for all of Nazi Europe run from 200,000 to 500,000, but historians are not sure of the total population in 1939. The proportion that perished, however, was certainly well below the two-thirds figure for Europe's Jews, probably between one-fifth and one-quarter.

The treatment of gays was also far less harsh and sweeping as a rule than the treatment of Jews. In the first place, the Nazi regime cared almost exclusively about gay German men and their same-sex partners. The number of people prosecuted in occupied countries was tiny. In the Netherlands from 1940 to 1943, for example, only 138 court cases occurred, and those resulted in 90 convictions. The German legal prohibition on same-sex acts, Paragraph 175 of the Criminal Code, did not extend to women, so relatively few lesbians attracted the regime's notice and hostility. And, outside of Germany, the Nazis reacted positively when a client regime issued new regulations that criminalized gay male sex, as Vichy France did in 1942, but Germany did not pressure governments to do this; it did, of course, pressure them to deport Jews. Even inside Germany, persecution was uneven. The Nazi authorities estimated the number of gay males in Germany in 1933 at two million, or about 6.25 percent of the German male population of almost 32 million at the time. That population increased to almost 38 million by 1939, thanks largely to the annexations of Austria and what had been western Czechoslovakia, and the same percentage of that population works out to almost 2.4 million gay men. But the Third Reich arrested only 100,000 men under Paragraph 175 between 1933 and 1945, convicted only 50,000 of them, and sent only about 10,000 of them to camps, where 6,000 of them perished.

The gay men caught in this system suffered excruciating punishments, but they constituted a tiny portion of the target population. Why? Because the Nazis cared only about their behavior, not their nature. Himmler actually believed until at least 1943, when some documentary evidence suggests that he began to have his doubts, that most gay men were "curable" if given the right incentives. The goal was to eliminate their behavior among Germans through intimidation, punishment, and reeducation and, in so-called incorrigible cases of repeat offenders, castration or death. Put in contemporary phrasing, Himmler believed that most gay men could be "scared straight." Killing them all was simply not necessary. It was even less necessary in the occupied countries, because the chief offense of a German gay man was non-procreation, but in the occupied countries, non-procreation of the native population was desirable. That is why the German authorities briefly toyed with the idea of decriminalizing sex among men in occupied Poland in 1939. A clear sense of what drove Nazi policy toward gay men comes across in the title of the Nazi organization founded in 1936 to conduct their persecution, the Reichszentrale zur Bekämpfung der Homosexualität und Abtreibung, the Central Office for Combating Homosexuality and Abortion. Unlike the Jews, all gay men did not have to die because they were immutable enemies of the German *Volk*. Closeted gay German men could live; foreign gay men who stayed away from German civilians or military personnel were a matter of indifference to the Nazis.

All of this amounts to saying that Nazism targeted many groups, but it did not target them all in the same way. But if Jehovah's Witnesses, Gypsies, and gays did get caught up in the camp machinery, they had much in common with each other and with Jews. These groups were the most exploited, the ones treated consistently worst, and the ones with the fewest ways of bettering their situation.

Another group whose numbers in the camp system increased exponentially as time passed was Slavs, but they did not have a distinguishing color for their triangles, largely because they were usually considered "political" prisoners or "asocial" ones. Their presence has led some observers to lump them with other victims of the Holocaust, most famously in Simon Wiesenthal's formulation that the Holocaust had eleven million victims, six million Jews and five million others, mostly Slavs. But that number is fictional—Soviet civilian casualties alone came to more than ten million people—and not all Slavs were the same in German eyes. Nazi theory doomed some—mostly Poles, Russians, and Serbs—to ultimate extinction, but only over time, as German settlers multiplied and their need for native slaves in the conquered East declined to the vanishing point. Himmler's General Plan East foresaw the reduction of the Polish population by 85 percent, the Belarussian by 75 percent, the Ukrainian by 65 percent, and the Czech by 50 percent. But the Nazis considered other Slavs valuable "racial" allies, notably Bulgarians, Croats, Slovaks, and some Ukrainians. Hitler and Himmler even considered many Czechs and some Poles to be capable of "Germanization" (*Germanisierung*), that is, of being turned into German speakers and racially assimilated.

In short, though the camps contained many different sorts of people, all of whom were subjected to terrible suffering, no other group was attacked as thoroughly and systematically as the Jews. And not even the population of Germany's mental institutions and sanatoria experienced a mortality rate comparable to that of Europe's Jews.

In discussing the camps, one must begin by remembering how people arrived at them: usually parched and starving, after train trips that lasted for days in stifling and overcrowded cars filled with often wailing, sometimes crazed people, many of them dying or already dead. The deportees from Polish ghettos endured all this after debilitating months of clinging to life under only slightly better conditions. Some of these people welcomed deportation as a relief, even when they feared the worst, and more or less embraced the German proverb "better an end with horror than a horror without end." To put the matter bluntly, little fight was left in people who had been subjected to this sort of brutal treatment prior to and during deportation. To expect mass resistance on their part as they debarked at Auschwitz or Belzec or Treblinka is utterly to fail to imagine what they had been through.

To understand the behavior of people admitted to the camps, one needs to remember the fundamental observation by historian Michael Marrus that they were "the most complete totalitarian structure to have been devised by man." Inmates were crushed beneath this structure, worn down by exhaustion, starvation, extreme heat and cold, and disease and wholly cut off from outside help. Any infraction of even the most trivial rules resulted in the application of the Nazi doctrine of collective responsibility—vicious punishment of whole groups of inmates, not just those who had stepped out of line. The punishments included beatings and floggings, endless roll calls in all kinds of weather, group hangings, and two particularly gruesome acts: throwing people alive into the crematoria and in wintertime tying inmates to posts or to suspended ropes and spraying them with water, which turned to ice and froze the victims to death. Not for nothing did one survivor call Auschwitz "a mixture of Hell and an insane asylum."

The inmates, like the inhabitants of the ghettos, were cowed and divided against themselves by the constant fear that any resistance to or even evasion of the Germans' mandates would provoke more suffering than was already prevalent. This has a lot to do with the hesitations that surrounded every underground organization in the camps and with their constant caution and changes of plan. For example, the inhabitants of the "family camp" for Czech Jews at Auschwitz, which lasted for several months, made elaborate preparations for launching an uprising at the moment when word came that gassing was imminent. But when it did come, the planners' will faltered because they feared harm to the children in a pitched battle. In the end, they went to the gas without incident.

All would-be resisters had to contend with the ubiquitous presence of spies, motivated by the prospect of extra bread or sleep or cigarettes or exemption from a selection in return for providing the German guards with information about plots. The prisoners also had to cope with their national and linguistic differences, which made coordination tense and communication difficult. And, as the Czech family camp example suggests, the Nazi guards were relatively few but vastly powerful, so highly intimidating. It is worth recalling that no camp rebellion ever really succeeded. Even at the very end of the war, on February 2, 1945, when 419 albeit much weakened Soviet POWs succeeded in breaking out of Mauthausen, the Nazi regime still hunted nearly all of them down. Only eleven were still alive when the war ended eight weeks later. We already have noted how few people survived the rebellions at Sobibor and Treblinka in 1943 and at Auschwitz in late 1944.

The only successful form of resistance in the camps was escape, although the odds were long. Only five people are known to have escaped Belzec, and the two of them who survived the war did not actually escape from the camp. Rudolf Reder got away when he was sent to a nearby town to collect building materials and left in the care of one sleepy guard while the rest went to dinner. Chaim Hirszman jumped from a train that was taking him from Belzec to Sobibor. Treblinka was more porous because its fencing was neither electric nor equipped with alarms, but only a handful of the dozens of people who got away survived for very long, either because they fled to ghettos that later were liquidated or because the Germans quickly recaptured them. The Germans surrounded Sobibor, on the other hand, with a minefield that made that camp particularly difficult to escape. At Auschwitz, the most extensively guarded of the death camps, prisoners made no fewer than 802 escape attempts, of which at least 144 succeeded. Jews, who made up half the camp's population in the second half of 1942 and a majority thereafter, accounted for only 115 of the tries (14 percent) and 4 of the known successes (3 percent). Those numbers tell a lot about the hierarchy, the gradations of treatment, and the limited role of Jews in resistance groups in the camps. At all of these sites, the reprisals for trying to escape were fierce, ranging from public beatings and hangings of recaptured prisoners or alleged planners of new attempts to the simple practice of killing ten inmates, or even every tenth remaining inmate, for each missing escapee. Such ratios might make the balance sheet of escape attempts seem problematic, except for one consideration: Escapees from the carbon monoxide death camps were virtually the only people remaining after World War II who could provide eyewitness testimony against the murderers and thus get some of them convicted and punished.

Within the camps, the Nazis could rely on three circumstances beyond firepower to retain complete control. The first was the way camp conditions were designed to strip people of their sense of dignity, indeed their sense of self, and to dehumanize them so that they became fatalistic and resigned. Everything from the insistence that inmates be addressed and identify themselves always by number, not by name, to the incessant verbal abuse by the *Kapos* and guards, to the refusal to let people go to the latrines when in need, to the filthy and lice-ridden clothing and bedding—all these things were intended to produce just such a degrading result. People so changed were called *Muselmänner*, which literally means Muslims, apparently because inmates who invented the term thought that Muslims were similarly accepting of all that happened to them. Once people lost the active will to live, they were useless to any potential resistance movement but also useless to the Nazis themselves, and thus destined for certain death. After the war, Hanna Lévy-Hass, who spent 1944–45 at Bergen-Belsen, recalled that camp life deadened people, even to their own memories. She wrote, "We no longer even remember our own past. No matter how hard I strive to reconstruct the slightest element . . . not a single human memory comes back to me. . . . They've managed to kill in us not only our right to life in the present . . . but . . . all sense of a human life in our past. . . . I turn things over in my mind, I want to . . . and I remember absolutely nothing."

The second key weapon in the hands of the guards was their ability to drive inmates to exhaustion. That was the point of the long marches to and from work, the even longer hours at the labor sites, the assignments to ditch digging and industrial construction, the endless roll calls, the overcrowded bunks, and the compulsory calisthenics at the beginning or end of the workday, all coupled with malnutrition. Prisoners were made too exhausted to think, let alone to plan resistance efforts.

A third instrument of the Nazi masters, some psychologists maintain, was inmates' awareness that they had been consigned to an arbitrary and negative universe through no fault of their own. This explains the powerful impact of the famous incident in which Primo Levi, a new arrival at Auschwitz, asks, "Why?" when faced with an act of unfathomable meanness and is told, "Here there is no why." Though prisoners were right to think they did not deserve their fates, that knowledge often provoked self-pity and paralysis. Obsessing about the injustice of the situation and recognizing that the Nazis were impervious to persuasion led to despair and abandonment of the desire to survive.

Who did survive, then? Broadly speaking, the late, the lucky, and the well connected. Those who entered the camps in, say, 1944 and were relatively (but not too) young had the best chance of emerging alive. So did those who drew fortunate labor assignments, such as the women sent to the Degussa subsidiary at Gleiwitz mentioned earlier in this book. And those who had allies in important trustee positions, which means that non-Jews survived more than Jews did. Non-Jews generally looked out for themselves and did little to aid Jews. Rudolf Vrba, who in April 1944 became one of the very few Jews who escaped from Auschwitz, recalled bluntly, "the Resistance in the camp is not geared for an uprising but for the survival of the members of the Resistance." Even where a camp underground existed, it did little to impede the Holocaust. Auschwitz consumed 75,000 Poles, which is perhaps one-third of those sent there, but it took the lives of probably four-fifths of the Jews ever registered in the camp. If we include the unregistered Jews killed immediately upon arrival, then the mortality rate of Jews at Auschwitz was over 90 percent.

Of course, we can never know the full reality of life in the camps or gauge accurately what it took to survive. In the first place, the evidence available is partial; it springs from the writings and testimony of people who did survive and thus may be skewed in some ways. What worked for them may not have worked for countless others, but we do not know how many tried the same methods and failed. In the second place, it is clear that survival was often arbitrary and purely fortuitous, a matter of having a skill the Germans desired at a certain moment, landing a particular work detail by some stroke of luck, or enjoying the favor of a key official in the camp or a pivotal *Kapo* for some reason or as a result of a whim on that person's part. Zev Weiss survived Auschwitz, he says, because he sensed something fishy about a particular assembly call for his barracks, so he wriggled through a crack in the wall of that building, mingled with another barrack's population, and got himself registered there in place of a missing or dead prisoner, which actually was a not uncommon form of camp resistance activity. To this day, he cannot say what made him act as he did at that moment, but he is sure it saved his life, because the call to assemble led to the gassing of nearly all the population of the barracks he had fled. As Göran Rosenberg, whose parents both survived Auschwitz, notes, "There are no roads from Auschwitz but those of improbability."

The most persuasive insights we have on this subject are still those of Terrence Des Pres, in *The Survivor*, published in 1976. Des Pres saw four key elements that determined who outlived the camps. The first was discovery of purpose—bearing witness. Recording daily events helped inmates both to preserve senses of the future and of hope and to transcend the horror around them. Thinking ahead also was an act of resistance; the Nazis repeatedly mocked the inmates by saying that no one would ever know what had happened to them. Simply proceeding as if the Nazis could be proven wrong may have helped inmates maintain a will to live and a self-respect born of their defiance of anonymity.

A second determinant of survival was the recognition that preserving appearances was essential. Central to this was appreciating that one purpose of the camps was to degrade people, to make them filthy and ashamed, and then to punish them for being those things. Facilities for washing were almost nonexistent, and latrines were both crude and withheld. Inmates were tortured by being denied the chance to relieve themselves except during two permitted times per day, but were fed and worked in a manner that made dysentery rampant. People either concealed their excrement in their own clothing or surreptitiously tried to deposit it in the only receptacles available, their eating dishes, and their thoughts became focused on controlling their bowels. Such an environment sapped self-respect and made daily urgencies loom so large that few people had the mental energy to contemplate overt resistance. Des Pres puts all of this under the heading of "excremental assault," and he argues that those who saw through it had the best chance of living. They washed, even in filthy water. They kept their wretched wooden clogs tied securely and bound up their ragged clothes, not only to avoid selection by the SS but also to preserve a sense of self.

A third key element in enduring the camp system was coping with the initial shock of arrival. Studies of prisoner mortality undertaken since Des Pres confirm his point: Those who made it through the first three months had an above-average chance of survival. If mourning or disgust did not produce a rejection of existence, a person might have time to pull together or, to put things another way, if fate saved a person long enough to recover from mourning and disgust, survival became possible. All of this was very difficult, since most people dumped into the unfamiliar environment of the camps were prone to deny its reality, to experience it as if it were a nightmare. This often proved fatal. Vigilance was the best protection; not giving in to shock became indispensable to existence. Those who managed this transition had a chance of developing the capacity to operate alertly and without illusion—to take each day as it came. The difference between living and dying was sometimes between those who calculated the odds and despaired and those who thought that one chance of survival in one hundred or one thousand was good enough. Unsurprisingly, statistical and memoir-based evidence indicates that the chances of surviving the initial shock were better if one arrived in relatively favorable weather—during the spring or the summer rather than in the depth of winter.

Des Pres argues that a fourth determinant of surviving the camps was the discovery of what he calls a means of living simultaneously with and against the terms of existence: with them enough to avoid being snuffed out, against them enough to do the same. One or the other extreme—complete abandonment to the rules or complete defiance—meant death. One had to learn to operate at the margins, "to organize," as camp jargon had it. One had to learn to use bribery, to smuggle, to carry out useful forms of barter, and all of these depended upon the ability to create or join little networks of prisoners who helped each other. In Auschwitz, survival networks generally involved some participant attached to the Canada detail. This was the group that sorted the goods of gassed deportees in giant warehouses along the edge of the Birkenau camp that the inmates called Canada because they imagined that land as overflowing with natural resources. Every day, these workers managed to pilfer food, clothing, and valuables despite at least three rounds of searches by the SS guards. Such thefts, along with corrupt deals with some of the guards, were the principal basis of the extensive black market within the camps, usually involving small possessions of value—everything from needles and knives to tablets of sugar, saccharine, boullion, and the like.

Another key aspect of learning to live with and against the system was knowing when to lie in order to get the sort of administrative post or desirable job in a warehouse that could keep one alive. When the Germans asked arriving prisoners if they were chemists or tailors or carpenters or machinists, an inmate had to be ready to step forward whether she or he was or not—virtually the only people to survive were those who eluded the hard physical work that either consumed prisoners, given the prevailing rations, or led to beatings or shootings at work sites. Still another form of with-and-against behavior was that of *Kapos* who learned to appear vicious to prisoners in front of the SS personnel, thereby shielding them from the latter. Memoirs tell of a system of counteradministration in which prisoner trustees in offices and camp hospitals appeared to follow SS orders to the letter but found ways to conceal or change prisoners' identities or falsify diagnoses. Of course, not every prisoner in a key position helped his fellow inmates, but the system of solidarity was enforced by the knowledge that prisoners could exact revenge on toadies when the SS was not looking. A favorite tactic at Auschwitz was to push collaborators into the open latrines, where they would drown, apparently by accident. Within virtually all the camps, an intelligence system also sprang up, consisting of prisoners working as clerks in the SS offices and specialists among the prisoners who did repair work on the barracks. While seeming to serve the camp administration, they gathered information about the workings of the camp or events in the wider world and spread it around.

Finally, Primo Levi and others stress that survival often depended on "pairing" with another inmate, looking out for each other, and simultaneously holding at bay the camp's multiple ways of crushing any sense of human solidarity.

Des Pres and survivors who have given us memoirs to these effects may be right. But numerous accounts also come from survivors who say that they do not know how they got through the camps, cannot remember adopting a strategy for survival, and cannot say why they lived and others died. They recall instead a kind of endless numbness, a state of almost suspended mental animation that was broken only by liberation at the end of the war.

In short, the camp inmates developed a host of survival mechanisms, but the odds always were stacked against them, just as they were in the ghettos. In both settings, the likely outcome was death, sooner or later, unless the Allies arrived first. The most important explanation of why resistance never crystallized into a form that interrupted the killing machinery or threatened German control is that the system of divide and conquer functioned in the camps to the same diabolical effect that it operated in the ghettos. Inmates were not only outgunned but also atomized and generally resigned. The Germans exploited internal divisions and individuals' will to live right up until the dissolution of the camps. As Imre Kertesz, a Hungarian Jewish novelist and survivor of Auschwitz, writes, "Provided that under the conditions of totalitarianism a person wants to remain alive, he will contribute with such an attitude to the preservation of totalitarianism: this is the simple trick of the organization."

CHAPTER 6

HOMELANDS:
Why Did Survival
Rates Diverge?

IF JEWS COULD do relatively little to deflect or break the force of the Holocaust, what of their non-Jewish fellow citizens in the countries affected? What did they try or fail to do, and why? Does the relative incidence of courage or lack thereof on the part of individuals explain why the survival rates of Jews diverged so widely by country?

Everyone knows or should know that freedom is indivisible; when taken away from someone, it can be taken away from anyone. But few people dare act on that principle—or think they need to do so—even under the best of circumstances. The temptation in times of persecution is for those not immediately subject to it to try to ride it out until the horrors end, and in the meantime to look away or to take advantage. This was all the more true in German-occupied Europe, because the Nazi regime made sure people understood the risks of helping Jews. In Western Europe, these included being sent to a concentration camp. In Eastern Europe, concealing or hiding Jews could result in the execution of one's entire family.

Such penalties lie behind one of the most uncomfortable truths of the Holocaust. For all our appropriate attention to the Righteous Among the Nations memorialized by Yad Vashem and the brave individuals who risked their lives to hide or otherwise save people, no more than 5–10 percent of the Jews who survived the Holocaust did so by virtue of someone's individual heroism.

VARIETIES OF BEHAVIOR

Although readiness to help Jews emerged within every country in Europe, the number of people willing to help, their proportion of the local population, and their attributes and motives varied greatly from place to place and over time. Germans may have hidden and saved 5,000–10,000 Jews during the war years, not counting those protected by marriages to non-Jews and other special provisions; Dutch people 7,000–8,000; and Poles anywhere from 20,000 to 65,000. But those totals represent much smaller shares of the native Jewish populations than those saved by Danes or Italians. Humanity was not the special property of any one or two nationalities nor altogether absent among any, but neither was it evenly distributed by place or over time. Especially in the first year and a half of the mass killing, when the carnage was at its peak and Jews most needed help, willingness to give aid was generally rare, including in areas where it later mounted.

Where such willingness did appear, it generally had its roots in one of three sorts of convictions: political, religious, and personal. Leftists tended to be more likely to help Jews than conservatives, in part because communist and socialist thought discouraged racist thinking, and in part because Communist Party discipline called for resisting all Nazi actions after the invasion of the Soviet Union. Minority religious status sometimes fostered identification with persecuted Jews. For example, Polish and Ukrainian Catholics living in western Ukraine were more likely to aid Jews there than were either Polish co-religionists in overwhelmingly Catholic Poland or the more numerous Orthodox Ukrainians who predominated further east. Similarly, Quakers and Baptists in Germany were much more active in smuggling Jews out of the country before 1939 and hiding them thereafter than their Catholic or Lutheran fellow Germans. And in Catholic France, the remote, predominantly Protestant village of Le Chambon-sur-Lignon and the surrounding region managed to save about 3,500 Jews, many of them children (along with 1,500 other people being pursued by the Gestapo), though one should note in this connection that some Catholics in the region also helped.

Minority status was not always necessary to remind the pious to stand up for the persecuted. The Protestant bishops of Lutheran Norway protested collectively as deportations from that country were being prepared in November 1942. The Orthodox Primate of Bulgaria—the head of the official church of that country—played a central role in preventing deportations there. And although the Pope refused to speak out forcefully against the treatment of Jews and most Catholic cardinals and archbishops in majority Catholic countries remained silent, not all did. Cardinal Jozef-Ernest van Roey in Belgium and Cardinal Pierre Gerlier of Lyon, Archbishop Jules-Gérard Saliège of Toulouse, and Bishop Pierre Théas of Montauban in France were among the Catholic prelates who openly denounced German racism.

As for the personal motives that led to attempts to protect Jews, certain character traits and behavioral records were better predictors of willingness to act than others. The sociologist Nechama Tec's *When Light Pierced the Darkness* concluded, on the basis of a study of 754 Polish rescuers of Jews, that people with a strong sense of individualism and empathy and long records of helping the needy were more protective of Jews than people who took their behavioral standards from their environment and were more self-centered. That judgment is, perhaps unavoidably, rather circular. But another close examination of rescuers, Samuel and Pearl Oliner's *The Altruistic Personality*, which rests on a similarly small sample but includes rescuers from across occupied Europe, reinforces Tec's conclusions in one important respect: People who rescued Jews tended to come from families that instilled strong moral and ethical values, empathy, and concern for the common good. Both these studies suggest that solidarity and courage were not spontaneous, as they often appeared to be, but rather the long-gestating products of a person's upbringing. Otto Jodmin, a German superintendent of an apartment building in Berlin who hid Jews in its cellars and vouched for others as bombing victims so they could obtain identity and ration cards, attributed his actions to the way he had been brought up, which made him think, "I simply had to do it. . . . I just couldn't act in any other way." A Polish researcher named Teresa Prekerowa took issue with this line of analysis in the late 1990s on the basis of a much bigger sample of 3,300 people she considered "typical" of those who helped Jews. She concluded that helpers "were ordinary people who differed greatly from each other, as ordinary people do, and I do not think it is possible to find any characteristics they shared in common." Perhaps, but a great deal of social psychology research reinforces the idea that altruism has to be ingrained and practiced or it atrophies. Think of it as a kind of muscle memory. When a person wonders, "What would I have done?," the best clue to the answer may be his or her record of putting time and energy into helping people at risk.

We do not know enough about the youths of several diplomats who aided Jews in 1940–42 to say that they all fit this overall pattern, but some of them did. As the Nazis were sweeping over Europe, virtually the only effective rescue stemmed from the swift and unauthorized decisions of exceptional foreign diplomats to issue entry visas to their homelands to fleeing Jews. A notable example from mid-1940 was Aristides de Sousa Mendes, the Portuguese consul in Bordeaux, who, defying direct and repeated orders from his government, signed thousands of such documents as the German army bore down on that city. He was a *marrano*, a Catholic whose ancestors had converted from Judaism under duress centuries earlier, and he was deeply devoted to the adopted faith. The combination of religious conviction and family sentiment may have accounted for his remarkable display of courage and empathy. A similar, almost simultaneous, and remarkable tag-team effort occurred just beyond the opposite end of the Nazi empire at the time. This was the joint action of the Dutch and Japanese consuls Jan Zwartendijk and Chiune Sugihara, in Kovno, Lithuania, which the Soviets recently had occupied, to provide partially specious documentation that enabled almost 2,000 Jews to escape across the USSR to Shanghai and other destinations. Another celebrated individual, quasi-official rescue effort was that of the American journalist Varian Fry, who went to France on behalf of the newly formed Emergency Rescue Committee and funded the escapes of some 2,000 people, most of them Jews and many of them famous artists and intellectuals, across the Pyrenees Mountains into Spain in 1940–41. A Swiss consular official in Austria named Ernest Prodolliet helped Jews gain admission to his homeland in 1938. Reprimanded and transferred to Amsterdam, he once more deftly evaded his orders by issuing a number of transit visas through Switzerland to Dutch Jews after Germany occupied the Netherlands. Just before his office was closed in 1942, he turned over the remaining available consular funds, worth about $180,000 in 2014 dollars, to Gertrude van Tijn, the head of the Dutch Jewish Council's still-functioning emigration department. In return, he sought only an unenforceable (but ultimately honored) promise of repayment by the representatives of the American Jewish Joint Distribution Committee in Switzerland.

Sad to say, not enough people in Europe possessed the same humanitarian reflexes as these individuals did, and there were not enough people like Oskar Schindler, either, the Sudeten German opportunist and would-be war profiteer who took over an enamelware factory in Cracow and gradually resolved to save the lives of some 1,300 Jews who worked for him. His heroism is inexplicable because it seems out of keeping with his self-indulgent and disorderly life both before and after. But he displayed great ingenuity and nerve in outwitting the SS. His story stands out not just because he tried to help Jews but also because he succeeded. He did so primarily because he owned his company and did not have to explain or justify his actions to any superiors who might have tipped the Nazis off to what he was up to. In contrast, Berthold Beitz, a German who managed a Karpathian Oil Corporation drilling site in Boryslaw in eastern Galicia, where he protected hundreds of Jews who worked for him for almost two years, did not work for himself. He could not arrange for the Jews' withdrawal to another factory when the Germans retreated in 1944, lest some superior denounce him to the Gestapo for that action. The most he could do was warn his employees just before the SS moved against them, enabling many of them to go into hiding. Alfred Rossner, a German who ran a number of uniform factories in Bedzin in eastern Upper Silesia, bribed and wheedled the local Nazi authorities successfully from May 1942 until August 1943 to keep his Jewish workers from the deportation trains, sometimes even hiding them in his shops. But in the end, not only were most rounded up and deported in the final clearing of the Upper Silesian ghettos, but also the Gestapo caught on to Rossner. Arrested in December 1943, he died in prison in 1944, hanged either by his warders or by his own hand.

Perhaps the most remarkable story of an employer who tried and often succeeded in rescuing his Jewish workers comes from the very heart of the Third Reich, the capital city of Berlin, from a workshop on Rosenthaler Strasse in the middle of town. There Otto Weidt managed an operation that made brushes and brooms and employed at any one time about thirty deaf and mute Jews from a local home. Altogether during the war some fifty-six people from his workshop were slated for destruction by the Nazi state on grounds of both disability and heritage. He argued with the Gestapo each time one of his worker's names appeared on a deportation list, insisting that their work was vital to the war effort, and even bribed Nazi officials to get their names removed. In the end, half of his workers outlived the war, and so did he.

Individual heroism could achieve only so much in the face of the Nazi onslaught, yet about one-quarter of the European Jews in Nazi-occupied or -allied states and one-third of all the European Jews as of 1939 survived the Holocaust. How and why? We can begin to answer that question by looking at figure 7. It sorts Nazi-occupied or -allied countries in Europe according to two characteristics: whether more or less than the continent-wide average of two-thirds of the Jewish inhabitants were killed in each place, and whether each was ruled directly by the Germans or by a collaborating government.

The pattern that emerges is unmistakable, but not quite self-explanatory. That the most lethal parts of the continent were those directly occupied and administered by German officials does not mean that collaboration there was unimportant. In Serbia and Greece, veteran military leaders agreed to head puppet regimes that carried out German orders; similar arrangements arose in the Baltic states. In all of these areas, local police forces and/or mili-

FIGURE 7: GOVERNANCE AND HOLOCAUST MORTALITY RATES

	DEATH RATE OVER 2/3	DEATH RATE UNDER 2/3
Under German Administration	Baltic states, Belarus, Holland, Germany, Greece, Luxembourg, Czech Protectorate, Poland, Serbia, Ukraine	Belgium
Under Collaborating Governments	Slovakia, Croatia, Hungary in 1944	Bulgaria, Romania, Denmark, Finland, Norway, France, Italy, Hungary until 1944

tias continued to function and often to participate in rounding up Jews, and residents eager to denounce Jews in hiding were numerous. A particularly notorious example was the Dutch staff of an organization called the Recherchegruppe (or Colonne) Henneicke, which tracked down and turned in 8,000–9,000 Jews who tried to hide in the Netherlands—that is, more Jews than survived under cover in that country. Conversely, the generally lower death rates under indigenous collaborating governments do not imply that their personnel or citizens refrained from persecuting Jews. On the contrary, Vichy France under Philippe Pétain, Hungary under Regent Miklos Horthy, Romania under Marshal Ion Antonescu, and Bulgaria under Tsar Boris III independently enacted virulently anti-semitic legislation, stripped many Jews of citizenship, and delivered certain groups of Jews to Germany and/or engaged in killing them.

The decisive variable that determined the mortality rate in any given country was usually time—more specifically, whether the Nazi state attacked the resident Jews in 1941–42. Where Germans ruled directly, they almost always mobilized in pursuit of Jews promptly and thoroughly, unencumbered by an interest in preserving smooth working relations with local governments and populations. An exception was Belgium, and it was not really much of one. Though under German administration, authority over the police and so-called racial policy was in the hands of the German army, not the SS or the Nazi Party, until May 1942. And though a collaborating government did not actually rule Belgium, since the country's cabinet (but not its monarch) had fled to Britain, the indigenous civil service continued to function, and the Germans found working with it convenient and worth preserving. Still, Belgium did prove a great anomaly in one sense: More than 90 percent of the Jews there were foreigners, the sort of people usually deported first from most places, yet half of them survived. Another exception of a quite different sort was Greece, where a puppet government nominally existed after the country capitulated to Germany and Italy but where German control of the Nazi-occupied regions was very tight. Nonetheless, the Germans did not begin to deport Jews until March 1943; the somewhat smaller number in the Italian-occupied zone were not deported until 1944. Despite the delays, the death toll ultimately came to between 80 and 90 percent.

Where local administrations remained in place and were more autonomous, however, the Germans at first preferred to let native antisemitism run its course while they concentrated on the larger populations of Jews in the Reich's grasp elsewhere. By late 1942, when most of those other Jews were dead and Germany became insistent, the tide of war was turning and affiliated governments were growing wary of further persecution, since they might have to answer to the Allies if Hitler went down to defeat. Emblematic of the changing climate are the deportation statistics from two countries where the final death toll proved relatively low: The majority of the Jews ever deported from both France and Belgium departed in 1942, and then the pace from both places slowed. Equally telling was the behavior of Hitler's Balkan allies. Bulgaria, Hungary, and Romania each handed over to the Nazis some or all of the Jewish populations of regions taken in 1938–41 from neighboring states under German auspices but declined to turn over the Jewish inhabitants of their core territories in 1942–43. Even Slovakia, which in early 1942 eagerly agreed to deport most Jews—in fact, actually paid Nazi Germany for taking them—also had second thoughts toward the end of that year and suspended the deliveries, most of which had gone directly to Auschwitz.

In other words, the four chief determinants of the differing rates of Jews' rescue and mortality in Nazi Europe were: (1) how swiftly the Germans moved—if they began massively killing in 1941–42, they got almost all the Jews in any given area; (2) how long the Germans remained—their presence enabled the events in Hungary in May–July 1944 and would have enabled the slaughter of the French Jews had D-Day not interfered with their general deportation, which the Germans finally mandated less than two months earlier; (3) whether the Germans had to deal with an indigenous and at least quasi-autonomous government interested in surviving the war; and (4) whether most Jews were still alive in an area by the time of the battles of El Alamein and Stalingrad 1942–43—the interval that Winston Churchill called "the hinge of fate"—and the onset of Germany's forced labor drafts. These are the moments when the likelihood that the Third Reich would win the war dwindled, and the Jews' interests and national interests began to coincide around resistance to Germany. If enough Jews were still alive, these developments began working to their benefit.

The importance of national and Jewish interests seeming congruent emerges clearly from the fate of Jews in an area where and at a time when the opposite was the case—where national interests seemed to favor cooperation with the Nazis and the sacrifice of the Jews, notably the Baltic states and Ukraine in 1941–43. Ukrainian nationalists had seen their aspirations for independence crushed by the Bolshevik regime in 1919–21 and had endured a series of famines and purges in the 1930s that had deepened alienation from the Soviet state. Lithuanian, Latvian, and Estonian nationalists had lost their independence to occupation by the USSR in 1940. To them, the Germans came as potential liberators from Soviet enslavement, all the more so as Germany had allowed various national liberation groups to set up offices in Berlin and thus implied support for their goals. But because nearly all of these nationalist movements were historically antisemitic, Soviet rule in 1940–41 had an upside to the Jewish citizens of these states, some of whom found opportunities for advancement when the less discriminatory Soviet regime arrived, even though many other Jews suffered from the nationalization of their property by communism and from the deportations to Siberia that the Soviets conducted. As a result, Jews were overrepresented compared to their share of the Lithuanian population not only in the Communist Party and secret police there in 1940–41 but also among the people the communists sent to the Russian interior.

The consequence in most of the former Pale of Settlement was a situation in which Jewish and local nationalist interests seemed to conflict. To the Jews, the Soviet occupation of 1940 seemed the lesser of two possible evils; as one Jew from the region said at the time, the Soviet Union brought life in prison, but Nazi Germany brought the death sentence. But to Ukrainian and Baltic nationalists, even initially to the Catholic Metropolitan Archbishop Andrei Sheptytsky, who later tried to protect Jews, occupation by Germany appeared the lesser evil. These seekers of independence were only too ready to cooperate in removing a population that they disliked anyway in order to curry favor with the Germans. Well before the German invasion of Ukraine, both factions of the Organization of Ukrainian Nationalists (OUN), the Banderites and the Melnykites, had branded Jews as the allies of Bolshevism and endorsed killing Jewish males. On July 1, 1941, the day after the Germans occupied Lviv, the OUN issued a leaflet calling on Ukrainians to "destroy" Jewry, and a pogrom took place. Similarly, in March 1941, the Lithuanian Activist Front declared that Jews had "betrayed" the country and thus had no future there.

Although the SS had some initial difficulty carrying out its orders to stimulate pogroms in Baltic cities captured by German troops, local militias soon recognized what the Germans wanted them to do to Jews and began bludgeoning and hacking them to death in Vilna, Kovno, and Riga, the largest cities of Lithuania and Latvia. Lithuanian militiamen probably killed more of the 180,000 Jews who died in that country by the end of 1941 than Germans did. Ukrainian police and militias played an active part in the massacres in their homeland during 1941, including at Babi Yar in September, even though by that time the Germans already had made their opposition to Ukrainian independence clear and even arrested Stepan Bandera, the leader of one wing of the OUN. So long as Germany remained on the offensive on the Eastern Front, it had no shortage of willing local volunteers for militias and security forces that hunted and killed Jews. In 1943, in fact, Himmler had about 300,000 mostly cooperative local policemen under his command in the occupied East, and Russian scholars have put the number of citizens of the occupied USSR who served in Wehrmacht and SS units during the war at 1.2 million. By the time the tide of the war turned, and the Baltic and Ukrainian nationalists finally recognized that a Nazi New Order in Europe was not going to restore their independence, nearly all of the Jews in Ukraine and the Baltic states were dead. Even then, many of the collaborators continued to fight for Hitler because they had become so complicit in his crimes that they had no alternative and, in the case of the Ukrainians, because they still aspired to eliminate Poles and Jews from their lands. These men and their families retreated with the German armies in 1944–45 and made up a significant proportion of the people in displaced persons camps there after the war ended.

This is not to say that national interests were the only driver of widespread popular participation in killing Jews in the occupied East. The availability of plunder also served as a strong inducement. A Pole who lived on the outskirts of Vilna and witnessed the massacres there observed, "For the Germans 300 Jews are 300 enemies of humanity; for the Lithuanians they are 300 pairs of shoes, trousers, and the like." Nonetheless, the force that unleashed and claimed to legitimize covetous motives was perceived national interest.

Another sign of the decisive importance of national political considerations to the fate of Jews was the way that states officially or tacitly allied with Nazi Germany drew policy distinctions, albeit to varying degrees, between native-born Jewish citizens of their countries, especially veterans, and immigrant Jews of different nationalities. Vichy France, for example, was willing, even eager, to treat alien Jews as fit subjects for deportation but more resistant to giving up French citizens, though it did so on some occasions. Of the roughly 350,000 Jews in France in 1940, more than half had immigrated or fled illegally to the country since the beginning of the twentieth century. Drawing on mounting xenophobia during the 1930s and the convenient scapegoating of Jews for France's defeat in 1940, the collaborationist government headquartered in Vichy enacted antisemitic legislation voluntarily and in a form that was in some respects even more restrictive than Germany's. Vichy also accepted the arrests of foreign Jews in the occupied northern part of France beginning in October 1940; in fact, French police often carried out the roundups. French police also collected and handed over to the Germans 10,000 foreign Jews from unoccupied France during the summer of 1942. Deportations had begun in March of that year and resulted eventually in the transportation of approximately 76,000 Jews in France to concentration camps; only about 2,500 survived, and more than two-thirds of the deportees were foreigners. In the end, more Polish Jews who had sought refuge in France died at Nazi hands than did French Jews. The survival rate among foreign Jews in France ultimately came to about 50 percent, whereas for Jews who had French citizenship it came to a little less than 90 percent. But once more than half of the unfortunates left in 1942, the French government dragged its feet, partly as a matter of asserting its status as an independent, sovereign entity and partly as a matter of hedging its bets about the outcome of the war.

Similarly, the three German allies in southeastern Europe—Romania, Bulgaria, and Hungary prior to 1944—drew distinctions between Jews Germany could have and ones it could not and tailored national policies toward Jews to each country's political interests. The three states had leaders who held antisemitic views of varying intensity, and all three agreed to hand over Jews in lands acquired from neighboring countries in 1938–41 under German auspices. Thus in August 1941, Hungary pushed 17,000 Jews from the parts of Slovakia it had annexed in 1938–39 across its borders into German-occupied Poland and Ukraine, where the SS massacred 11,000 of them. Early in 1942, Hungary killed another 1,000 or so Jews in territory acquired during the dismemberment of Yugoslavia in April

1941. After Bulgaria received Thrace from Greece, Macedonia from Yugoslavia, and Dobrudja from Romania in 1940–41, it delivered 11,384 Jews from these regions to the Germans in early 1943. In all these instances, the principal and cynically self-interested motivation was demographic. Where killing Jews would reduce the size of the non-Hungarian and non-Bulgarian populations and speed the absorption of territory into their states, the acquiring countries were ready to cooperate.

Both Bulgaria and Hungary also enacted antisemitic laws designed to strip Jews of their property and exclude them from the civil services; Hungary's legislation went so far as to restrict the share of Jews in any profession to 6 percent and forbade sexual relations and new marriages between Jews and Magyars. But the countries' policies diverged even in 1941–42 regarding further deportations, with the Bulgarians promising to begin them in 1943 and the Hungarians steadfastly refusing, although they drafted adult Hungarian Jews for labor service on the Russian front, where about 42,000 of them died or were murdered. The Bulgarians bought the Germans off for a time by conscripting Bulgaria's Jews for work in the countryside but then reversed their position on deportations in March and April of 1943, partly because of intense and widespread domestic opposition and partly because of mounting concern that Germany might not win the war. Nearly all of the Bulgarian Jews ultimately survived because the Germans did not force the issue by occupying the country.

In Hungary, however, opposition to deportations crumbled after March 1944, when German troops poured into the nation, ostensibly to defend it from an impending Soviet invasion but really because Hungary was considering following Italy's example and finding a way out of the Axis alliance. Following an initial period of isolating and pillaging the Hungarian Jews, almost 60 percent of them, approximately 437,000 people, were deported in the space of only fifty-five days, between May 15 and July 9. At Auschwitz-Birkenau, about 25 percent of these people were selected for work and generally shipped onward to labor in Germany; perhaps half of them, about 55,000 people, survived the war. The rest of the deportees, more than 325,000 people, perished in the gas chambers upon arrival, making the total death toll from this round of Hungarian deportations roughly 380,000 and the total number of Hungarian Jews killed in the Holocaust, following another round in late 1944 and then a series of horrific death marches, between 500,000 and 565,000.

Even though most of the victims died at the hands of Germans, not Hungarians, the thoroughness of this operation, which netted 97 percent of the Jews in the Hungarian countryside and annexed areas and left virtually the only survivors in the Hungarian capital of Budapest, was largely homegrown. Only 150–200 German SS personnel were involved in the Hungarian roundups that the nation's own national and local police forces, supplemented by civil servants and volunteers, carried out under the direction of a Ministry of the Interior led and staffed by extreme right-wing Magyar antisemites. The concentration of Jews across the country into fifty-five short-lived ghettos proceeded according to a plan for the successive clearing of six different sections of the country. Finalized by Adolf Eichmann and several Hungarian policemen, that plan closely resembled a program that two nationalist Hungarian generals had devised in 1942, almost two years before the German occupation. In the apt summation of Peter Kenez, a historian of modern Hungary and himself a refugee from that country, "The German role in the destruction of Hungarian Jewry is best understood as giving an opportunity to some determined [Hungarian] antisemites to carry out a policy that they had long desired and planned."

How can one explain the scale and speed of the carnage in Hungary, comparable only to the liquidation of most of the Warsaw ghetto in fifty-three days during the summer of 1942, and so fast that Commandant Höss at Auschwitz repeatedly sought to slow the overwhelming pace? One part of the answer is that the RSHA could focus its efforts—after all, most of the other Jews of Europe were dead or out of reach by May–July 1944—and the killing center at Birkenau was very close by and more swiftly murderous than ever, thanks to the recently completed rail spur that ran into the camp almost to the doors of two of the gas chambers. A second, somewhat technical, explanation is that the deportation had a war-related purpose, which helps to account for so many trains—147 over the course of the operation, 3–6 per day—being made available. Auschwitz was supposed to cull 100,000 able-bodied workers, 10–15 percent of the anticipated deportees, and send them on immediately to Germany to labor on the massive effort to put war-producing factories underground. But still a third important component of a response lies in the history of antisemitism in Hungary. As in Germany, prior to World War I Jews in Hungary enjoyed apparently ever-expanding acceptance, opportunities, and prosperity, only to experience rising hostility following defeat and territorial losses in 1918-19 and the bloody suppression of a communist revolution in which Jews played conspicuous parts. In interwar Hungary, as in Germany, nationalist forces harped continuously on a supposed link between Jews, disloyalty, and unrest and fanned resentment at the prominence of Jews in commerce, industry, law, and medicine. As a result of such agitation, the installation of an authoritarian government, the inauguration of antisemitic restrictions, and the rise of a mass antisemitic political movement, the Association of Awakening Hungarians (EME), all occurred more than a decade before Hitler came to power in Germany.

When German diplomatic successes in 1938–41 led to the dismemberment of first Czechoslovakia and later Yugoslavia and meanwhile to the arbitration of Hungary's and Romania's competing claims to Transylvania, the Hungarian rulers were happy to express their gratitude for the pieces of territory that Hitler threw their way with the enactment of further restrictions on Jews' civil rights and economic activities. But the new territories nearly doubled the Hungarian Jewish population, from 401,000 to 725,000 (or from

491,000 to 825,000, counting converts of Jewish descent), making it larger than the entire Jewish population of Western Europe. That the additional Jews were much less likely to speak Magyar, and to resemble in dress and religious practices their co-religionists inside the previous borders, stoked the antisemitism that already prevailed in military and some government circles, including around the head of state, Admiral Horthy. When he finally capitulated in March 1944 to Nazi demands that he furnish 100,000–300,000 "Jewish workers for German war production purposes," the first two parts of the nation combed were the annexed regions to the northeast that happened to be closest to the advancing Russian troops; the last region scheduled for purging was the capital city, where the most assimilated and economically valuable Jews lived. In short, Hungarian desires, as well as Hungarian personnel, not only accelerated the deportations but also determined their course. Conversely, when Hungarian officials withdrew their cooperation with the Germans between July and October 1944, Eichmann and his aides could achieve almost nothing further except the deportation of 2,700 prisoners already interned in camps on Hungarian soil.

By far, the most contradictory and confusing policies toward Jews were those carried out in and by Romania in 1940–45, and to understand them, one needs to pay close attention to figure 8. Marshal Antonescu, the country's dictator, was an inveterate antisemite who blamed Jews for all of his country's weaknesses. In particular, he claimed that they had welcomed Romania's losses, in 1940, of the northern province of Bukovina, the northeastern province of Bessarabia (also then called eastern Moldova), and of northern Transylvania. The first two losses came as a result of a Soviet ultimatum and the third because of a German-Italian arbitration of border claims that gave this region to Hungary. Determined to regain all three territories, Antonescu joined in the invasion of the USSR in June 1941 and set out to murder the Jews of Bukovina and Bessarabia, both in punishment for their supposed pro-Soviet

FIGURE 8: ROMANIA, 1941–44

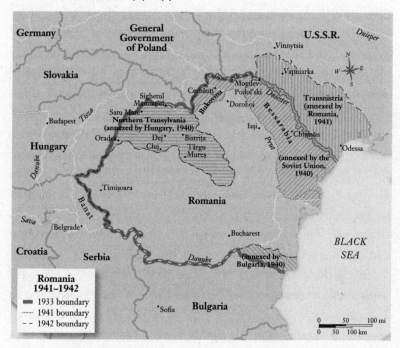

stance and as a means of speeding the Romanianization of the regions. He also hoped to use willingness to deport and kill Jews as leverage in persuading Hitler to give him back northern Transylvania. As a result, Romania acquired the dubious honor of becoming the German ally that killed the largest number of Jews, about 400,000 in Bukovina and Bessarabia and a territory the Romanians called Transnistria, the portion of Ukraine that Hitler awarded Antonescu in compensation for his loss of part of Transylvania.

But in 1942, when the Germans began requesting a schedule for the deportation of the Jews from the core provinces of Romania, an area called the Regat, Antonescu demurred. His generals on the Eastern Front already had begun warning him of impending disaster there, and he wanted to extort every last penny from the local

Jews before he sent them off. So he played for time, deferring the first deportations scheduled for October 1942 until spring 1943, at which point he joined the Bulgarians in reneging on his earlier promises. He never gave up his crazed dream of ultimately sending the Romanian Jews to Transnistria and thus creating an ethnically pure Romanian heartland, but he did not hand over the Jews in the Regat to the Nazis. This engendered one of the greatest ironies of the Holocaust: The nation that next to Germany killed the largest number of Jews also was the nation that had the largest surviving Jewish population in Europe in 1945. Whereas 80 percent of the Jews in Bukovina, Bessarabia, and Transnistria died at Romanian hands, 80 percent of the Jews in the Regat remained alive at the end of the war. Their situation was wretched, as the Romanian regime had terrified and impoverished them, but they still lived.

In all these instances, cynical and practical politics played a greater role in deciding the fate of Jews than moral considerations. In fact, taking a strong moral stand in solidarity with Jews proved counterproductive when the timing was not right. Early mass resistance to Nazi discrimination could backfire, as it did in Holland. A general strike there in February 1941 in protest against the persecution process led to its acceleration, and the objection of Catholic bishops to the deportation of Jewish converts to Catholicism triggered expedited arrests of such people. Provoked by this opposition, the German administrators in the Netherlands, many of whom had acquired experience with persecuting Jews in Austria in 1938–39, now moved with a fury unmatched in any other occupied Western European country. Between July 1942 and September 1943, they rounded up and deported 110,000 Dutch Jews out of a total population of 140,000.

Finally, as a demonstration of both the importance of politics to the fate of Jews and the difficulties of individual rescue efforts, consider what happened in the two countries where Jews enjoyed unusually high survival rates thanks largely to popular solidarity, namely

Denmark and Italy. Denmark is, of course, famous for concealing almost all the nearly 8,000 resident Jews and ferrying them across the narrow strait between that country and Sweden, and Italy for resolutely refusing, even while Mussolini was enacting antisemitic laws, to let anyone be deported, not only out of Italy but also out of the parts of France, Yugoslavia, Albania, and Greece that Italy occupied and administered. In both countries, roundups of the Jews were delayed by special political circumstances. Until 1943, a Danish government continued to function and to cooperate with the German occupation, Mussolini's regime was an Axis ally, and the Germans thought preserving these arrangements more important than forcing these countries even to compile lists of Jews or make them wear identifying badges, let alone to begin deportations. Only when the political conditions changed in late 1943—in Denmark when the cabinet resigned because the Germans imposed martial law in response to mounting popular resistance, in Italy when the Germans rushed to occupy the country because the king had dismissed the Duce and his successor had concluded an armistice with the Allies—only then could and did the Germans strike against Jews. All this meant that the assaults occurred precisely at the moment when helping Jews became an act of national resistance against an oppressive foreigner.

Many other pieces of good fortune were involved: the Danes had the virtual collusion of the leading German administrator in the country, Werner Best, and the opposition to the operation of both the military commander in Denmark, General Hermann von Hanneken, and the Gestapo chief there, Rudolf Mildner. Caught between Himmler's impatience to begin deportations and his own belief that they would complicate the job of managing the occupation, Best played a double game. He advocated action to the SS in Berlin in order to please Himmler, but he leaked news of the impending roundups to the Danish Jews via a German named Georg Duckwitz four days in advance in order to preserve a good working relationship with the Danish bureaucracy and police. This gave the Jews time to get away from their homes before the German police came to apprehend them on the evening of October 1, 1943. During the ensuing weeks, the Jewish Danes had two more price-less advantages in making their escape: an offer of asylum from the Swedish government for anyone who got to its shores, and only a narrow body of water to cross. Even so, most of them got away only because German navy patrol boats off the Danish coast made no attempt to interfere with the roughly 700 vessels—mainly fishing boats—that carried the exodus. Only 284 Danish Jews fell into Nazi hands in the roundup of October 1, and 22 more drowned while trying to escape. Ultimately, 7,742 reached Sweden, including 1,376 German Jewish refugees, along with 686 non-Jewish spouses. Per-haps even more amazing than these numbers is the fact that after the war, when these people returned to Denmark, they found their homes and property not only unmolested but also often carefully tended in their absence.

In Italy, Mussolini had just announced the imposition of forced labor on Italian Jews and was on the verge of commanding deporta-tions when he was overthrown in July 1943, and the Jews in Italian-occupied Croatia already had been interned in a potential transit camp. But in the chaos that surrounded the influx of the German army, the remaining 2,600 Croatian Jews could escape, and most of the 32,000 Italian ones remaining in the northern two-thirds of the country had time to go underground. They then had the geographi-cal advantages of rugged mountains— namely, the Apennines in the center of the country and the Alps in the north that provided ideal hiding places—and proximity to the Allied front lines advancing up the Italian boot.

Nevertheless, the latest studies suggest that about one-quarter of those still vulnerable Jews were killed during the Holocaust, that many of those deported after the Germans occupied the coun-try were apprehended by Italian collaborators, and that in regions where the German presence was greatest, for example around Trieste in the northeast, Italian attitudes hardly mattered and 90 percent of the Jewish community perished. One reason for the German thoroughness in that region is that the SS units from Operation Reinhard were transferred there when those camps in Poland closed. Local heroism was no match for German ruthlessness, as indicated by the fate of Giovanni Palatucci, a commissioner in the police headquarters in nearby Fiume. He used his office to impede roundups and help Jews escape by boat to southern Italy until the Gestapo arrested him in September 1944 and sent him to Dachau, where he died shortly before the liberation of that camp.

Timing, geography, and small numbers were factors that favored relatively high rates of survival among Jews in Denmark and Italy. So did the fact that by the fall of 1943, the likelihood that Germany would lose the war became strong. But other circumstances played a role, and they were important in Bulgaria, too. In none of these countries were Jews notably prominent in commercial or cultural life or in communist politics and thus representable as profiteers or threats. Moreover, all three Jewish communities were highly acculturated. The members of all three routinely spoke the national language and dressed like the majority population. Unlike a majority of the Jews of Ukraine, Poland, Lithuania, Romania, and rural Hungary, Yiddish was not their lingua franca, and traditional Orthodox garb was rare. In Italy in 1938, more than one-third of all married Jews had non-Jewish spouses. Sometimes, the fate of Germany's and Hungary's urbanized Jews is invoked as a warning against acculturation, a proof that it does not protect Jews from the hostility of others. Certainly in those instances, it did not. But acculturation did not always fail as a safeguard. The different experiences of the highly integrated Jewish communities of Bulgaria, Denmark, and Italy, where much of the gentile population mobilized to shelter Jews, bear paying attention to as well.

THE CASE OF POLAND

Probably no subset of issues related to the behavior of non-Jewish populations during the Holocaust is touchier than those surrounding what happened in Poland. The country was, after all, the epicenter of the Holocaust: the location of the death camps, the homeland before World War II of half the victims, and the graveyard of fully 90 percent of the Jews who lived there in 1939. Among the Jews who survived, the sense that Christian Poles had done little to help, indeed in many cases had favored and even encouraged the outcome, has been strong.

That perception drew strength from Claude Lanzmann's monumental, nine-hour-long documentary film of the 1980s, *Shoah*, which showed some Polish peasants near Chelmno explaining that the Jews died because they had killed Christ centuries before and others near Auschwitz grinning as they recalled the arrival of deportation trains there. In 2001, the publication of Jan Gross's book *Neighbors* brought renewed attention to the fraught nature of communal relations in Poland under the Nazis. Gross recounted a savage massacre of Jews by Christian Polish peasants in the village of Jedwabne, in the Soviet-annexed part of Poland, just after the Germans arrived in 1941. He overstated the numbers of both victims and perpetrators and minimized the instigating role of the Germans but established that local residents did the killing, often in bestial fashion. Works such as Lanzmann's and Gross's may have something to do with a curious feature of survivors' testimonies that Christopher Browning came across when he studied the Starachowice labor camp: Accounts of Poles' behavior given by Jews immediately after the war were generally far milder and less angry than those collected later. The sense of bitterness and betrayal grew more intense with the passage of time.

At the same time, aside from Belarus, Poland was the place where the German occupation was worst for everyone subjected to it. During the invasion, German troops repeatedly machine-gunned civilians and prisoners of war. In the parts of Poland seized by Germany, the death toll came to at least 50,000 people and perhaps more than 60,000 by December 1939 alone. Before the massacre of the Jews began, the Germans intentionally liquidated much of the Polish intelligentsia, killing one-third to two-thirds of the professors, journalists, lawyers, priests, leading politicians, and so on and thus greatly weakening the country that later emerged from World War II. The concentration camp at Auschwitz actually was established initially for these people, not for Jews. A few statistics give a sense of how complete the purge at some local levels was: In the Catholic diocese of Poznan (Posen in German), in the Warthegau, 77 percent of the priests were put in concentration camps, deported, or killed outright between 1939 and 1945. In the six dioceses that Nazi Germany annexed from Poland, the death rate for priests during the war varied from a low of 30 percent to a high of just over 50 percent. Moreover, Himmler established a program that essentially stole thousands of blond-haired, blue-eyed, racially German-looking children from their Polish parents and placed them in adoptive Nazi families within the Reich. His demographic engineering efforts in the Warthegau involved the displacement and impoverishment of 300,000 Poles, and the arbitrary nature of Nazi rule in the General Government assured that thousands more died at German hands. About two million more Poles were brought to the Reich for forced labor and exploited and mistreated there to varying degrees.

The lot of those left at home was not much better; hundreds at a time were shot and their farms or villages burned in reprisal actions against any resistance to German measures or harm to German troops. Secondary education for Poles was almost entirely banned, and all universities closed and plundered. Hans Frank, the Nazi master of the General Government, openly declared that he did not care whether Poles "had anything to eat or not." As a result, in 1941 official rations provided Poles with only 29 percent of the daily calorie norms set by the League of Nations; in 1943, the figure was 17 percent. Most Poles survived by buying on the black market, but the search for food was time-consuming and exhausting, and the prices exorbitant. Martin Winstone, who has written the most thorough recent study of the GG, reports that "bread prices—the supreme barometer of the black market—hovered at around 4,000 per cent of prewar levels" from 1941 until the end of the German occupation. In just the first few months of German rule, the resources and machinery of the GG were stripped so clean that Frank described the region in March 1940 as "economically speaking, an empty body. What there was. . . has, as far as possible, been taken out by the [German] Four Year Plan." Though the Nazis came to recognize a contradiction between keeping order in the country and impoverishing it, they never resolved the conflict, and living standards continued to plummet during the occupation.

Policy was one reason the annexed and occupied parts of Poland suffered grievously, but personnel was another. Germany generally staffed the GG with district leaders who were long-time, deeply committed National Socialists, usually of the most racist sort, and often the most incompetent, greedy, or scandal-ridden. Frank, the governor general, was prototypical in all these respects. Although this pattern made Nazi administrators occasionally susceptible to bribery that might ameliorate conditions, it also made the new overlords even more determined to extract everything they could, both for the Reich and for themselves, from the occupied region. Fritz Cuhorst, the first Nazi-appointed head of the city of Lublin, spoke for many of them in December 1939 when he remarked, "[W]e have decided to behave as officials exactly the opposite of at home, that is, like bastards." As a result, according to the contemporary account of an anonymous Polish doctor, "[I]t was like living in a country where all the thieves and gangsters had been let loose and the operation of the law entirely suspended."

Perhaps one can get the best sense of the extent of the damage to Poland in World War II by comparing events there to two of the war's greatest conflagrations: the air wars against Germany and Japan. More Poles died in the bombing of Warsaw in 1939 than Germans in the firebombing of Dresden in 1945; in fact, more inhabitants of Warsaw alone, about 720,000 people, perished in the Second World War than did Germans in all Allied air raids. Even more shockingly, more Poles may have been killed in the suppression of the Warsaw Rising of 1944 than Japanese people were in the atomic bombing of Hiroshima and Nagasaki a year later. In the end, approximately two million non-Jewish Polish citizens perished during the Nazi occupation between 1939 and 1945, a staggering total, but not as many as the number of Polish Jews who were killed, and hardly comparable as a percentage of the prewar population. The oft-quoted statement that as many Christian as Jewish Polish citizens died under Nazi rule is false. Jakub Berman, a Polish communist leader who was Jewish, simply cooked up the number in December 1946 for political reasons, and it has been disproven by close statistical analysis. Even so, a great many non-Jews died in annexed and occupied Poland. Moreover, while this was happening, Polish gentiles also hid and saved tens of thousands of Jews. To put the matter in a superficially surprising form: The Jewish survival rate in Warsaw was equal to that in Amsterdam.

Since 1945, competing claims to greater suffering and mutual indifference under the Nazis have perpetuated the sense of distance between the Jewish and non-Jewish Polish communities. To a regrettable degree, many Jews have talked as if the Poles were worse than the Germans during the Holocaust, and many non-Jewish Poles have treated every criticism of their behavior as a treasonous and ungrateful insult to a beleaguered nation. In April 2015, the Polish foreign minister went so far as to summon the American ambassador to complain that a reference to "the murderers and accomplices of . . . Poland" in a speech and newspaper column by FBI Director James Comey—a remark that this chapter shows is entirely justified—constituted an insult to the many heroic Poles who had resisted Nazi Germany. Of course, Poles exhibited both complicity and heroism during World War II; to cite one is not to deny the other. Moreover, as we will see, resistance to Nazism in Poland and implication in the Holocaust sometimes went hand in hand. But Comey decided to do the politic thing and apologize. Even in contemporary academic circles outside of Poland, these sensitivities have surfaced in the critical reaction to Timothy Snyder's important book *Bloodlands*, which appeared in 2010. Snyder juxtaposed the suffering of Jews at Nazi hands with the suffering of Poles, Ukrainians, and other Eastern Europeans primarily at Soviet hands in the former Pale of Settlement between 1933 and 1945. In response, a number of prominent Jewish scholars, both here and in Israel, charged him with downplaying Polish antisemitism and generally presenting an excessively pro-Polish account of the carnage.

How can we sort through the mutual recrimination fairly and come to a measured assessment of what happened? I think such an effort has to keep seven essential and somewhat contradictory sets of facts in mind.

First, antisemitism in Poland was considerable before 1939 and on the rise. To be sure, it was not universal. The popular Peasant Party and the elitist Democratic Party that emerged just before World War II advocated toleration and discouraged persecution. But the chief proponent of discrimination against Jews was Roman Dmowski. His National Party (known until 1928 as the National Democrats, or Endecja) gained influence from 1935 on, as the government that succeeded that of the deceased Marshal Jozef Pilsudski adopted a series of measures aimed at driving Jews out of the Polish economy and, indeed, the country. Recurrent small-scale pogroms flared up in the late 1930s, most of them in small towns in the center of Poland, resulting in the deaths of fourteen Jews and the wounding of 2,000 more. A government decree requiring businesses to post the full names of their owners facilitated boycotting Jewish enterprises, as did the division of municipal market halls into Jewish and non-Jewish sections. Discriminatory admissions policies drove down the share of Jews among university students in Poland by almost two-thirds (from 20.4 percent to 7.5 percent) between 1928 and 1938. Those who enrolled had to sit on specially designated benches in the lecture halls after 1937 and sometimes were subjected to violent attack. Between 1936 and 1939, the Polish parliament first limited, and then banned, kosher slaughtering. Meanwhile, virtually no Jews held positions in Polish governmental or municipal offices, the railway and postal systems, and the government monopoly industries, such as tobacco, alcohol, and lumber. Aside from two baptized generals of Jewish descent, the Jewish officers in the regular Polish army were almost all medical doctors. National legislation restricted Jewish actors to Yiddish theaters and Jewish journalists to Jewish-owned newspapers, and various professional associations, including those for electrical engineers and physicians, voted to exclude Jews henceforth. The political organization founded in 1936 to support the post-Pilsudski regime, the Camp of National Unity (OZON), also barred Jewish members.

In 1937, the Conservative Party leader, Prince Janusz Radziwill, endorsed the "forcible emigration of the Jews," and the Polish government actually sent a delegation to Madagascar to explore the possibility of sending Jews there. The Polish foreign minister even discussed the idea with his French counterpart the following year and tried to lease roughly a million acres of land on the island to support the emigration of 30,000 Jewish families per year during the next five or six years, some 500,000 to 600,000 people all told. Shortly thereafter, the Polish ambassador in the United States opened talks with a group of wealthy and influential American Jews about their purchasing the Portuguese colony of Angola as a "supplemental Jewish homeland." So eager was the Polish government to drive out Jews that it actually trained right-wing Zionist fighters in Poland in 1938–39 and then sent them off to Palestine. The hope was that they would perpetrate enough violence to persuade the British either to leave that territory or relax restrictions on immigration to it.

The depth and breadth of Polish antisemitism reflected the close link between Polish nationalism and Polish Catholicism. In the eyes of many Poles, one simply could not be Polish without being Catholic, and the nation's priests heartily concurred. As the most outspokenly antisemitic Catholic clergy in Europe, they usually threw their political weight behind Dmowski and his Nationalists. Church leaders and publications tied the Jews repeatedly to every alien and supposedly corrupting or polluting force in modern life and thus to every current of opinion or behavior that threatened the authority, power, and income of the Church. Poland's cardinals were particularly unabashed about blaming Jews for the nation's problems. The Church's official stance toward Jews remained unchanged since the Middle Ages: They were evil and seditious people who should be shunned, but not harmed physically.

Typical of the entrenched animosity toward Jews among Catholic leaders in Poland was the pastoral letter entitled "On Catholic Moral Principles" that Cardinal August Hlond, the Primate of Poland, issued in February 1936. It read, in part, as follows:

> It is a fact that the Jews . . . constitute the avant-garde of godlessness, the Bolshevik movement, and revolutionary activities. It is a fact that Jewish influence on morality is pernicious, and that their publishing houses spread pornography. It is true that the Jews permit fraud and usury. . . . But let us be fair. Not all Jews are like that. . . . One may love one's own nation more, but one may not hate anyone. In commercial matters it is good to prefer your own ahead of others, avoiding Jewish stores and Jewish booths at the market, but one may not plunder Jewish shops. . . . One must close oneself off to the harmful moral influences of Jewry . . . in particular boycott the Jewish press and corrupting Jewish publishing houses, but it is not permitted to attack the Jews, beat them, wound them, injure them, defame them.

Two years later, Father Jozef Kruszynski, the former rector of the Catholic University of Lublin and the chief intellectual propagator of the *Protocols of the Elders of Zion* in interwar Poland, summarized the ambivalent teachings of the Church toward Jews. He described their persecution in Germany as barbaric but added, "Hitler called the Jews the microbe of the world. The accusation is unusually harsh but we must admit that it is correct." In short, traditional religious antisemitism remained vivid and strong in Poland, and very few Catholic priests, especially at the parish level, spoke up in defense of the Jews or urged their parishioners to help them. On the contrary, the Church hierarchy repeatedly excused what it called the "regrettable excesses" of Polish antisemites by depicting them as understandable reactions to the Jews' disrespect "for the faith and traditions of Christians."

Second, Jews and Poles tended to live as separate ethnic communities in much of prewar Poland, and there was little sense of solidarity between them. Only 12 percent of Polish Jews described Polish as their native language in a survey conducted before the war. The ambiguous phrasing of the questions asked suggests that this figure may be an understatement, and records of library borrowing indicate that Jews were reading more in Polish than in Yiddish. Nonetheless, most Jews spoke Yiddish primarily, and most who spoke Polish did so with an identifiable accent. Intermarriage and conversion were rare. Jews operated their own choirs, cooperatives, credit unions, cultural societies, hospitals, orchestras, orphanages, newspapers, publishing houses, sports clubs, and theater companies.

In much of the country, Jews and Poles were divided by residence and occupations. Although Jews came to 10 percent of the prewar national population, they made up 33 percent of the urban dwellers in western and central Poland and between 40 percent and 60 percent in different parts of the eastern half of the country, the area that fell to the Soviet Union in 1939. Although only 1 percent of the Jews were professionals, these Jews accounted for 63 percent of the people employed in commerce as of 1921, and 56 percent of the MDs ten years later, along with 43 percent of the teachers, 33.5 percent of the lawyers, and 22 percent of the journalists and publishers. On the eve of World War II, firms owned by Jews employed more than 40 percent of the Polish workforce, and Jews paid 35–40 percent of Poland's taxes. Class resentment and envy, in other words, along with ethnic distinctness and religious differences, created distance between the two communities. In Poland, the belief flourished that Jews had grown disproportionately wealthy by unfair collusion and thus that Poles were justified in repossessing what remained rightfully theirs. Yet much of the Jewish population remained poor, sometimes grindingly so, in part as a result of discriminatory employment and taxation policies enforced by the government. When World War II began, perhaps one-third of the Jews in Poland were dependent on relief aid, most of it coming from Jewish organizations in the United States.

All of this was less true in Warsaw than elsewhere: Jews in the nation's relatively cosmopolitan capital were more acculturated, more likely to speak Polish and interact with non-Jews, and less uniformly envied or resented. In fact, the relative frequency of contacts across communal lines largely accounts for the number of Jews concealed and saved in the city, which came to around 11,500, perhaps more. Gunnar S. Paulsson, the closest student of the rescue of Jews in Warsaw, has calculated that 70,000–90,000 non-Jews must have been involved in the effort. There were so many Jews successfully hiding in Warsaw in June 1943—probably more than 25,000—that the Nazis resorted to a trick. They claimed to have entry documents to various Latin American countries and to be willing to sell them to Jews who would then be exchanged with the Allies for German nationals abroad. The Germans even installed a number of Jews to live comfortably in the Hotel Polski, supposedly the collection point for the exchange. About 3,500 Jews emerged from hiding to fall into this trap and then die at Auschwitz.

Third, politics divided Poles and Jews, too. As early as the Polish-Soviet War of 1919–20, the Polish army interned its Jewish troops in a detention camp as security risks. During the interwar period, a greater percentage of Jews than non-Jews stood on the political left in Poland, and in the 1930s, Jews composed more than half of the Polish Communist Party's local leaders and most of the members of its Central Committee, though most Jews did not belong to the Party. Most Poles believed that Jews were pro-communist in 1939–41, and, given the Germans' intentions toward Jews, the belief was not unfounded. Yehuda Bauer's book on the Soviet-annexed portion of Poland shows that Jews there did recognize that for them the Russians presented the lesser of two evils in Eastern Europe and generally behaved with corresponding cooperativeness when the Soviets arrived. Writing of 1939 in 1943, Calel Perechodnik described the "immense happiness" with which Jews greeted the Soviet occupation of eastern Poland and added, "This is nothing to be surprised at. From one direction a German invaded, proclaiming slogans of merciless destruction and murder of all Jews. From the other direction, a Bolshevik invaded, proclaiming slogans that for him all people were equal under the law. There was nothing to compare here."

Given the depth of Polish hatred of Russia, born of both the long tsarist occupation in the nineteenth century and the Soviet deportation of some one-half million Poles from the annexed regions to Siberia in 1940–41, the general Jewish stance was bound to split the two communities even wider apart. In the case of Jedwabne, allegedly pro-Soviet behavior by local Jews in 1939–41 provided the pretext for the murders. And the massacre there was hardly an isolated occurrence: It was one of sixty-six nearly simultaneous such attacks in the province of Suwalki alone and some two hundred similar incidents in the Soviet-annexed eastern provinces. As Stefan Rowecki, a general in the Polish resistance, reported to the Polish government-in-exile in London on July 4, 1941, while the German armies were sweeping across the formerly Polish territory taken by the Soviets, many Poles were ready to offer "administrative and economic cooperation with the Germans in these areas . . . [as] a knee-jerk reaction of gratitude to their liberators from the Bolshevist oppression in which the Jews had played a big part." Ironically, as Yehuda Bauer has argued, two forces—the appeal of Soviet society to Jews in eastern Poland, especially to younger elements of the population, and the economic and antireligious measures that the communists adopted—undermined the cohesion of the Jewish community there between 1939 and 1941. This sapped its capacity to resist the Germans when the invasion came, just as divisions over the Soviet occupation eroded solidarity between Jews and Poles in the region.

Jan Kozielewski, a valiant non-Jewish resister during the war who operated under the code name Jan Karski, wrote a report to the government-in-exile in London in February 1940 that made clear how deep this sort of division between Jewish and non-Jewish Poles already had become. He concluded that "'[t]he solution of the Jewish question' by the Germans. . . . is creating something of a narrow bridge upon which the Germans and a large portion of Polish society are finding agreement." In consequence, almost everywhere outside of Warsaw, the principal resistance organization, the Armia Krajowa (AK), or Home Army, excluded Jews from its ranks on the assumption that they were security risks and potentially pro-Soviet. As the Russian armies pushed the Germans back toward Poland's borders, this attitude made some Home Army commanders, who were now fighting a two-front war against the Germans and the pro-Soviet Polish People's Army, even more hostile to Jews. As a result, no fewer than twenty-two of the Jewish inmates who escaped Sobibor during the uprising there in October 1943 died at Polish hands in subsequent days, at least eight of them killed by a unit of the Armia Krajowa. In August 1944, the Barwy Biale detachment of the Home Army, now part of the 2nd Legions Infantry Regiment, discovered three to four dozen Jewish escapees from the Skarzysko-Kamienna munitions factory hiding in a forest and slaughtered every one of them in cold blood.

Whether for religious, social, personal, or political reasons, many peasants and even resistance units in rural areas also routinely killed or turned in hundreds of Jews who tried to hide from the Nazis. In fact, these Poles did this increasingly as time passed and right up until the end of the German occupation. Zygmunt Klukowski, a physician in a small town near Lublin, wrote in his diary on November 26, 1942:

> The farmers are seizing the Jews hiding in the villages, out of fear of possible reprisals, and are taking them to the town, or sometimes simply killing them on the spot. In general, there has been a strange brutalization in relation to the Jews. A psychosis has seized hold of people, and, following the German example, they do not consider the Jews to be human, regarding them rather as an injurious pest that must be exterminated using all available means, like a dog sick with rabies or a rat.

On many occasions, the so-called Blue Police, the remaining Polish cops on the beat, and local units of voluntary firefighters were also involved in flushing out hidden Jews or picking them up after locals reported their locations. Whenever a successful hunt for Jews in hiding occurred, the local Polish leaders who led it got the right to distribute any property obtained, including the clothing of the victims. Meanwhile, the Germans offered rewards for each Jew delivered up, sometimes kilograms of sugar, sometimes money, and sometimes vodka, and threatened communities in which Germans found concealed Jews with collective punishment. Fear of such punishment had a lot to do with the collective psychosis that Klukowski noticed.

The evidence that is accumulating suggests that, at a conservative estimate, at least as many non-Jewish Poles turned Jews in as hid Jews from the Nazis. The vast majority of Polish Christians did neither of these things, but the minorities that helped or harmed Jews appear to have been unevenly balanced. Particularly in rural areas, the chances of being protected long enough to survive were slight. One study of what happened in Dabrowa Tarnowska County, about fifty miles east of Cracow, traced in the Polish and German archives and the records of postwar trials the destinies of some 337 Jews who tried to hide there after the liquidation of the ghettos. Fifty-one succeeded and emerged alive after the Soviet armies arrived, but 286 perished between 1942 and 1945. Among those killed, people who died at the hands of Polish civilians and police outnumbered those murdered by Germans 122 to 105. Tellingly, the underground press divided sharply in commenting on this sort of collaboration, with some resistance papers condemning it as shameful while others proclaimed, "[W]e have to punish those who want to hide Jews and declare them [that is, the protectors] traitors." That divergence may account for something else apparent from those figures regarding Dabrowa Tarnowska: Most people who hid Jews there did so in return for money or other payments, yet very few of the Jews hidden on that basis— only 9 percent—actually managed to survive the war. This suggests that they were turned in when they ran out of valuables to exchange for protection.

Fourth, during the German occupation, the Polish resistance did rather little to help Poland's Jews, even though it was fully and quickly informed, first, about the conditions in the ghettos and, later, about the deportations and the death camps. The AK did pass its knowledge, including specific references to gassings, to the Polish government-in-exile in London, which publicized it, and did make sure that the underground press within the country disseminated the information. Official proclamations warned Poles against collaborating with the persecution of Jews or blackmailing those in hiding, and late in the war AK units carried out executions for such offenses. Moreover, that government sent Jan Karski to Britain in November 1942 and on to the United States in July 1943 to brief leaders on what was happening in Poland. But in keeping with the Home Army's strategy of hoarding strength until Nazi rule in Poland was on the verge of collapse, the AK made no effort to impede the transports from Warsaw or to blow up the rail lines to Belzec, Sobibor, and Treblinka. For the same reason, the AK provided only modest support for the Warsaw Ghetto Uprising in the spring of 1943: a total of fifty pistols, fifty hand grenades, about ten pounds of explosives, two unsuccessful attempts during the fighting to blow holes in the ghetto walls, and several sniper attacks on German guards. This level of assistance actually marked the high point of AK help to Poland's Jews. After Tadeusz Komorowski succeeded the captured General Rowecki as commander of the Home Army in July 1943, its willingness to aid Poland's few surviving Jews declined. Instead, the AK displayed greater eagerness to combat the so-called banditry of Jewish fugitives and partisan units that survived by requisitioning from peasants.

Perhaps the most powerful demonstration of the halfhearted nature of the Polish resistance's support for Jews is the story of the organization that the government-in-exile formed for that very purpose. Zegota, the Committee to Aid the Jews, was supposed to do so by funding forged papers and hiding places. Not only did it come into existence rather late, in the autumn of 1942, after most Polish Jews had been killed, but its effectiveness was limited. Estimates of how many people the group actually saved vary widely but top out at several thousand, most of them children. Even the leaflet that called for public protests against the deportations and led to the formation of Zegota betrayed the ambivalence toward rescue that undermined such efforts. Zofia Kossak, the author, could not resist noting: "Our feelings toward the Jews have not changed. We continue to deem them political, economic, and ideological enemies of Poland." The Catholic Church hierarchy provided no support and took little notice of the organization, and most of its funds—certainly most of those that actually got to Poland—came from Jewish sources abroad, not the London-based Polish government. One reason for this was that the faction of the National Party in the Polish government-in-exile refused to join or support Zegota and kept up a constant drumbeat of underground antisemitic propaganda.

The National Party's presence and actions undermined the government-in-exile's declarations that postwar Poland would be a state in which all citizens had equal rights. In fact, one of the most remarkable aspects of the Holocaust in Poland is how little impact the carnage had on the attitudes that had prevailed toward the nation's Jews before World War II. A survey of the leaders of thirteen political groups in the Polish resistance at the end of 1943 established that they favored liquidation or emigration of the Jews over integration and equality in a postwar state by a ratio of nine to four. Even among political prisoners in the concentration camps, according to Hermann Langbein, the persistent antisemitism of the Poles stood out.

Fifth, precisely because there were more Jews in Poland than anywhere else, more people stood to gain by their disappearance than anywhere else, and this, too, undercut any sense of solidarity. In fact, the Nazis consciously set out to buy the loyalty of non-Jews, especially in the regions conquered from the USSR in 1941, by swiftly giving away Jews' household possessions to the local populations and by turning schools, community houses, synagogues, and hospitals into service facilities for the local non-Jewish population. And even the death camps became sources of local enrichment, since the surrounding villages profited from the spending of guards and sometimes from the black market in goods taken from the people killed. Thanks to rumors that spread through the occupied country, currency and jewelry dealers set up shop around Treblinka in 1942–43, and prostitutes were drawn to the area. The extent to which many ordinary Polish citizens benefited from the murders is apparent even today in the Polish restitution laws, which stipulate that no one can reclaim property stolen from Jews unless the applicant is a resident of Poland. Given that most surviving Jews left after 1945 or were driven out by the late 1960s, this law effectively protects a massive degree of theft, and it was designed to do so precisely because the theft was so massive.

Sixth, antisemitism in Poland outlasted the Holocaust and continued afterward. Nechama Tec, who studied rescuers and who survived wartime Poland thanks to several of them, recalls in her memoir, *Dry Tears*, that the first thing her protectors asked of her after the Russians liberated their town was not to tell anyone who had hidden her. Many other hidden children in Poland have reported the same thing, and when the Jewish Historical Commission in Cracow began to publish the names of rescuers in 1947, many of them requested that the organization omit them in the future. Polish rescuers often expected disdain from their neighbors for their kindness, not praise or respect, and often got what they expected. The only family to hide Jews from the massacre in Jedwabne in 1941 experienced so much disapproval after the war that most of the members emigrated to Chicago.

Multiple pogroms broke out in Poland after the war; one of them took the life of Chaim Hirszman, one of only two survivors of Belzec. The Kielce pogrom of 1946 erupted when someone claimed that the Jews who had returned to live in the city's Jewish community center had kidnapped and killed a gentile child, just as the ancient blood libel alleged. Jan Gross, who has closely studied what happened in a book called *Fear*, argues that the pogrom was not just an outbreak of endemic Jew hatred but also an attempt to remove witnesses to the extent of previous Polish complicity in the Holocaust. Indeed, a good deal of prosopographical evidence suggests that some of the most enthusiastic Polish antisemites in 1942 and 1946 tried to cover their tracks after the war by becoming some of the most enthusiastic Polish collaborators with communism. Meanwhile, other antisemites simply carried on the old tradition of depicting Jews as people ready to betray Poland to the Reds and spread stories—once more exaggerated, but not completely unfounded—of Jewish "overrepresentation" in the communist security services.

As a result of the pervasively antisemitic atmosphere, some 250,000 Jews, including many who had just returned to the country from their earlier refuge in the Soviet Union, fled westward from Poland in the first years after the war ended. In the late 1960s, the communist government of postwar Poland organized a so-called anti-Zionist campaign, largely in order to divert mounting popular unrest but also to disprove the regime's lingering reputation with the Polish public as a tool of Jews. After 1989 and the fall of communism in Poland, Lech Walesa, the hero of the Solidarity movement, showed how persistent antisemitism remained in parts of Polish society. He tried to discredit a competing candidate for the presidency of Poland by asserting that he was of Jewish descent and later dismissed Jan Gross's findings about Jedwabne as the work of "a Jew who tries to make money."

Seventh, more Poles are commemorated at Yad Vashem for saving Jews than any other nationality. In part, this simply follows from the fact that Jews were more numerous in Poland than anywhere else, so even a lower than average number of would-be rescuers would have saved more people or died trying than elsewhere. Still, Tec's studies and those of other scholars contain thousands of stories of Polish courage in defense of Jews in a place where this was especially dangerous. Emanuel Ringelblum, the creator of the Oyneg Shabes archive in the Warsaw ghetto, was hidden, along with his wife and son and thirty-four other Jews, in a hideout prepared and owned by a non-Jew named Mieczyslaw Wolski. He and his nephew were killed with those Jews when the Germans discovered the bunker in March 1944. Polish and German researchers have identified reliably almost 1,000 cases of Poles executed for helping Jews in hiding, nearly all of them not included in the Yad Vashem total.

So, to what conclusion do these seven points lead? Above all, to a call for understanding and for suspending the mutual blaming and competing claims to having suffered worst. The key point to remember is that the Nazis created a Hobbesian world in annexed and occupied Poland, where no indigenous government existed to exert restraint and different parts of the population were constantly pitted against each other in a desperate struggle to survive. This was not fertile ground for the growth of a sense of common interest. The environment was far more conducive to preoccupation with one's own interests and taking advantage of opportunities. That is why the fact that the Nazis victimized Poles in many ways did not immunize some Poles from several sorts of complicity in the Germans' crimes.

Achieving this kind of balanced perspective has been and will continue to be much harder for people in Poland than it should be for those living elsewhere. This is because interpreting a nation's history is generally a high-stakes political game to its citizens; as William Faulkner famously observed, "The past is never dead. It's not even past." Ever since 1945, descriptions of non-Jewish Poles' behavior toward Jewish ones during the Holocaust have provoked considerable controversy in Poland. People on the left, considering themselves increasingly secular and progressive and perhaps less embittered by the experience and memory of communism, have dwelled upon the hostility or indifference of the Catholic Church and the antipathy of the Home Army toward Jews. People on the right, closely identified with Catholicism and traditional values and still mistrusting the supposed Jewish-Bolshevik connection, have focused on every remotely demonstrable image of Christian charity and national generosity toward persecuted people in wartime Poland. Because these views of history function as sources of both identity and legitimacy in the present, Poles will continue to argue intensely over who did what to whom on their soil in the years 1939–45.

But the rest of us should have less difficulty acknowledging and empathizing with the suffering of nearly all parties, without asserting a false equivalence. The fate of the non-Jews who largely survived the war was not the same as that of the Jews who were, at least in Poland, virtually wiped out. Jews in occupied Poland were fifteen times more likely to be killed than non-Jews. And an ideological reason accounts for the difference: In the Nazi New Order, the Jews were destined for swift death, the Poles for enslavement and exploitation, but for extinction only when the time came that Germany no longer needed their labor.

CHAPTER 7

ONLOOKERS:
Why Such Limited
Help from Outside?

IF THE NAZIS meant what they said during the 1930s, namely that their goal was to "remove" Jews from German territory, then the best chance to save large numbers of Jews from what later became the Holocaust lay in their escape to other countries. As it happened, 60 percent of the Jews of Germany did get away in this fashion, along with 67 percent of the Jews of Austria, and about 25 percent of the Jews in Bohemia and Moravia. But very few Jews in Hitler's path toward living space could emigrate in the 1930s—even fewer once the murders began. Instead, Jews discovered that no outside power would or later could offer them much beyond rhetorical support and promises of reprisal, and even this sort of backing was quite measured. Why couldn't more people get out of harm's way? Why did the Jews receive such limited help?

The short answer is that a combination of antisemitism and economic and political interests worked to restrict the admission of Jews to other countries throughout the Holocaust and to inhibit other action on their behalf. Sooner or later, every nation that might have helped decided that it had higher priorities than aiding or defending Jews. So did the League of Nations, headquartered in Geneva; most non-governmental organizations, such as the International Olympic Committee and the International Committee of the Red Cross; and almost every transnational religious institution, including the Catholic Church. The result was an erratic line of possibility for those persecuted within Germany's borders. Opportunities to get out of Nazi hands were widest in 1933–34 and again in 1938–39, but very narrow in the years in between or afterward. For the Jews of Eastern and southeastern Europe in the 1930s, the prospects were even worse.

PREWAR EVASIONS

The initial opportunity for Germany's Jews stemmed from the hospitality of four democracies on the Reich's periphery: France, the Netherlands, Belgium, and Czechoslovakia. Revulsion at Nazi brutality arose in all four places, reinforced, in the case of the French, who took in 55,000 Jews between 1933 and 1939, by the same receptiveness to other immigrants that France had shown since the Great War depleted the nation's population. But in all four instances, sympathy declined over time, especially in France, where the late onset of the Depression compared to other countries meant that hostility to economic competition from refugees peaked just as the need for asylum did. By the mid-1930s, France enacted various rules that made immigration less appealing, restricting the practice of medicine to citizens and placing quotas on foreign artisans who could enter the country, for example.

After 1936, four other arguments arose and gradually narrowed the passage through France's gates. First, the popularity of the policy of appeasing Nazi Germany—that is, allowing changes to some of the terms of the Versailles Treaty in order to avoid war—made the presence of Jewish refugees politically inconvenient. Second, the election in 1936 of Léon Blum, a Jew, as prime minister of a leftist government called the Popular Front mobilized antisemitic feeling among French conservatives. Third, opponents of immigration stoked suspicion that escapees from Nazi Germany would include spies who would undermine French security. And fourth, critics pointed out that letting in German refugees would lead to admitting far more numerous Jews seeking to escape from Poland. The influential journalist Emmanuel Berl, himself a Jew, argued in November 1938 that such people were "taken as a whole not very desirable." Opening the borders to them, he said, would be an act of "crazy generosity." Even the French Jewish Committee split over the advisability of increasing Jewish immigration and failed to make a strong case for it. After *Kristallnacht*, France actually made getting into and staying in that country more, not less, difficult for refugees, imposed prison sentences on illegal residents, and even sentenced the aunt and uncle of Herschel Grynszpan to six months in prison for having let him live in their home as an unauthorized immigrant.

The trend of events in the Netherlands, Belgium, and Czechoslovakia was similar, though not for exactly the same reasons. In Holland, the general policy was to take in any refugees who crossed the border but to make sure that the local Jewish community, through its Jewish Refugee Committee, formed in 1933, paid for their upkeep, and then to hasten them on their way. Thus the Dutch government progressively narrowed work opportunities for Jews in Holland during the 1930s. The 22,000 German Jews who were in or had passed through the Netherlands by the end of 1937 depended almost completely on charity, much of it obtained from the American Jewish Joint Distribution Committee, usually referred to as "the Joint." The name reflected the organization's origins as an alliance of philanthropic groups associated with differing strains of political and religious opinion within the American Jewish community. Following the German pogrom of November 1938, the Dutch government decided to intern all new immigrants in camps for which the Refugee Committee would have to provide a million guilders ($550,000 at the time) in construction and maintenance funds. Though Holland generally did not enforce its threat to turn away all refugees at its borders beginning in December 1938, construction of a central internment camp at Westerbork began for the estimated 23,000 to 30,000 German Jewish refugees in the country as of early 1939. Of that number, 7,000–8,000 got away before the Germans invaded in May 1940. Belgium also took in about 30,000 German Jews between 1933 and 1939, about half before and half after the pogrom, but also made entering the country and staying progressively more difficult. Statistics from Czechoslovakia highlight its hardening policies: 60,000 Austrian Jews applied for residence following the pogrom of November 1938, but only about 6,000 got in, most of them illegally. In short, the chances of finding refuge in Western Europe declined as desperation to escape Nazi Germany rose.

Switzerland provided the most glaring illustration of this tendency to close the escape hatches precisely when they were most needed. Never very receptive to Jewish refugees during the 1930s, thanks largely to the efforts of an antisemite named Heinrich Rothmund, who headed the Swiss Federal Police for Foreigners, the country actually sealed its borders on August 19, 1938, and deployed troops to catch and repatriate anyone trying to enter from Nazi-occupied Austria without the appropriate visa. Paul Grüninger, a courageous police captain in the frontier canton of St. Gallen, was one of the rare officials who refused to comply with these instructions. As a result, about 1,000 Jewish refugees slipped into Switzerland via his jurisdiction before his conduct cost him his job early in 1939. Meanwhile, in order to preserve normal tourist traffic with Nazi Germany while keeping Jews from there out, the Swiss persuaded the Germans to stamp the passports of German Jews with a large *J* and began categorically refusing them admission. One month later, in October 1938, the Swedes adopted the same practice.

Throughout the 1930s, the USSR declined to offer a haven to all but a handful of ranking Jewish communists. The Soviet Union declared that Jewish refugees were unsuited to life in an unfamiliar socialist society and, in any case, not the USSR's responsibility, since their persecution was a product of capitalist quarreling. From September 1935 on, Jews entering the socialist motherland had to satisfy several discouraging and, at least in part, mutually contradictory preconditions: proletarian ancestry, possession of substantial amounts of money, and willingness to become Soviet citizens and perform manual labor on construction sites in northern or eastern parts of the USSR.

Britain saw its role in the crisis of German Jewry as that of a "transit nation," one that might allow refugees to land on the "tight little island" but not to stay very long. Given the reluctance of the Dominions, such as Canada, Australia, New Zealand, and South Africa, to provide destinations—South Africa, for example, accepted only 6,000–7,000 Jewish refugees during the 1930s and Canada fewer than 5,000 in the entire period of 1933–45, including a grand total of only 23 from Germany and Austria during 1938, the year of the *Kristallnacht* pogrom—this self-image meant that Britain was not a frequent refuge for Jews seeking to get out of Germany. The country took in only about 70,000 European Jews during the 1930s, only 10,000 of them up until the end of 1937, and fully 50,000 of them just in the short time from January to September 1939, including some 10,000 young people on the famous *Kindertransport*, the Children's Transport.

Moreover, Britain pursued similarly restrictive policies in Palestine, the territory in the Middle East from which the Romans had driven most Jews in ancient times and to which Zionists wanted to return, but which for the present was subject to British rule under a mandate from the League of Nations. To be sure, in the Balfour Declaration of 1917, the British government had declared its rhetorical support for a future "national home for the Jewish people" in the region, largely and cynically for two reasons. First, Britain wanted to bolster its claims to the territory after the war. Second, the British cabinet hoped the declaration would prompt allegedly influential Jews in the United States and elsewhere to support the countries then at war with Germany and Austria. Ironically, Edwin Montagu, the only Jewish member of the cabinet at the time, voted against the declaration, in part because he was appalled by the antisemitic overtones of this fantasy of Jewish power, in part because he rejected Zionism as likely to bring strife and misery to Palestine. Partly in consequence of the declaration, the Jewish population in the region rose to around 400,000 by the mid-1930s. This growth set off the violent backlash that Montagu had predicted in the form of the Arab Revolt (1936–39). Henceforth, the British thought that their control, not only of Palestine but also of the Suez Canal, the jugular vein of the British Empire, depended on placating Arab opinion, so they reduced the already low permissible annual quota of Jewish immigrants. Whereas 149,076 Jews from all countries got into Palestine from 1933 to 1935, only 54,899 did in 1936–38. The annual intake rose again in 1939, but only to 31,195, and a government white paper of May 1939, issued just after the revolt finally was suppressed, set the quota for the ensuing five years at 15,000 per annum for a total of only 75,000 more places, after which Jewish immigration to the region would cease altogether. The British explicitly stated that their goal was to confine the Jewish proportion of the population in Palestine to one-third.

In Britain, as virtually everywhere else, the people who made these restrictive policies claimed to be haunted by the specter of what might happen if they were more generous. They feared that more open borders would prompt Eastern European governments, especially those in Poland, Hungary, Romania, and Lithuania, to enact even more antisemitic measures than they already had and thus to set off an exodus of almost five million Jews, which is to say 5.5 times the combined Jewish population of Germany, Austria, and western Czechoslovakia in 1933. Such concerns were not imaginary. At the meeting of the Council of the League of Nations in May 1938, Poland and Romania explicitly expressed the desire to reduce the size of their Jewish populations and requested aid in doing so. The following October, Poland's ambassador in London tried to blackmail Britain into allowing 100,000 Polish Jews into its colonies per year by stating that otherwise his government would be "inevitably forced to adopt the same kind of policy as the German government."

The fate of these Eastern European Jews also haunted the Jewish Agency in Palestine, to which the British occupation authority delegated the distribution of the annual allotment of legal entry permits, and that fact further narrowed the access of German Jews to the region. Because the Jews of Poland and Romania seemed equally in danger but were historically more pro-Zionist and currently had fewer avenues of escape than the Jews of Germany, the agency restricted the latter population's share of the permits awarded annually from 1933 to 1938 to an average of only 22 percent. The proportion exceeded one-third in only the last of those years, when it topped 40 percent. In short, Nazi racism set off a vicious circle in which partial success in driving Jews out of Germany encouraged imitation by bigots in countries to the east that, in turn, pressured potentially hospitable places into scaling back possible exit opportunities for German Jews.

Fear of a refugee flood also prevailed in the United States, along with other obstacles to generosity toward refugees from Nazi persecution. The problem was not at the top of the American government; President Franklin D. Roosevelt was no antisemite—indeed, he appointed more Jews to senior positions in government than any president before him. He was anti-German, an attitude born of both bad experiences with a German governess in his youth and his service as assistant secretary of the navy while the United States fought Germany in 1917–18. But existing American law and public opinion hamstrung him from doing much to help Jewish refugees during the 1930s, and he avoided taking political risks for the sake of Jews abroad.

The legal obstacles stemmed from the quota system of immigration that the United States introduced during the 1920s. It set a maximum total of 150,000 legal entrants to the country annually and apportioned that figure almost entirely among European nations according to the share of the American population that traced its descent to each of them in the census of 1890. The year was not an accidental or arbitrary choice but an intentional and eugenicist one. Congress selected 1890 because it antedated a great influx of immigration from Italy, the Balkans, and Russia around the turn of the century. America's legislators wanted to give preference to predominantly White Anglo-Saxon Protestants over all others. Ironically, this resulted in a relatively large permissible number of arrivals from Germany per year, 25,957 people—relatively large as a share of the number of entrants allowed annually (more than one-sixth) but, of course, tiny in relation to the need in the 1930s, since Germany had 560,000 inhabitants whom the Nazis considered Jews when Hitler came to power and later added some 300,000 Jews in Austria, the Sudetenland, and Bohemia-Moravia. At almost 26,000 German Jewish immigrants a year, admitting everyone in this population would have required thirty-three years; admitting even the almost 310,000 German, Austrian, and Czech Jews who actually applied for entrance by 1939 would have required almost twelve years.

But the United States had no intention of admitting the full quota of German immigrants annually, let alone of allowing Jews to fill the full allotment. In fact, from 1933 to 1939, when the quota permitted the admission of up to 156,000 people, the United States let in only 77,000, including about 65,000 Jews. From all of Europe in this interval, the United States took in only 92,000 Jews. If one extends the time frame to 1933–44, the immigration total for America is probably about 225,000 Jews from all of Europe, including

120,000 Jews from Germany and Austria, and the number of unused German quota slots rises to 190,000.

These admission figures are paltry compared to the European Jewish population of nine million in 1939 or the six million Jews killed in the Holocaust. But 225,000 is three times the number of people Great Britain took in and almost fifty times the number that Canada accepted; 120,000 Jews is more than any other country admitted from the German Reich; the number the United States took rose annually from 1933 to 1940; and the total admitted from 1937 to 1941 was more than four times the total of the preceding four years. In 1938, President Franklin Roosevelt combined the immigration quotas for Germany and Austria to raise the permissible number of entrants to 27,370 and thus improve the odds of Jews getting out, and in 1939, he issued an executive order indefinitely extending the visitors' visas of all Jews then in the United States, thereby saving another 15,000 Jews from repatriation and death. The most authoritative study of FDR and the Jews concludes that between 1937 and 1941, "FDR's second-term policies likely helped save the lives of well over 100,000 Jews." In other words, America performed terribly in the face of the crisis of European Jewry, except in comparison to every other country. Moreover, at least until World War II broke out, American receptivity gradually increased, precisely as refuge in Europe was growing generally harder to find.

Why didn't the United States do better? The short answer is that both powerful individuals and public opinion opposed doing better, with the results that no serious move to change the immigration quotas arose, and strict enforcement of immigration rules held down the numbers admitted until very late during the 1930s. American policy was not as harsh as British, which assured that that country admitted more than five-sevenths of its total refugees at the last minute before World War II began. Still, in the United States, the comparable figure was one-half in the short interval between *Kristallnacht* and mid-1939.

Opposition to immigration fed on three primary causes: fear of economic competition, popular nativism and isolationism, and elite antisemitism. The fear of economic competition was expressed in many quarters. For example, the dentists of Westchester County lobbied FDR's political advisor Samuel Rosenman to prevent the admission of any more refugee dentists into the country, and the national conventions of the Veterans of Foreign Wars and the American Legion passed resolutions against further immigration so long as unemployment persisted in the United States. Such resistance resulted in strict enforcement of the Likely to Become a Public Charge, or LPC, rule, which denied immigration to people considered so lacking in funds that they would become dependent on welfare. U.S. consular officials abroad, who received applications to immigrate, required extensive data on each person's likely financial resources after arrival and generally set, as their superiors in Washington required, a high standard for economic security before granting a visa. Frances Perkins, the secretary of labor, argued vehemently for a relaxation of these standards, but the State Department argued equally forcefully in their favor. FDR sided with State except in two brief intervals, one during late 1936 and the second in 1938–39 after the *Anschluss* and *Kristallnacht*.

The rationale behind FDR's stance was straightforward: The American public opposed letting more people in. Throughout the 1930s, every national public opinion poll on the question showed that two-thirds to three-quarters or more of Americans rejected the relaxation of the quotas and the admission of more refugees. As a result, early in 1939, Congress defeated the Wagner-Rogers Bill, which would have admitted 20,000 Jewish children under the age of fourteen to the United States. Not only was the general public hard-hearted, but student opinion followed: the *Daily Northwestern* of December 13, 1938, reported that 68 percent of American students were against more admissions for fear of "imperiling U.S. living conditions." The sad truth is that virtually no politician outside of a few urban centers on the East Coast could get elected in the United States during the 1930s on a platform of offering asylum to the Jews of Europe. FDR was a politician who had to win across the nation, not just in these pockets of empathy.

Nativism and isolationism were revved up by the radio broadcasts of a Detroit-area priest named Father Charles Coughlin, who peddled the same charge against Jews that others had leveled at his Irish forebears decades earlier, namely that they could not fit into American life. He had an audience of three million fans listening weekly and cited (and republished) the infamous *Protocols of the Elders of Zion* to make his point. The Catholic hierarchy did not muzzle him until 1942. Meanwhile, far more mainstream figures played on American antisemitism, including those leaders of the Republican Party who declared that, thanks to FDR's appointment of many Jews to office, he was offering the public, not the New Deal but the Jew Deal. Given such attitudes, perhaps one should not be surprised that a poll in 1938 found that 58 percent of Americans considered Jews in Europe at least "partly" at fault for their own persecution. Another survey in July 1939 showed that 32 percent of Americans believed Jews had too much influence in business, while another 10 percent favored deporting Jews. The prevalence of these views caused even the proponents of helping Jewish refugees to sanitize their vocabulary and to speak of "persecutees" who needed help, not of Jews.

A telling illustration of the forms antisemitism could take comes from the history of the university where I taught for thirty-six years, which had restrictions on the number of Jews admitted annually until the 1960s. In January 1939, the *Daily Northwestern* ran an article about a class in the Medill School of Journalism that had compiled a list of the ten greatest news stories of 1938. The group considered worthy of inclusion such by now long forgotten events as the wrong-way flight of Douglas Corrigan—he ostensibly set out to fly to California from New York but went to Ireland instead—and the Lima Conference of Pan-American states, but not the *Kristallnacht* pogrom, even though the burning of the synagogues in Germany in November 1938 had made the front page of the *Chicago Tribune*. On the almost universally white and predominantly Protestant students of Medill, the attack on Jews in Germany seems hardly to have registered.

Attitudes at Northwestern testified to the power of antisemitism among American elites in the 1930s. Especially important as a representative of this current was an assistant secretary of state with the sonorously white Anglo-Saxon Protestant name of Breckenridge Long. A former ambassador to Italy and a fervent admirer of Mussolini, he fought hard to keep down the number of Jews admitted to the United States annually. His most convenient and effective argument was the possibility that relatives remaining in Germany could be used to blackmail refugee Jews into becoming spies for the Reich. Every train or boat carrying Jews out of Nazi Europe, he said, "is a perfect opening to Germany to load the United States with agents." As a result, early in June 1941, the U.S. State Department instructed its consuls worldwide to deny visas to foreigners who had close relatives in Germany or the countries it controlled.

Against these impediments to accepting more refugees, no political force arose that was strong enough to prevail. FDR chose at key moments to offer modest help, but he did not want to incur political costs. Immediately after the *Anschluss*, he asked his cabinet whether Congress would support an expansion of the German immigration quota but backed off when the members answered in the negative. He became even more cautious after the Republicans, including many isolationists, gained eighty-one seats in the House and eight in the Senate the following November, a few days before *Kristallnacht*. In 1939, he encouraged several Latin American states, notably Bolivia, Brazil, the Dominican Republic, and Paraguay, to admit more Jewish refugees. But he also refused to issue a special order to let the refugee ship *St. Louis* land in the United States or even in the U.S. Virgin Islands, as offered by that territory's governor and legislative assembly and advocated by two members of FDR's cabinet. He also declined to endorse the Wagner-Rogers Bill. Taking the long view, he decided that such actions would undermine his effort to get Congress to repeal America's Neutrality Acts and thus would prevent him from helping countries to resist Hitler's aggression later. Shortly thereafter, he backed away from the idea of using Alaska as a refuge for Jews once he learned that he would then have to set up new restrictions on travel between there and the continental United States. At a press conference in June 1940, he even repeated Long's claim that the German government was threatening to shoot the relatives still in the Reich of refugees who declined to work as spies for Germany. Finally, in March 1941, FDR did nothing to reverse the U.S. Maritime Commission's denial of permission for an ocean liner, the *S.S. Washington*, with a capacity of 1,700 passengers, to add a direct route to New York from Lisbon, almost the last escape hatch from Europe.

Interestingly enough, German intelligence offices in occupied Holland did concoct a scheme for smuggling agents into the Americas under the cover of releasing Jews, and some 486 of them got permission to leave the Netherlands for Spain, the Caribbean, and South America between May 1941 and January 1942. But in view of the time frame, this project clearly was an outgrowth of Long's often publicly expressed fears as much as a vindication of them.

The American Jewish community proved on its own incapable of rallying popular solidarity with Europe's Jews. Though Jews then constituted a slightly larger percentage of the U.S. population than they do now, they were divided by heritage between the American Jewish Committee, whose members traced their lineage back to Germany for the most part, and the American Jewish Congress, headed by Stephen Wise, whose members hailed primarily from Eastern Europe. The former group feared that too much agitation for Jewish immigration would stoke antisemitism and preferred behind the scenes, high-level efforts to exert influence. The latter group favored public rallies and boycotts of German goods to put pressure on the Nazi regime. Neither organization had much effect on U.S. policy toward refugees. The two groups also differed in their attitudes toward the creation of a Jewish state: the committee's leaders were non-Zionist or sometimes anti-Zionist, whereas the congress favored settlement and eventually a Jewish state in Palestine. That stance on the part of the congress meant that it had conflicting priorities: Escape to the United States was not escape to the prospective Jewish homeland, so it was both desirable and not. Even David Ben-Gurion, the principal Jewish leader in Palestine, feared that too much receptivity to Jewish refugees elsewhere would endanger the Zionist project. Conversely, the American Jewish Joint Distribution Committee, dominated by the American Jewish Committee, preferred to concentrate its resources on supporting the increasingly impoverished German and Eastern European Jewish communities and on sustaining refugees in Europe and the Western Hemisphere rather than on aiding immigration to Palestine.

The difficulties of getting out of Germany gave rise to an improbable escape route in late 1938, one of the few that remained available in the early years of World War II. Perhaps 17,000–20,000 European Jews found refuge in Shanghai, on China's east coast, more specifically in the part of the city called the International Settlement, which a consortium of eleven countries ruled until December 1941, when Japanese troops marched in. People who reached the International Settlement needed no visa to enter, just transit visas through any countries en route, which were usually the USSR plus the Japanese puppet state of Manchukuo, in northern China, and both were happy to collect the fees. The Japanese occupiers confined the Jews to a slum neighborhood called Hongkew, where most of them survived the war through complicated transfers of aid from the Joint Distribution Committee.

The futile Evian Conference of 1938 reflected a widespread tendency of nations to pass the buck when it came to offering a haven to Jews. The outcome confirmed the observation two years earlier by

Chaim Weizmann, the president of the World Zionist Organization, that Jews confronted a globe "divided into places where they cannot live and places they cannot enter." During the late 1930s, as historian Bernard Wasserstein writes, "Dutch Guiana, Angola, Cyprus, the Philippines, the Belgian Congo, the Dominican Republic, Mexico, Haiti, Ethiopia—each was broached, researched, and hailed as a potential haven. In each case obstacles were discovered and globes twirled again, until eyes fixed anew on the latest, ever more improbable land of redemption." In view of all this, the remarkable thing is how many people got out, not how few. The fate of the passengers on the refugee ship *St. Louis* was prototypical, in this sense. Of the 937 Jews on board, 28 got off in Cuba, and one committed suicide. Of the 908 remaining, 620 were admitted to France, Belgium, and Holland, where 365 survived the war. Britain admitted 288, all of whom were similarly fortunate. In short, about three-quarters of the once apparently doomed passengers in fact found secure refuge from the Germans, and about half eventually found their way to the United States. But these were German Jews, and the large share of them who got out mirrored the relatively high overall escape rate of their fellows. Farther east, the chances were far worse. In the year 1937, for example, only 9,000 Jews managed to emigrate legally from Poland to any new homeland, and the annual U.S. immigration quota for that country came to only about 6,000 people.

A similar sense of ambiguity surrounds the actions of another international player that might have done more to help the Jews in the 1930s, namely the Roman Catholic Church, especially its spiritual head in the Vatican. The Church's record has both up and down sides, but in the end, like most of the countries discussed thus far, it looked out for itself first and did not do nearly as much not only as it could have done but also as its leaders at one time or another actually thought of doing.

From the start, the Church's leaders in Rome recognized that Nazism represented a barbaric force. They had to be talked into

signing the Concordat with Hitler in July 1933 by Germany's Catholic cardinals, a majority of whom favored the agreement as the only
way to limit Nazi incursions on Church activities. Almost immediately after Hitler came to power, a group of Jesuits began drafting
a condemnation of Nazism for the pope to issue. Four years later,
this document became the encyclical entitled *Mit brennender Sorge*
(*With Burning Sorrow* is the official translation, but *Sorge* actually
means "concern" or "anxiety"). Despite that dramatic label, the
wording was considerably watered-down from what the Jesuits had
prepared. Though it denounced the glorification of race and nation
as "idolatrous," the text did not mention Nazism by name and was
far less critical of Germany's ruling regime than another encyclical
condemning communism issued only a few days earlier. The juxta-
position was telling: However much the Church's leaders in Rome
despised Nazism, they always hated and feared communism more,
and this fact consistently caused the Vatican to pull its punches in
dealing with Hitler's regime. When the Nuremberg Laws appeared
in 1935, the Church said nothing. It was likewise silent in 1938,
when Nazi mobs burned synagogues, smashed homes and shops,
and arrested and beat Jews.

Church authorities hardly could mount a full-throated defense of
Jewry from persecution because they had so long advocated and indeed
enforced forms of it. As Mussolini pointed out when he inaugurated
Italy's first antisemitic laws in 1938—which excluded Jews from the
Fascist Party, the military, and public education, ejected them from
honorary societies, revoked grants of citizenship to them since 1919,
and limited the size of businesses or estates they could own—these
restrictions were not as severe as the ones the popes had imposed in
the lands they ruled until 1870, including the city of Rome. Moreover,
the limits on Jewish activity were quite similar to those that major
Catholic publications, including *La Civiltà Cattolica*, the biweekly
Jesuit publication whose contents had to be cleared by the Vatican
before printing, had been advocating for more than fifty years. Behind

that advocacy stood the Church's traditional conviction that contact with Jews could corrupt the faith of believers, now reinforced by the view that Jews, Freemasons, and Bolsheviks constituted an unholy modern and conspiratorial alliance against all that the Holy Mother Church stood for. Shortly before the publication of *Mit brennender Sorge*, *La Civiltà Cattolica* published "The Jewish Question," an article that denounced the Jews' supposed "domination over money and their preponderance in socialism and communism" and concluded by suggesting that the only way to contain their influence was to strip them of citizenship in Christian nations. In May 1937, another article began with this sentence, "It is an evident fact that the Jews are a disruptive element due to their spirit of domination and their preponderance in revolutionary movements," and went on to advocate segregating Jews from Christians. And, in mid-July 1938, the journal wrote of the Jews' "messianic craving for world domination" before endorsing the recent enactment of laws in Hungary designed to restrict Jews' professional opportunities.

Nonetheless, Pope Pius XI, who reigned until February 1939 and grew increasingly appalled at Nazi violations of the terms of the Concordat and glorification of the Aryan race, contemplated speaking out. In September 1938, he told a group of Belgians visiting the Vatican, "antisemitism is inadmissible. Spiritually, we are all Semites," and just before Christmas that year, he referred to the Nazi swastika, for which the German word is *Hakenkreuz* (hooked cross), as "a cross that is the enemy of the Cross of Christ." But these remarks remained known only to the few who heard them and passed them on. Temporizers and outright antisemites in the Vatican not only made sure of that but also undercut an initiative the pope had taken the previous June, when he asked an American Jesuit named John LaFarge to draft an encyclical tentatively titled "The Unity of the Human Race." Wlodzimierz Ledochowski, the vehemently antisemitic head of the Jesuit order, first assigned two more traditionalist clergymen to assist LaFarge and then held up the completed text for months before reluctantly passing it on in January 1939, less than a month before the pope died. The document went no further than his bedside table. The text has survived, however, and it suggests that neither the Church nor the reigning pope could break free of the policy of caution toward Nazism or the doctrinal inheritance of certain forms of antisemitism. The text contained an ambivalent argument that on the one hand condemned racism as heretical and called for an end to the persecution of the Jews, but on the other, repeatedly referred to the supposed moral failings of Jews and the danger to the faithful of paying attention to or coming into close contact with them.

Even that was too much criticism of Nazi racism for Pius XI's successor, the former Vatican secretary of state Cardinal Eugenio Pacelli, who took the papal name of Pius XII. In 1936, Pacelli had opposed issuing *Mit brennender Sorge* as an encyclical to be read in German churches and suggested a mere pastoral letter to just the German bishops. Not without reason was he the candidate the Nazi envoys in Rome hoped would prevail in the conclave that chose the new pope. After his election on the third ballot, in March 1939, he destroyed not only all the copies of his predecessor's draft encyclical that his aides could find, but also the very plates on which a speech Pius XI had been planning on the subject had been printed. A Roman aristocrat by descent and a diplomat by training, Pius XII was a deeply cautious and conservative man with regard to both politics and theology. As the papal nuncio in Germany prior to Hitler's accession, he had grown fond of the country and critical of the Catholic Center Party for its participation in democratic politics, which he disliked, and for its longtime opposition to becoming part of a coalition government with the Nazis, which he advocated. Though not happy with the form the Concordat took and disappointed that it contained no protection for Jewish converts to Catholicism, he negotiated the agreement and then clung to it in subsequent years as the best hope for the Church's survival in the Third Reich. Above all, he abhorred "godless communism" and sought to coexist with any political regime that combated it.

Pius XII considered his chief duty to be to the Church and to Catholics, not to suffering people in general, and some critics have reproached him therefore for practicing parochial rather than pastoral politics. Not all of these critics have spoken in hindsight or from outside the Church. Some of the leading German clerics, notably Bishop Konrad von Preysing in Berlin, advised him to display greater firmness in dealing with the Nazi regime and to express greater solidarity with German Jews, but others overrode such arguments. The dominant voice was that of Cardinal Adolf Bertram in Breslau, who feared provoking a renewed persecution of the Catholic Church in Germany along the lines of Chancellor Otto von Bismarck's *Kulturkampf* during the 1880s. Thus, although Preysing, for example, organized various efforts to help Jews in Berlin, especially ones who had converted to Christianity, the Vatican encouraged neither these actions nor their imitation by other dioceses.

To appreciate the constraints that Church leaders felt in the 1930s and 1940s, one has to grasp the importance of the sacraments in Catholic religious teaching. Broadly speaking, the Church's doctrine was "no salvation without the sacraments"; that is, one cannot go to heaven without having had access to baptism, communion, confirmation, confession, marriage, holy orders, and extreme unction or the last rites (now called the anointing of the sick). Moreover, one cannot have the sacraments without the clergy who administer them: no salvation without priests. Graham Greene's novel *The Power and the Glory* (1940) provides an excellent testimony to the importance of the sacraments to Catholic doctrine. The flawed, alcoholic, and unchaste "whisky priest" at the heart of the plot goes underground in a corner of Mexico during the 1930s, when that country's government was trying to suppress the Church. In the story, his determination to risk his life to keep the means of salvation available to the faithful overrides his personal flaws and transforms a sinner into a holy man. The deliverer is essential; the power of the sacraments outweighs and cancels both his sins and those of his flock.

This indispensability of the sacraments is a doctrine that can disarm the Church in the face of ruthless and violent political movements. The threat to remove priests and suppress the Church is, given Catholic doctrine, a threat to deprive all Catholics in the areas affected of any hope of salvation. Fear of this threat propelled both the Church's anticommunism, since communists appeared intent on suppressing the Church, and its caution in challenging Nazism, lest it resort to suppression. And the Nazi regime proved adroit at exploiting these fears. It displayed animosity toward the Church on occasion, especially when it tried to remove crucifixes from school classrooms and engaged in show trials of supposed immorality among monks in the 1930s. But it always stopped just short in Germany of wholesale persecution. Like many other Germans and German institutions, as we have seen, Catholic leaders therefore tried to steer as clear as possible of challenging the regime "in order to avoid worse." But worse for whom or what? Generally for them and their Church.

WARTIME PRIORITIES

As German policymakers inched toward the decision to murder the European Jews, the worldwide failure to rally to their defense largely continued. To be sure, the Nazis permitted emigration from the continent until October 1941, and approximately 72,000 Jews got out of Greater Germany between the outbreak of the war and that date. But that was a relatively small number compared to the need. And after the slaughter began, the countries allied against Nazi Germany, the papacy, neutral countries, and Jews abroad did little to contain the carnage. Why?

Allied passivity was not the result of ignorance of what was happening in Nazi-occupied Europe. Diplomats and journalists from neutral countries, a category that included the United States until December 1941, could read about ghettos in the German press, and businessmen from these nations, such as Swiss factory owners in Poland, witnessed the condition of Jews there and reported on the matter to their head offices. Once the killing began, the Allies learned of it almost immediately. British intelligence intercepted the reports of mass shootings in Russia by the Order Police as they began and passed summaries on to Winston Churchill every morning during the summer of 1941. Both he and the code breakers concluded on September 12 that continuing to do so was superfluous because he could do nothing in response. He could not even reveal the gruesome information for fear of tipping off the Germans to the deciphering of their messages. In October of that year, apostolic delegate Giuseppe Burzio, the Vatican's ambassador in Slovakia, reported the killings to the pope. By March of 1942, a representative of the Joint Distribution Committee in Budapest described the mass murders in Russia at a press conference in New York City, and many American newspapers picked up and publicized the information. That same month marked the beginnings of large-scale deportations to the first death camps, and the papal nuncio in Bern, Switzerland, gathered enough information about what was happening to report to the Vatican that deportation was tantamount to execution. The first published report of murders by gas appeared in the *Times* of London on March 10, 1942, very shortly after they began on a large scale.

By May 1942, the flow of information was thickening. Father Pirro Scavizzi, a military chaplain with the Italian troops that participated in the invasion of the Soviet Union, came home on leave, secured an audience with the pope, and told him of the mass shootings. Meanwhile, the Jewish Bund Party in Poland smuggled out to the Polish government-in-exile in London an account of the gassings at Chelmno in particular and the massacre of the Polish Jews in general, which was then publicized by the British government and picked up by the American press. By June and July of 1942, the BBC and American newspapers were carrying fairly frequent reports of mass murder, though knowledge of gassing was not yet widespread, and Auschwitz had not been identified publicly by name.

But the information ran into considerable emotional and psychological resistance, and even among Jewish leaders disbelief prevailed for a long time. Mass annihilation seemed inconceivable, and those who did not want to accept its occurrence recalled the exaggerated stories that had been told in 1914–18, about the brutality of the German occupation of Belgium, as an example of how inflated tales circulate in wartime. As late as December 1944, a majority of the British public did not believe in the so-called atrocity reports coming out of occupied Europe. Incredulity persisted, even though all grounds for it fell away in the period between August and November 1942. In August, Gerhart Riegner, the representative of the World Jewish Congress in Switzerland, told the American vice consul there and Jewish leaders in London that he had received a reliable report that the Nazis planned to "exterminate" all the Jews in the East in one swift operation using prussic acid gas, which is the generic name for Zyklon. His source for this broadly but not completely accurate information, not revealed until long after the war, was Eduard Schulte, the chief executive of a German steel and mining firm headquartered in Upper Silesia, not far from Auschwitz, whose talkative second-in-command was a close friend of the region's Gauleiter. Schulte was an unlikely person to pass information to foreigners, an old-fashioned German nationalist whose sons were fighting on the Eastern Front. But he had grown so disgusted by the conduct of the Nazi regime that he decided to use his periodic business trips to Switzerland to begin transmitting intelligence to his country's enemies, not only about mass murder but later also about troop movements and the like.

In November 1942, confirmation of the revelations about gassing in the East came from three unimpeachable sources: The first was

Carl Burckhardt, then the vice chairman and later the chairman of the International Committee of the Red Cross in Geneva, who relayed his knowledge to the U.S. State Department, and the second was a series of leaks from the officially secretive Vatican. The third source swept away the last doubts among Jewish leaders; it consisted of a group of Palestinian Jews whom the Germans had interned in Europe and then exchanged for Germans captured by the Allies. These repatriated Jews recounted what they had seen with their own eyes in ghettos and camps. The result was the United Nations declaration of December 17, 1942, in which the Allies acknowledged and denounced the massacre, thus informing every neutral or Nazi-allied government in Europe of what was happening and of the Allies' intention to exact postwar punishment. This was followed by a radio broadcast in German on the BBC by Thomas Mann, the exiled Nobel Prize–winning novelist, that notified anyone listening of what the Nazi regime was doing to Jews.

Even so, Allied operatives had trouble grasping the reality. This is most strikingly apparent with regard to a message intercepted by British intelligence on January 11, 1943. It contained a tally by Höfle, the Eichmann of the General Government, of the total number of Jews killed at the Operation Reinhard camps to date: a figure of 1,274,166. That's a stunning number, considering that it refers to the deaths at only Belzec, Sobibor, and Treblinka, none of which had been in operation for even ten months. But the code breakers did not know the names of the camps or recognize the initials that identified them in the document, so the information remained unpublicized and classified for the duration of the war.

Grasping was not the only problem; deciding what to do with the information was also difficult. The principal Allies worried that making too much of Jewish suffering would play into the claims of Nazi propaganda that Churchill, Roosevelt, and Stalin were fighting for the Jews, indeed were their agents. Thus the Allies were reluctant to see, let alone to stress, the special nature of the Nazi attack on Jews, preferring to talk always—and this continued even after the war—about the suffering of "citizens" in the occupied states. Given the speed of the German onslaught and its geographical concentration out of the reach of Allied aircraft, there is little the Allies could have done to impede the process except to spread the word, mobilize neutral states to help, and encourage resistance to what the Germans were doing, but worries about seeming too pro-Jewish inhibited such actions.

Nor was that the only constraint on Allied rhetoric. The USSR continued to refuse to recognize ethnic distinctions among the victims of Nazism. Stalin spoke only once during the entire Second World War about the fate of the Jews—in a speech on November 7, 1941, accusing the Germans of having carried out pogroms. Neither he nor any other Soviet military leader encouraged partisan units to aid Jews or to interfere with attacks on them. The USSR never considered the idea of bombing railroads to the camps or launching offensives aimed in their direction. The Russians first learned of Auschwitz by name in November 1943, about eight months before the Western Allies acknowledged its existence. By August 1944, when Soviet troops were only 160 kilometers (about 100 miles) away, the leaders of the NKVD, the Soviet secret police, were well versed in the camp's operations and tasks. Yet that information did not flow down the chain of command, and capturing the camp did not become a military objective. In 1944, various Jewish representatives lobbied Soviet diplomats to encourage a raid on the site. At the time on the Eastern Front, the USSR's planes outnumbered the Germans' by seven to one, and Auschwitz was within range of all Soviet light bombers, including the Pe-2 dive-bombers that were ideally suited to hitting narrow targets like the camp's crematoria. But nothing happened, and the principal reason appears to be that Stalin did not want to highlight the situation of the Jews. The Soviets' attitude was summed up by their behavior after they liberated Auschwitz in January 1945—they maintained complete silence about the camp until May, when they issued a report and broadcast a description that did not even mention the word "Jew."

Meanwhile, the top ranks of Great Britain's government exhibited sympathy for the plight of the Jews but remained constrained by worries about holding the loyalty of Arabs. Churchill, who had opposed the white paper of May 1939 that limited Jewish immigration to Palestine, was the most vocal in urging British action to impede the Holocaust. The United Nations' declaration of December 1942 that condemned the murders occurred largely at Britain's instigation, and Churchill insisted that the British seriously consider how to attack Auschwitz in 1944. But he got equivocal support from his own foreign secretary Anthony Eden, who was personally antisemitic and very pro-Arab, and almost no backing from lower down in the British bureaucracy, where Air Secretary Sir Archibald Sinclair blocked the bombing plans and other officials stymied assorted relief efforts. In 1943, one British official called the possible "release" of 70,000 Jews from Romania a "frightful prospect" because they might go to Palestine and upset the delicate political balance there. The same worry made the British strong opponents of various plans toward the end of the war to ransom Jews still in the Nazi grip. Only 37,451 Jews succeeded in legally immigrating to Palestine between the outbreak of World War II and the end of 1944, and more than a third of them got in only in that last year. Most remarkably, the British reluctance to seem to be defending Jews accounts for the fact that both the United States and the UK purposefully ignored for more than a year after April 1943 consistent reports from Polish intelligence identifying Auschwitz as a site of mass murder.

One of the reasons the British and other Allies hesitated to emphasize Jewish suffering and the need for Jews to escape Europe was a man named Hajj Muhammad Amin al-Husseini, the Grand Mufti or highest authority on Islamic law in Jerusalem since 1921. One of the leaders of the Arab revolt in Palestine from 1936 to 1939, he had been driven by the British first out of Palestine, then Iraq, and finally Iran. In November 1941 he found asylum, along with several other Arab nationalists, in Berlin. His propaganda writings and broadcasts depicting America, Britain, communism, and the Jews as the common enemies of Arabs and the Axis powers had little practical effect, except possibly in provoking a spike in desertions by Palestinians from British army units in the run-up to the Battle of El Alamein in the fall of 1942. Whether exiled or not, Arab leaders were so internally divided and contentious during World War II that none of them, including the Mufti, could speak for very large segments of the public in the Middle East. But the British especially feared that demonstrative support for Jews and their interests might change the situation, provoking anything from increased sabotage of Allied military units and operations in the region to an uprising that would divert precious troops and resources from the war effort.

Like the Eastern European nationalists who imagined that allying with the Nazis would increase their chances for future independence, and the several hundred thousand Muslims of the southern Soviet Union who joined the Wehrmacht and the SS in order to shake off Stalin's yoke, the Mufti had his hopes for affiliation with the Axis disappointed. Hitler put off giving him anything more than oral support for an end to colonial rule in the Middle East, not least because the Reich's Italian ally intended not only to retain Libya and Ethiopia after the war but also to expand its holdings in the region. The Germans also steadily refused to sanction an Arab-led army to fight with them. Instead, they confined their support to the raising of a few Muslim Bosnian and Albanian SS units (with German officers) and a tiny German-Arab Battalion that by August 1942 had attracted a mere 243 volunteers. These forces proved ineffective. Transferred in 1943 to North Africa and swollen, through local recruitment efforts, to about 2,000 men, the German-Arab Battalion fought so badly that the officers broke it up into labor units. By the fall of 1944, rampant desertion led the Germans to disband the

Bosnian and Albanian forces, which the Mufti had encouraged and helped to organize. The desperate Third Reich finally announced its "recognition of the independence of the Arab countries" in November 1944, but the moment for rallying Arab or Muslim support to the Nazi cause long since had passed. All told, far more Arabs fought for the Allies in World War II than for the Axis, and probably more Muslims did, too.

In the meantime, the Mufti scored a few victories, notably in late 1942, when he used his influence with Himmler to block an exchange of Jewish children from Slovakia, Poland, and Hungary for German civilians in Palestine under the auspices of the Red Cross. Husseini also in the following months successfully discouraged the German allies Romania and Bulgaria from accepting monetary payments in return for permitting thousands of Jews to emigrate to Palestine. He even suggested to the Bulgarian foreign minister that the children should go to Poland instead, even though the Mufti had learned directly from Himmler what happened to Jews transported there. But these were limited, short-term triumphs, and the Mufti's association with the Axis ultimately had larger, long-term, and disastrous consequences for his goal of a Palestinian state, let alone one over which he would rule, as he hoped to do after the war. Although he managed to escape to Cairo after Germany's defeat and thus live on, his wartime linkage of Arab and Nazi interests helped move the United Nations toward the partition of Palestine in 1947 and the United States and UK toward siding with the Jews in the civil war there in 1948. Husseini's active political career came to an end due to his adamant refusal to accept partition, his disastrous leadership during the fighting that year, and his unacceptability to the former allies against Nazi Germany. King Abdullah of Jordan replaced him as Grand Mufti in December 1948.

If the British were more worried about their position in Palestine and the Middle East than the fate of the Jews, Pope Pius XII was more worried about protecting the city of Rome, finding a way to mediate an end to the war before the atheistic Soviets penetrated to the heart of Europe, and preserving his standing as the "Common Father" of Catholics everywhere, even those perpetrating atrocities. He therefore carefully maintained public silence about the killing of the Jews, on which he was thoroughly informed. He also did not speak publicly about the arrests of Catholic priests in various parts of occupied Europe or the murders of the Sinti and Roma and of the Soviet prisoners of war. He was only slightly more overt in opposing the German euthanasia campaign, even though some of the victims were Catholics and Bishop von Galen condemned it from within the Reich. His only public utterance on the subject of the Jews came in his Christmas message of 1942, which made oblique and brief reference (twenty-seven words in a document of twenty-six pages) to the tragedy of hundreds of thousands of innocent people dying on account of their race. Quietly and behind the scenes, however, he tried to exert some influence against German persecution. He had his ambassador to Vichy France, for instance, tell Marshal Philippe Pétain in July 1942 that the pope did not approve of deportations, and a few months later, Pétain agreed to limit them to foreign Jews in the German-occupied parts of the country. But the achievement evaporated when the Germans extended their occupation to all of France in November 1942. In August 1943, following an audience with a remarkable French monk and rescuer named Father Marie-Benôit, Pius XII used Vatican diplomatic channels to persuade Spain to grant entry visas to and repatriate all Spanish Jews in occupied France, even those who had fought against the ruling regime in the Spanish Civil War a few years earlier.

But for the most part, the pope left decisions about whether and how to aid Jews to individual bishops, abbots, prioresses, and nuncios throughout the Catholic world, while he at the same time withheld from them the information he was accumulating about the murders. Even more strikingly, he declined to intervene with the Germans when they began deporting Jews from Rome in 1943, although he did get the Nazi representatives to promise to respect sanctuary in many Roman churches. Pius also put off pressing the ruler of Hungary, Admiral Horthy, to stop the deportations from that country in 1944 until after the Allies liberated Rome. By the time the pope finally appealed to Horthy on June 25—three full weeks after U.S. troops entered Vatican City—115 trains carrying more than 340,000 Hungarian Jews already had arrived at the selection ramp of Birkenau. When the deportations resumed after Horthy's overthrow that fall, Pius refused to send another protest.

Timid, prudent, and hoping to play the role of intermediary who could broker a peace that would end the fighting, Pius XII behaved more like a politician—and a rather petulant one at that—than a prelate, more like the keeper to the keys to Rome's sumptuous churches than the keeper of the keys to the Kingdom of Heaven, and thus more like a provincial Roman than a prince of the universal church. Whether one endorses or condemns his conduct depends to a large degree on what one considers his primary responsibilities or obligations. He thought they were to Catholics and the accumulated patrimony of St. Peter. How one judges him also depends on whether one agrees with the Polish president-in-exile, Wladislaw Raczkiewicz, who contradicted Pius XII's refusal to denounce Nazi atrocities by asserting that "divine law knows no compromise." Does it? Perhaps it does not to a religious figure who sees himself as the Vicar of Christ on earth, but surely it does to someone who sees himself as the CEO of a morally and materially valuable institution. Pius XII's actions suggest that he saw himself more as the latter than the former. The historian Michael Bess has summed up the pope's conduct: "Push never came to shove because the Nazis pushed, but the Vatican did not shove back."

The upside of Pius's generally hands-off policy regarding the persecution of the Jews is that his conduct opened the way for some of the clerics to whom he left the matter to behave better than he did. As we have seen, several French and Dutch bishops spoke out against the mistreatment and murder of Jews. These brave souls came to nowhere near a majority of the bishops in either country, most of whom remained silent, but they demonstrated that at least some prelates' priorities differed from the pope's. We also already have encountered Metropolitan Sheptytsky in Lviv, who tried to impede Ukrainian collaboration in the murders in two extraordinary ways. First, he wrote to Himmler in February 1942 to request that Ukrainian Catholic police not be used in actions against Jews. Second, he issued a pastoral letter the following month that deprived parish priests of the power to absolve parishioners of murder after confession. Reserving that power to himself alone, Sheptytsky directed the faithful to treat Catholics involved in killing with "the disgust and disgrace they deserve."

Archbishop Aloysius Stepinac of Zagreb in Croatia also spoke out, complaining to that country's leader in November 1941 about the "inhuman and cruel treatment of non-Aryans" and delivering sermons in subsequent years that forbade participation in killing Roma and Jews and condemned racism. Going beyond words, Stepinac also provided baptismal certificates and work permits to Jews and hid many of them in Catholic buildings. In France, the first roundups and deportations in mid-1942 triggered a protest on the part of the Assembly of French Catholic bishops, in the form of a letter from Cardinal Emmanuel Célestin Suhard, the head of the assembly, to Marshal Pétain. It read, in part, "Deeply moved by the information reaching us about the massive arrests of Israelites that took place last week and by the harsh treatment inflicted upon them . . . our voice is raised to protest in favor of the inalienable rights of human beings. It is also an anguished call for pity for . . . mothers and children." But the letter asked for nothing more specific, and the papal nuncio in Vichy, Monsignor Valerio Valeri, dismissed the document as "platonic." The church hierarchy in Slovakia was even slower to perceive its Christian duty. A pastoral letter distributed by the bishops of that country in 1942 defended only Jews who had converted to Catholicism and otherwise invoked antisemitic arguments to justify deportations. But the authors reversed themselves less than a year later. In March 1943, they issued a new letter that denounced the shipments as an unwarranted application of collective guilt that violated the Golden Rule. The deportations from Slovakia already had stopped, but the clerics' intervention tied the hands of the Slovak president, Jozef Tiso, an antisemitic Catholic priest who periodically toyed with resuming the deliveries, and no more occurred until the death rattle of Tiso's regime in the latter part of 1944.

The further down the Catholic Church hierarchy one looks, the more brave and principled behavior one finds. In Poland, for example, about two-thirds of the convents offered refuge to Jewish children and adults. The nuns saved, according to the best estimate, no fewer than 1,500 people in this fashion. In Lithuania during the carnage of 1941, several parish priests berated their flocks for having brutalized and stolen from Jews, even though their bishops took at first an equivocal stance and did not begin to condemn the persecution and organize rescue efforts until 1943. In Belgium, a network led by two Catholic laymen, Albert van den Berg and Georges Fonsny, and supported by Capuchin and Franciscan friars and the Sisters of St. Vincent de Paul, placed about 400 children in various Catholic institutions and thus rescued them. It was one of at least six such primarily Catholic groups that worked to conceal Jews in Belgium during the war. And in Rome, perhaps 4,000 Jews found refuge in monasteries, convents, and churches in 1943–44. But much more could have been achieved had the pope made rescue the Church's official policy, enjoined the faithful to carry it out, and used some of the Holy See's convertible currency to aid operations aimed at saving Jews, all of which the Vatican steadfastly declined to do.

When pressed by foreign diplomats as to why he did not do more, Pius XII always emphasized the dangers that might flow from speaking out. Perhaps it would only enrage the Germans and provoke even more violence, like—although the pope never explicitly drew this comparison—the Dutch bishops' protest against the deportation of Jewish converts to Catholicism that resulted in an acceleration of the practice. Yet neither the Dutch prime minister nor the queen of the Netherlands was cowed into silence. Only days after the deportation trains began to roll east from Holland in July 1942, the prime minister condemned the practice, and a follow-up broadcast on Radio Orange, the voice of the Dutch government in exile, spoke of gas chambers; in October, Queen Wilhelmina told her people over the same sender that she felt "personally affected [by] the systematic extermination" of Dutch Jewry. Still, these leaders spoke from the safety of exile, and events in Germany highlighted the risks of reprisal. Although the Gestapo left Bishop von Galen alone after he spoke out against the euthanasia campaign, police arrested thirty-seven clerics in his diocese and sent them to camps, where six of them died.

Alternatively, the pope sometimes claimed that an open protest might cause patriotic Germans to desert their faith, either during the war or in anger after a German defeat, for which they might blame him. That is what some of the German bishops and cardinals feared, and, like them, Pius XII opted to avoid confrontation "in order to avoid worse." Once again, the sacraments functioned as an inhibition: The pope felt responsible not only to keep them available to the faithful but also to keep the faithful open to them and thus to salvation. But such fears did not stop Bernhard Lichtenberg, the provost of the Catholic cathedral in Berlin, St. Hedwig's, from praying publicly for the Jews being deported and from drafting a denunciation of a pamphlet written by Goebbels that condemned any expression of sympathy for Jews. For these offenses, the Gestapo arrested Lichtenberg in October 1941, jailed him for two years, then put him in a work camp, and finally shipped him to Dachau. Incarceration and mistreatment had shattered his health, and he died in transit on November 5, 1943. To Lichtenberg, unlike the pope, the prospect of mass apostasy could not outweigh the commandment to love one's neighbor here and now. Far better than Pius XII himself, Lichtenberg lived up to the ringing words of the new pope's first encyclical, "*Summi Pontificatus*: On the Unity of Human Society" (October 1939): "In the fulfillment of this, Our duty, we shall not let Ourselves be influenced by earthly considerations nor be held back by mistrust or opposition . . . nor yet by fear of misconceptions or misinterpretations. . . . The Ecclesiastical Hierarchy . . . in union with the Successor of Peter . . . [is] firm when, even at the cost of torments or martyrdom, it has to say: *Non licet*; it is not allowed!"

When all other arguments for inaction failed, the pope played his final card in fending off Allied calls for greater forthrightness: the assertion that if he criticized Nazi crimes, he would have to criticize Soviet ones, and the Allies could not want that while the fighting still raged. But of course he never relented in his vocal opposition to communism, so Allied representatives found this a particularly infuriating pretext.

The best hope for outside help for Jews caught up in the Holocaust was probably the United States, but it responded to the crisis hesitantly, partly for reasons already apparent before the war, partly for new ones. First, the incidence of antisemitism in the American population actually increased during the conflict. A Gallup poll in July 1942 found that 44 percent of the respondents thought that Jews had too much power and influence; two years later, another such survey reported that the same proportion—44 percent—considered Jews "a threat" to the United States. Second, Breckenridge Long remained in office until 1944 and in opposition to anything that would increase the flow of Jews into the United States, and FDR, who had known Long since their common service in the Department of the Navy in World War I, remained deferential toward him, especially toward his argument that refugees presented security risks. As a result, in 1940–41, the two years before America entered World War II, only about 30,000 German Jews got into the country, along with perhaps an equal number from elsewhere in Europe. Third, military planners, in particular, took the line that the only way to help Jews was to win the war as quickly as possible, and then used this argument to rule out small actions that might have helped at the margins. For example, suggestions to transport more immigrants to the United States were rejected repeatedly from 1941 to 1944 because of an alleged shortage of shipping. But 400,000 German POWs were brought across the Atlantic to the United States, and many munitions ships returned empty from Europe.

Washington's attitude softened in late 1943 as a result of several developments. Jan Karski, the Polish resister who earlier had reported to his government-in-exile about rising antisemitism in occupied Poland, also briefly had managed to smuggle himself into the Izbica ghetto, near Lublin, to see what was happening. When he met with FDR personally and told him of what he had witnessed in 1943, the president did not display particular interest in the subject, but the meeting lasted twice as long as planned, and after the conversation FDR seemed aroused as never before by the killings. At the same time, the turn of the tide of war in the Allies' favor indicated that action was becoming possible: Pressure from Congress began to mount, prompted partly by the activism of the outspoken representative of right-wing Zionism in the United States, Peter Bergson; and Treasury Secretary Henry Morgenthau and others persuaded FDR that Long had to go after he gave clearly misleading testimony to a congressional committee. In January 1944, a War Refugee Board came into existence, equipped with large amounts of money, almost all of it provided by the Joint Distribution Committee and other American Jewish organizations. The funds aided Jews through means that ran from bribing Nazi officials to financing the creation of protective identities for individuals, lobbying foreign and neutral governments to help Jews, and supporting escape efforts. Although the board could not stop the Hungarian deportations in the first half of 1944, it did underwrite the efforts of Raoul Wallenberg, the

Swedish businessman-turned-diplomat who went to Budapest later that year and organized efforts to issue thousands of Swedish and Swiss protective documents to Jews in that city. In early 1945, the food that the board paid for and stockpiled in Swedish ports saved thousands of lives when Himmler briefly tried to open a negotiating channel to the Western Allies by allowing the International Red Cross to provision prisoners at Ravensbrück and other camps in northern Germany. In retrospect, it seems clear that the board was created relatively late, but perhaps as early as it could make any difference to people's fates.

Even the War Refugee Board's growing influence in Washington could not suffice, however, to persuade the War Department to order the bombing of Auschwitz and the train lines to the camp. The United States first recognized its function and location only in March 1944, despite earlier Polish underground attempts to alert Americans to the camp's operations. This was at about the same time that the refitting of captured air bases in Italy first permitted aircraft to get from American or British lines to the camp and back without running out of fuel. The first bombing proposals by Jewish groups in the United States reached the State Department and the Department of the Army between May 16 and June 2, 1944, and John Pehle, the director of the War Refugee Board, forwarded other such requests to U.S. Assistant Secretary of War John McCloy in late June. A few weeks later, on July 7, British Foreign Secretary Anthony Eden asked British Air Secretary Sinclair whether bombing runs could stop the murder of Hungary's Jews. It was, in fact, already nearly over, since the last deportation trains from Hungary departed on July 9. In early August, the chief of the U.S. Air Staff requested reconnaissance photos of the Auschwitz-Birkenau area, which had been taken on April 4, May 31, June 26, and July 8 but not yet developed. A formal request to bomb Auschwitz, again to McCloy, came from the World Jewish Congress in New York on August 9, but John Pehle undermined the request on August 11 for fear that large numbers of inmates would die in any air raid. Three days later, McCloy turned down the proposal, saying that it was "impracticable," even though low-flying bombers that could have hit the crematoria were at Italian bases at the time. McCloy also maintained that the idea represented an unwarranted diversion of military assets to a nonmilitary target.

The military argument actually had some force, especially as things looked at the time. One needs to remember that Allied air-power had three principal preoccupations in the months just prior to September 1944: smashing development and launching sites for the German V-1 and V-2 rockets that were terrorizing England; aiding the Allied advance up the Italian boot, which had been very slow; and breaking German resistance in Normandy, which finally occurred on August 12, more than two months after D-Day and just as McCloy was considering the WJC's proposal. Thereafter, while the Allies were hurtling toward the German borders on the west and east, and when Pehle first on October 1 transmitted a Polish request that Auschwitz be targeted and then on November 8 added his own such plea, most American bombers were fixed on smashing Germany's fuel production in order to bring the Reich's armies to a halt. That was, in fact, the mission of American bombers that flew directly over and took pictures of the Auschwitz camp on August 20 and September 13 on their way to hitting the nearby IG Farben factory at Monowitz, only three to four miles east of the gas chambers.

In the end, bombing the camp might not have saved many lives. By the time those planes appeared, about 90 percent of Auschwitz's victims already were dead. The SS transferred more than half of the population of the camp complex—and of the core sites at Auschwitz-Birkenau in particular—to camps further inside Germany between July 1944 and the end of the year. Though transports of Jews continued to arrive and to provide, along with inmates, victims for the gas chambers, the Germans could have murdered the numbers involved (30,000 in October, for example) by other means without difficulty. And the gassings were almost over, in any case: Himmler terminated them at Auschwitz on November 2. Had Allied warplanes attacked the camp, collateral damage would have occurred, as it did when U.S. aircraft bombed a V-2 guidance factory adjacent to Buchenwald on August 24, 1944, and 315 prisoners died, and in early 1945, when planes hit suspected atomic energy facilities near Sachsenhausen and killed some 250 prisoners. The fortified perimeter of Auschwitz was so wide that few people could have broken out while the crematoria were being hit.

But planners did not know all this at the time, so the question remains, why did they not try? The answer with regard to the military authorities, as with regard to the governments herein described and the papacy, is simple: Trying just was not important enough to them; other needs or goals always took precedence. Even with regard to the one thing that the Allies and the pope might have done in 1942 that would have worked—publicizing Nazi crimes against Jews more—political and theological inhibitions prevailed.

Should we include the behavior of American or Palestinian Jewry among the reasons for the insufficiency of the world's response? It is true that the American Jewish community was divided and did not concentrate its lobbying effort. Stephen Wise of the American Jewish Congress held FDR in awe and refused to pressure him. Similarly, Yehuda Bauer, the author of a multivolume history of the Joint Distribution Committee, describes the people who worked at its headquarters in New York as "constitutionally incapable of serious questioning, let alone serious criticism, of an administration that stood between the Jewish community and antisemitism or worse." But Jews came to only 3.6 percent of an increasingly antisemitic American population during the war. They plainly lacked the power antisemites constantly ascribed to them. Something similar must be said about the Jews of the *Yishuv*, who also largely failed to rise to the challenge. They, too, were a relatively small population, around 400,000 people in 1940, more than 85 percent of them living in only three urban areas: Haifa, Tel Aviv, and Jerusalem. Also in an exposed and vulnerable position, Jewish leaders in Palestine recognized that they had few material resources to bring to bear in rescue attempts and achieved little success with these until 1944. All told, their clandestine program of *Aliyah Bet*, or illegal immigration to Palestine, managed to smuggle no more than 19,000 Jews into the territory between 1939 and 1945. One problem was fragmentation: The *Yishuv* was as deeply politically divided as the Jews in the ghettos, in part along the same lines, so coordination around a coherent strategy was lacking. A second problem was mounting fatalism. The advocates of a future Jewish state understood by 1943 the depressing implications for them of what the Nazis already had accomplished, namely that the population the Zionists had counted on to provide the overwhelming majority of future settlers had been largely eradicated. Henceforth, the demographic future of a Jewish homeland seemed to them to lie with the then 800,000 Jews of North African and Arab lands and to depend, even more than before, on not alienating the Allies by protesting against their perceived inaction in bringing the Nazi killings to a stop.

The tragedy of 1939–45 is that the fate of the Jews of Europe was always a matter of secondary importance to everyone but themselves and the regime that wished to kill them. This was especially true of Switzerland, almost the last remaining potential refuge for Jews left in a Nazi-dominated Europe. The Alpine confederation's official policy during World War II read, "Refugees who have fled purely on racial grounds, e.g., Jews, cannot be considered political refugees." But enforcement was inconsistent. About 2,000 Jews got into the country legally between 1939 and 1945. Almost 20,000 more were admitted and held in internment camps, while approximately 24,500 were turned back at the borders, even though the Swiss government possessed ample information about their likely fate thereafter.

A similarly uncaring attitude initially prevailed in the one country that ultimately rose to the challenge: Sweden. Until late 1942 and the Nazi roundup of Norway's Jews, Sweden and its diplomats were distinctly indifferent to the Jewish catastrophe and intent on not jeopardizing their country's neutrality during the war and its lucrative sales of such items as iron ore and ball bearings to Nazi Germany. But thereafter the Swedish government began successively extending its protection to ever-widening groups of Jews. Its first move in this direction came in December 1942, when the Swedish cabinet informed the German government that Sweden would open its borders to all remaining Jews in Norway, regardless of their country of citizenship, and offer asylum. Almost exactly eleven months later, in early October 1943, Sweden announced the same policy regarding all Jews in Denmark, which opened the way for their mass flight across the Baltic Sea. The Swedes even tried unsuccessfully to persuade the German government to divert its ship carrying some of the few arrested Danish Jews to a Swedish port.

As the exodus from Denmark began, the Swedish embassy in Copenhagen commenced issuing provisional passports to Jews who could establish some connection with Sweden, and these documents sometimes sufficed to prevent Germans from detaining the bearers. That precedent proved highly important in March 1944, when Germany occupied Hungary and fearful Jews began besieging the Swedish embassy. But provisional passports required some commercial or residential basis and approval in Stockholm; they could not be issued to just anyone, and thus were inadequate to the need. Ambassador Carl Ivar Danielsson and his chief aide, Per Anger, now improvised a hierarchy of protective documents modeled on ones called *Schutzpässe*, which the Swiss vice consul in Budapest, Carl Lutz, had been issuing since 1942. These were simply official-looking pieces of paper with the Swedish coat of arms in color and assorted stamps, all designed to impress upon Hungarian police that the bearer was exempt from deportation by virtue of not being a Hungarian citizen. But the Hungarian deportations started in the outer provinces, far away from the Swedish embassy, so this sort of protection initially was not of much help; neither was the Swedish decision, in mid-June, to allow the embassy to issue provisional passports and entry visas without prior approval from Stockholm.

More efficacious was a letter from King Gustav V of Sweden to Miklos Horthy, delivered on July 3, urging him to put a stop to the deportations. Along with messages from the pope and the U.S. government, this document helped to push Horthy, on July 7, into ordering the suspension of the deportations, thus providing breathing room for the not yet arrested Jews of Budapest. Two days later Raoul Wallenberg arrived in the Hungarian capital, and his continuation of the practices that Swedish diplomats had developed proved instrumental in saving thousands of Jews after Horthy's overthrow on October 15, 1944. These heroic efforts were the culmination of a two-year-long process of recognizing Sweden's responsibility to act that was virtually unparalleled by any other nation.

That is not to say that the Swedes were the only diplomats who tried to impede the Holocaust in Hungary. From Switzerland, an equally extraordinary effort was led by George Mantello, a Romanian Jewish refugee serving as the first secretary in the Salvadoran consulate in Geneva. In 1943, backed by his superiors, he began issuing at no cost Salvadoran citizenship papers to between 20,000 and 30,000 mostly Jewish applicants in Hungary and Romania, thus obstructing their deportation. Then, in the late spring of 1944, he sent an emissary to Budapest who obtained copies of two eyewitness reports on the functioning of Auschwitz and the extent of the Hungarian deportations. He immediately released these to Swiss newspapers and with the help of four prominent Swiss theologians whipped up a press campaign exposing and denouncing the murders. To claim that he thus became "the man who stopped the trains to Auschwitz," as the title of a recent study of his actions asserts, goes too far, but the outcry surely played a part in persuading Admiral Horthy to suspend the deportations in July. After they resumed the following fall, the papers Mantello had issued became significant again, not because of further action on his part but because Carl Lutz of the Swiss consulate took over representing Salvadoran interests in Hungary and persuaded the new Arrow Cross regime to honor the documents. They were then supplemented by thousands of comparable papers being issued by the Portuguese and Vatican representatives in Budapest and by a remarkable Italian, Giorgio Perlasca, who had obtained political asylum in the Spanish embassy in Hungary's capital. From November 1944 to January 1945, he posed as a Spanish diplomat, and in that capacity he issued thousands of safe conduct documents, supposedly on the basis of a Spanish law that extended citizenship to Jews descended from those expelled from Spain in the fifteenth century. Of the 140,000–150,000 Jews who survived the Holocaust in Budapest, roughly 120,000 owed their lives, at least in large part, to the protective papers that Salvadoran, Spanish, Swedish, and Swiss diplomats provided.

CHAPTER 8

AFTERMATH:
What Legacies,
What Lessons?

THE TRAGEDY OF THE Holocaust did not end with Germany's surrender in May 1945. Conditions on the death marches from abandoned camps and in the camps that continued to operate until the Allies arrived were so atrocious that tens of thousands of Jews died even afterward. The toll at Belsen was prototypical: 35,000 inmates expired in the final few weeks of the war, including Anne Frank, and more than 14,000 died after liberation, sometimes from disease but mostly because their bodies could no longer absorb the food that now was available to them. As a result, by mid-1945, only about 200,000 Jews had survived the camps, roughly 100,000 of whom had been at Auschwitz at one time or another.

RETURN, RESETTLEMENT, RETRIBUTION, AND RESTITUTION

Even this number was too much for the unprepared Allies to cope with. They had set up the United Nations Relief and Rehabilitation

Administration (UNRRA) in 1943, but neither this organization nor the military units that liberated the camps in 1945 were ready for what they found. Indeed, the shock to the U.S. troops that liberated Dachau at the end of April 1945 was so profound that some of them went on a rampage, murdering between 40 and 122 of the guards discovered on the site. Two weeks earlier, when British units had reached Bergen-Belsen, they used bayonets and rifle butts to make the remaining German guards collect and bury the bodies strewn around the camp. Of the treatment meted out, an accompanying journalist wrote, "The punishment they got was in the best Nazi tradition, and few of them survived it; but it made one pensive to see British soldiers beating and kicking men and women, even under such provocation."

But the object of Allied revulsion soon changed from the perpetrators to the victims, since many of the camp inmates had been demoralized, in both senses of the word, by what they had experienced and now behaved in ways that aroused more antipathy than sympathy on the part of those who had freed them. Such behavior prompted General George Patton, the commander of U.S. troops in southern Germany, to call "the Jewish type of Displaced Person . . . a sub-human species without any of the cultural or social refinements of our time." But Patton was a notorious loudmouth and bigot who was looking for such opportunities. He later called the Nuremberg trials of Nazi war criminals a "semitic" event, accused the American press of being under "semitic influence," and stated that the purpose of that influence was to "implement Communism."

Patton's antisemitism was more overt than most, but prejudice played a part in shaping the initial American and British incomprehension of the differences among the two million displaced persons (DPs) in Germany at the end of 1945. Many of them were survivors of Nazi labor camps, but many others were refugees who had fled Eastern Europe with the German armies, including 600,000 people from the Baltic states alone, among whom were numerous former collaborators with the Germans. Once more, Jews were treated as just one persecuted group among many. At some 2,500 UNRRA installations, a lot of them identical to places where the Nazis had caged people, all DPs were initially thrown in together, without regard to whether they had been victims or servants of the Nazis. The tensions that arose were particularly high between Jews and the far more numerous Christian refugees from Eastern Europe who feared to return to their now Soviet-occupied homelands.

So bad were the conditions in the refugee camps at the middle of 1945 that Earl Harrison, President Harry S. Truman's inspector, issued a scathing report that included a passage that, in retrospect, is astounding: "As matters now stand, we appear to be treating the Jews as the Nazis treated them except that we do not exterminate them. They are in concentration camps in large numbers under our military guard instead of SS troops. One is led to wonder whether the German people, seeing this, are not supposing that we are following or at least condoning Nazi policy." Truman instructed General Eisenhower, the overall commander of American forces in Europe, to improve the situation of Jewish DPs. Some progress was made, including the establishment of thirteen separate camps for Jews, no fewer than twelve of them in the American occupation zone, but U.S. policy remained constrained by its chief goals: (1) to keep the residents confined so that the German populace, who feared them, would not be alienated; and (2) to keep conditions uncomfortable enough to encourage DPs to return to their lands of origin.

Return proved short-lived for many Jews because of events like the pogrom at Kielce in Poland in July 1946 and because of the hardships that accompanied the tightening Soviet grip on Eastern Europe. As a result, the problem of Jewish refugees actually increased after 1945. Whereas only 18,000 Jewish survivors were in UNRRA camps in Germany and Austria in December 1945, that number swelled to over 97,000 a year later and to more than 167,000 at the end of 1947. Many of these people were Polish Jews who had escaped the Nazis by retreating with Soviet forces in 1941, returned to Poland in 1945–46, and then decided to flee westward. Others were Hungarian and Romanian Jews who had survived homegrown persecution and now took the first chance to get away. Still others were Jews from Ukraine who had fled with the Red Army in 1941, returned with it in 1944, and encountered the same sort of reluctance to vacate their former residences that the new occupants showed virtually everywhere else. The large numbers were increasingly expensive to support—UNRRA spent almost $4 billion in the late 1940s, a staggering sum at the time, most of it from the United States. Yet the refugees seemed to have nowhere else to go. Because the United States continued to enforce its quota system of immigration, only 15,000 Jewish DPs were admitted between May 1945 and June 1947. Meanwhile, Britain and the Dominions proved more hospitable to non-Jewish refugees from Eastern Europe than to Jewish ones, though Australia was a partial exception, and the British continued to enforce the white paper limit of 15,000 Jewish immigrants to Palestine per year.

The United States, to which Britain was heavily indebted at the end of World War II, tried to persuade Prime Minister Clement Attlee to allow 100,000 Jewish refugees into Palestine, but he set two preconditions: that the United States pay to transport and support them, and that the Jewish fighters then seeking to drive Britain out of Palestine lay down their arms. Neither party cooperated, so no deal occurred. But the point became moot when the British decided in early 1947 to turn the question of Palestine over to the fledgling United Nations. It voted nine months later to partition the region between Jews and Arabs. Between 1945 and 1951, by a combination of legal and illegal means, somewhere between 133,000 and 200,000 European Jewish refugees got to the territory that became the State of Israel in 1948. They were often received somewhat insensitively—either suspected of having collaborated with the Nazis in order to survive, or pitied as the remnant of a weak and failed diaspora. Either way, they were regarded as living proof of the need for Zionism and an independent and self-reliant Jewish state.

Meanwhile, resistance to the immigration of DPs to the United States softened somewhat as a result of growing public sympathy with their plight and an increased perception among American officials that their continued presence on German soil was politically inconvenient and embarrassing. Even so, the price of greater openness was readiness to turn a blind eye to earlier collaboration with Nazism on the part of many of the tens of thousands of non-Jewish Latvian, Lithuanian, Ukrainian, and *Volksdeutsche* residents of German DP camps, who were also allowed into the United States under the terms of the Displaced Persons Act of 1948 and the amendments passed in 1950. Now admired as refugees from communism, these people actually outnumbered the Jews who gained entrance to America under the new legislation. Altogether, the United States admitted between 80,000 and 137,000 Jewish Displaced Persons by 1953, a not inconsiderable total but about the same share of the total number of Jews who found refuge worldwide as in the 1930s. Think about that for a minute: The United States actually was, in relative terms, no more open to Jewish immigrants from 1945 to 1953 than from 1933 to 1939. Of course, most of them were no longer in mortal danger after World War II, so one might argue that their need had become less acute, but they were often homeless and destitute.

Those who got here faced incomprehension of their experience akin to the attitudes exhibited earlier by the U.S. military commanders in Germany. Most Americans simply could not imagine what survivors had been through. The sense of isolation that many of them felt was compounded by two policies on the part of well-meaning Jewish social service agencies. The first was a conscious decision to disperse survivors among disparate Jewish communities that volunteered as sponsors. Many Jewish survivors thus found themselves in places, such as Columbia, South Carolina, and Denver, Colorado, that were worlds apart from their places of origin.

Once there, they ran up against another conscious policy that the agencies encouraged sponsors to adopt: an emphasis on persuading survivors to "move on" and not dwell on or talk about the past and its losses. A great deal of emotional and psychological pain remained unresolved in the process of rebuilding lives.

It is, of course, not true that the Holocaust was forgotten in the 1950s and 1960s. By the time I graduated from high school in 1964, the subject was already a conspicuous topic in American popular culture. I first learned about it in junior high in the late 1950s from reading Leon Uris's novel *Exodus*, the biggest bestseller in the United States since *Gone with the Wind*. This highly fictionalized account of the voyage of a real illegal refugee ship to Palestine became a film starring Paul Newman. I saw it, as I did *The Diary of Anne Frank* (1959). When I was in high school, *Judgment at Nuremberg* with Spencer Tracy was a box-office success, and so was *The Pawnbroker*, with Rod Steiger, during my first year in college. But it is true that the Holocaust did not yet stand out sharply from the enormous cataclysm of World War II. This is an example of what I call the optic of history. Most Americans thought, after 1945, that the real story of World War II was the story they had been part of—namely, the war in the Pacific and the invasions of Europe, not what had occurred in Poland and Ukraine. According to family lore, my father ended World War II on the island of Tinian, having been trained in New Mexico in 1944–45 to drop an atomic bomb on Japan. Fortunately, he did not in the end do so because there were only two bombs for five trained crews, but I grew up hearing a lot more about defeating Japan than fighting Nazis, even though almost twice as many Americans died in the war against Germany than in the Pacific theater. Besides, the cold war put a damper on paying attention to the Holocaust, since most Germans were now America's allies, and political convenience argued for not raking up the past. Decades had to pass before survivors felt that they had an audience for their recollections.

Postwar politics also worked against extensive retribution to per-petrators and demands for restitution to the victims, but in both instances, as with the myth of silence about the Holocaust follow-ing the war, more happened than people tend now to remember. It is simply untrue that many major perpetrators of the Holocaust escaped punishment afterwards, just as it is untrue that Germans, especially those in the eastern half of their country, paid little or no price for what their nation had done. Both legends are the opposite of reality. Germany was a badly damaged country in 1945, and it remained that way for many years after, despite the economic revival of the 1950s. When I first visited, in 1968–69, I saw numerous empty, bombed-out lots in Düsseldorf, as well as trees growing from the roofs of the Frankfurt Opera House and the twin churches on the Gendarmenmarkt in Berlin. Those edifices were ruins twenty-four years after World War II ended.

So tenacious is the legend of perpetrators escaping punishment that it seems to blind the people who retell it to even their own evi-dence. A case in point is Donald McKale's *Nazis after Hitler: How Perpetrators of the Holocaust Cheated Justice and Truth*, an extended philippic about Nazis who supposedly avoided punishment after World War II and advanced self-justifications that aided the cause of Holocaust denial. Yet of the thirty-one individuals on whom the author focuses to make his case, his own text shows that twelve were executed for their deeds, two committed suicide, four died in captiv-ity, two died as they were about to be arrested and prosecuted, one died on the run, and four went to jail. Only six went unpunished. The mortality rate came to two-thirds by the time Adolf Eichmann was executed in Jerusalem in 1962.

In fact, in the early postwar years, the reckoning was pretty intense. Altogether, European courts condemned and sentenced approximately 100,000 Germans and Austrians for wartime criminality of one sort of another. The four victorious Allies convicted another 8,812 Germans and Austrians in proceedings held in occupied Germany. American prosecutions of 1,030 camp officials and guards on atrocity charges in 1945–47 produced 885 convictions; 261 of the 432 defendants condemned to death for these offenses or for harming American military personnel ultimately died on the gallows. The hanging at Dachau on May 27–28, 1947, of forty-eight German personnel from Mauthausen constitutes the largest mass execution in American history. Among those also executed by the United States were Paul Blobel, who had commanded *Sonderkommando* 1005, the unit charged with exhuming the bodies of camp victims, burning them, and destroying all traces of Belzec, Sobibor, and Treblinka; Otto Moll, among other things the commandant of several gassing installations and of the slave labor camps at IG Farben's murderous mines near Auschwitz; and Oswald Pohl, the head of the SS Economics and Administration Main Office and, as such, the architect of the SS camp labor system. The British tried 989 people on war crimes charges and hanged eleven members of the camp administration at Belsen. The executees included Franz Hössler, who had commanded the first gas chambers at Auschwitz and later supervised the exhumation and burning of 100,000 bodies there, as well as two businessmen who sold Zyklon to the SS. The Soviets hanged Friedrich Jeckeln, the SS man who presided over the murders at Babi Yar, on the site of the Riga ghetto in 1946. They also executed six of the former *Hiwis* at Sobibor even before the war ended and ten more of them after a trial in 1962. Altogether, Soviet courts convicted almost 26,000 Germans and Austrians and about 11,000 local collaborators.

The Poles tried 5,358 German nationals between 1945 and 1957. Among the people executed were Rudolf Höss, the longest-serving commandant of Auschwitz; Jürgen Stroop, the SS commander who put down the Warsaw Ghetto Uprising; Hans Biebow, the German administrator of the Lodz ghetto; Amon Göth, the sadistic commandant of the Plaszow concentration camp made famous in *Schindler's List*; Arthur Greiser, the Nazi governor of the Warthegau; the two top-ranking officials of the General Government; the four senior

German figures in occupied Warsaw; Heinrich Josten, the commander of the SS guard force at Auschwitz; Erwin von Helmersen, an SS doctor at Birkenau; Werner Händler, the man in charge of food for the inmates of both those camps; and Maximilian Grabner, the head of the Political Section of the Auschwitz-Birkenau camp administration from 1940 to 1943, which was the subunit responsible for torture and executions. Poland also sentenced two of the men who poured Zyklon into the gas chambers to long prison terms; one of them died in his cell in 1955, and the other was released in 1958.

Arthur Seyss-Inquart, the German administrator of the occupied Netherlands, was condemned to death at the Nuremberg trials and executed. The Dutch followed up by putting to death forty Nazi officials and collaborators, including Hanns Rauter, the SS chief in Amsterdam. The death sentences of Ferdinand aus der Fünten, who directed the deportations from Holland, and of Willy Lages, the chief of the SS Security Service there, were commuted in 1951 to life in prison. Lages served fifteen years, then died five years later. Aus der Fünten served thirty-nine years until the Dutch released him on grounds of ill health two months before he died. Albert Gemmeker, the commandant of the camp at Westerbork from which most Dutch Jews were sent to their deaths, got off more lightly with a ten-year prison term, of which he spent six behind bars before his release in 1955.

In general, the chances of high-ranking perpetrators being punished were quite high. Consider the fates of the sixteen people who at one time or another had independent command of a death camp: thirteen were killed one way or another during the 1940s, one received a death sentence in 1954 and promptly died of a heart attack, and two escaped justice for a time, only to be caught ultimately and given life sentences. The figures for the fourteen people who commanded an *Einsatzgruppe* are similar: Seven perished during the war, two committed suicide in custody, and three were executed, for a total of twelve fatalities. The remaining two were sentenced to prison, albeit for what turned out to be only brief terms. In both categories, no one got off scot-free. Of the forty-two individuals who ever commanded one of the thirteen most notorious concentration camps—Bergen-Belsen, Buchenwald, Dachau, Dora-Mittelbau, Flossenbürg, Gross-Rosen, Mauthausen, Natzweiler, Neuengamme, Ravensbrück, Sachsenhausen, Stutthof, and Theresienstadt—fourteen died before 1945, eighteen were executed or committed suicide, four served prison terms, and only six (14 percent) went unpunished or unaccounted for after the war. Nikolaus Wachsmann, the author of a definitive history of the Nazi concentration camps published in 2015, says that only seven of the former wartime commandants of the twenty-seven main SS concentration camps were still alive in 1950. Though not a perfect record, this is hardly a terrible one.

With regard to euthanasia killings and slave labor, the attrition among order-givers was also extensive. The three chief figures in T4, Philipp Bouhler, Viktor Brack, and Karl Brandt, died shortly after the war, Bouhler by suicide after his capture by the United States in 1945 and Brack and Brandt by hanging in 1948 after their condemnation by an American court. Both Albrecht Schmelt, who devised the SS's sliding charges for different categories of Jews leased out as slave laborers, and Hans Kammler, the SS man in charge of the enslaved workforce at Dora-Mittelbau and the other Fighter Staff Program factories, perished as the war was ending.

In addition, courts in their homelands condemned to death the Vichy prime minister Pierre Laval and the Romanian dictator Ion Antonescu, both of whom had delivered Jews to the Nazis and then thought better of it. Vichy's chief of state Philippe Pétain escaped the same fate only because Charles de Gaulle commuted his sentence to life in prison, where he died. Norway's collaborationist leader Vidkun Quisling was shot by a firing squad; Slovakia's Jozef Tiso was hanged; and so was Hungary's Ferenc Szalasi, who took over its government and resumed the deportation of Jews in late

1944, along with the three chief figures of the Hungarian Interior Ministry who organized the mass deportations earlier that year. In the meantime, every one of the German envoys to Croatia, Slovakia, Hungary, Bulgaria, and Romania who lobbied those governments to kill or deport Jews during the war had been killed either upon capture or following a trial in 1945–47.

Finally, the Germans themselves accounted for a considerable number of prosecutions. West Germany sent 6,479 people to prison between 1945 and 1986, and the East Germans convicted 12,861 individuals between 1945 and 1976. Still, there were notable omissions and lapses, especially during the 1950s. Only about 10 percent of the Germans who ever worked at Auschwitz went on trial anywhere after the war, and the mid- to low-ranking personnel at most concentration camps were largely ignored later or given light sentences—at least by American standards—when tried. Of the 50,000 members of the Police Battalions that killed about half a million people in occupied Eastern Europe, only 64 men were ever charged and 41 ever sentenced. And most of the SS officers who were imprisoned shortly after the war were out by 1958. But exceptions occurred: Hermann Krumey, a key figure in the deportations from Hungary, got a life sentence in the late 1960s and served it. Hans Höfle, Globocnik's chief of staff during Operation Reinhard and the man who drew up the infamous statistical tally of the killings during 1942, evaded justice until his arrest in 1961 but killed himself the following year. In 1969, East Germany executed Josef Blösche, the SS man pointing a machine gun toward the boy with a cloth cap (see chapter 5, figure 6) during the suppression of the Warsaw Ghetto Uprising. Though most of the district-level Nazi administrators who presided over deportations in the General Government went unpunished, two who were investigated in the 1960s also committed suicide. Only a few of the high-ranking figures at Auschwitz got away, notably Josef Mengele, the doctor who conducted selections at the arrival ramp and vicious experiments on inmates and who hid out in South America until he drowned in 1979. Wilhelm Boger, the infamous interrogation officer in the Political Section of the Auschwitz camp, was not quite as lucky. After he escaped from American custody in 1947, he managed to remain at large until 1959, when the German authorities caught up with him. Sentenced in 1965 to life in prison, he died there twelve years later.

The record also is mixed, but not negligible, regarding the 121 men from T4 who staffed the Operation Reinhard camps. Forty-two (that is, more than a third) of them died during the war, in Soviet captivity, or immediately after 1945, mostly by their own hands. Twenty-two were sentenced after the war, nine to life in prison, twelve to terms of three to twelve years, and one, who committed suicide, to death. One other former T4 man killed himself during the preliminaries to his trial in 1965. Among those caught and punished was Hermann Bauer, who called himself the "gas master" of Sobibor. Condemned to death in 1950 but saved by the abolition of capital punishment in West Germany, he served out a life sentence, dying in West Berlin's Tegel prison in 1980. Still, about fifty-seven (47 percent) of these participants in murder escaped punishment. According to Michael Bryant, the most recent and careful student of their prosecutions, German courts would have convicted as many as twenty-one more of them as accomplices to murder in the three successive trials of Reinhard camp guards in 1963–66 and another of Majdanek personnel in 1966–71 if more eyewitness testimony, to which those courts generally were deferential, had been available. Where relevant survivors who could implicate individual guards in cruelty or killing were in short supply, however, the courts had no alternative under West German law than to give defendants the benefit of the doubt regarding their claims to have "inwardly opposed" Nazi actions and been uninvolved in the gassings.

Of course, a number of infamous figures did escape punishment, many of them through the efforts of an entity that also had been less than consistently helpful to Jews during the Holocaust: the Roman

Catholic Church. Driven by the view that any ally against communism was worth assisting, Catholics developed several escape routes, known colloquially as ratlines, for Nazis and their European allies. All of these itineraries ran out of Germany through South Tyrol, the German-speaking area in northeastern Italy, and then either directly to the port city of Genoa or first to Rome and then to that port. From there, the escape routes went either to Franco's Spain via Barcelona and sometimes then on to Juan Peron's Argentina or directly to Buenos Aires. Along the way, the International Red Cross and the Vatican Relief Commission, the latter run by Monsignor Giovanni Montini, the future Pope Paul VI, provided new identities and travel documents, and Giuseppi Siri, the Archbishop of Genoa, furnished food and shelter there. Most of the money for the operation, about $5 million at the time, came from unwitting donations on the part of the National Catholic Welfare Committee in the United States, spurred on by Cardinal Francis Spellman of New York City.

Some of that American funding also went to a Nazi sympathizer in Rome, an Austrian bishop named Alois Hudal, the rector of a seminary for German-speaking priests. Among the notorious criminals that Hudal helped get away were Josef Mengele and Adolf Eichmann; Gerhard Bohne, one of the principal organizers of the T4 program, who ultimately returned to Germany and escaped punishment; and Eduard Roschmann, the vicious commandant of the Riga ghetto, who lived in Argentina from 1948 to July 1977. The prospect of extradition drove Roschmann to Paraguay, where he died within about a month of his arrival. Another beneficiary of Hudal's aid was Erich Priebke, who led a massacre of 335 Italians during the German retreat from Rome and then spent fifty years in Argentina before finally being extradited to Italy in 1995, tried, and sentenced to life imprisonment under house arrest, which is where he died, in 2013, at the age of 100. Hudal also hid Franz Stangl, the former commander of the Sobibor and Treblinka death camps, at the seminary until he could make his escape to Syria and later to Brazil. He finally was arrested there in 1967, extradited to West Germany, and sentenced to life imprisonment in 1970. Stangl's escape, as well as that of one of his deputies at Sobibor, Gustav Wagner, was the work of another old Nazi who worked out of Hudal's seminary, Walter Rauff, the inventor of the motor-fed gas van. They, too, initially went to Syria, but, unlike Stangl, both Wagner and Rauff lived out their lives in safety, the former in Brazil, where he died in 1980, the latter in Chile until he succumbed to lung cancer in May 1984.

A similar ratline emanated from a pontifical college for Croatian priests in Rome, where Father Krunoslav Draganovic funneled both the remaining funds of the brutal Ustasha state to the Vatican Bank and thousands of Ustasha veterans and a few Nazis to safety abroad. Two of his more infamous successes were Klaus Barbie, known as "the butcher of Lyon" for his role as a wartime torturer for the SS in that city, and Ante Pavelic, the former ruler of Croatia, who had presided over the slaughter of thousands of Jews, Sinti and Roma, and Serbs. Justice did not catch up to Barbie until 1983, partly because he was protected by both American and West German intelligence agencies and a succession of military rulers in Bolivia. When that country returned to democracy that year, the new government arrested and extradited Barbie to France, where he was sentenced to life in prison four years later. He died there of multiple cancers in 1991. Meanwhile, Pavelic had escaped retribution far more briefly, despite the fact that he, too, had additional help from a Western intelligence agency, in his case Britain's. After an assassin sent by the Yugoslavian secret police nearly killed Pavelic in Argentina in 1957, he fled to Chile and then Spain and died of his wounds two years later.

Even more Nazis and their allies would have escaped if Catholic leaders had gotten their way. Pius XII pleaded repeatedly for clemency for condemned war criminals, both in general and in specific instances. He thus held to the theory of pastoral responsibility that he had followed throughout World War II, a theory that historian Jacques Kornberg has shown assigned less importance to condemning sin that to keeping open possibilities of forgiveness and redemption. Most German bishops, including Clemens von Galen, the man who had criticized the euthanasia program, went even further by denouncing the war crimes trials themselves as unjust. So did Bishop (later Cardinal) Aloisius Muench, the antisemitic, German-speaking son of Bavarian immigrants to the United States who served both as liaison between the American occupation administration and the German Catholic Church and as the papal representative in occupied Germany. He wrote a pastoral letter that contrasted "Christ's law of love" with the "Mosaic idea of an eye for an eye." But when the pope and German Catholic leaders pressured John McCloy, the U.S. High Commissioner for Germany from 1949 to 1952, to commute the sentence of Otto Ohlendorf, who had commanded an *Einsatzgruppe* and a section of the RSHA, their advocacy was too much for even Muench. Quietly but firmly, he advised the German prelates and the Vatican to back off, lest their stance become public and embarrass the Church.

One other famous group long supposed to have enabled escapes by war criminals, the *Organisation der ehemaligen SS-Angehörigen* (Organization of Former Members of the SS), known by the acronym ODESSA, appears to have been largely mythical. That did not prevent the famous "Nazi hunter" Simon Wiesenthal from believing it was real and from encouraging the novelist Frederick Forsyth to place it and the aforementioned Eduard Roschmann at the center of a gripping bestseller called *The Odessa File*. In 1974, it became a hit movie of the same name starring Jon Voight. Although grist for a vivid story, ODESSA was the sort of fantasy that fevered postwar imaginations conjured up, and its nonexistence helps explain why, in the end, few major Nazi war criminals got away. An independent historians' commission entrusted in the late 1990s with an exhaustive examination of Nazi activities in Argentina combed the archival record there and in Europe and reached the conclusion that only 180 likely war criminals or collaborators had gained entry to that South American country, of whom about 100 were French and Belgian, about 50 Croat, and only 23 German or Austrian. That assessment gains credibility from a recent detailed study of the case of Aribert Heim, an SS doctor who killed prisoners at Mauthausen and got away to live out his years in Cairo until 1992. The authors, two investigative journalists, argued that the success of people like Heim in eluding capture owed much more to the efforts of their friends and families than to any organization's support. A peculiarity that helped make this so was the provision in postwar German law that barred charging close relatives of suspects with aiding and abetting their escape. In consequence, immediate families could refuse to cooperate with investigators without fear of punishment.

That the Western powers did not hold more people responsible was partly a matter of cold war politics. To combat the Soviet Union, the United States wanted to exploit the expertise of some compromised individuals, not only people like Barbie and Pavelic but also scientists such as Wernher von Braun of Germany's V-2 rocket program. Braun's connection to the use of slave labor at Dora-Mittelbau seemed less important to America after 1945 than his ability to design ballistic missiles and, ultimately, the spacecraft that took John Glenn into orbit around the earth. More generally, the United States sought to embed West Germany in the West and the NATO alliance and considered continuing prosecutions counterproductive to that purpose. But leniency also reflected a domestic German democracy-building strategy. Konrad Adenauer, West Germany's first postwar leader and a man with impeccable anti-Nazi credentials, believed that integrating former Nazis into the new political order was the best way of reconciling them to a democratic system and alliance with the West. He wished to prevent the rise of a sense of victimization comparable to the one Germans had nursed after World War I. Thus he accepted prosecution of only the most obviously criminal actors, but argued for forbearance otherwise and for a kind of collective amnesia about the degree to which Germans had supported the Nazi Führer and shared his hatreds. Adenauer saw to it that former perpetrators and their widows received state pensions and that some even returned to positions in the West German government. His own right-hand man in the 1950s was Hans Globke, who had written the manual for implementing the Nuremberg Laws.

Adenauer's strategy largely succeeded in political terms but only temporarily in historical ones. Beginning in the late 1950s and accelerating thereafter, pressure to confront the details of the past and in some cases the perpetrators themselves rose dramatically in West Germany, as East German propagandists exposed the questionable pasts of many officials and people born after the war reached maturity and began posing painful questions. By the time they did this, the country's democratic institutions were strong enough to withstand the call for honesty about the past. Since the 1970s, openness about what Germans did and about the reality of the Holocaust has been part of what Germans call their "constitutional patriotism," and memorials reminding Germans of the worst of which they were capable now dot the nation's capital, as well as most of its large cities.

German restitution policy toward victims of the Holocaust followed a similarly halting course toward a similarly accepting endpoint. From 1945 on, the Germans conceded that they had to pay something in the form of restitution or compensation for all the misery that they had caused, but they sought consistently to keep the bill as low as possible. As a result, every concession came in response to outside pressure and was confined to relieving it, but the pressure never really stopped, and the ultimate bill came to a staggering sum. Since 1945, total payments to survivors, their heirs, and the state of Israel have come to more than $100 billion, not counting the value of returned objects, such as art works. Yet certain categories of victims benefited disproportionately, some received nothing at all because they died before compensation was extended to them, and even $100 billion falls well short of the worth of the damages the Germans inflicted.

The survivors who came off best were Jewish Germans who managed to flee the country before the Holocaust or who survived it somehow on German soil. Under Allied occupation rules as well as laws passed by the fledgling German state in the early 1950s, such people were entitled to the return of their old property, such as homes, businesses, furniture, jewelry, and other assets, or a cash payment equal to its worth. The total payout for identifiable and lost property came to 7.5 billion deutsche mark by the mid-1960s, which was just shy of two billion U.S. dollars at the time. German Jews whose careers had suffered by virtue of being driven out of the country were entitled to a lump-sum payment of 10,000 deutsche mark for "damage to education," and those expelled from the practice of law or university faculties were granted the lifelong pension of someone who had reached the senior ranks of the judiciary or the professoriate. Hannah Arendt lived comfortably in New York City in part off of such income. In the first years of this century, 100,000 people worldwide were still receiving such payments.

Other categories of victims came away with much less, if anything. Jewish refugee organizations got 120 million marks worth of German foreign assets to use in the immediate postwar years to aid resettlement of Jewish survivors, along with the proceeds of refining and selling the gold that had been shipped to Berlin from the death camps in Poland but not smelted by the end of the war. Israel received three billion marks to support survivors as a result of the Luxembourg Agreement of 1952, and the Jewish Claims Conference another 450 million marks for the same purpose. Between 1958 and 1961, in accordance with the usual rule in international law that only countries, not individuals, can get compensation from other countries, West Germany signed treaties with sixteen non-communist European states that provided them with 2.5 billion marks to distribute to Holocaust survivors within their borders.

Substantial as these amounts were, they excluded large groups of survivors, primarily those in Eastern Europe. The West Germans insisted until unification in 1990 that they were responsible only for survivors who met two criteria: (1) they had lived within Germany, defined by its borders in 1937, at some time between 1933 and 1945 or moved to the Western occupation zones or West Berlin between 1945 and 1952; and (2) they currently resided in West Germany or in a country that had diplomatic relations with West Germany. The second rule disqualified most Eastern European survivors until the 1970s, since most of their countries had diplomatic ties only with communist East Germany until then. The first rule excluded many survivors in Eastern Europe altogether.

A second major category of survivors who were left out of the German compensation schemes comprised people who had been slave laborers for German private industry. For many years, German courts refused to hold German firms liable to pay such people, contending that the companies had been acting on government orders and that the state, not the firms, was the proper address for claims. Largely in order to limit damage to their reputations in foreign markets, a few companies made token postwar payments to former slave laborers as a gesture, not an admission of obligation or guilt. The legal remnant of IG Farben, along with the Krupp, Siemens, AEG, and Rheinstahl companies gave the Jewish Claims Conference 51.5 million marks between 1957 and 1962 to aid approximately 15,000 Jews who had toiled for these enterprises during World War II, but the average payout converted to a rather paltry $850 at the time. Two decades later, Daimler-Benz and Volkswagen did something similar.

Both gaps in the German compensation system were filled in the 1990s. The German government first extended payments to survivors who had fled Eastern Europe after 1965 and to severely injured survivors still in the region. Then, in 1999, Germany worked out a deal with the United States that traded the suspension of class-action suits in American courts—legal efforts to seize German assets in the

United States to pay survivors—in return for the establishment of a fund to pay their claims. The fund would contain ten billion marks, half from the German government and half from private German corporations. Some of that money collected for this German Foundation Initiative went to non-Jewish Eastern European forced laborers, but three billion marks, or about 1.5 billion U.S. dollars at the time, went to Jewish survivors in compensation for both former slave labor and confiscated monetary assets, notably insurance policies.

In short, the history of recompense by Germany for the crimes of the Holocaust is an ambiguous one. On the one hand, buoyed by the extraordinary postwar revival of its economy and motivated by an initially self-interested desire for integration into NATO and the new Europe, Germany consented to pay an overall indemnity for the Holocaust that no one would have thought possible in 1945. On the other hand, the German record is clouded by the highly variable support provided to individuals, along with the halting and grudging way in which compensation expanded, which meant that hundreds of thousands of victims died before they became eligible.

Something similar happened in other European countries. Throughout Eastern Europe, of course, the record was far worse, as communist governments nationalized property rather than returned it, and most of them quickly drove out their surviving Jewish populations. Ninety percent of Bulgaria's remaining Jews had emigrated by 1949, nearly all of Romania's and Poland's by the 1960s. After the fall of communism, most of these countries then established residency and citizenship requirements for restitution of confiscated possessions, mostly real estate, which conveniently meant that they would not have to give anything back, since few Jews wished to return and many had lost their citizenship automatically upon emigrating.

In Western Europe, an initial flurry of attention to restoring homes and physical assets soon gave way to insensitivity and indifference that lasted into the 1990s. Backed by the Vatican, Catholic religious institutions and orphanages in Holland and France often declined to relinquish the Jewish children consigned to them by parents who had perished to other relatives or Jewish community institutions. So-called heirless assets—ones whose owners never came back—notably thousands of art works, remained in the hands of whatever person or institution held them when the war ended. Only in the 1990s were the postwar deficiencies made up. For example, the Dutch state provided compensation for the stocks and bonds that had been seized from Jews in Holland in the 1940s and sold to Dutch citizens, and the French government endowed a new Foundation for the Memory of the Shoah with 2.5 billion francs, a sum thought to be the value of property formerly owned by Jews in France that had remained unclaimed after the war.

Switzerland presented a particularly awkward case of restitution because it had been formally neutral during World War II but had purchased considerable quantities of plundered gold from the Third Reich and had served as the salesroom for much of the art, furs, jewelry, and commercial paper that the Nazis stole from Jews. Moreover, Switzerland's banks were suspected of having pocketed the contents of numerous "dormant" accounts opened by Jews who later were killed in the Holocaust. These issues were largely swept under the rug in the immediate postwar years. The United States acceded to the Washington Agreement of 1946, by which the Swiss promised to liquidate frozen German assets in their country, transfer half their value to a fund for stateless Nazi victims, and hand over one-sixth of the gold acquired from Nazi Germany in return for rehabilitation as an acceptable trading partner. Although the Swiss government passed a law in 1946 that ordered restitution of stolen art even if the purchase had been made in good faith, the legislation allowed only a short interval for making claims and applied only to works bought after 1939 in occupied areas, not in Germany proper.

During the 1990s, the World Jewish Congress succeeded in turning a spotlight on Switzerland's involvement with the Nazi regime,

AFTERMATH: WHAT LEGACIES, WHAT LESSONS? | 321

especially the issues of stolen gold, dormant bank accounts, production of war materials, and hostility to refugees. A series of commissions of inquiry were named, notably one under Paul Volcker on the conduct of Swiss banks and another led by Jean-François Bergier on the broad subject of Swiss policy and actions during World War II. The associated research teams demonstrated that the number of bank accounts opened by Jews during the Nazi era, unclaimed after the war, and then drained by the banks through fees probably was lower than Switzerland's critics had claimed, but that Swiss banks had conspired to frustrate postwar inquiries about them. The Bergier Commission also found that the Swiss National Bank knowingly had accepted plundered gold from the Nazi regime and afterward repeatedly mischaracterized—that is, lied about—its policies and conduct.

As these findings emerged, they played a significant role in setting the terms of the settlement of a U.S. court case against the Union Bank of Switzerland in 1999 by which the bank agreed to pay $1.25 billion into a fund administered by a U.S. District Court: $800 million for restitution of dormant bank accounts; $100 million for compensation for looted assets; and $325 million for payments to former slave laborers at Swiss-owned companies in occupied Europe or at German firms that had put their revenue in Swiss banks and for refugees mistreated by the Swiss. By December 31, 2015, the Claims Conference had disbursed the entire sum, mostly in the first two categories.

In retrospect, the recurrent pursuit of recompense for the victims of the Holocaust has proven both impossible and necessary—impossible because so much of what was lost was intangible and irremediable, necessary because so little of what could be given back or paid for was treated as such in the early postwar years, when every European nation was preoccupied with reconstruction. And because thousands of victims died before being able to benefit, the justice achieved was incomplete. Moreover, the monetization of loss is always approximate and grows more so as the interval between offense and redress increases, and many of the countries where the thefts were most extensive, notably Poland and Romania, have yet to grapple seriously with their obligations.

So despite enormous expenditures, gaps still yawn between what people suffered and what they got back and between what a perpetrating entity did or gained and what it ultimately paid. Every major restitution or compensation settlement since 1950 has been an instance of "negotiated justice," in which the amounts made available have had less to do with what real compensation required or real criminality deserved than with the momentary bargaining strength of the parties. This was as true of the sums distributed pursuant to the Luxembourg Agreement of 1952 as of those raised by the German Foundation Initiative of 2000. Political realities also explain why Switzerland never has been forced to indemnify any person or agency for the agreements that the Alpine republic signed with the governments of Poland and Hungary shortly after World War II. These deals allowed Switzerland to seize the heirless Swiss assets of dead Polish and Hungarian citizens, most of whom were Jews, as compensation for the nationalization of Swiss property in these newly communist states.

Moreover, the settlements involving corporations have been instances of rough justice: The enterprises bought valuable advantages by paying arbitrarily determined sums that bore no relation to the firms' earlier conduct, while sometimes guiltier parties walked away untouched. The Union Bank of Switzerland, in effect, purchased the right to complete a merger and do further business in the United States in return for a payment that exceeded the value of all Holocaust-related dormant bank accounts and gold deposits in the country's commercial banks. Yet the National Bank of Switzerland, the recipient of 92 percent of the gold in Switzerland that came from Nazi Germany, escaped with its underpayment under the Washington Agreement because it had no business interests in the United States that later could be threatened. German companies are not obligated to contribute to the Foundation Initiative, regardless of their involvement in slave labor or other dimensions of the Holocaust, and the extent of each voluntary contribution is pegged to a company's recent annual sales, not its degree of culpability, and is tax-deductible.

These are not the only blemishes on the quest for recompense. Although lawyers for restitution plaintiffs provoked numerous German firms into opening their archives and thus precipitated many significant historical studies, these advocates also spread a lot of misconceptions about the origin and worth of several forms of spoliation. Historians will be busy correcting the record for a long time. The admiring accounts of class-action suits that have been published also warrant rebuttal, not least because several lawyers in those and other restitution proceedings of the 1990s turned out to be awful role models for their profession. A number of them were censured, disbarred, forced to resign their positions, or sentenced to jail in subsequent years for legal and financial misconduct. Finally, recent settlements have opened old wounds within the Jewish community worldwide regarding the propriety of accepting money as indemnification for death and whether funds received should go exclusively to survivors or, at least in part, to Jewish cultural undertakings.

All that said, hundreds of thousands of survivors and heirs have benefited from the persistence of people who refused to settle for the first round of restitution and compensation in the immediate postwar years, and, as with regard to the relentless pursuit of the last Nazi war criminals at large, an important point has been made. That point is that statutes of limitations do not apply to the crimes of mass murder and mammoth larceny. Sooner or later, the repressed returns and, contrary to the legal axiom, justice delayed is not necessarily justice denied.

MEMORY, MYTHS, AND MEANINGS

Why? has examined a subject full of pain: pain of separation and exile, of persecution and torture, of degradation and murder, and of harrowing and haunted survival. To enter into the Holocaust is to risk enormous disillusionment with human beings and to awaken deep anxiety about how badly things can go wrong in this world. How can we sum up what we can and should learn from putting ourselves through this experience? What are the lessons and legacies of the topic?

In seeking an answer to that large question, perhaps we should begin by asking why anyone should study the Holocaust. The answer is not self-evident, and many people criticize our culture's fascination with the topic. In fact, Peter Novick's bestselling *The Holocaust in American Life* insisted that we can learn almost nothing useful from human conduct in so extreme a historical situation. Elsewhere, specialists in the field have been charged with engaging in "shoah business," and courses like the one on the Holocaust that I taught at Northwestern for many years have been derided as a form of special pleading that puts the miseries of Jews above those of many other populations that have suffered grievous onslaughts. Essentially, most responses to these criticisms stress that what makes the Holocaust stand out from other mass murders of the twentieth century is the sort of place that perpetrated it (an advanced and ostensibly civilized country) and the cause that propelled it (race, the most pressing issue of our time, not just in a polyglot country like the United States but also in a globalizing world). One should study the Holocaust, in other words, because its setting and impetus are highly relevant to the modern world.

The implicit corollary to that argument is that the Holocaust is a deadly precedent (after all, anything that has happened once can happen again), so we must learn about it in order to act effectively to prevent a recurrence. This practical argument can come in both universal and parochial variations. Some evidence vindicates the universal one, which emphasizes how learning can impede genocide, since the memory of the Holocaust helped impel Americans and Europeans to intervene, however belatedly, to stop the killing in Bosnia and Kosovo during the 1990s. But examples from outside Europe suggest that learning goes, literally, only so far. It clearly made no difference to the course of events in Rwanda in the 1990s, only slightly more to that in Darfur in the 2000s, and, thus far, very little to what has happened in Syria in the 2010s. The parochial version of the practical justification for studying the Holocaust—because the Holocaust is a warning against Jews depending on others—has been far more consistently consequential, but for both good and ill. It has stiffened the resolve of the citizens of a Jewish state in a hostile region, but it also has reinforced condescension toward Jews in the diaspora and an "us alone against the world" attitude that threatens to become self-fulfilling.

A related and important preliminary question is: How should we study the Holocaust? I have tried to indicate that I think the answer is "carefully and soberly," with a mix of precision and feeling, and without engaging in sentimentality or sanctification. Unfortunately, a certain amount of sanctification is built into the word "Holocaust," which derives from the ancient Greek term for "an offering totally consumed by fire"—in other words, a religious sacrifice. But many of those who were killed would have rejected an attribution of religious meaning to their deaths. To avoid this sort of ascription of meaning, even holiness, to mass murder, the Hebrew word "*Shoah*," which means "destruction," probably would be preferable. But the biblical uses of that word also are religiously inflected. In any case, the terminology has become firmly entrenched. Despite that, I hope readers of *Why?* come to see what happened as a set of historical events, to be recovered, studied, and comprehended by the usual historical means. We have to approach the record neither in awe nor in anger if we hope to learn anything valuable, rather than merely to have our preconceptions confirmed and our righteousness aroused.

Yes, the subject challenges our sense of the comprehensible, but that is because of our revulsion. We reflexively call the Holocaust unfathomable or unbelievable as a way of distancing ourselves from it and expressing our disgust. Nonetheless, the *Shoah* is comprehensible in the same way that any other catastrophic human or life experience is: with difficulty, patience, and application to the task. To say that the subject is incomprehensible is to despair, to give up, to admit to being too lazy to make the long effort, and, worst of all, to duck the challenge to our most cherished illusions about ourselves and each other that looking into the abyss of this subject entails. And the alternative to trying to understand how and why the Holocaust happened is to capitulate to a belief in fate, divine purpose, or sheer randomness in human events.

Why? has approached the problem of comprehensibility by breaking the topic down into four primary questions:

1. *Why the Jews?* Because their emancipation in the nineteenth century from centuries of residential and occupational confinement aroused a backlash that gave new impetus and new form to a chimerical hatred—that is, to a belief that they constituted the single cause for everything that others opposed and feared.

2. *Why the Germans?* Because a massive and multidimensional national crisis, a perfect storm of economic, political, cultural, and social upheavals, opened the way for believers in this hatred to acquire power in Germany and to reinforce or indoctrinate others in their views.

3. *Why murder and with these means?* Because of a process of problem-solving mission creep, a cumulative radicalization of policy, as increasingly harsh efforts to "remove" Jews from German territory proved insufficient or unworkable and gave way to ever more extreme methods of "elimination."

4. *Why was the eradication of the Jews so nearly successful,
resulting in the deaths of two-thirds of those in Europe and
at least three-quarters of those within reach of the Nazis?*
Because indifference and self-interest in Germany and
then the occupied or satellite states during World War
II cleared the way for the haters; because the logistics
of murder proved uncomplicated and self-financing;
because the Nazis' ferocious onslaught peaked during
the period of their greatest military success; and because
most of the killing was done when the Allies against
Germany could neither observe nor interdict it.

Along the way, we have debunked or at least complicated a number of myths. A few years back, I developed a lecture about how wide the gap has grown between what specialists know and what much of the public believes about the Holocaust. I was not alone in sensing this problem. Paul Levine also has perceived a growing "gap between scholarship and public memory" and called it a veritable "clash between 'town' and 'gown.'" My talk listed nine prevailing myths and misconceptions about the Holocaust and tried to explain why they are not so. As I list the first eight erroneous propositions, you will notice that much of this book has sought to undermine them:

First, that antisemitism played a primary or decisive role in bringing Hitler to power; it did not. Its persistence undermined and corroded a sense of solidarity between Jewish and non-Jewish Germans, but belief in an international Jewish conspiracy or a need to "remove" Jews from the German body politic was never strong or widespread enough in Germany to propel Hitler to high office. Without the Depression and the collusion of conservative leaders who expected to use Hitler for their purposes, he would not have come to power.

Second, that Hitler planned to murder the Jews from the day he took office, if not before; as far as historians can tell, he did not.

Massacre was always a possibility implicit in Nazi ideology, but only gradually became a semi-explicit policy of the German state—as a result of the clash between the ethnic mathematics of Hitler's drive for living space and his conviction that military victory depended on the disappearance of Jews from his realm.

Third, that the Allies could have done much to impede the killing once it began; given where and when most of the slaughter took place—in the northeast quadrant of the European continent and in the eighteen months following Germany's invasion of the Soviet Union, when the Reich was continuously on the offensive and winning—they could not. As David Cesarani has shown, the only ways Germany's opponents could have reduced the carnage significantly were for the British and/or the Soviets to lose the war in 1941, thus salvaging the prospect of deporting Jews elsewhere, or for the Allies to win the conflict in 1942–43, which was clearly beyond their power.

Fourth, that greater passive or active resistance by Jews could have reduced the death toll considerably; not realistically speaking. Such behavior would have required an almost unimaginable degree of clairvoyance on the part of Jews, an equally unimaginable degree of solidarity among them, and a far different balance of forces between Jews and their Nazi captors.

Fifth, that popular attitudes toward Jews, rather than political structures and interests, were the principal determinants of survival; not in the aggregate. More courage to help on the part of non-Jews would have produced more survivors, but nowhere near as many as remained alive because of the cynical political and personal calculations of collaborationist regimes in Europe.

Sixth, that the Holocaust diverted resources from the German war effort and weakened it in significant ways; not really. Germany sent more trains to the staging areas of Operation Barbarossa, the invasion of the Soviet Union, every day in mid-1941 (2,500) than the SS deployed to transport Jews to camps during the entire Holocaust (2,000), so clearly the deportations did not stress the capacity of the

Reich's railroads. The nation's reliance on forced and slave labor would have been just as chaotic, inefficient, and insufficient with the retention of the murdered Jews as it proved to be without them.

Seventh, that the slave labor system was driven principally by greed; it was not. It was the creation of a regime that lacked the population to sustain the massive war on which Germany had embarked and the imagination and generosity to enlist enough other Europeans in the cause.

Eighth, that most of the leading perpetrators of the Holocaust escaped punishment after World War II; in fact, the great majority of the vilest ones were already dead by 1945 or caught and penalized fairly shortly thereafter. To be sure, the Germans and the victors of World War II could have tried harder to find the killers who got away and could have rested less content with punishment that concentrated more on the order givers than the order executers in the camps and the shooting units. But the reckoning after 1945 for the Holocaust was more comprehensive than for any other modern instance of genocide.

At one point or another, the chapters in *Why?* have presented detailed evidence that refutes each of those assertions. Nonetheless, I do not expect them to disappear. Sometimes historical work is an extended game of whack-a-mole.

But *Why?* has said little thus far about the ninth common misconception. This is the idea, associated with the widely read books of Zygmunt Bauman and Detlev Peukert, that the Holocaust was a product of modernity and a demonstration of its dangers. The prevailing image is of mechanized murder, epitomized by ubiquitous references to "factories of death." But, although Auschwitz was a human disassembly line, it resembled a nineteenth-century slaughterhouse more than a modern manufacturing plant, and the other killing centers, with the partial exception of Majdanek, were ramshackle affairs. Most of the camps killed with a rather simple and at most early industrial device: a gasoline engine. Even the designation of the intended victims was done the old-fashioned way: by drawing up deportation lists with ink on paper, a task that was usually delegated to Jewish organizations in Western Europe and Germany and to Jewish Councils in the ghettos, if it was done at all. In occupied Russia and Ukraine, the non-Jewish locals just pointed out the Jewish ones. Finally, almost half of the killing occurred by starvation and exposure or by one-on-one bludgeoning or shooting—in short, by rather primitive means.

Neither is the broader form of this identification of the Holocaust with modernity accurate—namely, that the Holocaust represented the modern world's aspiration and achievement of the means to carry out vast forms of social engineering. The ambition to wipe out a whole group is not specifically modern: The goal is as old as the Israelites' extirpation of the Amalekites and the Romans' erasure of the Carthaginians, both of which were more complete than the Nazi murder of the Jews, despite being accomplished with mere fire and sword. Moreover, the pseudoscience that gave a supposedly modern gloss to the attempt at racial purification—eugenics—was, in fact, the very opposite of modern. It was the application of animal husbandry to human society, an argument that people can and should be bred like racehorses, and nationalities can and should be considered as breeds. Nazi racism was fundamentally rooted in an agricultural, not an industrial, world, and in an understanding of genetics that approximated that of the medieval or pre-modern eras. Furthermore, in scientific terms, eugenics was a fraud. Far from being modern in either conception or means, the Holocaust was an outbreak of extraordinary primitivism, a fitting product of an ideology that believed that all life is governed by the law of the jungle. In the astute words of Dan Stone, "Modernity was less the driving force of the Holocaust than the setting for it."

Finally, of course, the biggest myth about the Holocaust is another one not yet discussed, the claim that it never happened, and this book cannot close without discussing how ridiculous this claim is and why it continues to get made. On the ridiculousness, the first point to make emphatically is that the Holocaust is, quite simply, one of the most amply documented events in world history. To be sure, historians had to dig for several decades to arrive at as complete a picture of what happened as we now have, and, along the way, interpretations evolved as the state of our knowledge did. After all, the perpetrators went to considerable trouble to destroy the evidence of what they had done, though it was fortunately too voluminous to eradicate. Thus, to cite the most significant examples, we still have many of the passenger lists of the deportation trains, the prisoner death registries at Auschwitz and Mauthausen, some of the receipts for orders of Zyklon, most of the *Einsatzgruppen* reports that itemized and categorized the dead, photos of the victims' belongings piled up at Babi Yar, Lodz, and Birkenau, the minutes of the Wannsee Conference, Höfle's tally of the death toll at the Reinhard camps, SS statistician Richard Korherr's report from the spring of 1943 on the extent of the final solution to date, a vinyl recording of Himmler delivering his speech at Posen in 1943, Joseph Goebbels' extensive diaries, Alfred Rosenberg's somewhat more episodic ones, the postwar confessions of Rudolf Höss and numerous other killers, and so on.

Yet a vocal group of deniers persists in asserting that gas chambers did not exist and genocide did not occur during the Third Reich, that the number of Jews who died in World War II was small and an incidental outcome of the fighting, that the evidence mentioned above consists of forgeries or coerced testimonies, and that Jews and communists contrived the "hoax" of the Holocaust after World War II in order to discredit Germany, extract money from it, and gain support for a Jewish state in Palestine. Calling themselves "revisionists," these deniers drape themselves in the trappings of scholarship, but their strained arguments so clearly resemble the conspiracy theories that animated nineteenth-century antisemitism that their role as the real driving force behind denial shows through.

A British judge examined the claims of David Irving, perhaps the leading Holocaust denier of recent decades, during a libel trial in 2000 and pronounced them a deliberate falsification of the historical record. More recently, Bettina Stangneth's *Eichmann Before Jerusalem* has shown how a group of Nazi exiles and sympathizers in Argentina assembled most of the core arguments of denial and published them under a pseudonym in an émigré German journal called *Der Weg* (The Way) in 1954. Their article, "On the Streets of Truth," bearing the byline of a fictitious American journalist named Warwick Hester, who revisionists later claimed was the equally imaginary "American jurist Stephen F. Pinter," still circulates on the Internet. Stangneth considers it "the principal source text" for Holocaust deniers. Arguing with people who believe this nonsense is pointless, because the real source of their belief is not evidence or reasoning but incorrigible and circular fantasies about Jewish power and malevolence.

The title of a fine book by Eva Hoffman, the daughter of Holocaust survivors, is *After Such Knowledge*, and a way to bring this book to an end is to put that title in the form of a question. What should we do "after such knowledge"? What are the implications of all that we have learned about the Holocaust? Few subjects seem to cry out more for an attempt to establish their "meaning" or "message," and few subjects can make the person trying to formulate such conclusions feel so inadequate. Raul Hilberg often said that he was afraid to address the big questions raised by the *Shoah* for fear of giving small answers. Can we nonetheless draw any larger conclusions from our examination of these terrible events, despite all appropriate cautiousness about the attempt?

I think we can, but before I try, let me underline three features of our world that have profoundly changed since the end of the Second World War and that have affected the potential for renewed outbreaks of antisemitism.

First, the European world of the first half of the twentieth century was caught up in a kind of civil war between ideologies that prized individualism, discussion, and fulfillment—such as liberalism, representative government, and free enterprise—and ones that prioritized collectivism, obedience to group goals, and submission to authority: for example, fascism, Nazism, communism, and in those days most forms of Christianity. Many of the dangers to the Jews arose out of the way they were used in this conflict, as symbols of individualism or wealth or communism or freethinking and unbelief. These days are largely gone. Western nations are nearly all individualist, secular, and capitalist now. It is difficult to depict Jews as threats because the ideologies once tied to them have either triumphed and become generally shared or, in the case of communism, collapsed. That does not mean that antisemitism has disappeared, only that it has become, for the moment, largely powerless in the Western world.

Other parts of the globe are another matter, however. Wherever individualism, religious or ethnic pluralism, and enterprise remain ideologically suspect or are perceived as alien, Jews and all other minorities remain endangered, and the wretched lies of the *Protocols of the Elders of Zion* continue to be circulated and believed, as they are currently in Russia and many predominantly Muslim lands and among non-Jewish immigrants from these lands to other places. Just as in nineteenth- and twentieth-century Central and Eastern Europe, in the rest of the world today, the security of Jews, like that of most minorities, is least wherever the liberal values of toleration, coexistence, and openness to change are weak. To prevent other Holocausts, it is not enough to combat antisemitism; one has also to fight for these broader values, and not only at home. This is one of the central insights of the much-maligned European Union, which has insisted on increased protections of minority rights, especially for Roma and gay people, as preconditions for admitting countries to its ranks. In an increasingly globalized world, the obligation to combat and reduce parochialism and intolerance is an increasingly global matter.

Second, even in Western Europe and North America, the lessons drawn after 1945 about the world that spawned the Holocaust and the countermeasures put in place then are now under attack. In economically difficult times, Europe is experiencing a widespread resurgence of nationalism in the forms of hostility to foreigners, especially immigrants and the bureaucrats of the European Union, and a retreat from the welfare state under the cover of reducing debts. The current condition of Greek and Hungarian politics gives us a sense of what we have to look forward to if these trends continue and strengthen: the rise of neo-fascist parties and the enlistment of the energies of young and often unemployed men in brutality. Antisemitism, remember, rises and falls in inverse relationship to the stock market. Moreover, in this country and in Europe, economic inequality is growing, as the proponents of a certain version of free market capitalism increasingly lose sight of the implicit contract that most Western nations made with their populations in response to World War II. That contract traded a promise that governments would provide basic services and security in return for citizens abandoning political extremism. Communism and fascism were the outgrowths of societies in which the distribution of wealth and opportunity were massively unequal, and the postwar architects of European unification and social safety nets knew that reducing inequality was the essential prerequisite for social peace. As governments cease to keep their part of this bargain, they invite citizens to cease to keep theirs, and in such a context, no minority (and perhaps no democracy) will be safe. This is why the sort of political rhetoric that categorizes people as "makers vs. takers," often implying that the latter group consists heavily of immigrants, is a profoundly dangerous and ignorant throwback to a vastly destructive era.

Third, something else has changed in the past sixty years that may provide cause for worry. Ironically, that something else is the existence of a Jewish state. Nowadays, hostility to the existence and policies of the state of Israel tends in some quarters to slide into hostility to Jews in general and to the revival of vicious stereotypes about them. A potential for antisemitism to grow, a temptation to depict Jews once more as aliens with different purposes and priorities from those of their fellow citizens, exists in Europe (and to a lesser extent in the United States) because of a gap between European and Israeli interests and sensitivities.

For non-Jews in Europe, the top priority in the Middle East is not the survival of a Jewish state; the top priorities are political calm, access to oil, and sufficient economic development of the region so that its burgeoning and overwhelmingly young population does not swamp Europe's declining and aging one. Non-Jewish Europeans would prefer the problem of who gets what parts of what used to be Palestine simply to go away because the problem not only poses a threat of war on their doorstep, but also engenders militancy and unrest among the millions of Muslim immigrants already in Europe. At the same time, many American and European Jews, for emotional and practical reasons, including the memory of the Holocaust and the view that Israel is a potential home of last resort in the event of new eruptions of antisemitism, do not think they can afford such indifference.

In this division of interest lies a danger that demagogues may arise to accuse Jews of divided loyalties and of dragging the entire nations of which they are part into conflicts in which more is at stake for them than for those nations. Should that happen, a situation not unlike that of the 1930s will arise, antisemites will have an opening, and the strength of inclusive and liberal values will face powerful challenges. In other words, the existence of a Jewish state, especially one in which the most insular segments of the population play an increasingly decisive role, presents dangers to Jews elsewhere as well as benefits. In 2003, Tony Judt, a distinguished historian of Jewish descent, aroused an explosive debate by implicitly asking, in the *New York Review of Books*, "Is Israel good for the Jews?" and more or less answering no. Peter Beinart, the author of *The Crisis of Zionism* and himself an Orthodox Jew, has now taken Judt's place in highlighting the divergence between many Israeli practices and the liberal values that protect Jews elsewhere and in urging Jews to face up to the implications of this divergence as a matter of both principle and prudence.

In short, current conditions differ in hopeful and worrisome ways from those that produced the Holocaust. What, then, are the implications today of what we have learned for those of us fortunate enough to be living in relatively free societies? I think the Holocaust has two important lessons for minorities in the United States in general and for Jews in particular.

Lesson One is: Be alert but not afraid. Some degree of antisemitism is ineradicable for the foreseeable future; it has too long a pedigree and is too much the dark side of apartness and normal social frictions to disappear. But antisemitism is not necessarily always dangerous; it made Hitler possible, but it did not make him succeed. An irony of the history of antisemitism is that this ideology that called Jews parasites always has been a parasitic issue. To succeed, it has needed a host that it can exploit—a pervasive sense of crisis and victimization that allegedly justifies lashing out in reprisal. That is the essential prerequisite for widespread demonizing of Jews as the root of all evil, and the presence of this sort of sweeping crisis is what brought Hitler to power.

One can argue that the Great Recession sorely tested America, yet demonstrated that the will to demonize cannot get the upper hand in this country for several reasons. First, we have the example of the Holocaust to serve as a warning of what happens when such demonization triumphs. If Holocaust education has any prophylactic value, it probably lies in dampening impulses to attack Jews and in multiplying the number of antiantisemites. Second, the spread of education and of more complicated notions of causation may have made more people resistant to simplified blame games. I hope this is so. Third, we benefit from the freedom of the media to expose stereotyping, but with the fragmentation of news outlets and market segments into increasingly walled-off camps, this protection may be waning. Fourth, and above all, the internal diversity of American culture is a form of protection against demonization. We have no dominant faith or ethnic group anymore—in a sense, we are all members of some minority or another. As a result, many and perhaps most of us should and often do behave like those groups during the Holocaust whose own minority status led them to sympathize with Jews.

Consider what has NOT happened regarding Jews in the United States in recent years. At the heart of three of the nation's most sensational recent corruption scandals were three Jews, Andrew Fastow at Enron, Jack Abramoff of the congressional lobbying payoffs, and Bernard Madoff, who perpetrated the largest Ponzi scheme of all time. Moreover, a majority of the heads of the big banks and brokerage houses that recklessly sold derivative contracts and mortgage-backed securities and thus brought on the recent recession also were Jews. Yet outside of several neo-Nazi websites, no one has been idiotic enough to advance the proposition that these people are typical of American Jewry, and no political movement has arisen around a program of reforming Wall Street by "cleansing" it and the nation of Jews. Look how far we have come from the Strousberg and Panama affairs of the late 1800s.

Some commentators have noted the prominence of Jews among the proponents of an unnecessary and enormously costly war in Iraq, figures such as Paul Wolfowitz, Scooter Libby, and former senator Joseph Lieberman. Their role has given rise to muted suggestions that such people have been motivated by a desire to protect Israel and to muffled debates about the supposed power of pro-Israeli lobbying groups, such as AIPAC (American Israel Public Affairs Committee), to suppress discussion in the United States over Israeli policy in the occupied territories. But none of this conversation has turned virulent or violent. Most importantly, no political movement has emerged that presents any person's behavior as the expression of categorical beliefs and flaws rather than individual ones.

And consider the situation of the American minority that is in some ways most comparable to the Jews in Germany prior to 1933: gay people. They, too, say no to fundamental beliefs—in this case about gender roles; they, too, are present in small enough numbers to be easily attackable; they, too, have been depicted as degenerate and corrupting—the Bible contains scriptural passages frequently invoked to stigmatize gay people just as the Gospel of John and the Easter service used to be quoted to stigmatize Jews; they, too, are simultaneously derided for supposedly hanging together but also trying to blend in; and above all, gays, too, are often depicted as threatening—associated with child molestation and AIDS, as Jews once were with the blood libel and plague, and decried as people so unclean that they subvert and sully marriage by seeking to engage in it. Yet a "chimerical" image of gay people has failed to take hold in the United States, and resistance to a supposed "homosexual agenda" appears to be losing even its primary function of rallying the religious right now that "godless communism" is no longer available. The so-called defense of marriage and the hypocritical and cruel policy of "don't ask, don't tell" are gone.

Nonetheless, to expect bigotry to evaporate as if it had never existed would be foolhardy. Look at the way anti-immigrant feeling, much of it echoing the rhetoric of the nineteenth-century Know-Nothing Party, has surged in America in recent years, now turned not against Irish, Italians, and Jews but against Latinos, Muslims, and people of color. Overcoming these ugly repetitions of American exclusionism will take time, but it will happen, and in the same way it always has in the past, by sheer force of numbers. So, the first lesson of the study of the Holocaust for all minority groups in American society is "be alert, but not afraid." The general trend in America remains toward pluralism, freedom, and Jefferson's right to "the pursuit of happiness" for each person in his or her own way. We all have a responsibility to see to it that the trend continues; its opposite is the oppression, the stasis, and the homogeneity that Nazism prized.

Lesson Two of the Holocaust for minority groups in America and Jews in particular is: Be self-reliant but not isolationist. That means taking care with two very dangerous and common words nowadays: memory and identity. We tend to glorify both with cries such as "never again" or "never forget" and assertions of our heritage or loyalties before every utterance. But both practices have downsides.

This may sound like an odd, even heretical thing for a historian to write, but there is such a thing, in every culture as in every life, as too much memory. It can block learning, change, and trust. Looking perpetually back can seem to justify endless bitterness and to authorize fatalism. But, as Susan Sontag once wrote, "To make peace is to forget." The assumption that the future cannot help but resemble the past, that people who once hated me always will hate me, is often self-confirming. George Mitchell, the architect of the Good Friday agreement that brought peace to Northern Ireland, notes in his memoirs that on the eve of the deal, 83 percent of the people there thought a resolution of their civil war impossible. Sometimes one of the most valuable skills in life is the ability to think outside the box of the past, as Mitchell did. Not always, of course, but sometimes, and one of the purposes of studying history is to acquire a feel for the difference.

There is also such a thing, in every culture as in every life, as too much pride in what one's kind has been and currently is, rather than in what it can achieve in concert with others. The history of the Holocaust suggests that minorities run risks when they depend too much on others, since the others generally will be guided by self-interest, but also that cutting oneself off from others poses its own, perhaps equal, dangers. Groups, like individuals, cannot make their ways alone; they need friends.

In addition to those two lessons with special relevance to members of minority groups, I believe that the study of the Holocaust has three broad implications for all citizens, whether members of minorities or not. First, the Holocaust highlights the primacy of avoiding situational causes. The veneer of civilization is thin, the rule of law is fragile, and the precondition of both is economic and political calm. This means that politics matters, and none of us can ever afford to fail to participate in making responsible public policy. Nazism stemmed from German racism, but that ideology would never have become national policy without the presence of an economic, national, and ideological crisis that fostered demagoguery and irresponsibility. Everyone's first goal in a decent society must be to avoid contributing to such a crisis or to those responses. Remember, more Germans became antisemites because they became Nazis than vice versa. Some of them became Nazis before 1933 because of the mess and the impasse in which their country found itself, and even more of them did so later because the Nazis became the apparently rather successful holders of power.

I have often thought that one of the great injustices of the Nuremberg trials was that Franz von Papen, the man who did more to bring about Hitler's appointment as chancellor of Germany than anyone else, was acquitted because he had not committed an actual war crime. True, but he had made all the war crimes possible. The court held that political misjudgment is not a criminal offense, and I concede the point. But historians rightly vilify Papen, and his name will be forever odious. Something similar can be said of the financiers and bankers whose recklessness brought on the stock market crash of 1929 and the collapse of Germany's banks in 1931. Like Papen, they are permanent reminders that our first responsibility as citizens, regardless of our walk of life, is to do no harm. That is not a doctrine of passivity. *Why?* has shown how much harm doing nothing can do. It is a doctrine of activity informed by seriousness, prudence, restraint, and unselfishness. These were not Franz von Papen's chief attributes, any more than they were the chief attributes of the German financial wizards of the 1920s or, for that matter, of the American ones during the first decade of this century.

Second, the Holocaust illustrates the fundamental importance and difficulty of individual courage and imagination. This dreadful history shows the necessity of standing up to categorization and conspiracy peddling, of refusing to turn a blind eye or a deaf ear to defamation. There can be no drawing of distinctions between citizens when it comes to fundamental human rights, no hair-splitting about who gets to have them and who does not. In fact, such rights are for the people whom we fear or dislike because they are the people who need them. But this dreadful history also shows that doing the right thing can have costs that are multiplied by the unwillingness of most people to pay them, so bravery is not enough—wit, wiliness, shrewd judgment, persistence, and creativity in challenging evil are also indispensable. Resistance is never easy and seldom comfortable, and compassion has to be practiced in order to hold up when challenged. Rising to that challenge begins with a refusal to be cowed, followed by alertness to opportunity. According to the philosopher Philip Hallie, who several decades ago wrote a powerful account of the villagers in Le Chambon-sur-Lignon, their principal leader, Pastor André Trocmé, "believed that if you choose to resist evil, and you choose this firmly, then ways of carrying out that resistance will open up around you. His kind of originality generated originality in others."

Third, the Holocaust testifies to the need to preserve the essential distinction between means and ends. Antinomianism—the idea that moral restrictions do not apply to us because of some special nobility or necessity of our purposes—is the fatal temptation that the Nazis proffered and the fateful rationalization they used. Still endemic, it always feeds on fear. In times of extreme crisis, the history of the Holocaust demonstrates, a person's most profound moral commitments—to family, faith, community, country, organization, party, and principle, for example—can be made to seem like reasons to choose to do great harm, can be deeply corrupted. Franz Neumann, one of the pioneer analysts of National Socialism, highlighted

its adeptness at "surrounding every perfidy with the halo of idealism." The dreadful events of the Holocaust should be a reminder
that calls to self-defense and for retribution are among the most
corruptible of ideals. As William Pitt, a British prime minister in
the mid-eighteenth century, once warned: "Necessity is the plea for
every infringement of human freedom. It is the argument of tyrants;
it is the creed of slaves." The politics of division and emergency, of
bullying and rage—the politics that says desperate times require the
political equivalent of "stand-your-ground" laws—that sort of politics always deserves opposition and scorn because it is the politics
that is just itching to get out of hand.

The Holocaust was not mysterious and inscrutable; it was the
work of humans acting on familiar human weaknesses and motives:
wounded pride, fear, self-righteousness, prejudice, and personal
ambition being among the most obvious. Once persecution gathered momentum, however, it was unstoppable without the death of
millions of people, the expenditure of vast sums of money, and the
near destruction of the European continent. Perhaps no event in history, therefore, better confirms that very difficult warning embed-
ded in a German proverb that captures the meaning I hope readers
will take away from this book: *Wehret den Anfängen*, "Beware the
beginnings."

That proverb comes to mind whenever I am asked at public
forums when and how I think the Holocaust could have been prevented or stopped. My response is to name a time and place exactly:
April 1–5, 1933, in Berlin. April 1 is well known as the date of the
Nazi boycott of Jewish-owned shops across Germany. But something else occurred that day, the occupation by a company of Nazi
storm troopers of the offices of the National Association of German
Industry, headed by Gustav Krupp von Bohlen und Halbach, who
also was the leader of the Krupp armaments and steel firm. The
thugs made clear their intention to stay and disrupt the association's
work until it dismissed all its employees who were Jews or affiliated

with other political parties. When Krupp, who was a very powerful and prominent man, tried to persuade Hitler to call off his dogs, the Nazi Führer simply declined, explaining that he could not restrain the enthusiasm of people who had been through thick and thin with him as he rose to power. Krupp then gave in, firing everyone of whom the Nazis disapproved on April 5 and thus breaking his contracts with each of those people.

One of the members of the National Association's governing board, a man named Georg Müller-Oerlinghausen, wrote a prophetic protest to Krupp eight days later, saying that his actions amounted to capitulation to bullying and that they deprived the organization of all basis for future noncompliance with Nazi demands. If the German industrialists would not stand up for the contractual legal rights of their own personnel, Müller-Oerlinghausen asked, for whom would they stand up and on what grounds? He was right, and the more powerful the Nazis became, the more irreversibly right he was.

Beware the beginnings.

ACKNOWLEDGMENTS

Naturally, a book that took shape over almost thirty years owes a lot to a great many people, too many to list most of them by name. I have the privilege of working in a vibrant field, full of indefatigable and intelligent researchers from whom I have learned something new every day, so I want to express my appreciation to the scholars on whose publications I have drawn heavily in this book, both explicitly and implicitly. I also thank the thousands of Northwestern University students who completed History 349 between 1987 and 2015 and whose curiosity and eagerness to learn motivated me to keep trying, year after year, to make my presentation of the evidence and my reasoning from it ever clearer and tighter. Many colleagues and graduate students contributed valuable input at a History Department workshop on chapter 3 in Evanston in May 2015. I am especially indebted to Professor Amy Stanley for prompting me to rethink one minor and one major issue and to Professor Robert Lerner for alerting me to a significant omission. Thanks, too, to the participants in the Silberman Seminar at the United States Holocaust Memorial Museum in June 2015, who heard these chapters as lectures and provided useful feedback. Several generous colleagues and friends read the manuscript and offered numerous suggestions that enhanced it: Christopher Browning, Benjamin Frommer, Richard Levy, Wendy Lower, Thomas Lys, and Michael Marrus. The Jewish Foundation for the Righteous and Oxford University Press kindly granted permission to reprint several passages that I wrote for the chapter introductions in *How Was It Possible? A Holocaust Reader* (2015) and Chapter 35 of *The Oxford Handbook of Holocaust Studies* (2010). My agent, Peter Bernstein, and my editor, John Glusman, saw exactly the virtues in the manuscript that I tried to put there, and that carried me over the finish line. Everyone mentioned here earned and has my gratitude, but I alone am responsible for any errors or defects that remain.

Special thanks to Volt and the dogs: Offsetting the bleakness of what I was working on, they made each day a pleasure.

NOTES

INTRODUCTION
(xiv) **"Impossible to remember,"** Judt, *Postwar*, 830.

CHAPTER 1: TARGETS
(3) **A professor of mine**; he put the matter more elegantly in writing: "antisemitism is a cluster of behaviors with a single name;" Gay, *Freud, Jews and Other Germans*, 13.
(4) **Germany took pains**, Motadel, *Islam*, 56–60.
(5) **xenophobic and chimerical forms**, Langmuir, *Toward*, 306, 328–52.
(5) **Ancient Roman attitudes**, Lindemann and Levy, *Antisemitism*, 38–40.
(9) **Freud, Samuel, Poliakov, and Cohn**, Hand and Katz, *Post-Holocaust France*, 177–84.
(9) **"doctrine of Jewish witness,"** Lindemann and Levy, *Antisemitism*, 64–65; Bauer, *History*, 9.
(11) **surge of attacks . . . blood libel**, Lindemann and Levy, *Antisemitism*, 68–70, 74.
(12) **Luther and Erasmus**, Nirenberg, *Anti-Judaism*, 254, 262, 266.
(16) **"beliefs in racial or ethnic determinism,"** Lindemann, *Esau's Tears*, xiv.
(16) **"A Jew can no more,"** Stern, *Politics*, 141.
(17) **On Gobineau and Schlegel**, see Weitz, *Century*, 33–35; Arvidsson, *Aryan*, 26–30.
(19) **On Galton and Ploetz**, see Burleigh and Wippermann, *Racial State*, 29, 32.
(21) **Patents of Toleration**, Beller, *Antisemitism*, 33–34; Meyer, *German-Jewish History*, v. 2, 16–17.
(22) **Bavarian petition . . . opposing equality for Jews**, Hochstadt, *Sources*, 24.
(25) **Country and city population figures**, Mitchell, *Statistics*, 3–15.
(28) **Jews seemed disproportionately present . . . illustrative figures**, Slezkine, *Jewish Century*, 47–50; Pulzer, *Rise*, 12; Hamann, *Hitler's Vienna*, 327–28; Elon, *Pity*, 259.
(29) **That may have been what Albert Einstein had in mind**, Elon, *Pity*, 274.
(32) **Dreyfus and Beilis**, Lindemann, *Jew Accused*, passim.
(32) **3 percent**, ibid., 60.
(33) **"enemies of the antisemites, not of antisemitism,"** ibid., 126.

CHAPTER 2: ATTACKERS
(38) **On Herder**, see Burleigh and Wippermann, *Racial State*, 25; Smith, *Handbook*, 242–43; Arvidsson, *Aryan*, 26, 29, 74–75.
(39) **On Fichte**, see Katz, *Prejudice*, 57–59; Smith, *Handbook*, 245–46.
(39) **the most famous tales that the Grimms reproduced**, Smith, *Handbook*, 263.
(40) **"Jewishness in Music,"** Katz, *Darker Side*, 33–46.

(41) **On Hep-Hep**, see Hoffmann et al., *Exclusionary Violence*, 23–42

(41) **"freedom to choose their own trades,"** Aly, *Why*, 34.

(42) **"No longer should we tolerate,"** Katz, *Prejudice*, 252.

(42) **"almost exclusively in favor of our co-citizens,"** ibid., 253.

(43) **six editions**, ibid., 256.

(44) **"natural reaction. . . . misfortune,"** Hochstadt, *Sources*, 27.

(44) **265,000 German men signed**, Levy, *Antisemitism*, v. 1, 21.

(44) **Stoecker's party was overwhelmed**, Pulzer, *Rise*, 87.

(44) **Progressive Party gains**, Ritter, *Wahlgeschichtliches Arbeitsbuch*, 39.

(45) **figure 2**, ibid., 40–41, 146.

(46) **electoral base small . . . narrow**, Pulzer, *Rise*, 189–90; Lindemann and Levy, *Antisemitism*, 130.

(46) **"Gegen Junker und Juden,"** Levy, *Downfall*, 58.

(47) **Wilhelm Marr . . . "a business,"** Zimmermann, *Marr*, 103.

(48) **Krupp and the usual breakdown in election districts**, Ritter, *Wahlgeschichtliches Arbeitsbuch*, 133–35 (Prussia), 164–66 (Saxony).

(48) **63 percent**, Lindemann, *Esau's Tears*, 149.

(48) **Jewish population, birthrate, intermarriage, immigration, urbanization**, Richarz, *Leben*, v. 2, 12–23.

(50) **concentration of Jews' occupations**, ibid., 23–34.

(50) **Jewish immigrants from Poland**, ibid., 18–19.

(51) **"They lived like bankers,"** Elon, *Pity*, 255.

(52) **Jewish officers**, Vital, *People Apart*, 135.

(52) **2 percent of the professors**, Richarz, *Leben*, v. 2, 32.

(52) **"cultural code,"** Volkov, *Germans*, 115.

(52) **The Prussian state had taken firm action**, see Smith, *Butcher's Tale*.

(53) **Prominent Jewish industrialists**, Elon, *Pity*, 265–67.

(53) **election of 1912**, ibid., 293; Levy, *Downfall*, 250.

(53) **"Kinderkrankheit,"** Gay, *Freud, Jews, and Other Germans*, 15.

(53) **"Jew count,"** Levy, *Antisemitism*, v. 1, 371–72; Pulzer, *German State*, 205–6; Elon, *Pity*, 338–39; Rosenthal, *Ehre*, passim.

(54) **if only 12,000 or 15,000 more Jews**, Hitler, *Mein Kampf*, 679.

(54) **Wilhelm II and Ludendorff**, Tooze, *Deluge*, 135; Liulevicius, *War Land*, 198.

(54) **the incidence of violent acts**, see Walter, *Kriminalität*, and Hecht, *Juden*.

(55) **figure 3**, J. Falter et al., *Wahlen*, 44.

(56) **On the origins of the** *Protocols*, Segel, *A Lie*, 65–69; Bronner, *Rumor*, 80–88.

(57) **"the best proof,"** Hitler, *Mein Kampf*, 307.

(57) **Reparations and war debts**, Tooze, *Deluge*, 369, 444; Balderston, *Economics*, 20–21.

(58) **Scheunenviertel riot**, Hoffmann et al., *Exclusionary*, 123–40.

(61) **"theozoology,"** one of Hitler's ideological forerunners in Vienna, Jorg Lanz von Liebenfels, coined the term as the title of a book he published in 1904.

(61) **"His speeches,"** Konrad Heiden, quoted in Rees, *Charisma*, 28.

(61) **"biological materialism,"** Aly, *Why*, 11.

(62) **"We know only one people,"** Hamann, *Hitler's Vienna*, 212.

(62) **"thoughtlessness,"** Arendt, *Eichmann*, 49, 287–88; compare Stangneth, *Eichmann*, 201–2, 217–19.

(63) **"a blemish,"** Rauschning, *Voice*, 220.

(63) **Twenty-five Point Program**, Noakes and Pridham, *Nazism*, v. 1, 14–16.

(64) **programs laid down in 1931 and Göring's speech**, Adam, *Judenpolitik*, 26–31.

(64) **"racial tuberculosis" . . . Robert Koch**, Fest, *Hitler*, 212; Kershaw, *Hitler*, v. 2, 470.

(65) **downplayed antisemitism**, Allen, *Seizure*, 142; Wistrich, *Hitler*, 45.

(66) **"the opposite of what exists today,"** Fest, *Face*, 296.

(67) **On Hirschfeld**, see Beachy, *Gay Berlin*, 160–86; on Fromm, Aly and Sontheimer, *Fromms*.

(67) **unemployment . . . 15 percent**, Balderston, *Economics*, 79; Overy, *Recovery*, 20; and James, *Slump*, 357.

(68) **The way the Nazis campaigned**, Bracher, *Dictatorship*, 179, 182.

(69) **Northeim**, Allen, *Seizure*, 88–89, 126, 142.

(69) **40 percent**, Noakes and Pridham, *Nazism*, v. 1, 84.

(70) **Alone among the parties**, Mühlberger, *Social Bases*, 71–80.

(70) **"emancipate women,"** Stibbe, *Women*, 17.

(70) **Early in the new year**, *Simplicissimus*, January 8, 1933; Turner, *Thirty Days*, 1.

(71) **"were drawn to antisemitism,"** Allen, *Seizure*, 84.

CHAPTER 3: ESCALATION

(76) **two-tier approach**, Barkai, *Boycott*, Chapter 2.

(78) **"social death,"** Kaplan, *Between*, 5.

(79) **Since 1933 . . . working for themselves or each other**, Barkai, *Boycott*, 106–8, and Bajohr, *Aryanisation*, 108.

(79) **"A law making the whole of Jewry liable,"** Tooze, *Wages*, 221.

(79) **"in the event of his death,"** Noakes and Pridham, *Nazism*, v. 3, 73.

(79) **The gist was**, ibid., 72–79.

(82) **carted off to concentration camps**, Cesarani, *Final*, 164–65.

(83) **willing to join in the violence**, see Steinweis, *Kristallnacht*, and as background, Wildt, *Volksgemeinschaft*, chapters 5–7.

(83) **36,000, 26,000, and 600 men**, Wünschmann, *Before Auschwitz*, 197, 204.

(83) **allowed the German insurance companies to renege**, Feldman, *Allianz*, 221, 227.

(84) **emergence of a new word**, Hayes, *How*, 172–73.

(85) **he told the Czech foreign minister**, Adam, *Judenpolitik*, 235.

(85) **"[t]he Germans. . . . have embarked,"** Breitman and Lichtman, *FDR*, 120.

(86) **German planners actually**, Browning, *Origins*, 86; Gerwarth, *Hangman*, 179–81; Cesarani, *Final*, 300–1.

(86) **"the bolshevist method,"** Breitman, *Architect*, 119.

(88) **Hermann Göring charged Reinhard Heydrich**, Roseman, *Wannsee*, 53.

(89) **murders reached a crescendo**, Burds, *Rovno*, 20–21.

(89) **"the soldier must have full understanding,"** Megargee, *Annihilation*, 125.

(90) **Events proceeded along parallel lines in German-occupied Serbia**, Browning, *Origins*, 334–46.

(92) *Selbstgleichschaltung* **and the diplomats**, Hayes, *How*, 111–17.

(92) **group of leading business executives and Krupp**, Berenbaum and Peck, *Holocaust and History*, 198–99.

(92) **Degussa**, Hayes, *From Cooperation*, 38.

(93) **Weizsäcker's remarks**, Hayes, *How*, 113.

(93) **Roessler's remarks**, Hayes, *From Cooperation*, 26.

(94) **"you reckon that you,"** ibid., viii.

(94) **"Sind Sie arisch?,"** Haffner, *Defying*, 150–51.

(94) **comrade**, ibid., 290–91.

(95) **"From now on,"** Noakes and Pridham, *Nazism*, v. 2, 252.

(96) **cutting off contact with Jewish friends and neighbors**, Fulbrook, *Dissonant*, 103–13.

(96) **"work towards the Führer,"** Kershaw, *Hitler*, v. 1, 529.

(96) **warping . . . worked especially powerfully on young people**, Fulbrook, *Dissonant*, 136–39.

(97) **behavior of Ernst Busemann**, Hayes, *From Cooperation*, 88–90, 93–98 ("it is pointless," 90).

(98) **Potsdam and Kiel**, Bankier, *Germans*, 70–71.

(99) **Magdeburg**, Kulka and Jäckel, *Jews*, 155.

(99) **many farmers had to be forced**, Stephenson, *Home Front*, 139–40.

(99) **shame and disgust on the morning after**, Schrafstetter and Steinweis, *Germans*, 9, 60, 67–68.

(100) **"The images of the arrest of the Jews,"** Kulka and Jäckel, *Jews*, 529.

(100) **local offices from all around the country**, ibid., 537–42.

(100) **"our intellectuals,"** Browning, *Origins*, 390.

(100) **"Jew-friendly behavior,"** ibid; Stargardt, *German War*, 242; Bajohr and Pohl, *Holocaust*, 56.

(100) **the first contingents. . . . When the shipments resumed**, Morehouse, *Berlin*, 168, 171.

(101) **those descended from or in marriages to non-Jewish Germans**, Büttner, *Not*, 11–71; Tent, *Shadow*, 1–19; Meyer, *Balancing* Act, 346; and Gruner, *Widerstand*, 178–89.

(104) **Transfer Agreement, 20,000, and 1.5 percent**, Bauer, *Brother's*, 128–29; Barkai, *Boycott*, 51–53, 100–4; Barkai, "German Interests," 245, 251–52, 261–66; Yisraeli, "Third Reich," 139, 141–42, 147.

(105) **some people had better chances of being accepted elsewhere than others**, Barkai, *Boycott*, 55, 153–54; Kaplan, *Between*, 138–44; Richarz, *Leben*, v. 3, 49, 51–52; Wasserstein, *Eve*, 417.

(106) **They fought back the only way they collectively could**, Bauer, *Brother's*, 105–37, 257–58; Barkai, *Boycott*, 85–99; Barkai, *Centralverein*, 307–17; Richarz, *Leben*, v. 3, 42–47; Benz, *Juden*, Chapter 4.

(107) **the effort proved hopeless. . . . The Reichsvereinigung thus degenerated**, Meyer, *Balancing*, chapters 1–2; Richarz, *Leben*, v. 3, 58–64; Benz, *Juden*, 71–74.

(107) **In Vienna**, Rabinovici, *Eichmann's*, 2–3, 119, 129–31.

(108) **Emblematic of the viciousness**, Meyer, *Balancing*, 158–61; Moorhouse, *Berlin*, 268–71.

(108) **appeasers actually were inclined to blame Jews**, Cesarani, *Final*, 216.

(109) **France signed a new treaty**, Caron, *Uneasy*, 196–200; McCullough and Wilson, *Violence*, 54–69.

(109) **Joseph Lyons . . . resolutely refused**, ibid., 144.

(110) **the Hollywood film distribution companies**, Doherty, *Hollywood*, 38.

(112) **the Gestapo used the card files**, Meyer, *Balancing*, 127.

(112) **The SS experimented briefly in 1944**, Wachsmann, *KL*, 453.

(112) **GM's Opel division**, Turner, *General Motors*, 42–44, 86–103.

(112) **Ford-Werke in Cologne**, Ford Motor Co., *Findings*, 35–40.

CHAPTER 4: ANNIHILATION

(114) **how concentrated the time and place**, Browning, *Ordinary Men*, xv; Hilberg, *Destruction*, 1321; Stargardt, *Witnesses*, 9; Dwork, *Children*, xi.

(116) **the effect on his men**, Roseman, *Wannsee*, 63–64; Rhodes, *Masters*, 150–54, 167–68, 223–28.

(117) **None of the experts balked. . . . to assure the people involved of immunity**, Bryant, *Confronting*, 37–38.

(118) **propaganda campaign in the 1930s**, Proctor, *Racial Hygiene*, 181–85.

(118) **he expected potential religious objections to decline**, Bryant, *Confronting*, 27.

(118) **the MDs in charge of the program had decided**, ibid., 43–44.

(119) **Lange soon modified the killing process**, Browning, *Fateful*, 59.

(119) **14f13,** Wachsmann, *KL,* 250–58.

(120) **Dachau. . . . Most . . . were transported,** Morsch and Perz, *Studien,* 241, 338–40.

(120) **Tests on mental patients,** Browning, *Origins,* 283, 304.

(121) **whom he regarded in the typically Catholic fashion,** Griech-Polelle, *Bishop,* 107–8, 113–14, 118, 150–51.

(121) **Less than three weeks. . . . did not begin applying,** Berger, *Experten,* 30, 34–36; Bryant, *Eyewitness,* 3, 54, 78, 151, 159, 161; Arad, *Belzec,* 17–19.

(121) **were discussing setting up "gassing devices,"** Hochstadt, *Sources,* 116–17.

(121) **work began on the Belzec death camp,** Browning, *Origins,* 360–65; see also Witte et al., *Dienstkalendar,* 233–34.

(122) **identified the derelict manor house,** Montague, *Chelmno,* 49–53.

(122) **solved the carbon monoxide supply problem,** Browning, *Fateful Months,* 57–62; Cüppers, *Rauff,* 109–18.

(123) **1/3000th of an ounce,** Hayes, *From Cooperation,* 273.

(123) **the average cost of murder per head,** ibid., 293, 296–97.

(123) **an instruction . . . that forbade further emigration,** Arad et al., *Documents,* 153–54.

(124) **Beyond the addition of two officials,** Cesarani, *Final,* 454–55.

(124) **Heydrich laid out a plan,** Hochstadt, *Sources,* 132–36.

(124) **Rosenberg . . . had briefed trusted German reporters,** Browning, *Origins,* 403–4; Matthäus and Bajohr, *Political Diary,* 385–89, quotation at 388.

(124) **"this is as close . . . as historians will get,"** Fritzsche, "The Holocaust," 604.

(125) **As . . . Raul Hilberg emphasized,** Hilberg, *Destruction,* v. 1, 49–59.

(126) **Mortality at Chelmno,** Montague, *Chelmno,* 185–88.

(126) **jerry-rigged edifices,** Berger, *Experten,* 49, 96; Arad, *Belzec,* 25; Kuwalek, *Belzec,* 61–62, 66–67.

(127) **Death tolls and survivors of the Operation Reinhard camps,** Berger, *Experten,* 9, 52, 64, 116, 140–41, 177, 252–55, 272, 276, 388; Bryant, *Eyewitness,* 5–7, 99, 110, 113, 125; Arad, *Belzec,* 84, 87, 99, 127–30, 258–69, 341–48; Schelvis, *Sobibor,* 197–98; Kuwalek, *Belzec,* 14, 170, 225–27, 244–46.

(127) **second group of death camps,** Gruner, *Jewish,* 217–29, 255–56; Gutman and Berenbaum, *Anatomy,* 114; Hayes, *Industry,* 347–60; Dlugoborski and Piper, *Auschwitz,* v. 2, 100–136; Megargee, *Encyclopedia,* v. IB, 875–88; Morsch and Perz, *Studien,* 219–27; Mailänder, *Female,* 172–73.

(128) **deaths at and survivors of Auschwitz,** Hayes, "Capital," 330.

(129) **Majdanek was far less lethal,** Mailänder, *Female,* 44.

(130) **Mauthausen,** Wachsmann, *KL,* 163–66, 214; Morsch and Perz, *Studien,* 126–28, 244–59; Caplan and Wachsmann, *Camps,* 131; Jardim, *Mauthausen,* 54–56; Megargee, *Encyclopedia,* v. IB, 900–907; Horwitz, *Shadow,* 17–18.

(130) **Durchgangstrasse IV camps and Janowska,** Brandon and Lower, *Shoah,* 190–223, 324.

(131) **the camps took in enormous plunder,** Hayes, "Capital," 337; Hochstadt, *Sources,* 170–78; Arad, *Belzec,* 154–64; Berger, *Experten,* 180; Montague, *Chelmno,* 88.

(132) **the example of the Netherlands,** Dean, *Robbing,* 285.

(133) **Chelmno consisted,** Montague, *Chelmno,* 76–84.

(133) **obtained from IG Farben,** Dwork and van Pelt, *Auschwitz,* 207–8.

(133) **Potemkin villages,** see the keyed maps in Arad, *Belzec,* 34–35, 38–39.

(133) **Quantity and cost of the Zyklon used at Auschwitz,** Hayes, *From Cooperation,* 295.

(134) **some 7,000 Germans,** Dlugoborski and Piper, *Auschwitz,* v. 5, 102.

(134) **about one-third as many,** Hagen, *German History,* 343.

(134) **Germans and *Hiwis* at Belzec, Sobibor, and Treblinka,** Berger, *Experten,* 138, 218; Arad, *Belzec,* 19, 22; Kuwalek, *Belzec,* 79–80, 111.

(134) **4,750 of these people,** Black, "Foot Soldiers," 7.

(134) **earned substantially more,** Berger, *Experten*, 329–30.

(134) **operated in the black,** Bryant, *Confronting*, 39.

(135) **Priority, pace, and equipment of deportation trains,** Mierzejewski, *Asset*, v. 2, 117–19; Hilberg, *Sonderzüge*, 59, 81–82, 86; Gerlach and Aly, *Kapitel*, 273; Lichtenstein, *Tod*, 22, 34, 51–53, 96, 105, 135.

(135) **German and Hungarian train statistics,** Mierzejewski, *Asset*, v. 2, 127, 166; Gall and Pohl, *Eisenbahn*, 228, 239; Lichtenstein, *Tod*, 14; Pätzold and Schwarz, *Bahnhof*, 104–6.

(136) **the same one or two slow and rickety trains,** Hilberg, *Sonderzüge*, 208–12; Arad, *Belzec*, 52, 65–66; Mierzejewski, *Asset*, v. 2, 117; Lichtenstein, *Tod*, 67.

(138) **On the doctrine of "base motive,"** see Bryant, *Eyewitness*, 92–94.

(139) **"cognitive dissonance,"** see Newman and Erber, *Understanding*, 52–54.

(139) **"repulsive duty" . . . "horrible task,"** Breitman, *Architect*, 196.

(139) **"all had an intense need to talk,"** Lower, *Furies*, 93.

(140) **"political soldiers,"** Westermann, *Hitler's*, 15.

(141) **"dichotomist ethics," "moral grammar," "too weak,"** Kühne, *Belonging*, 59, 87, 167.

(141) **"By claiming weakness,"** Beorn, *Marching*, 241.

(141) **"they were always capable of such violence,"** Römer, *Kameraden*, 465.

(141) **"particular National Socialist morality,"** Welzer, *Täter*, 31.

(142) **they became willing . . . identified,** Berger, *Experten*, 312.

(142) **Neuser and Glas,** Mierzejewski, *Asset*, v. 2, 125–26.

(142) **Oskar Gröning,** Rees, *Auschwitz*, 155–58.

(143) **only 30 percent of the SS men . . . *Volksdeutsche* made up a large percentage,** Hayes, "Capital," 336. On the predominance of *Volksdeutsche* and *Hiwis* in the guard force at Majdanek, see Mailänder, *Female*, 67, 146–47.

(144) **Numbers of German women in the occupied East,** Lower, *Furies*, 6–7, 21.

(145) **"In favoring perceived duty over morality,"** Lower, ibid., 111. On the propensity for violence among the women guards at Majdanek, see Mailänder, *Female*, 71–72, 274–79.

(145) **"I did not want to stand behind the SS men,"** Lower, *Furies*, 155.

(145) **Major Karl Plagge,** Hayes, *How*, 658–74.

(145) **Anton Schmidt,** Wette, *Feldwebel*, 234–35

(146) **outcomes of this sort were rare,** ibid., 139–42.

(146) **"inner identification with evil,"** Segev, *Soldiers*, 214.

(147) **60 percent . . . and another 17 percent,** Wildt, *Generation*, 23, 458.

(147) **more than 83 percent of them,** Berger, *Experten*, 292–93.

(147) **upwardly mobile, well educated, and with long records of involvement,** Wildt, *Generation*, 38–47, 429–32. See also Ingrao, *Believe*, 17–31, and Perz, "Austrian Connection," 418–19.

(148) **the T4 personnel . . . constituted a highly indoctrinated group,** Berger, *Experten*, 302–4, 316–18.

(148) **"our India,"** Kershaw, *Hitler*, v. 2, 401–2.

(148) **likened Germany's eastward expansion to America's westward one,** Tooze, *Wages*, 8–11, and Fritzsche "The Holocaust," 601.

(148) **"the majority of Nazi genocide,"** Mann, *Dark Side*, 276, 278.

(149) **"If I looked like him,"** Breitman, *Architect*, 4.

(150) **"[I]f National Socialism had looked in the mirror,"** Smelser and Zitelmann, *Braune Elite*, 100.

(150) **His favorite adjective was *"unerhört,"*** ibid., 105.

(150) **Burckhardt's and Hitler's descriptions of Heydrich,** Fest, *Face*, 100, 110.

(151) **"I feel free of all guilt,"** Smelser and Zitelmann, *Braune Elite*, 111.

(151) **their removal was the job of another SS officer**, Berger, *Experten*, 79–81; Arad, *Belzec*, 44–45.

(152) **he had come, during the 1930s, to believe deeply**, Cesarani, *Becoming*, Chapter 2; Rabinovici, *Eichmann's*, 35–36.

(152) **how proud he was of his SS service in retrospect and how thoroughly he rationalized it**, Stangneth, *Before*, 221–30, 242–81, 302–7.

(153) **"a functionary in the true sense. . . . had never really wasted much thought,"** Fest, *Face*, 277, 284.

(153) **"Übervater,"** Smelser and Zitelmann, *Braune Elite*, 167.

(153) **Kaltenbrunner gave vent to his fervent Nazism by attesting**, ibid., 163; Mann, *Dark Side*, 243–44.

(154) **The last two figures**, the best treatments of these men are in Allen, *Business*, passim; the most thorough studies of the SS economic empire are Kaienburg, *Wirtschaft*, and Naasner, *SS-Wirtschaft*.

(154) **Himmler's speech to the assembled SS commanders**, Hochstadt, *Sources*, 163–65.

(155) **A nation is not only what it does**, Craig, *Germany*, 638.

(155) **Awareness . . . was widespread. . . . Germans spoke with open dread**, Bajohr and Pohl, *Holocaust*, 59–72; Longerich, *Davon*, 223–40.

(155) **diary entry by Curt Prüfer**, McKale, *Rewriting*, 11.

(156) **Klemperer diary entries**, Klemperer, *I Will*, v. II, 28, 41, 155, 371.

(156) **"the Nazis wanted to manage,"** Fritzsche, *Life*, 286.

(156) **Goebbels announced in the journal *Das Reich*. . . . the *Völkischer Beobachter* . . . reported**, Bajohr and Pohl, *Holocaust*, 57; Friedländer, *Nazi Germany*, v. 2, 276, 337–38.

(156) **Hitler reminded Germans**, Longerich, *Davon*, 201.

(156) **If such partial revelations had a purpose**, ibid., 325–26.

(157) **Perhaps 10,000. . . . Konrad Latte**, Schneider, "Saving," 52–57.

(157) **Arndt and Krakauer**, Moorhouse, *Berlin*, 180, 295.

(157) **plundered Jewish property sent to Hamburg**, Bajohr, *Aryanization*, 279; Aly, *Beneficiaries*, 127–29. See also Mierzejewski, *Asset*, v. 2, 127; Fritzsche, *Life*, 258–59.

(158) **food and goods shipped home by far-flung troops**, Aly, *Beneficiaries*, 94–152.

(159) **"silent protest" and "to the hardest manual labor,"** Gruner, *Rosenstraße*, 139, 200. See also Friedländer, *Nazi Germany*, v. 2, 425.

(159) **the reality of resistance generally goaded the Reich**: the classic example is the crackdown precipitated by the Dutch general strike of 1941; see Moore, *Victims*, 72–73; Presser, *Ashes*, 56–57.

(160) **Forced laborer statistics**, Hayes, *How*, 315–30.

(161) **they were not necessarily cheap**, Tooze, *Wages*, 534–37; Spoerer, *Zwangsarbeit*, 183–90; Hayes, *From Cooperation*, 262–64, 268–71; Wachsmann, *KL*, 452.

(162) **Relative fates of male and female slave laborers at Gleiwitz**, Hayes, *From Cooperation*, 267–68.

(162) **five to ten times more likely to die**, Neander, *Beispiel*, 59.

(162) **the mathematics of the German labor force during World War II**, Overy, *War*, 291–311.

(163) **compulsory labor program for German Jewish males**, Barkai, *Boycott*, 159–62.

(163) **extended this program to . . . Poland**, Browning, *Nazi Policy*, 61–65.

(164) **Autobahn and Organisation Schmelt**, Gruner, *Jewish*, 214–29; Gutterman, *Narrow*, 43–55.

(164) **first use of slave labor by German private industry**, Pohl, *Holzmann*, 264–65.

(164) **Volkswagen and IG Farben**, Mommsen, *Volkswagenwerk*, 433–41, 496–515, and Hayes, *Industry and Ideology*, 347–53.

(165) **Project Giant**, Pohl, *Holzmann*, 266–67; Gutterman, *Narrow*, ch. 8.

(165) **Alderney**, Deak, *Europe*, 59.

(165) **Half the inmates of Auschwitz never even got labor assignments**, Hayes, "Capital," 337.

(165) **SS companies were neither profitable, nor usually successful in their joint ventures . . . though one initiative . . . made money**, Wachsmann, *KL*, 405–6; Tooze, *Wages*, 630.

(166) **Changing female selection and mortality rates at Auschwitz**, Dlugoborski and Piper, *Auschwitz*, v. II, 180–82; Gutman and Berenbaum, *Anatomy*, 466; Wachsmann, *KL*, 353, 455, 477–78.

(166) **On Starachowice**, see Browning, *Remembering*, passim.

(166) **On Skarzysko-Kamienna**, see Ofer and Weitzman, *Women*, 285–309.

(167) **one-third of the German infantry's ammunition**, Karay, *Death*, 70.

(168) **On the design, conception, dimensions, and working conditions at Dora**, Sellier, *History*, 31–32, 511–15; Neander, *Mittelbau*, 179–84, 189–95; Allen, *Business*, 222–32; Neufeld, *Rocket*, 208–13, 224–28; Wachsmann, *KL*, 444–47; and Neander, *Beispiel*, passim.

(169) **Rocket production and deaths at Dora (26,500) and deaths from rockets (15,386)**, Wachsmann, *KL*, 453–54, and Seiler, *History*, 398, 403–4. On the additional murderous effects of V-2 production at Mauthausen, see Horwitz, *Shadow*, 20–21.

(169) **Fighter Staff Program**, Allen, *Business*, 232–39; Tooze, *Wages*, 627–34; Wachsmann, *KL*, 448–51.

(169) **mortality rates fluctuated**, Buggeln, *Slave*, 27–32.

(170) **to salvage their machinery**, Gregor, *Daimler-Benz*, 194–96, 221–52.

(170) **about 15 percent of the construction work**, Hayes, "Capital," 347.

(170) **principal profiteer from the slave labor program**, Neander, *Mittelbau*, 55;

(170) **estimated at 600 to 700 million reichsmark**, Wachsmann, *KL*, 410.

(171) **Marches from Auschwitz and Gross-Rosen**, Blatman, *Marches*, 81–105; Rees, *Auschwitz*, 264; Wachsmann, *KL*, 554–57.

(171) **Marches from Stutthof and killing at Palmnicken**, Blatman, *Marches*, 111–25.

(172) **the camps that received retreating prisoner groups**, Morsch and Perz, *Neue Studien*, 25; Stangneth, *Eichmann*, 53; Bessel, *1945*, 50; Blatman, *Marches*, 127–32; Buggeln, *Slave*, 60–61.

(172) **Bergen-Belsen**, Blatman, *Marches*, 132–36; Rees, *Auschwitz*, 265–67; Stone, *Liberation*, 83.

(173) **These decisions were Heinrich Himmler's**, Blatman, *Marches*, 53–54, 137; Wachsmann, *KL*, 572–76.

(173) **"no inmate may fall into the enemy's hands alive,"** Blatman, *Marches*, 154, 181.

(173) **Not all of them . . . but most did**, Blatman, *Marches*, 155–79; Wachsmann, *KL*, 580.

(173) **Deaths at Buchenwald**, Blatman, *Marches*, 152.

(173) **When the British bombed the city**, Bessel, *1945*, 52.

(174) **Dachau, Mauthausen, and their subcamps**, Blatman, *Marches*, 197–217; Jardim, *Mauthausen*, 59–60.

(174) **"many of the living people look dead,"** Blatman, *Marches*, 242.

CHAPTER 5: VICTIMS

(177) **in Cracow**, Henry, *Resistance*, 51.

(177) **inmate killed a German**, Arad, *Belzec*, 98–99.

(177) **twentieth transport**, Henry, *Resistance*, 129–30, and Gilbert, *Holocaust*, 574–75.

(177) **Number of underground movements in Polish ghettos and camps**, Gutman and Krakowski, *Unequal*, 106.

(177) **Arendt quotations**, *Eichmann*, 117.

(178) *amidah*, Bauer, *Rethinking*, 120.

(178) **Hilberg is probably right**, Hilberg, *Destruction*, 1106.

(178) **Numbers of Jews in resistance units**, Henry, *Resistance*, xix, xxv, xxvii, xxxiii, 142–57, 168–75, 201–19, 432–37; Bauer, *Rethinking*, 137–39.

(179) **"the concentration of the Jews,"** Hochstadt, *Sources*, 87–89.

(179) **modeled on the body . . . in Vienna**, Rabinovici, *Eichmann's*, 40.

(180) **In Lodz, for instance, twenty-two of the first thirty council members were killed**, Dobroszycki, *Chronicle*, xlvi; Trunk, *Judenrat*, 23; Trunk, *Lodz*, xxxiii, 34.

(181) **Lodz ghetto area**, ibid., 16

(181) **Lodz ghetto population**, Dobroszycki, *Chronicle*, xxxix, but Horwitz, *Ghettostadt*, 335, gives 163,777, and Trunk, *Lodz*, xxx, says "about 164,000."

(181) **Warsaw ghetto population and area**, Engelking and Leociak, *Warsaw*, 49; Gutman, *Jews*, 63

(181) **permeability . . . remained much greater. . . . at many of the smaller sites**, Perechodnik, *Am I?*, 68.

(181) **villages of the largely rural Lublin district**, Silberklang, *Gates*, 29, 212–14.

(181) **attritionists and productionists**, Browning, *Path*, 28–56.

(182) **figure 5**, Dobroszycki, *Chronicle*, xxxix, lxvi, 50, 52, 107, 193, 314, 352, 444, 519; Trunk, *Lodz*, xlvi–xlvii.

(182) **pitted against each other**, Redner, *Policeman*, 86, 106.

(182) **his own father seized and ate**, Adelson, *Diary*, 176–77.

(184) **Internal disunity among Jews**, Trunk, *Judenrat*, 29–35, 368–87; Corni, *Ghettos*, 172–89; Wasserstein, *Ambiguity*, 154.

(184) **"the community's social structure disintegrated,"** Lensky, *Physician*, 163.

(185) **Why would the Germans kill people who could be useful**, Redner, *Policeman*, 127–28.

(185) **refusal of ghetto residents in both Lodz and Bialystok**, Hayes, *Lessons I*, 11.

(186) **the extent of Jews' denial**, Perechodnik, *Am I?*, 12, with slight corrections to the translation from Polish by my colleague Jacek Nowakowski. See also Redner, *Policeman*, 175.

(187) **Nazi camouflage measures**, for example, Horwitz, *Ghettostadt*, 283–84; Wasserstein, *Ambiguity*, 141–42; Redner, *Policeman*, 166.

(187) **mixture of bait and threats**, Dawidowicz, *War*, 301; Dobroszycki, *Chronicle*, 125, 164–65; Horwitz, *Ghettostadt*, 277–79; Corni, *Ghettos*, 69; Wasserstein, *Ambiguity*, 141.

(187) **procedure re deportations from the Netherlands**, Moore, *Victims*, 91–97, 109; Wasserstein, *Ambiguity*, 138–39, 193, 195.

(188) **Rosenblatt quotation**, Bauer, *Rethinking*, 80–81.

(188) **the conduct of Asscher and Cohen**, Wasserstein, *Ambiguity*, 174–76.

(189) **According to David Daube's**, ibid., 251.

(189) **Rumkowski's "give me your children!" speech**, Trunk, *Lodz*, 272–75.

(190) **Administration and police numbers in Lodz**, ibid., 38, 40, 44; **in Warsaw**, Gutman, *Encyclopedia*, 1609; Engelking and Leociak, *Ghetto*, 409. See also Corni, *Ghettos*, 74.

(190) **On Szerynski and the Warsaw ghetto police**, Trunk, *Judenrat*, 475–94, 498–501, 552–53; Gutman, *Jews*, 88–90, 237–40; Corni, *Ghettos*, 107–11; Perechodnik, *Am I?*, 104.

(190) **increasingly corrupt and extortionist . . . these police did the footwork**, Redner, *Policeman*, 130–35, 155–60.

(191) **Composition of the Dutch Jewish police**, Moore, *Victims*, 220–21; Wasserstein, *Ambiguity*, 190–91; Cesarani, *Final*, 679, 681–82.

(191) **Daily food intake . . . hovered**, ibid., 274–75.

(191) **in Warsaw in 1941**, the lower estimate is in Gutman, *Encyclopedia*, 1609, the higher in Bauer, *History*, 170.

(191) **at Otwock**, Perechodnik, *Am I?*, 232–33.

(191) **5,550 people were dying in the Warsaw ghetto per month**, Gutman, *Jews*, 64.

(192) **German and Jewish casualties in the Warsaw Ghetto Uprising**, Engelking and Leociak, *Ghetto*, 51; Henry, *Resistance*, 31 (Hilberg, *Destruction*, 1105, gives slightly lower German figures, so does Friedländer, *Nazi Germany*, v. 2, 526).

(192) **resistance against the German drive to empty the Bialystok ghetto resulted in**, Bender, *Bialystok*, 258–65.

(192) **Outcomes of Treblinka and Sobibor uprisings**, Arad, *Belzec*, 363–64; Schelvis, *Sobibor*, 168, 175, 231–42.

(193) **Shootings at Majdanek and Poniatowa**, Silberklang, *Gates*, 402–7.

(193) **On the extent of smuggling in and out of the Warsaw ghetto**, see Hilberg et al., *Czerniakow*, 306; Cesarani, *Final*, 435–36.

(193) **On Ringelblum and Oyneg Shabes**, see Kassow, *Who?*

(193) **On Lodz**, Dobroszycki, *Chronicle*.

(194) **several Jewish ghetto administrations adopted different survival strategies ... but ... they ultimately came to the same end**, Bauer, *History*, 157–67; Polonsky, *Jews*, v. III, 479–500.

(195) **"No Jewish action caused any significant difference,"** Silberklang, *Gates*, 440.

(196) **"living in the expectation of death,"** Arendt, *Eichmann*, 119.

(196) **"running a race against time,"** Vagi et al., *Hungary*, 256.

(197) **2 percent of the French population**, Paxton, *Vichy*, 294–95.

(197) **Dutch civil servants and police**, Wasserstein, *Ambiguity*, 143; Romijn et al., *Persecution*, 13–26.

(198) **Population figures for the Warsaw ghetto**, Engelking and Leociak, *Warsaw Ghetto*, 50–51; Gutman, *Jews of Warsaw*, 270–71.

(200) **Her last name was Neyer, and she is walking beside**, according to Yisrael Gutman in Laqueur, *Encyclopedia*, 693.

(200) **Courts of Honor in Italy, Germany, and the Netherlands**, Trunk, *Judenrat*, 553–55; Jockusch and Finder, *Honor*, 107–36; Wasserstein, *Ambiguity*, 253–54.

(200) **Kastner case**, Segev, *Seventh*, Part V; the quotations appear on pp. 283 and 318, respectively.

(201) **who fell into the hands of the Soviet Union**, Anonymous, *Clandestine*, xv; Meyer, *Balancing*, 359.

(202) **Ben-Gurion's letters**, Segev, *Seventh*, 294.

(202) **the last prosecution**, Jockusch and Finder, *Honor*, 320–21.

(203) **the number of camps**, van Pelt, "Nazi," 150.

(203) **Such installations and their satellites ... about one million died**, Wachsmann, *KL*, 627.

(203) **at most, about 150,000 Jewish veterans**, estimated from Wachsmann, *KL*, 771.

(203) **survival rates were infinitesimal**, Montagu, *Chelmno*, 126–41, 195; Arad, *Belzec*, 258–69; Bryant, *Eyewitness*, 35, 42–43; Kuwalek, *Belzec*, 14, 170, 225–27.

(204) **a hierarchy of prisoner categories developed ... constant struggle to control the most important trustee assignments**, Orth, *System*, 57–61, Wachsmann, *KL*, 122–35.

(204) **Hermann Langbein ... has left a vivid account**, Langbein, *People*, 12–14.

(205) **Sinti and Roma**, Hayes and Roth, *Handbook*, 275–81; Lewy, *Persecution*, 221–26; Hayes, *How*, 495–505; Weiss-Wendt, *Genocide*, 2, 16–17; Weiss-Wendt, *Murder*, 144–48; Bryant, *Eyewitness*, 41; Deletant, *Forgotten*, 187–96.

(206) **The treatment of gays**, Hayes and Roth, *Handbook*, 281–83; Jellonek, *Homosexuelle*, 19–36, 327–32; Longerich, *Himmler*, 231–40; Gellately and Stoltzfus, *Outsiders*, 233–55; Berenbaum and Peck, *Holocaust*, 338–57; Wachsmann, *KL*, 127–28, 665.

(208) **not all Slavs were the same in German eyes**, Hayes and Roth, *Handbook*, 283–87.

(209) **how people arrived at them**, Gigliotti, *Train*, especially chapters 4–5.

(209) **"the most complete totalitarian structure to have been devised by man,"** Marrus, *History*, 147.

(209) **"a mixture of Hell and an insane asylum,"** Langbein, *People*, 477.

(210) **the inhabitants of the "family camp" for Czech Jews**, Henry, *Resistance*, 584.

(210) **when 419 . . . Soviet POWs succeeded in breaking out of Mauthausen**, Blatman, *Marches*, 400–401; Horwitz, *Shadow*, 124–43.

(210) **The only successful form of resistance in the camps was escape, although the odds were long**, Bryant, *Eyewitness*, 42–43; Arad, *Belzec*, 258–69; Schelvis, *Sobibor*, 135–42; Hayes, "Capital," 340; Wachsmann, *KL*, 534–36.

(212) **Hanna Lévy-Hass . . . wrote**, Confino, *World*, 203.

(212) **"Here there is no why,"** Levi, *Survival*, 25.

(213) **"the Resistance in the camp is not geared for an uprising,"** Henry, *Resistance*, 587.

(213) **Auschwitz consumed 75,000 Poles . . . but it took the lives of probably four-fifths of the Jews ever registered**, Hayes, "Capital," 330, 332.

(214) **"There are no roads from Auschwitz but those of improbability,"** Rosenberg, *Brief*, 106.

(214) **"excremental assault,"** Des Pres, *Survivor*, 51–71.

(217) **"pairing,"** Henry, *Resistance*, 566–67.

(217) **As Imre Kertesz . . . writes**, ibid., 580.

CHAPTER 6: HOMELANDS

(219) **Minority religious status**, Bauer, *History*, 286; Bauer, *Death*, 93–95, 106–7, 111; Engelmann, *Hitler's*, 71–78; Henry, *We Only*, 9–40.

(220) **Minority status was not always necessary**, Petrow, *Bitter*, 116; Todorov, *Fragility*, 9, 25, 97–101; Bar-Zohar, *Beyond*, 167–77; Rhodes, *Vatican*, 319; Marrus and Paxton, *Vichy*, 271–73; Dwork and van Pelt, *Holocaust*, 332–33.

(220) **certain character traits . . . were better predictors**, Tec, *Light*, 152–54, 188–91; Oliners, *Altruistic*, Chapter 6.

(221) **Otto Jodmin . . . "I simply had to do it,"** Moorhouse, *Berlin*, 297.

(221) **Teresa Prekerowa . . . "ordinary people who differed greatly,"** Libionka, "Polish Literature," 61–62.

(221) **Aristides de Sousa Mendes**, Gutman, *Encyclopedia*, 1381–82.

(222) **the Dutch and Japanese consuls . . . in Kovno**, Hayes, *How*, 648–57.

(222) **Varian Fry**, Wyman, *Paper*, 142.

(222) **Ernest Prodolliet**, Independent Commission, *Switzerland*, 109; Bauer, *Jewry*, 276; Wasserstein, *Ambiguity*, 165.

(223) **Berthold Beitz**, Käppner, *Beitz*, 47–113.

(223) **Alfred Rossner**, Fulbrook, *Small Town*, 156–58.

(223) **Otto Weidt**, Moorhouse, *Berlin*, 296.

(224) **puppet regimes that carried out German orders**, Pavlowitch, *Disorder*, 58–59; Mazower, *Inside*, 18–22; Müller, *Seite*, 159, 168–69, 174.

(225) **Recherchegruppe (or Colonne) Henneicke**, Dean, *Robbing*, 283; Moore, *Victims*, 207–10; Presser, *Ashes*, 354, 366, 392–93.

(226) **The majority of the Jews ever deported from both France and Belgium**, Benz, *Dimension*, 124, 127–28, 132–33, 135.

(226) **Even Slovakia . . . had second thoughts**, Ward, *Priest*, 224–35.

(227) **Germany had allowed various national liberation groups to set up offices in Berlin**, Friedländer, *Nazi Germany*, v. 2, 220; Polonsky, *Jews*, v. III, 409–11.

(227) **Jews were overrepresented compared to their share of the Lithuanian population**, Kosmala and Verbeeck, *Facing*, 79; Barkan et al., *Shared*, 380–81.

(228) **the Soviet Union brought life in prison, but Nazi Germany brought the death sentence**, Bauer, *Death*, 37–38.

(228) **to Ukrainian and Baltic nationalists ... Germany appeared the lesser evil**, Snyder, *Bloodlands*, 190–94, 397; Gitelman, *Bitter*, 67.

(228) **calling on Ukrainians to "destroy" Jewry, and a pogrom took place**, Petrovsky-Shtern and Polonsky, *Polin* 26, 339; Lower, *Empire-Building*, 94–95; Redner, *Policeman*, 34–37; Bartov and Weitz, *Shatterzone*, 371–73.

(228) **Lithuanian Activist Front declared that Jews had "betrayed,"** Dieckmann, *Litauen*, 252–53; see also Kühne, *Belonging*, 81; Polonsky, *Jews*, v. III, 406.

(228) **Ukrainian police and militias played an active part**, Struve, *Herrschaft*, passim.

(229) **Himmler had about 300,000**, Cesarani, *Final*, 382.

(229) **"For the Germans 300 Jews are ...,"** ibid., 394.

(229) **Of the roughly 350,000 Jews in France in 1940, more than half**, Marrus and Paxton, *Vichy*, 364.

(230) **Statistics on deportations from France**, Benz, *Dimension*, 127, 133–34; Paxton, "Jews: Vichy," 40–43.

(230) **the French government dragged its feet**, Marrus and Paxton, *Vichy*, 372.

(230) **Hungarian deportations and death toll**, Braham, *Politics*, 153, 251; Wachsmann, *KL*, 460.

(232) **the thoroughness of this operation ... was largely homegrown**, Braham, *Studies*, 71–78, 86.

(232) **the apt summation of Peter Kenez**, Kenez, *Coming*, 250.

(232) **Höss ... repeatedly sought to slow the overwhelming pace**, Wachsmann, *KL*, 459.

(233) **the deportation had a war-related purpose**, Buggeln, *Slave*, 46–49.

(233) **history of antisemitism in Hungary**, Braham, *Politics*, 20–25; Vagi et al., *Holocaust*, xxxviii–xliv.

(233) **the new territories nearly doubled the Hungarian Jewish population**, Vagi et al., *Holocaust*, 368–69.

(234) **"Jewish workers for German war production purposes,"** Braham, *Politics*, 59.

(234) **Antonescu's policies and motives**, Hayes, *How*, 445–65, excerpting the fundamental study by Ancel; Ioanid, *Romania*, especially 271–81; Deletant, *Forgotten*, 209–14.

(236) **a strong moral stand ... proved counterproductive when the timing was not right**, Moore, *Victims*, 73, 79–90; Presser, *Ashes*, 56–57; Friedländer, *Nazi Germany*, v. 2, 410–11.

(237) **Many other pieces of good fortune were involved**, Lidegaard, *Countrymen*, 31–35, 44–51, 65–73, 96–97, 154, 289, 329–332, 339–40; Friedländer, *Nazi Germany*, v. 2, 545–47.

(238) **In Italy, Mussolini had just announced**, Knox, "faschistische Italien," 56, 61, 65, 79; Schlemmer and Woller, "italienische Faschismus," 182–87.

(239) **around Trieste ... 90 percent of the Jewish community perished**, Zimmerman, *Italy*, 247–51.

(239) **Giovanni Palatucci**, Bess, *Choices*, 81.

(239) **In Italy ... more than one-third**, Sarfatti, *Jews*, 27–28; Zuccotti, *Italians*, 20.

(240) **Gross ... overstated ... but established**, Gross, *Neighbors*, 73–89; Bikont, *Crime*, 521–24; David-Fox, *Holocaust*, 19–20; **a curious feature of survivors' testimonies**, Browning, *Remembering*, 50.

(241) **50,000–60,000 by December 1939 ... liquidated much of the Polish intelligentsia**, Matthäus et al., *War*, 3; Rossino, *Hitler*, 234; Snyder, *Bloodlands*, 126–27, 153–54; Gross, *Neighbors*, 7.

(241) **how complete the purge at some local levels was**, Libionka, "Church Hierarchy," 86; see also Phayer, *Pius XII*, 23–24; and Huener, "Kirchenpolitik," 113–16, 128–29.

(241) **official rations provided Poles**, Winstone, *Dark*, 115.

(242) **"bread prices ... hovered,"** ibid., 118–19.

(242) **"economically speaking, an empty body,"** ibid., 73.

(242) **"[W]e have decided. . . . [I]t was like living in a country,"** ibid., 50, 53.

(243) **More Poles died in the bombing of Warsaw . . . more Poles may have been killed in the suppression,** Snyder, *Bloodlands*, 405–6.

(243) **about 720,000 people,** Paulsson, *Secret*, 1.

(243) **Jakub Berman . . . simply cooked up the number,** Snyder, *Bloodlands*, 356–57, 407; Gross, *Fear*, 4.

(243) **The Jewish survival rate in Warsaw was equal to that in Amsterdam,** Paulsson, *Secret*, 2, 5, 229–31.

(243) **newspaper column by FBI Director,** James Comey, "Why I Require FBI Agents to Visit the Holocaust Museum," *Washington Post*, April 16, 2015.

(244) **a number of prominent Jewish scholars,** e.g., the reviews by Dan Diner in *Contemporary European History* 21 (2012), 125–31, and Omer Bartov in *Slavic Review* 71 (2012), 424–28.

(244) **antisemitism in Poland was considerable before 1939 and on the rise,** Bauer, *Brother's*, 194; Polonsky, *Jews*, v. III, 80–81, 85–88; Blobaum, *Antisemitism*, 158–70; Mendelsohn, *Jews*, 71–76; Zimmerman, *Underground*, 16–20; Watt, *Bitter*, 361-66.

(245) **"forcible emigration of the Jews" . . . sent a delegation to Madagascar,** Wasserstein, *Eve*, 40, 359; Hamerow, *Why*, 62.

(245) **The Polish foreign minister even discussed . . . and tried to lease . . . "supplemental Jewish homeland,"** Bauer, *Brother's*, 193; Zimmerman, *Contested*, 22–23; Hamerow, *Why*, 62, 87.

(245) **trained right-wing Zionist fighters in Poland,** Snyder, *Black*, 64–66, 281.

(246) **Church leaders and publications. . . . "It is a fact that,"** Polonsky, *Jews*, v. III, 81–84; Libionka, "Church Hierarchy," 77–86.

(247) **"Hitler called the Jews the microbe of the world,"** Blobaum, *Antisemitism*, 261.

(247) **"regrettable excesses" . . . disrespect "for the faith and traditions of Christians,"** Libionka, "Church Hierarchy," 81.

(247) **separate ethnic communities . . . survey conducted before the war,** Wasserstein, *Eve*, 224, 330.

(247) **Jews and Poles were divided by residence and occupations,** Mendelsohn, *Jews*, 23–32, 42–43; Bauer, *Brother's*, 180–89; Watt, *Bitter*, 365.

(248) **11,500, 70,000–90,000, 25,000, 3,500,** Paulsson, *Secret*, 229–31, 236.

(249) **the Polish army interned,** Hamerow, *Why*, 44.

(249) **Jews composed more than half,** Gross, *Fear*, 195–97.

(249) **Jews there did recognize,** Bauer, *Death*, 35–41; Zimmerman, *Contested*, 61–68.

(249) **"This is nothing to be surprised at,"** Perechodnik, *Am I?*, 2, with slight corrections to the translation from the Polish by my colleague Jacek Nowakowski.

(249) **the massacre there was hardly an isolated occurrence,** Polonsky, *Jews*, v. III, 421, 425; Bauer, *Death*, 92–120; Zimmerman, *Underground*, 95–98; Barkan et al., *Shared*, 306, 316.

(249) **Stefan Rowecki . . . reported,** Kosmala and Verbeeck, *Facing*, 66.

(250) **"is creating something of a narrow bridge,"** Polonsky, *Jews*, v. III, 408; Zimmerman, *Underground*, 74–75.

(250) **Jewish inmates who escaped Sobibor,** Schelvis, *Sobibor*, 181–82.

(250) **Barwy Biale detachment . . . slaughtered,** Mazurek and Skibinska, "Barwy Biale," 433–80; Zimmerman, *Underground*, 290.

(251) **"The farmers are seizing the Jews,"** Polonsky, *Jews*, v. III, 450.

(251) **the so-called Blue Police. . . . Germans offered rewards . . . and threatened,** Grabowski, *Hunt*, 101–20.

(252) **what happened in Dabrowa Tarnowska County,** ibid., 61.

(252) "[W]e have to punish those who want to hide Jews," ibid., 58.

(252) Most people who hid Jews there did so in return for money, ibid., 135–48.

(252) The AK did pass its knowledge . . . warned Poles against . . . blackmailing . . . and . . . carried out executions, Fleming, *Auschwitz*, 27; Zimmerman, *Underground*, 84, 129–31, 134–39, 141–50, 154–60, 162, 224, 227, 264, 300–302; Polonsky, *Jews*, v. III, 461.

(253) made no effort to impede the transports . . . provided only modest support for the Warsaw Ghetto Uprising, Zimmerman, *Underground*, 54, 161, 167–68, 179, 197–209, 214–17, 241; Fleming, *Auschwitz*, 254–55; Polonsky, *Jews*, v. III, 463, 511–12; Friedländer, *Nazi Germany*, v. 2, 523.

(253) Komorowski . . . banditry, Zimmerman, *Underground*, 251–56, 262, 267–86, 297–98, 417–18.

(253) Zegota . . . "Our feelings toward the Jews have not changed." . . . most of its funds, Zimmerman, *Underground*, 175–78, 184, 303–12; Bauer, *American*, 332–33.

(254) favored liquidation or emigration . . . by a ratio of nine to four, Polonsky, *Jews*, v. III, 445.

(254) Even among political prisoners in the concentration camps, Langbein, *Against*, 146, and *People*, 75–76.

(254) currency and jewelry dealers set up shop around Treblinka, Gross and Gross, *Golden*, 28–38.

(255) the first thing her protectors asked, Tec, *Tears*, 214.

(255) omit them in the future, David-Fox, *Holocaust*, 13.

(255) emigrated to Chicago, Gross, *Neighbors*, 131; Polonsky, *Jews*, v. III, 424.

(255) Hirszman. . . . Kielce pogrom. . . . tried to cover their tracks, Bryant, *Eyewitness*, 35; Gross, *Neighbors*, 152–67; Grabowski, *Hunt*, 86. Cf. Kuwalek, *Belzec*, 315–17.

(256) Jewish "overrepresentation," Gross, *Fear*, 220–22, 226–31

(256) to discredit a competing candidate . . . "a Jew who tries to make money," Gross, *Fear*, 30; Judt, *Postwar*, 827.

(256) Ringelblum . . . was hidden . . . by a non-Jew, Gutman and Krakowki, *Unequal*, iii; Kassow, *Who?*, 362–65, 383–85.

(256) almost 1,000 cases of Poles executed for helping, Wette, *Feldwebel*, 154; Grabowski, *Hunt*, 56, gives "slightly more than seven hundred" as the figure arrived at by Polish researchers.

(258) fifteen times more likely, Snyder, *Bloodlands*, 406.

CHAPTER 7: ONLOOKERS

(260) France enacted various rules that made immigration less appealing, Caron, *Uneasy*, 28–33.

(260) After 1936, four other arguments . . . narrowed, Hamerow, *Why*, 72–89; Weber, *Hollow*, 87–110; Caron, *Uneasy*, 187–205.

(261) "taken as a whole not very desirable," Wasserstein, *Eve*, 218.

(261) even sentenced the aunt and uncle, McCullough and Wilson, *Violence*, 59.

(261) The trend . . . in the Netherlands, Belgium, and Czechoslovakia, Bauer, *Brother's*, 170–72, 177, 243, 267; Hamerow, *Why*, 61.

(262) Switzerland provided the most glaring illustration, Independent Commission, *Switzerland*, 105–9, 128–30; Caestecker and Moore, *Refugees*, 82–102; Bauer, *Brother's*, 172–76, 239–40, 267–68.

(263) several discouraging and . . . mutually contradictory preconditions, David-Fox, *Holocaust*, 37.

(263) Britain saw its role . . . as that of a "transit nation," London, *Whitehall*, chapters 3–5; Hamerow, *Why*, 90–119, 156–61; McCullough and Wilson, *Violence*, 108–50; Abella and Troper, *None*, xx, 6–9, 48–49.

(263) **Britain pursued similarly restrictive policies in Palestine**, Dwork and van Pelt, *Flight*, 28–51; Bauer, *History*, 127–28; Wasserstein, *Eve*, 339, 363, 413.

(264) **haunted by the specter of what might happen**, Hamerow, *Why*, 104, 112, 114–16; Caestecker and Moore, *Refugees*, 64; London, *Whitehall*, 95.

(265) **Poland's ambassador in London tried to blackmail Britain**, Wistrich, *Hitler*, 21; Hamerow, *Why*, 63; London, *Whitehall*, 91.

(265) **an average of only 22 percent**, Bauer, *Brother's*, 163.

(266) **the almost 310,000 . . . Jews who actually applied for entrance by 1939**, Breitman and Kraut, *American*, 74.

(266) **probably about 225,000**, Friedländer, *Nazi Germany*, v. 2, 783, says 211,000 as of the end of 1943; London, *Whitehall*, 12, says "no more than 250,000 . . . in the years 1933–45." Wyman, *Paper*, 218–19, calculates that just over 250,000 "refugees from Nazism" got into the U.S. by the autumn of 1944, but not all of these people were Jews.

(267) **"FDR's second-term policies likely helped save the lives of well over 100,000 Jews,"** Breitman, *FDR*, 317.

(267) **more than five-sevenths of its total refugees at the last minute**, London, *Whitehall*, 11–12, 103, 115–18, 131–34, 141; Bauer, *Brother's*, 270–71.

(268) **fear of economic competition**, Wyman, *Paper*, 3–9; Breitman and Kraut, *American*, 11–17, 21–22, 33–37, 49–50; see Hamerow, *Why*, 252–53.

(268) **The American public opposed letting more people in**, Breitman and Kraut, *American*, 58; Breitman and Lichtman, *FDR*, 116.

(269) **Father Charles Coughlin. . . . Jew Deal . . . polls of 1938 and 1939**, Wyman, *Paper*, 17–19, 22; Breitman and Lichtman, *FDR*, 75–77; Hamerow, *Why*, 251 (on the Jew Deal).

(270) **"is a perfect opening to Germany to load the United States with agents,"** Hamerow, *Why*, 281; Breitman and Kraut, *American*, 112–45.

(270) **State Department instructed its consuls worldwide**, Wasserstein, *Ambiguity*, 110.

(270) **FDR's caution**, Breitman and Kraut, *American*, 222–35.

(271) **a scheme for smuggling agents into the Americas under the cover of releasing Jews**, Wasserstein, *Ambiguity*, 118.

(272) **The two groups also differed in their attitudes toward the creation of a Jewish state. . . . Joint Distribution Committee . . . preferred**, Bauer, *Brother's*, 157–66.

(272) **Shanghai**, Hochstadt, *Exodus*, especially chapters 3–4; Caestecker and Moore, *Refugees*, 109–21.

(273) **"divided into places where they cannot live and places they cannot enter" . . . "Dutch Guiana, Angola, Cyprus,"** Wasserstein, *Eve*, 360, 403.

(273) **Statistics on the *St. Louis***, Vincent, "Voyage," 255, 270–71, 274, 288; Breitman and Lichtman, *FDR*, 138.

(273) **Emigrants from Poland in 1937 and U.S. quota**, Bauer, *Brother's*, 194, 249.

(273) **the Church's leaders in Rome recognized . . . glorification of race and nation as "idolatrous,"** Wolf, *Pope*, 230, 268; Kornberg, *Dilemma*, 228–29; Godman, *Vatican*, 102–6, 129, 141–53.

(274) **As Mussolini pointed out**, Kertzer, *Mussolini*, 307–15.

(275) **"The Jewish Question," . . . "It is an evident fact." . . . "messianic craving for world domination,"** Kertzer, *Mussolini*, 211, 289–91.

(275) **"Spiritually, we are all Semites" . . . "the enemy of the Cross of Christ,"** Kertzer, *Popes*, 280.

(275) **Content and fate of "The Unity of the Human Race,"** Kertzer, *Popes*, 280–82; Wolf, *Pope*, 206–12; Passelecq and Suchecky, *Hidden*, passim.

(276) **Pacelli had opposed issuing *Mit brennender Sorge* . . . suggested a mere pastoral letter**, Wolf, *Pope*, 265–68.

(276) **was he the candidate the Nazi envoys in Rome hoped would prevail . . .**

destroyed the copies and plates, Kertzer, *Mussolini*, 370–81; Ventresca, *Soldier*, 130–32, 134–35.

(276) **A Roman aristocrat by descent . . . and critical of the Catholic Center Party,** Ventresca, *Soldier*, 7–18, 38–65, 72–84.

(276) **Though not happy with the form the Concordat took,** Wolf, *Pope*, 170–78.

(277) **Pius XII considered his chief duty to be to the Church and to Catholics,** Kornberg, *Dilemma*, 4–6, 255–67; Godman, *Vatican*, 82–83.

(277) **Preysing vs. Bertram,** Hayes and Roth, *Handbook*, 238–41; Phayer, *Catholic*, 67–81.

(277) **On the importance of the sacraments to the Church's political conduct,** Kornberg, *Dilemma*, 3–4, 272–73; Spicer, *Resisting*, 6–9.

(278) **approximately 72,000 Jews,** Bauer, *Jewry*, 66.

(279) **Swiss factory owners in Poland . . . reported,** Straumann and Wildmann, *Schweizer*, 116–20.

(279) **British intelligence intercepted,** Breitman, *Official*, 89–98.

(279) **the Vatican's ambassador in Slovakia,** Kornberg, *Dilemma*, 81.

(279) **Father Pirro Scavizzi . . . the Jewish Bund Party in Poland,** Phayer, *Catholic*, 47–48.

(280) **As late as December 1944, a majority of the British public did not believe,** see Hamerow, *Why*, 410; Stone, *Liberation*, 68.

(280) **Gerhart Riegner and Eduard Schulte,** Breitman and Laqueur, *Breaking*, passim; Riegner, *Never*, 35–43, 50.

(280) **three unimpeachable sources,** Friedländer, *Nazi Germany*, v. 2, 458–61; Riegner *Never*, 48–50.

(281) **BBC broadcast by Thomas Mann,** Longerich, *Davon*, 240–45.

(281) **a tally by Höfle,** Friedländer, *Nazi Germany*, v. 2, 479–80.

(281) **making too much of Jewish suffering would play into the claims of Nazi propaganda,** Aronson, *Hitler*, passim; Hamerow, *Why*, 398, 400–403, 409, 411–12, 414.

(282) **the USSR never considered the idea,** David-Fox, *Holocaust*, 31–36.

(282) **The Russians first learned. . . . But nothing happened,** Orbach and Solonin, "Calculated," 90–113.

(283) **Churchill, Eden, and Sinclair,** Wasserstein, *Britain*, 307–20; Neufeld and Berenbaum, *Bombing*, 261–71.

(283) **"frightful prospect,"** see Wasserstein, *Britain*, 340–41.

(283) **Only 37,451,** Ofer, *Escaping*, 319.

(283) **both the United States and the UK purposefully ignored,** Fleming, *Auschwitz*, 167–218.

(284) **The Mufti and his effects on the British,** Wasserstein, *Britain*, 28–29, 71, 79–80.

(284) **The Mufti's hopes and disappointments,** Motadel, *Islam*, 41–43, 87–92, 96–97, 107–8, 113–14, 188–94, 226–35, 250, 274–82; Nicosia, *Nazi*, 71, 267, 276–79.

(285) **the Mufti scored a few victories . . . [his] association with the Axis ultimately had . . . disastrous consequences,** Motadel, *Islam*, 43–44; Nicosia, *Nazi*, 242–57; Achcar, *Arabs*, 150–73.

(285) **Pope Pius XII was more worried about,** Phayer, *Catholic*, 57–66; Kornberg, *Dilemma*, 253.

(286) **He had his ambassador to Vichy . . . tell its leader,** Marrus and Paxton, *Vichy*, 262.

(286) **used Vatican diplomatic channels to persuade Spain,** Zuccotti, *Père*, 127–28; Ventresca, *Soldier*, 199–200.

(286) **left decisions . . . withheld . . . information,** Phayer, *Catholic*, 43, 46, 49.

(286) **declined to intervene . . . put off pressing . . . Horthy . . . refused to send another protest,** ibid., 104–9; Phayer, *Pius*, 91–93.

(287) **"divine law knows no compromise,"** "Pius XII," 16; see also Ventresca, *Soldier*, 174.

(287) **"Push never came to shove,"** Bess, *Choices*, 86.

(288) **Sheptytsky . . . tried to impede Ukrainian collaboration . . . in two extraordinary ways**, Petrovsky-Shtern and Polonsky, *Polin* 26, 347–49.

(288) **"Deeply moved. . . . platonic,"** Friedländer, *Nazi Germany*, v. 2, 420.

(288) **Catholic hierarchy in Slovakia**, Ward, *Tiso*, 225–28, 232–39; Kornberg, *Dilemma*, 78–86.

(289) **In Belgium, a network**, Moore, *Survivors*, 276–95.

(289) **in Rome**, Schlemmer and Woller, "italienische Faschismus," 195.

(289) **emphasized the dangers that might flow**, Ventresca, *Soldier*, 162–70, 174–76.

(290) **although the pope never explicitly drew this comparison**, Kornberg, *Dilemma*, 253.

(290) **neither the Dutch prime minister nor the queen of the Netherlands was cowed**, Wasserstein, *Ambiguity*, 244.

(290) **arrested thirty-seven clerics . . . six of them died**, Griech-Polelle, *Galen*, 217; Spicer, *Resisting*, 137.

(290) **such fears did not stop Bernhard Lichtenberg**, Hayes and Roth, *Handbook*, 239; Spicer, *Resisting*, 171–82.

(291) **"In the fulfillment of . . . Our duty . . . it is not allowed,"** Kornberg, *Dilemma*, 266.

(291) **the incidence of antisemitism in the American population actually increased during the conflict**, Dinnerstein, *Antisemitism*, 128–49; Wyman, *Abandonment*, 14–15, Dinnerstein, *Survivors*, 6; Hamerow, *Why*, 311.

(291) **in 1940–41 . . . only about 30,000 German Jews got into the country**, Bauer, *Jewry*, 66.

(292) **many munitions ships returned empty from Europe**, Wyman, *Abandonment*, 335.

(292) **Karski in Izbica and with FDR**, Karski, *Story*, 368–84, 419, 446–47.

(292) **War Refugee Board funding**, Bauer, *American*, 407

(293) **food that the board paid for and stockpiled in Swedish ports saved thousands of lives**, Rosenberg, *Brief*, 139–40, 149–50.

(294) **The non-bombing of Auschwitz**, Hamerow, *Why*, 402–18; Neufeld and Berenbaum, *Bombing*, passim, but especially 249–60, 271–80.

(294) **bombing the camp might not have saved many lives**, Rees, *Auschwitz*, 246–47.

(294) **The SS transferred**, Czech, *Kalendarium*, 701, 821.

(294) **30,000 in October, for example**; Steinbacher, *Auschwitz*, 124.

(295) **collateral damage would have occurred**, Wachsmann, *KL*, 586; Hayes, *From Cooperation*, 256.

(295) **Stephen Wise . . . refused to pressure him**, Hamerow, *Why*, 269, 345; Riegner, *Never*, 71.

(295) **"constitutionally incapable of serious questioning,"** Bauer, *American Jewry*, 52.

(295) **the *Yishuv***, Porat, *Blue*, 251, 256–58, 261–62; Ofer, *Escaping*, 23–31, 318–19.

(296) **"Refugees who have fled purely on racial grounds,"** Independent Commission, *Switzerland*, 114.

(296) **enforcement was inconsistent**, ibid., 110, 117.

(297) **Evolution of Swedish policy**, Hayes, *How*, 735–52, excerpting the fundamental work of Paul Levine.

(298) **George Mantello**, Kranzler, *Man*, chapters 7–11.

(299) **Giorgio Perlasca**, Levine, *Wallenberg*, 310–11, 324–48.

CHAPTER 8: AFTERMATH

(300) **The toll at Belsen**, Stone, *Liberation*, 83–85, 107–8, 111–12.

(301) **some of them went on a rampage . . . used bayonets and rifle butts**, Abzug, *Inside*, 93; Bessel, *1945*, 162–64.

(301) **"The punishment they got,"** Stone, *Liberation*, 100.

(301) **the object of Allied revulsion soon changed**, Fritz, *Endkampf*, 53–56, 227–38; Abzug, *Inside*, 154–55.

(301) **Patton's remarks**, ibid., 157.

(302) **"As matters now stand,"** Brenner, *After*, 11; Fritz, *Endkampf*, 236–37.

(302) **18,000/97,000/167,000**, Wyman, *DPs*, 149.

(303) **encountered the same sort of reluctance**, Petrovsky-Shtern and Polonsky, *Polin* 26, 368–79.

(303) **UNRRA spent almost $4 billion**, Gutman, *Encyclopedia*, 1540.

(303) **They were often received somewhat insensitively**, Hayes, *How?*, 775–87.

(304) **readiness to turn a blind eye**, Douglas, *Right*, 28; Dinnerstein, *America*, 251–71.

(304) **faced incomprehension of their experience**, Cohen, *Case*, passim.

(306) **the reckoning was pretty intense**, Frei, *Transnationale*, 31–32; Heberer and Matthäus, *Atrocities*, 49–71; Jardim, *Mauthausen*, 1, 197.

(307) **The British tried**, Wachsmann, *KL*, 608.

(307) **Soviet courts convicted**, Frei, *Transnationale*, 193; Bazyler and Tuerkheimer, *Forgotten*, 40–41.

(307) **The Poles tried**, Wachsmann, *KL*, 608–9.

(308) **The Dutch followed up**, Wasserstein, *Ambiguity*, 223–24; Deak, *On Trial*, 204.

(309) **only seven . . . were still alive in 1950**, Wachsmann, *KL*, 612.

(310) **Only about 10 percent of the Germans who ever worked at Auschwitz**, Dlugoborski and Piper, *Auschwitz*, v. 5, 102–3, 108, 116 (789 out of perhaps 7,200 Germans ever stationed there).

(310) **In 1969, East Germany executed**, Raskin, *Child*, 94–98.

(311) **The record . . . regarding the 121 men from T4**, Berger, *Experten*, 363–71; Bryant, *Eyewitness*, 13–19.

(312) **Catholics developed several escape routes**, Phayer, *Pius XII*, 173–94; Phayer, *Catholic*, 165–75; Stangneth, *Eichmann*, 79, 90–92, 292–93.

(312) **Alois Hudal**, Phayer, *Pius XII*, 195–207.

(313) **Draganovic, Barbie, Pavelic**, ibid., 208–51; Deak, *On Trial*, 217–18.

(313) **Pius XII . . . held to the theory of pastoral responsibility that he had followed**, Kornberg, *Dilemma*, 235, 255–74

(314) **Galen . . . went even further**, Phayer, *Catholic*, 139, 162–63.

(314) **Muench . . . wrote a pastoral letter that contrasted**, Brown-Fleming, *Conscience*, 5–6.

(314) **their advocacy was too much for even Muench**, Phayer, *Pius XII*, 165.

(314) **ODESSA, appears to have been largely mythical**, Stangneth, *Eichmann*, 89–90.

(314) **An independent historians' commission . . . reached the conclusion**, Schneppen, *Odessa*, 208–9. For evidence of a higher number of Croatian criminal immigrants, see Phayer, *Pius XII*, 246.

(315) **owed much more to the efforts of their friends and families**, Kulish and Mekhennet, *Eternal*, 83–86, 91–94, 210–14.

(316) **total payments . . . have come**, Marrus, *Measure*, 68–76; Dean et al., *Robbery*, 99–133; Goschler, *Schuld*, 474–75, 539.

(317) **The survivors who came off best**, Hayes and Roth, *Handbook*, 548–50.

(317) **Other categories of victims came away with much less**, ibid., 551–54.

(318) **a few companies made token postwar payments**, Ferenc, *Less*, 188.

(319) **German Foundation Initiative**, see Spiliotis, *Verantwortung*, passim; Eizenstat, *Imperfect*, 243–78; Dean et al., *Robbery*, 128.

(319) **Catholic religious institutions and orphanages . . . often declined**, Marrus, "Custody," 378–403; Ventresca, *Soldier*, 222–27.

(320) **the French government endowed a new Foundation**, Dean et al., *Robbery*, 139.

(321) **Switzerland and its payments**, Eizenstat, *Imperfect*, 90–186; Independent Commission, *Switzerland*, 274–79, 442–49.

(322) **"negotiated justice,"** Barkan, *Guilt*, 309.

(322) **The Union Bank of Switzerland, in effect . . . the National Bank of Switzerland, the recipient of 92 percent of the gold**, Spiliotis, *Verantwortung*, 54; Independent Commission, *Switzerland*, 238, 252–53.

(323) **these advocates also spread a lot of misconceptions . . . awful role models**, Marrus, *Measure*, 124–26; Petropoulos and Roth, *Gray*, 7–9; Bazyler and Alford, *Restitution*, 197–204; Eizenstat, *Imperfect*, 182.

(327) **"gap" . . . "clash,"** Levine, *Wallenberg*, 12–13.

(328) **As David Cesarani has shown**, Cesarani, *Final*, passim.

(328) **more trains to the staging areas of Operation Barbarossa . . . every day**, Gall and Pohl, *Eisenbahn*, 227.

(330) **"less the driving force . . . than the setting,"** Stone, *Histories*, 126.

(332) **A British judge**, Lipstadt, *History*, passim; Evans, *Lying*, 104–48; van Pelt, *Case*, 488–506.

(332) **"On the Streets of Truth" . . . "principal source text,"** Stangneth, *Before*, 152–53, see also 142–44.

(335) **Tony Judt . . . aroused an explosive debate**, reprinted in Judt, *Change*, 115–23; see also Judt, *Reappraisals*, 286–95.

(339) **"To make peace is to forget,"** Sontag, *Pain*, 103.

(339) **83 percent of the people there thought a resolution . . . impossible**, Mitchell, *Negotiator*, 315.

(341) **"believed that if you choose to resist evil . . . ways . . . will open up around you,"** Bess, *Choices*, 129.

(342) **"surrounding every perfidy,"** Neumann, *Behemoth*, 379.

(343) **wrote a prophetic protest**, Hayes "Industry under the Swastika," 28.

SELECTED BIBLIOGRAPHY

ABELLA, IRVING, AND HAROLD TROPER. *None Is Too Many: Canada and the Jews of Europe, 1933–1948.* Toronto: University of Toronto Press, 2012.

ABZUG, ROBERT H. *America Views the Holocaust 1933–1945.* Boston: Bedford/St. Martin's, 1999.

———. *Inside the Vicious Heart: Americans and the Liberation of the Concentration Camps.* New York: Oxford University Press, 1987.

ACHCAR, GILBERT. *The Arabs and the Holocaust.* New York: Metropolitan Books, 2009.

ADAM, UWE DIETRICH. *Judenpolitik im Dritten Reich.* Königstein: Athenäum/Droste, 1979.

ADELSON, ALAN, ED. *The Diary of Dawid Sierakowiak: Five Notebooks from the Lodz Ghetto.* New York: Oxford University Press, 1996.

ADELSON, ALAN, AND ROBERT LAPIDES, EDS. *Lodz Ghetto: Inside a Community under Siege.* New York: Viking, 1989.

ALLEN, MICHAEL THAD. *The Business of Genocide.* Chapel Hill: University of North Carolina Press, 2002.

ALLEN, WILLIAM SHERIDAN. *The Nazi Seizure of Power.* New York: Franklin Watts, 1984.

ALY, GÖTZ. *Final Solution: Nazi Population Policy and the Murder of the European Jews.* London: Arnold, 1999.

———. *Hitler's Beneficiaries.* New York: Metropolitan Books, 2006.

———. *Why the Germans? Why the Jews?* New York: Metropolitan Books, 2014.

ALY, GÖTZ, PETER CHROUST, AND CHRISTIAN PROSS. *Cleansing the Fatherland: Nazi Medicine and Racial Hygiene.* Baltimore: Johns Hopkins University Press, 1994.

ALY, GÖTZ, AND SUSANNE HEIM. *Architects of Annihilation.* Princeton, NJ: Princeton University Press, 2002.

ALY, GÖTZ, AND MICHAEL SONTHEIMER. *Fromms: Wie der jüdischen Kondomfabrikant Julius F. unter die deutschen Räuber fiel*. Frankfurt am Main: S. Fischer, 2007.

ANCEL, JEAN. *The History of the Holocaust in Romania*. Lincoln: University of Nebraska Press, 2011.

ANONYMOUS. *The Clandestine History of the Kovno Jewish Ghetto Police*. Bloomington: Indiana University Press, 2014.

ARAD, YITZHAK. *Belzec, Sobibor, Treblinka: The Operation Reinhard Death Camps*. Bloomington: Indiana University Press, 1987.

———. *The Holocaust in the Soviet Union*. Lincoln: University of Nebraska Press, 2009.

ARAD, YITZHAK, ISRAEL GUTMAN, AND ABRAHAM MARGALIOT, EDS. *Documents on the Holocaust*. Lincoln: University of Nebraska Press, 1999.

ARENDT, HANNAH. *Eichmann in Jerusalem*. New York: Penguin Books, 1964.

ARONSON, SHLOMO. *Hitler, the Allies, and the Jews*. New York: Cambridge University Press, 2004.

ARVIDSSON, STEFAN. *Aryan Idols: Indo-European Mythology as Ideology and Science*. Chicago: University of Chicago Press, 2006.

BAJOHR, FRANK. *"Aryanization" in Hamburg*. New York: Berghahn Books, 2002.

BAJOHR, FRANK, AND DIETER POHL. *Der Holocaust als offenes Geheimnis*. Munich: C. H. Beck, 2006.

BALDERSTON, THEO. *Economics and Politics in the Weimar Republic*. Cambridge: Cambridge University Press, 2002.

BANKIER, DAVID. *The Germans and the Final Solution*. Oxford: Blackwell, 1992.

BANKIER, DAVID, ED. *Probing the Depths of German Antisemitism*. New York: Berghahn, 2000.

BARKAI, AVRAHAM. *From Boycott to Annihilation: The Economic Struggle of German Jews, 1933–1943*. Hanover, NH: University Press of New England, 1989.

———. "German Interests in the Haavara-Transfer Agreement 1933–1939." *Leo Baeck Yearbook* 35 (1990): 245–66.

———. *"Wehr Dich!" Der Centralverein deutscher Staatsbürger jüdischen Glaubens 1893–1938*. Munich: C. H. Beck, 2002.

BARKAN, ELAZAR. *The Guilt of Nations*. New York: W. W. Norton & Company, 2000.

BARKAN, ELAZAR, ELIZABETH A. COLE, AND KAI STRUVE, EDS. *Shared History—Divided Memory. Jews and Others in Soviet-Occupied Poland, 1939–1941*. Leipzig: Leipziger Universitätsverlag, 2007.

BARNETT, VICTORIA J. *Bystanders: Conscience and Complicity During the Holocaust*. Westport, CT: Praeger, 1999.

BARON, LAWRENCE. "Tarnishing Tinseltown: Hollywood's Responses to Nazi Germany." *Journal of Jewish Identities* 7 (2014): 61–80.

Bartov, Omer. *The Eastern Front, 1941–45: German Troops and the Barbarization of Warfare.* New York: St. Martin's, 1986.

Bartov, Omer, and Eric D. Weitz, eds. *Shatterzone of Empires: Coexistence and Violence in the German, Habsburg, Russian, and Ottoman Borderlands.* Bloomington: Indiana University Press, 2013.

Bar-Zohar, Michael. *Beyond Hitler's Grasp: The Heroic Rescue of Bulgaria's Jews.* Holbrook, MA: Adams Media, 1998.

Bauer, Yehuda. *American Jewry and the Holocaust: The American Jewish Joint Distribution Committee, 1939–1945.* Detroit: Wayne State University Press, 1981.

———. *The Death of the Shtetl.* New Haven, CT: Yale University Press, 2009.

———. *A History of the Holocaust.* New York: Franklin Watts, 1982.

———. *My Brother's Keeper: A History of the American Jewish Joint Distribution Committee, 1929–1939.* Philadelphia: Jewish Publication Society, 1974.

———. *Rethinking the Holocaust.* New Haven, CT: Yale University Press, 2001.

Bazyler, Michael J., and Roger P. Alford, eds. *Holocaust Restitution: Perspectives on the Litigation and Its Legacy.* New York: New York University Press, 2006.

Bazyler, Michael J., and Frank M. Tuerkheimer. *Forgotten Trials of the Holocaust.* New York: New York University Press, 2014.

Beachy, Robert. *Gay Berlin: Birthplace of a Modern Identity.* New York: Alfred A. Knopf, 2014.

Beller, Steven. *Antisemitism: A Very Short Introduction.* New York: Oxford University Press, 2007.

Bender, Sara. *The Jews of Bialystok during World War II and the Holocaust.* Hanover, NH: University Press of New England, 2008.

Benz, Wolfgang, ed. *Dimension des Völkermords: Die Zahl der jüdischen Opfer des Nationalsozialismus.* Munich: Oldenbourg, 1991.

———. *Die Juden in Deutschland 1933–1945.* Munich: C. H. Beck, 1989.

Beorn, Waitman. *Marching Into Darkness: The Wehrmacht and the Holocaust in Belarus.* Cambridge, MA: Harvard University Press, 2014.

Berenbaum, Michael, ed. *A Mosaic of Victims.* New York: New York University Press, 1990.

Berenbaum, Michael, and Abraham J. Peck, eds. *The Holocaust and History.* Bloomington: Indiana University Press, 1998.

Berger, Sara. *Experten der Vernichtung: Das T4-Reinhardt-Netzwerk in den Lagern Belzec, Sobibor und Treblinka.* Hamburg: Hamburger Edition, 2013.

Berger, Stefan. *Germany: Inventing the Nation.* London: Hodder Arnold, 2004.

Bess, Michael. *Choices Under Fire: Moral Dimensions of World War II.* New York: Vintage, 2006.

Bessel, Richard. *Germany 1945: From War to Peace.* New York: HarperCollins, 2009.

BIKONT, ANNA. *The Crime and the Silence: Confronting the Massacre of Jews in Wartime Jedwabne.* New York: Farrar, Straus and Giroux, 2015.

BLACK, PETER. "Foot Soldiers of the Final Solution: The Trawniki Training Camp and Operation Reinhard." *Holocaust and Genocide Studies* 25 (2011): 1–99.

BLATMAN, DANIEL. *The Death Marches.* Cambridge, MA: Harvard University Press, 2011.

BLATT, THOMAS TOIVI. *From the Ashes of Sobibor: A Story of Survival.* Evanston: Northwestern University Press, 1997.

BLOBAUM, ROBERT, ED. *Antisemitism and its Opponents in Modern Poland.* Ithaca: Cornell University Press, 2005.

BOEHLING, REBECCA, AND UTA LARKEY. *Life and Loss in the Shadow of the Holocaust.* New York: Cambridge University Press, 2011.

BRACHER, KARL DIETRICH. *The German Dictatorship.* New York: Praeger, 1970.

BRAHAM, RANDOLPH. *The Politics of Genocide: The Holocaust in Hungary.* Detroit: Wayne State University Press, 2000.

———. *Studies on the Holocaust.* Boulder: Social Science Monographs, 2000.

BRAHAM, RANDOLPH, ED. *The Geographical Encyclopedia of the Holocaust in Hungary.* 3 vols. Evanston: Northwestern University Press, 2013.

BREITMAN, RICHARD. *The Architect of Genocide: Himmler and the Final Solution.* New York: Alfred A. Knopf, 1991.

———. *Official Secrets: What the Nazis Planned, What the British and the Americans Knew.* New York: Hill and Wang, 1998.

BREITMAN, RICHARD, AND ALAN M. KRAUT. *American Refugee Policy and European Jewry: 1933–1945.* Blooomington: Indiana University Press, 1987.

BREITMAN, RICHARD, AND ALLAN J. LICHTMAN. *FDR and the Jews.* Cambridge, MA: Harvard University Press, 2013.

BRENNER, MICHAEL. *After the Holocaust: Rebuilding Jewish Lives in Postwar Germany.* Princeton, NJ: Princeton University Press, 1997.

BRONNER, STEPHEN ERIC. *A Rumor about the Jews: Reflections on Antisemitism and the Protocols of the Elders of Zion.* New York: St. Martin's Press, 2000.

BROWN-FLEMING, SUZANNE. *The Holocaust and Catholic Conscience: Cardinal Aloisius Muench and the Guilt Question in Germany.* South Bend: University of Notre Dame Press, 2005.

BROWNING, CHRISTOPHER R. *Fateful Months: Essays on the Emergence of the Final Solution.* New York: Holmes & Meier, 1991.

———. *Nazi Policy, Jewish Workers, German Killers.* New York: Cambridge University Press, 2000.

———. *Ordinary Men: Reserve Police Battalion 101 and the Final Solution in Poland.* New York: HarperCollins, 1992.

———. *The Origins of the Final Solution.* Lincoln: University of Nebraska Press, 2004.

————. *The Path to Genocide.* New York: Cambridge University Press, 1992.

————. *Remembering Survival: Inside a Nazi Slave-Labor Camp.* New York: W. W. Norton & Company, 2010.

BRYANT, MICHAEL S. *Confronting the "Good Death": Nazi Euthanasia on Trial, 1945–1953.* Boulder: University Press of Colorado, 2005.

————. *Eyewitness to Genocide: The Operation Reinhard Death Camp Trials, 1955–1966.* Knoxville: University Press of Tennessee, 2014.

BUGGELN, MARC. *Slave Labor in Nazi Concentration Camps.* New York: Oxford University Press, 2014.

BURDS, JEFFREY. *Holocaust in Rovno: The Massacre at Sosenski Forest, November 1941.* New York: Palgrave Macmillan, 2013.

BURLEIGH, MICHAEL. *Death and Deliverance: 'Euthanasia' in Germany 1900–1945.* Cambridge: Cambridge University Press, 1994.

BURLEIGH, MICHAEL, AND WOLFGANG WIPPERMANN. *The Racial State: Germany 1933–1945.* Cambridge: Cambridge University Press, 1991.

BURRIN, PHILIPPE. *Hitler and the Jews: The Genesis of the Holocaust.* London: Arnold, 1994.

————. *Nazi Anti-Semitism.* New York: The New Press, 2005.

BÜTTNER, URSULA. *Die Not der Juden teilen: Christlich-jüdische Familien im Dritten Reich.* Hamburg: Christians, 1988.

CAESTECKER, FRANK, AND BOB MOORE, EDS. *Refugees from Nazi Germany and the Liberal European States.* New York: Berghahn, 2010.

CAPLAN, JANE, AND NIKOLAUS WACHSMANN, EDS. *Concentration Camps in Nazi Germany.* New York: Routledge, 2010.

CARON, VICKI. *Uneasy Asylum: France and the Jewish Refugee Crisis, 1933–1942.* Palo Alto: Stanford University Press, 1999.

CESARANI, DAVID. *Becoming Eichmann.* New York: DaCapo Press, 2004.

————. *Final Solution: The Fate of the Jews 1933-1949.* London: Macmillan, 2016.

COHEN, BETH. *Case Closed: Holocaust Survivors in Postwar America.* New Brunswick: Rutgers University Press, 2007.

COHN, NORMAN. *Warrant for Genocide: The Myth of the Jewish World Conspiracy and the Protocols of the Elders of Zion.* London: Serif, 1996.

CONFINO, ALON. *A World Without Jews: The Nazi Imagination from Persecution to Genocide.* New Haven, CT: Yale University Press, 2014.

CONZE, ECKART, NORBERT FREI, PETER HAYES, AND MOSHE ZIMMERMANN. *Das Amt und die Vergangenheit: Deutsche Diplomaten im Dritten Reich und in der Bundesrepublik.* Munich: Karl Blessing, 2010.

CORNI, GUSTAVO. *Hitler's Ghettos.* London: Arnold, 2002.

CRAIG, GORDON A. *Germany 1866–1945.* New York: Oxford University Press, 1978.

CÜPPERS, MARTIN. *Walter Rauff—in deutschen Diensten.* Darmstadt: Wissenschaftliche Buchgesellschaft, 2013.

CZECH, DANUTA. *Kalendarium der Ereignisse im Konzentrationslager Auschwitz-Birkenau 1939–1945*. Hamburg: Rowohlt, 1989.

DAVID-FOX, MICHAEL, PETER HOLQUIST, AND ALEXANDER M. MARTIN, EDS. *The Holocaust in the East: Local Perpetrators and Soviet Responses*. Pittsburgh: University of Pittsburgh Press, 2014.

DAWIDOWICZ, LUCY S. *The War Against the Jews 1933–1945*. New York: Holt, Rinehart and Winston, 1975.

DEAK, ISTVAN. *Essays on Hitler's Europe*. Lincoln: University of Nebraska Press, 2001.

———. *Europe on Trial: The Story of Collaboration, Resistance, and Retribution During World War II*. Philadelphia: Westview Press, 2015.

DEAN, MARTIN. *Robbing the Jews: The Confiscation of Jewish Property in the Holocaust, 1933–1945*. New York: Cambridge University Press, 2008.

DEAN, MARTIN, CONSTANTIN GOSCHLER, AND PHILIPP THER, EDS. *Robbery and Restitution: The Conflict over Jewish Property in Europe*. New York: Berghahn Books, 2007.

DELETANT, DENNIS. *Hitler's Forgotten Ally: Ion Antonescu and His Regime, Romania 1940–1944*. New York: Palgrave Macmillan, 2006.

DES PRES, TERRENCE. *The Survivor: An Anatomy of Life in the Death Camps*. New York: Oxford University Press, 1976.

DIECKMANN, CHRISTOPH. *Deutsche Besatzungspolitik in Litauen 1941–1944*. 2 vols. Berlin: Wallstein, 2011.

DINNERSTEIN, LEONARD. *America and the Survivors of the Holocaust*. New York: Columbia University Press, 1982.

———. *Anti-Semitism in America*. New York: Oxford University Press, 1994.

DLUGOBORSKI, WACŁAW, AND FRANCISZEK PIPER, EDS. *Auschwitz 1940–1945: Central Issues in the History of the Camp*. 5 vols. Oświęcim: Auschwitz-Birkenau State Museum, 2000.

DOBROSZYCKI, LUCJAN, ED. *The Chronicle of the Lodz Ghetto 1941–1944*. New Haven, CT: Yale University Press, 1984.

DOHERTY, THOMAS. *Hollywood and Hitler, 1933–1939*. New York: Columbia University Press, 2013.

DOUGLAS, LAWRENCE. *The Right Wrong Man: John Demjanjuk and the Last Great Nazi War Crimes Trial*. Princeton, NJ: Princeton University Press, 2016.

DWORK, DEBORAH, *Children With a Star: Jewish Youth in Nazi Europe*. New Haven: Yale University Press, 1991.

DWORK, DEBORAH, AND ROBERT JAN VAN PELT. *Auschwitz: 1270 to the Present*. New York: W. W. Norton & Company, 1996.

———. *Flight from the Reich: Refugee Jews, 1933–1946*. New York: W. W. Norton & Company, 2009.

EARL, HILARY. *The Nuremberg SS-Einsatzgruppen Trial, 1945–1958.* New York: Cambridge University Press, 2009.

EIZENSTAT, STUART E. *Imperfect Justice: Looted Assets, Slave Labor, and the Unfinished Business of World War II.* New York: Public Affairs, 2003.

EKSTEINS, MODRIS. *Walking since Daybreak: A Story of Eastern Europe, World War II, and the Heart of our Century.* Boston: Houghton Mifflin, 1999.

ELON, AMOS. *The Pity of It All: A History of Jews in Germany, 1743–1933.* New York: Henry Holt & Company, 2002.

ENGEL, DAVID. *The Holocaust: The Third Reich and the Jews.* Harlow: Longman, 2000.

ENGELKING, BARBARA AND JACEK LEOCIAK. *The Warsaw Ghetto: A Guide to the Perished City.* New Haven, CT: Yale University Press, 2009.

ENGELMANN, BERNT. *In Hitler's Germany: Everyday Life in the Third Reich.* New York: Pantheon, 1986.

EPSTEIN, CATHERINE. *Model Nazi: Arthur Greiser and the Occupation of Western Poland.* New York: Oxford University Press, 2010.

EVANS, RICHARD J. *Lying about Hitler: History, Holocaust, and the David Irving Trial.* New York: Basic Books, 2001.

———. *The Third Reich at War.* New York: Penguin Press, 2009.

FALTER, JÜRGEN ET AL., EDS. *Wahlen und Abstimmungen in der Weimarer Republik.* Munich: C. H. Beck, 1986.

FATTORINI, EMMA. *Hitler, Mussolini, and the Vatican: Pope Pius XI and the Speech That Was Never Made.* Cambridge: Polity Press, 2011.

FAVEZ, JEAN-CLAUDE. *The Red Cross and the Holocaust.* New York: Cambridge University Press, 1999.

FELDMAN, GERALD D. *Allianz and the German Insurance Business, 1933–1945.* New York: Cambridge University Press, 2001.

FERENCZ, BENJAMIN B. *Less Than Slaves: Jewish Forced Labor and the Quest for Compensation.* Cambridge, MA: Harvard University Press, 1979.

FEST, JOACHIM. *The Face of the Third Reich.* London: Weidenfeld & Nicolson, 1970.

———. *Hitler.* New York: Vintage Books, 1975.

FLEMING, MICHAEL. *Auschwitz, the Allies and the Censorship of the Holocaust.* Cambridge: Cambridge University Press, 2014.

FORD MOTOR COMPANY ARCHIVES. *Research Findings about Ford-Werke under the Nazi Regime.* Dearborn, MI: Ford Motor Company, 2001.

FREI, NORBERT. *Adenauer's Germany and the Nazi Past: The Politics of Amnesty and Integration.* New York: Columbia University Press, 2002.

FREI, NORBERT, ED. *Transnationale Vergangenheitspolitik: Der Umgang mit deutschen Kriegsverbrechern in Europa nach dem Zweiten Weltkrieg.* Göttingen: Wallstein, 2006.

FRIEDLANDER, HENRY. *The Origins of Nazi Genocide: From Euthanasia to the Final Solution* Chapel Hill: University of North Carolina Press, 1995.

FRIEDLÄNDER, SAUL. *Nazi Germany and the Jews*, 2 vols. New York: HarperCollins, 1997, 2007.

FRIEDMAN, JONATHAN C., ED. *The Routledge History of the Holocaust*. New York: Routledge, 2011.

FRITZ, STEPHEN G. *Endkampf: Soldiers, Civilians, and the Death of the Third Reich*. Lexington: University Press of Kentucky, 2004.

FRITZSCHE, PETER. "The Holocaust and the Knowledge of Murder." *Journal of Modern History* 80 (2008): 594–613.

———. *Life and Death in the Third Reich*. Cambridge, MA: Harvard University Press, 2008.

FULBROOK, MARY. *A Small Town near Auschwitz: Ordinary Nazis and the Holocaust*. New York: Oxford University Press, 2012.

———. *Dissonant Lives: Generations and Violence through the German Dictatorships*. New York: Oxford University Press, 2011.

GALL, LOTHAR, AND MANFRED POHL, EDS. *Die Eisenbahn in Deutschland*. Munich: C. H. Beck, 1999.

GAY, PETER. *Freud, Jews and Other Germans*. New York: Oxford University Press, 1978.

———. *My German Question: Growing Up in Nazi Berlin*. New Haven, CT: Yale University Press, 1998.

GELLATELY, ROBERT, AND NATHAN STOLTZFUS, EDS. *Social Outsiders in Nazi Germany*. Princeton, NJ: Princeton University Press, 2001.

GERLACH, CHRISTIAN. *Kalkulierte Morde: Die deutsche Wirtschafts- und Vernichtungspolitik in Weißrusland 1941 bis 1944*. Hamburg: Hamburger Edition, 1999.

GERLACH, CHRISTIAN, AND GÖTZ ALY. *Das letzte Kapitel: Der Mord an den ungarischen Juden*. Stuttgart: Deutsche Verlags-Anstalt, 2002.

GERWARTH, ROBERT. *Hitler's Hangman: The Life of Heydrich*. New Haven, CT: Yale University Press, 2011.

GIGLIOTTI, SIMONE. *The Train Journey: Transit, Captivity, and Witnessing in the Holocaust*. New York: Berghahn, 2009.

GILBERT, MARTIN. *The Holocaust: A History of the Jews of Europe During the Second World War*. New York: Henry Holt and Company, 1985.

GILBERT, MARTIN, ED. *Surviving the Holocaust: The Kovno Ghetto Diary of Avraham Tory*. Cambridge, MA: Harvard University Press, 1990.

GINSBERG, BENJAMIN. *How the Jews Defeated Hitler: Exploding the Myth of Jewish Passivity in the Face of Nazism*. Lanham, MD: Rowman & Littlefield, 2013.

GITELMAN, ZVI, ED. *Bitter Legacy: Confronting the Holocaust in the USSR*. Bloomington: Indiana University Press, 1997.

GLAZAR, RICHARD. *Trap with a Green Fence: Survival in Treblinka.* Evanston: Northwestern University Press, 1995.

GODMAN, PETER. *Hitler and the Vatican.* New York: Free Press, 2004.

GORDON, SARAH. *Hitler, Germans, and the "Jewish Question."* Princeton, NJ: Princeton University Press, 1984.

GOSCHLER, CONSTANTIN. *Schuld und Schulden: Die Politik der Wiedergutmachung für NS-Verfolgte seit 1945.* Göttingen: Wallstein, 2005.

GOTTWALDT, ALFRED, AND DIANA SCHULLE. *Die "Judendeportationen" aus dem Deutschen Reich 1941–1945.* Wiesbaden: Marix Verlag, 2005.

GOULD, STEPHEN JAY. *The Mismeasure of Man.* New York: W. W. Norton & Company, 1981.

GRABOWSKI, JAN. *Hunt for the Jews: Betrayal and Murder in German-Occupied Poland.* Bloomington: Indiana University Press, 2013.

GREGOR, NEIL. *Daimler-Benz in the Third Reich.* New Haven, CT: Yale University Press, 1998.

———. *How to Read Hitler.* New York: W. W. Norton & Company, 2005.

GRIECH-POLELLE, BETH A. *Bishop von Galen: German Catholicism and National Socialism.* New Haven, CT: Yale University Press, 2002.

GROSS, JAN T. *Fear: Anti-Semitism in Poland after Auschwitz.* New York: Random House, 2006.

———. *Neighbors: The Destruction of the Jewish Community in Jedwabne, Poland.* Princeton, NJ: Princeton University Press, 2001.

GROSS, JAN T., and Irena Grudzinska Gross. *Golden Harvest.* New York: Oxford University Press, 2012.

GRUNER, WOLF. *Jewish Forced Labor under the Nazis.* New York: Cambridge University Press, 2006.

———. *Widerstand in der Rosenstraße: Die Fabrik-Aktion und die Verfolgung der "Mischehen" 1943.* Frankfurt am Main: S. Fischer, 2005.

GUTMAN, ISRAEL, ED. *Encyclopedia of the Holocaust.* 4 vols. New York: Macmillan, 1990.

GUTMAN, YISRAEL. *The Jews of Warsaw 1939–1943.* Bloomington: Indiana University Press, 1982.

GUTMAN, YISRAEL, AND MICHAEL BERENBAUM, EDS. *Anatomy of the Auschwitz Death Camp.* Bloomington: Indiana University Press, 1994.

GUTMAN, YISRAEL, AND SHMUEL KRAKOWSKI. *Unequal Victims: Poles and Jews During World War II.* New York: Holocaust Library, 1986.

GUTMAN, YISRAEL, EZRA MENDELSOHN, JEHUDA REINHARZ, AND CHONE SHMERUK, EDS. *The Jews of Poland Between Two World Wars.* Hanover, NH: University Press of New England, 1989.

GUTTERMAN, BELLA. *A Narrow Bridge to Life: Jewish Forced Labor and Survival in the Gross-Rosen Camp System 1940–1945.* New York: Berghahn, 2008.

HAFFNER, SEBASTIAN. *Defying Hitler.* New York: Farrar, Straus and Giroux, 2002.

———. *The Meaning of Hitler.* New York: Macmillan, 1979.

HAGEN, WILLIAM H. *German History in Modern Times.* New York: Cambridge University Press, 2012.

HAMANN, BRIGITTE. *Hitler's Vienna: A Dictator's Apprenticeship.* New York: Oxford University Press, 1999.

HAMEROW, THEODORE S. *Why We Watched: Europe, America, and the Holocaust.* New York: W. W. Norton & Company, 2008.

HAND, SEAN, AND STEVEN T. KATZ, EDS. *Post-Holocaust France and the Jews.* New York: New York University Press, 2015.

HAYES, PETER. "Auschwitz: Capital of the Holocaust." *Holocaust and Genocide Studies* 17 (2003): 330–50.

———. *From Cooperation to Complicity: Degussa in the Third Reich.* New York: Cambridge University Press, 2004.

———. *Industry and Ideology: IG Farben in the Nazi Era.* New York: Cambridge University Press, 2001.

———. "Industry under the Swastika." In *Enterprise in the Period of Fascism in Europe,* edited by Harold James and Jakob Tanner, 26–37. Burlington, VT: Ashgate, 2002.

HAYES, PETER, ED. *How Was It Possible? A Holocaust Reader.* Lincoln: University of Nebraska Press, 2015.

———. *Lessons and Legacies I: The Meaning of the Holocaust in a Changing World.* Evanston: Northwestern University Press, 1991.

HAYES, PETER, AND JOHN K. ROTH, EDS. *The Oxford Handbook of Holocaust Studies.* New York: Oxford University Press, 2010.

HEBERER, PATRICIA. *Children During the Holocaust.* Lanham, MD: AltaMira, 2011.

HEBERER, PATRICIA, AND JÜRGEN MATTHÄUS, EDS. *Atrocities on Trial.* Lincoln: University of Nebraska Press, 2008.

HECHT, CORNELIA. *Deutsche Juden und Antisemitismus in der Weimarer Republik.* Bonn: J. H. W. Dietz Nachfolger, 2003.

HEDGEPETH, SONIA M. AND ROCHELLE G. SEIDEL, EDS. *Sexual Violence against Jewish Women during the Holocaust.* Lebanon, NH: University Press of New England, 2010.

HENRY, PATRICK. *We Only Know Men: The Rescue of Jews in France during the Holocaust.* Washington: Catholic University of America Press, 2007.

HENRY, PATRICK, ED. *Jewish Resistance against the Nazis.* Washington: Catholic University of America Press, 2014.

HERBERT, ULRICH. *Best.* Bonn: J. H. W. Dietz Nachfolger, 1996.

———. *Hitler's Foreign Workers.* Cambridge: Cambridge University Press, 1997.

HERBERT, ULRICH, ED. *National Socialist Extermination Policies.* New York: Berghahn, 2000.

HERF, JEFFREY. *Divided Memory: The Nazi Past in the Two Germanys*. Cambridge, MA: Harvard University Press, 1997.

———. *The Jewish Enemy: Nazi Propaganda During World War II and the Holocaust*. Cambridge, MA: Harvard University Press, 2006.

HILBERG, RAUL. *The Destruction of the European Jews*, 3 vols. New Haven, CT: Yale University Press, 2003.

———. *Sonderzüge nach Auschwitz*. Frankfurt am Main: Ullstein, 1987.

HILBERG, RAUL, STANISLAW STARON, AND JOSEF KERMISZ, EDS. *The Warsaw Diary of Adam Czerniakow: Prelude to Doom*. New York: Stein and Day, 1979.

HITLER, ADOLF. *Hitler's Secret Book*. New York: Grove Press, 1983.

———. *Mein Kampf*. Boston: Houghton Mifflin, 1943.

HOCHSTADT, STEVE. *Exodus to Shanghai: Stories of Escape from the Third Reich*. New York: Palgrave Macmillan, 2012.

HOCHSTADT, STEVE, ED. *Sources of the Holocaust*. New York: Palgrave Macmillan, 2004.

HOFFMAN, EVA. *After Such Knowledge: Memory, History, and the Legacy of the Holocaust*. New York: Public Affairs, 2004.

HOFFMANN, CHRISTHARD, ET AL., EDS. *Exclusionary Violence: Antisemitic Riots in Modern German History*. Ann Arbor: University of Michigan Press, 2002.

HORWITZ, GORDON J. *Ghettostadt: Lodz and the Making of a Nazi City*. Cambridge, MA: Harvard University Press, 2008.

———. *In the Shadow of Death: Living Outside the Gates of Mauthausen*. New York: Free Press, 1990.

HUENER, JONATHAN. "Nazi *Kirchenpolitik* and Polish Catholicism in the Reichsgau Wartheland, 1939–1941." *Central European History* 47 (2014): 105–37.

INDEPENDENT COMMISSION OF EXPERTS. *Switzerland, National Socialism and the Second World War*. Zurich: Pendo, 2002.

INGRAO, CHRISTIAN. *Believe and Destroy: Intellectuals in the SS War Machine*. Malden: Polity Press, 2013.

IOANID, RADU. *The Holocaust in Romania*. Chicago: Ivan R. Dee, 2000.

JÄCKEL, EBERHARD. *Hitler in History*. Hanover, NH: University Press of New England, 1984.

———. *Hitler's Weltanschauung*. Middletown: Wesleyan University Press, 1972.

JAMES, HAROLD. *The German Slump: Politics and Economics 1924–1936*. Oxford: Oxford University Press, 1986.

JARDIM, TOMAZ. *The Mauthausen Trial: American Military Justice in Germany*. Cambridge, MA: Harvard University Press, 2012.

JASKOT, PAUL B. *The Architecture of Oppression: The SS, Forced Labor and the Nazi Monumental Building Economy*. New York: Routledge, 2000.

JELLONNEK, BURKHARD. *Homosexuelle unter dem Hakenkreuz.* Paderborn: Ferdinand Schöningh, 1990.

JOCKUSCH, LAURA, AND GABRIEL N. FINDER, EDS. *Jewish Honor Courts: Revenge, Retribution, and Reconciliation in Europe and Israel after the Holocaust.* Detroit: Wayne State University Press, 2015.

JUDT, TONY. *Postwar: A History of Europe since 1945.* New York: Penguin, 2005.

———. *Reappraisals: Reflections on the Forgotten Twentieth Century.* New York: Penguin, 2008.

———. *When the Facts Change: Essays 1995–2010.* New York: Penguin, 2015.

KAIENBURG, HERMANN. *Die Wirtschaft der SS.* Berlin: Metropol, 2003.

KAPLAN, MARION. *Between Dignity and Despair: Jewish Life in Nazi Germany.* New York: Oxford University Press, 1998.

KÄPPNER, JOACHIM. *Berthold Beitz, die Biographie.* Berlin: Berlin Verlag, 2010.

KARAY, FELICJA. *Death Comes in Yellow: Skarzysko-Kamienna Slave Labor Camp.* London: Routledge, 2004.

KARSKI, JAN. *Story of a Secret State.* New York: Penguin Books, 2011.

KASSOW, SAMUEL D. *Who Will Write Our History? Emanuel Ringelblum, the Warsaw Ghetto, and the Oyneg Shabes Archive.* Bloomington: Indiana University Press, 2007.

KATSH, ABRAHAM I., ED. *Scroll of Agony: The Warsaw Diary of Chaim A. Kaplan.* Bloomington: Indiana University Press, 1999.

KATZ, JACOB. *The Darker Side of Genius: Richard Wagner's Anti-Semitism.* Hanover, NH: University Press of New England, 1986.

———. *From Prejudice to Destruction: Anti-Semitism, 1700–1933.* Cambridge, MA: Harvard University Press, 1980.

KENEZ, PETER. *The Coming of the Holocaust.* New York: Cambridge University Press, 2013.

KERSHAW, IAN. *Hitler.* 2 vols. New York: W. W. Norton & Company, 1999–2000.

———. *Popular Opinion and Political Dissent in the Third Reich: Bavaria 1933–1945.* Oxford: Oxford University Press, 1983.

KERTZER, DAVID I. *The Pope and Mussolini.* New York: Random House, 2014.

———. *The Popes Against the Jews.* New York: Alfred A. Knopf, 2001.

KEVLES, DANIEL J. *In the Name of Eugenics.* Berkeley: University of California Press, 1986.

KLEMPERER, VICTOR. *I Will Bear Witness.* 2 vols. New York: Random House, 1998–99.

KNOX, MACGREGOR. "Das faschistische Italien und die 'Endlösung' 1942/43." *Vierteljahrshefte für Zeitgeschichte* 55 (2007): 53–92.

KOEHL, ROBERT E. *RKFDV: German Resettlement and Population Policy 1939–1945.* Cambridge, MA: Harvard University Press, 1957.

KOONZ, CLAUDIA. *The Nazi Conscience.* Cambridge, MA: Harvard University Press, 2003.

KORNBERG, JACQUES. *The Pope's Dilemma.* Toronto: University of Toronto Press, 2015.

KOSMALA, BEATE, AND GEORGI VERBEECK. *Facing the Catastrophe: Jews and Non-Jews in Europe during World War II.* New York: Berg, 2011.

KRANZLER, DAVID. *The Man Who Stopped the Trains to Auschwitz: George Mantello, El Salvador, and Switzerland's Finest Hour.* Syracuse: Syracuse University Press, 2000.

KÜHNE, THOMAS. *Belonging and Genocide: Hitler's Community, 1918–1945.* New Haven, CT: Yale University Press, 2010.

KULISH, NICHOLAS, AND SOUAD MEKHENNET. *The Eternal Nazi: From Mauthausen to Cairo, the Relentless Pursuit of SS Doctor Aribert Heim.* New York: Doubleday, 2014.

KULKA, OTTO DOV, AND EBERHARD JÄCKEL, EDS. *The Jews in the Secret Nazi Reports on Popular Opinion in Germany, 1933–1945.* New Haven, CT: Yale University Press, 2010.

KUWALEK, ROBERT. *Das Vernichtungslager Belzec.* Berlin: Metropol, 2014.

LANGBEIN, HERMANN. *Against All Hope: Resistance in the Nazi Concentration Camps 1938–1945.* New York: Paragon House, 1994.

———. *People in Auschwitz.* Chapel Hill: University of North Carolina Press, 2004.

LANGMUIR, GAVIN I. *Toward a Definition of Antisemitism.* Berkeley: University of California Press, 1990.

LAQUEUR, WALTER, ED. *The Holocaust Encyclopedia.* New Haven, CT: Yale University Press, 2001.

LENSKY, MORDECHAI. *A Physician Inside the Warsaw Ghetto.* Jerusalem: Yad Vashem, 2009.

LEVI, PRIMO. *Survival in Auschwitz.* New York: Collier Books, 1961.

LEVINE, PAUL A. *From Indifference to Activism: Swedish Diplomacy and the Holocaust, 1938–1944.* Uppsala: Uppsala University Library, 1998.

———. *Raoul Wallenberg in Budapest: Myth, History and Holocaust.* Portland, OR: Vallentine Mitchell, 2010.

LEVY, RICHARD S. *The Downfall of the Anti-Semitic Political Parties in Imperial Germany.* New Haven, CT: Yale University Press, 1975.

LEVY, RICHARD S., ED. *Antisemitism: A Historical Encyclopedia of Prejudice and Persecution.* 2 vols. Santa Barbara: ABC-Clio, 2005.

———. *Antisemitism in the Modern World.* Lexington: D. C. Heath, 1991.

LEWY, GUENTER. *The Nazi Persecution of the Gypsies.* New York: Oxford University Press, 2000.

LIBIONKA, DARIUSZ. "Polish Church Hierarchy and the Holocaust—an Essay from a Critical Perspective." *Holocaust Studies and Materials 2010* (Warsaw: Polish Center for Holocaust Research, 2010): 76–127.

———. "Polish Literature on Organized and Individual Help to the Jews (1945–2008)." *Holocaust Studies and Materials 2010* (Warsaw: Polish Center for Holocaust Research, 2010): 11–75.

LICHTENSTEIN, HEINER. *Mit der Reichsbahn in den Tod: Massentransporte in den Holocaust.* Cologne: Bund-Verlag, 1985.

LIDEGAARD, BO. *Countrymen: The Untold Story of How Denmark's Jews Escaped the Nazis.*.New York: Alfred A. Knopf, 2013.

LINDEMANN, ALBERT S. *Esau's Tears: Modern Anti-Semitism and the Rise of the Jews.* New York: Cambridge University Press, 1997.

———. *The Jew Accused: Three Anti-Semitic Affairs (Dreyfus, Beilis, Frank), 1894–1915.* New York: Cambridge University Press, 1991.

LINDEMANN, ALBERT S., AND RICHARD S. LEVY, EDS. *Antisemitism: A History.* New York: Oxford University Press, 2010.

LIPSTADT, DEBORAH E. *Beyond Belief: The American Press and the Coming of the Holocaust 1933–1945.* New York: Free Press, 1986.

———. *Denying the Holocaust.* New York: Free Press, 1993.

———. *The Eichmann Trial.* New York: Schocken, 2011.

———. *History on Trial: My Day in Court with a Holocaust Denier.* New York: HarperCollins, 2005.

LIULEVICIUS, VEJAS GABRIEL. *War Land on the Eastern Front: Culture, National Identity and German Occupation in World War I.* Cambridge: Cambridge University Press, 2000.

LIVINGSTON, MICHAEL A. *The Fascists and the Jews of Italy: Mussolini's Race Laws, 1938–1943.* New York: Cambridge University Press, 2014.

LONDON, LOUISE. *Whitehall and the Jews 1933–1948.* Cambridge: Cambridge University Press, 2000.

LONGERICH, PETER. *"Davon haben wir nichts gewusst!" Die Deutschen und die Judenverfolgung 1933–1945.* Munich: Siedler, 2006.

———. *Heinrich Himmler.* Oxford: Oxford University Press, 2012.

———. *Holocaust: The Nazi Persecution and Murder of the Jews.* Oxford: Oxford University Press, 2010.

LOWER, WENDY. *The Diary of Samuel Golfard and the Holocaust in Galicia.* Lanham, MD: AltaMira, 2011.

———. *Hitler's Furies: German Women in the Nazi Killing Fields.* New York: Houghton Mifflin Harcourt, 2013.

———. *Nazi Empire-Building and the Holocaust in Ukraine.* Chapel Hill: University of North Carolina Press, 2005.

LUDI, REGULA. *Reparations for Nazi Victims in Postwar Europe.* New York: Cambridge University Press, 2012.

Mahoney, Kevin A. "An American Operational Response to a Request to Bomb Rail Lines to Auschwitz." *Holocaust and Genocide Studies* 25 (2011): 438–46.

Mailänder, Elissa. *Female SS Guards and Workaday Violence: The Majdanek Concentration Camp 1942–1944*. East Lansing MI: Michigan State University Press, 2015.

Mallmann, Klaus-Michael, and Gerhard Paul, eds. *Karrieren der Gewalt: Nationalsozialistische Täterbiographien*. Darmstadt: Wissenschaftliche Buchgesellschaft, 2011.

Mann, Michael. *The Dark Side of Democracy: Explaining Ethnic Cleansing*. New York: Cambridge University Press, 2005.

Marrus, Michael R. *The Holocaust in History*. Hanover, NH: University Press of New England, 1987.

———. *Some Measure of Justice: The Holocaust Era Restitution Campaign of the 1990s*. Madison: University of Wisconsin Press, 2009.

———. "The Vatican and the Custody of Jewish Child Survivors after the Holocaust." *Holocaust and Genocide Studies* 21 (2007): 378–403.

Marrus, Michael R., and Robert O. Paxton. *Vichy France and the Jews*. New York: Basic Books, 1981.

Mason, Tim. *Nazism, Fascism and the Working Class*. Cambridge: Cambridge University Press, 1995.

Matthäus, Jürgen, and Frank Bajohr. *The Political Diary of Alfred Rosenberg and the Onset of the Holocaust*. Lanham, MD: Rowman & Littlefield, 2015.

Matthäus, Jürgen, Jochen Böhler, and Klaus-Michael Mallman, eds. *War, Pacification, and Mass Murder, 1939: The Einsatzgruppen in Poland*. Lanham, MD: Rowman & Littlefield, 2014.

Mazower, Mark. *Hitler's Empire: How the Nazis Ruled Europe*. New York: Penguin, 2008.

———. *Inside Hitler's Greece: The Experience of Occupation 1941–44*. New Haven, CT: Yale University Press, 1993.

Mazurek, Jerzy, and Alina Skibinska. "'Barwy Biale' on their Way to Aid Fighting Warsaw: The Crimes of the Home Army against the Jews." *Holocaust Studies and Materials 2013* (Warsaw: Polish Center for Holocaust Research, 2013): 433–80.

McCullough, Colin, and Nathan Wilson, eds. *Violence, Memory, and History: Western Perceptions of Kristallnacht*. New York: Routledge, 2015.

McKale, Donald M. *Nazis after Hitler: How Perpetrators of the Holocaust Cheated Justice and Truth*. Lanham, MD: Rowman & Littlefield, 2012.

McKale, Donald M., ed. *Rewriting History: The Original and Revised World War II Diaries of Curt Prüfer, Nazi Diplomat*. Kent, OH: Kent State University Press, 1988.

MEGARGEE, GEOFFREY P. *War of Annihilation: Combat and Genocide on the Eastern Front, 1941.* Landham, MD: Rowman & Littlefield, 2006.

MEGARGEE, GEOFFREY P., ED. *The United States Holocaust Memorial Museum Encyclopedia of Camps and Ghettos 1933–1945.* 2 vols. Bloomington: Indiana University Press, 2009, 2012.

MENDELSOHN, EZRA. *The Jews of East Central Europe Between the World Wars.* Bloomington: Indiana University Press, 1983.

MEYER, BEATE. *A Fatal Balancing Act: The Dilemma of the Reich Association of Jews in Germany, 1939–1945.* New York: Berghahn, 2013.

MEYER, MICHAEL, ED. *German-Jewish History in Modern Times.* 4 vols. New York: Columbia University Press, 1996–98.

MICHMAN, DAN. *The Emergence of Jewish Ghettos during the Holocaust.* New York: Cambridge University Press, 2011.

MIERZEJEWSKI, ALFRED C. *The Most Valuable Asset of the Reich: A History of the German National Railway,* vol. 2: *1933–1945.* Chapel Hill: University of North Carolina Press, 2000.

MILLER, JUDITH. *One By One, By One: Facing the Holocaust.* New York: Simon & Schuster, 1990.

MITCHELL, B. R. *European Historical Statistics 1750–1970.* London: Macmillan, 1978.

MITCHELL, GEORGE J. *The Negotiator: A Memoir.* New York: Simon & Schuster, 2015.

MOMMSEN, HANS, AND MANFRED GRIEGER. *Das Volkswagenwerk und seine Arbeiter im Dritten Reich.* Düsseldorf: Econ, 1996.

MONTAGUE, PATRICK. *Chelmno and the Holocaust.* Chapel Hill: University of North Carolina Press, 2012.

MOORE, BOB. *Survivors: Jewish Self-Help and Rescue in Nazi-Occupied Western Europe.* Oxford: Oxford University Press, 2010.

———. *Victims and Survivors: The Nazi Persecution of the Jews in the Netherlands 1940–1945.* London: Arnold, 1997.

MOORHOUSE, ROGER. *Berlin at War.* New York: Basic Books, 2010.

MORSCH, GÜNTER, AND BERTRAND PERZ, EDS. *Neue Studien zu nationalsozialistischen Massentötungen durch Giftgas.* Berlin: Metropol, 2012.

MOSSE, GEORGE. *The Crisis of German Ideology.* New York: Schocken, 1981.

MOSSE, W. E. *The German-Jewish Economic Elite 1820–1935.* Oxford: Clarendon Press, 1989.

———. *Jews in the German Economy: The German-Jewish Economic Elite 1820–1935.* Oxford: Clarendon Press, 1987.

MOTADEL, DAVID. *Islam and Nazi Germany's War.* Cambridge, MA: Harvard University Press, 2014.

MÜHLBERGER, DETLEF. *The Social Bases of Nazism 1919–1933.* Cambridge, MA: Cambridge University Press, 2003.

MULLER, JERRY Z. *Capitalism and the Jews*. Princeton, NJ: Princeton University Press, 2010.

MÜLLER, ROLF-DIETER. *An der Seite der Wehrmacht: Hitlers ausländische Helfer beim "Kreuzzug gegen den Bolschewismus."* Berlin: Christoph Links Verlag, 2007.

NAASNER, WALTER. *SS-Wirtschaft und SS-Verwaltung*. Düsseldorf: Droste, 1998.

NEANDER, JOACHIM. *"Hat in Europa kein annäherndes Beispiel": Mittelbau-Dora—ein KZ für Hitlers Krieg*. Berlin: Metropol, 2000.

———. *Das Konzentrationslager Mittelbau in der Endphase der NS-Diktatur*. Clausthal-Zellerfeld: Papierflieger, 1997.

NEUFELD, MICHAEL J. *The Rocket and the Reich*. New York: Free Press, 1995.

NEUFELD, MICHAEL J., AND MICHAEL BERENBAUM, EDS. *The Bombing of Auschwitz: Should the Allies Have Attempted It?* New York: St. Martin's Press, 2000.

NEUMANN, FRANZ. *Behemoth: The Structure and Practice of National Socialism, 1933–1944*. Chicago: Ivan R. Dee, 2009.

NEWMAN, LEONARD S., AND RALPH ERBER, EDS. *Understanding Genocide: The Social Psychology of the Holocaust*. New York: Oxford University Press, 2002.

NICOSIA, FRANCIS R. *Nazi Germany and the Arab World*. New York: Cambridge University Press, 2015.

NIEWYK, DONALD L. *The Jews in Weimar Germany*. Baton Rouge: Louisiana State University Press, 1980.

NIRENBERG, DAVID. *Anti-Judaism: The Western Tradition*. New York: W. W. Norton & Company, 2013.

NOAKES, JEREMY, AND GEOFFREY PRIDHAM, EDS. *Nazism 1919–1945*. 4 vols. Exeter: University of Exeter Press, 1998–2001.

NOVICK, PETER. *The Holocaust in American Life*. Boston: Houghton Mifflin, 1999.

OFER, DALIA, AND LENORE J. WEITZMAN, EDS. *Women in the Holocaust*. New Haven, CT: Yale University Press, 1998.

ORBACH, DANNY, AND MARK SOLONIN. "Calculated Indifference: The Soviet Union and Requests to Bomb Auschwitz." *Holocaust and Genocide Studies* 27 (2013): 90–113.

ORTH, KARIN. *Das System der nationalsozialistischen Konzentrationslager*. Hamburg: Hamburger Edition, 1999.

OVERY, R. J. *The Nazi Economic Recovery 1932–1938*. London: Macmillan, 1982.

———. *War and Economy in the Third Reich*. Oxford: Clarendon Press, 1994.

PASSELECQ, GEORGES, AND BERNARD SUCHECKY. *The Hidden Encyclical of Pius XI*. New York: Harcourt Brace & Co., 1997.

PATCH, WILLIAM. "The Catholic Church, the Third Reich, and the Origins of the Cold War: On the Utility and Limitations of Historical Evidence." *Journal of Modern History* 82 (2010): 396–433.

PÄTZOLD, KURT, AND ERIKA SCHWARZ. *"Auschwitz war für mich nur ein Bahnhof": Franz Novak—Der Transportoffizier Adolf Eichmanns.* Berlin: Metropol, 1994.

PAULSSON, GUNNAR S. *Secret City: The Hidden Jews of Warsaw 1940–1945.* New Haven, CT: Yale University Press, 2002.

PAVLOWITCH, STEVAN K. *Hitler's New Disorder: The Second World War in Yugoslavia.* New York: Columbia University Press, 2008.

PAXTON, ROBERT O. "Jews: How Vichy Made It Worse." *New York Review of Books,* March 6, 2014.

———. *Vichy France: Old Guard and New Order.* New York: Alfred A. Knopf, 1972.

PERECHODNIK, CALEL. *Am I a Murderer? Testament of a Jewish Ghetto Policeman.* Boulder, CO: Westview Press, 1996.

PERZ, BERTRAND. "The Austrian Connection: SS and Police Leader Odilo Globocnik and His Staff in the Lublin District." *Holocaust and Genocide Studies* 29 (2015): 400–30.

PETROPOULOS, JONATHAN, AND JOHN K. ROTH, EDS. *Gray Zones: Ambiguity and Compromise in the Holocaust and its Aftermath.* New York: Berghahn, 2005.

PETROVSKY-SHTERN, YOHANAN, AND ANTONY POLONSKY, EDS. *Polin 26: Jews and Ukrainians.* Oxford: Littman Library, 2014.

PETROW, RICHARD. *The Bitter Years: The Invasion and Occupation of Denmark and Norway April 1940–May 1945.* New York: Morrow Quill, 1979.

PHAYER, MICHAEL. *The Catholic Church and the Holocaust.* Bloomington: Indiana University Press, 2000.

———. *Pius XII, the Holocaust, and the Cold War.* Bloomington: Indiana University Press, 2008.

"PIUS XII AND THE HOLOCAUST." Letters. *Commentary* 113 (January 2002): 11–16.

POHL, MANFRED. *Philipp Holzmann: Geschichte eines Bauunternehmens 1849–1999.* Munich: C. H. Beck, 1999.

POLONSKY, ANTONY. *The Jews in Poland and Russia,* vol. 3: *1914–2008.* Oxford: Littman Library, 2012.

POLONSKY, ANTONY, AND JOANNA B. MICHLIC, EDS. *The Neighbors Respond: The Controversy over the Jedwabne Massacre in Poland.* Princeton, NJ: Princeton University Press, 2004.

PRESSER, J[ACOB]. *Ashes in the Wind: The Destruction of Dutch Jewry.* Detroit: Wayne State University Press, 1988.

PROCTOR, ROBERT N. *Racial Hygiene: Medicine under the Nazis.* Cambridge, MA: Harvard University Press, 1998.

PULZER, PETER. *Jews and the German State: The Political History of a Minority, 1848–1933.* Oxford: Blackwell, 1992.

————. *The Rise of Political Anti-Semitism in Germany and Austria.* Cambridge, MA: Harvard University Press, 1988.

RABINOVICI, DORON. *Eichmann's Jews: The Jewish Administration of Holocaust Vienna, 1938–1945.* Malden MA: Polity Press, 2011.

RASKIN, RICHARD. *A Child at Gunpoint.* Aarhus, Denmark: Aarhus University Press, 2004.

RAUSCHNING, HERMANN. *The Voice of Destruction.* New York: Putnam, 1940.

REDNER, BEN Z. *A Jewish Policeman in Lvov: An Early Account 1941–1943.* Jerusalem: Yad Vashem, 2015.

REES, LAURENCE. *Auschwitz: A New History.* New York: Public Affairs, 2005.

————. *Hitler's Charisma.* New York: Pantheon, 2012.

RHODES, ANTHONY. *The Vatican in the Age of the Dictators (1922–1945),* New York: Holt, Rinehart and Winston, 1973.

RHODES, RICHARD. *Masters of Death: The SS-Einsatzgruppen and the Invention of the Holocaust.* New York: Alfred A. Knopf, 2002.

RICHARZ, MONIKA, ED. *Jüdisches Leben in Deutschland,* vols. 2–3: *im Kaiserreich* and *1918–1945.* Stuttgart: Deutsche Verlags-Anstalt, 1979, 1982.

RIEGNER, GERHART M. *Never Despair.* Chicago: Ivan R. Dee, 2006.

RITTER, GERHARD A., ED. *Wahlgeschichtliches Arbeitsbuch . . . 1871–1918.* Munich: C. H. Beck, 1980.

RITTNER, CAROL, AND JOHN K. ROTH, EDS. *Different Voices: Women and the Holocaust.* New York: Paragon House, 1993.

————, EDS. *Pope Pius XII and the Holocaust.* London: Leicester University Press, 2002.

RÖMER, FELIX. *Kameraden: Die Wehrmacht von innen.* Munich: Piper, 2012.

ROMIJN, PETER, ET AL. *The Persecution of the Jews in the Netherlands, 1940–1945.* Amsterdam: Vossiuspers UvA, 2012.

ROSEMAN, MARK. *The Wannsee Conference and the Final Solution.* New York: Metropolitan Books, 2002.

ROSENBERG, GÖRAN. *A Brief Stop on the Road from Auschwitz.* New York: Other Press, 2015.

ROSENFELD, OSKAR. *In the Beginning Was the Ghetto: Notebooks from Lodz.* Evanston: Northwestern University Press, 2002.

ROSENTHAL, JACOB. *"Die Ehre des jüdischen Soldaten": Die Judenzählung im Ersten Weltkrieg und ihre Folgen.* Frankfurt: Campus Verlag, 2007.

ROSSINO, ALEXANDER B. *Hitler Strikes Poland: Blitzkrieg, Ideology, and Atrocity.* Lawrence: University Press of Kansas, 2003.

SAFRIAN, HANS. *Eichmann's Men.* New York: Cambridge University Press, 2010.

SARFATTI, MICHELE. *The Jews in Mussolini's Italy: From Equality to Persecution.* Madison: University of Wisconsin Press, 2006.

SCHELVIS, JULES. *Sobibor: A History of a Nazi Death Camp.* Oxford: Berg, 2007.

SCHLEMMER, THOMAS, AND HANS WOLLER, "Der italienische Faschismus und die Juden 1922 bis 1945," *Vierteljahreshefte für Zeitgeschichte* 53 (2005): 165–201.

SCHMIDT, ULF. *Karl Brandt: The Nazi Doctor.* New York: Continuum, 2007.

SCHNEIDER, PETER. "Saving Konrad Latte." *New York Times Magazine,* February 13, 2000.

SCHNEPPEN, HEINZ. *Odessa und das Vierte Reich: Mythen der Zeitgeschichte.* Berlin: Metropol, 2007.

SCHRAFSTETTER, SUSANNA, AND ALAN E. STEINWEIS, EDS. *The Germans and the Holocaust.* New York: Berghahn, 2016.

SEBASTIAN, MIHAIL. *Journal 1935–1944.* Chicago: Ivan R. Dee, 2000.

SEGAL, BINJAMIN W. *A Lie and a Libel: The History of the Protocols of the Elders of Zion.* Lincoln: University of Nebraska Press, 1995.

SEGEV, TOM. *The Seventh Million: The Israelis and the Holocaust.* New York: Hill and Wang, 1993.

———. *Simon Wiesenthal: The Life and Legends.* New York: Doubleday, 2010.

———. *Soldiers of Evil: The Commandants of the Nazi Concentration Camps.* New York: McGraw-Hill, 1987.

SELLIER, ANDRÉ. *A History of the Dora Camp.* Chicago: Ivan R. Dee, 2003.

SHAPIRO, PAUL. *The Kishinev Ghetto 1941-1942.* Tuscaloosa: University of Alabama Press, 2015.

SHNEIDERMAN, S. L., ED. *The Diary of Mary Berg: Growing up in the Warsaw Ghetto.* London: Oneworld, 2007.

SILBERKLANG, DAVID. *Gates of Tears: The Holocaust in the Lublin District.* Jerusalem: Yad Vashem, 2013.

SLEZKINE, YURI. *The Jewish Century.* Princeton, NJ: Princeton University Press, 2004.

SMELSER, RONALD, AND RAINER ZITELMANN, EDS. *Die Braune Elite.* Darmstadt: Wissenschaftliche Buchgesellschaft, 1989.

SMELSER, RONALD, ENRICO SYRING, AND RAINER ZITELMANN, EDS. *Die Braune Elite II.* Darmstadt: Wissenschaftliche Buchgesellschaft, 1993.

SMITH, HELMUT WALSER. *The Butcher's Tale.* New York: W. W. Norton & Company, 2002.

———. *The Continuities of German History.* New York: Cambridge University Press, 2008.

SMITH, HELMUT WALSER, ED. *The Oxford Handbook of Modern German History.* New York: Oxford University Press, 2011.

SNYDER, TIMOTHY. *Black Earth: The Holocaust as History and Warning.* New York: Tim Duggan Books, 2015.

———. *Bloodlands: Europe Between Hitler and Stalin.* New York: Basic Books, 2010.

Sontag, Susan. *Regarding the Pain of Others*. New York: Farrar, Straus and Giroux, 2002.

Spicer, Kevin P. *Hitler's Priests: Catholic Clergy and National Socialism*. DeKalb: Northern Illinois University Press, 2008.

——. *Resisting the Third Reich: The Catholic Clergy in Hitler's Berlin*. DeKalb: Northern Illinois University Press, 2004.

Spiliotis, Susanne-Sophia. *Verantwortung und Rechtfrieden: Die Stiftungsinitiative der deutschen Wirtschaft*. Frankfurt am Main: S. Fischer, 2003.

Spoerer, Mark. *Zwangsarbeit unter dem Hakenkreuz*. Stuttgart: Deutsche Verlags-Anstalt, 2001.

Stangneth, Bettina. *Eichmann Before Jerusalem*. New York: Alfred A. Knopf, 2014.

Stargardt, Nicholas. *The German War: A Nation under Arms, 1939–1945*. New York: Basic Books, 2015.

——. *Witnesses of War: Children's Lives under the Nazis*. New York: Alfred A. Knopf, 2006.

Staudinger, Hans. *The Inner Nazi: A Critical Analysis of Mein Kampf*. Baton Rouge: Louisiana State University Press, 1981.

Steinlauf, Michael C. *Bondage to the Dead: Poland and the Memory of the Holocaust*. Syracuse: Syracuse University Press, 1997.

Steinweis, Alan E. *Kristallnacht 1938*. Cambridge, MA: Harvard University Press, 2009.

Stephenson, Jill. *Hitler's Home Front: Württemberg under the Nazis*. London: Continuum, 2006.

Stern, Fritz. *The Politics of Cultural Despair*. Berkeley: University of California Press, 1974.

Stibbe, Matthew. *Women in the Third Reich*. London: Arnold, 2003.

Stone, Dan. *Histories of the Holocaust*. New York: Oxford University Press, 2010.

——. *The Liberation of the Camps*. New Haven, CT: Yale University Press, 2015.

Straumann, Lukas, and Daniel Wildmann. *Schweizer Chemieunternehmen im "Dritten Reich."* Zurich: Chronos, 2001.

Streit, Christian. *Keine Kameraden: Die Wehrmacht und die sowjetischen Kriegsgefangenen 1941–1945*. Bonn: J. H. W. Dietz Nachfolger, 1991.

Stroop, Jürgen. *The Stroop Report*. New York: Pantheon, 1979.

Struve, Kai. *Deutsche Herrschaft, ukrainischer Nationalismus, antijüdische Gewalt: Der Sommer 1941 in der Westukraine*. Berlin: Walter de Gruyter, 2015.

Tal, Uriel. *Christians and Jews in Germany: Religion, Politics, and Ideology in the Second Reich, 1870–1914*. Ithaca: Cornell University Press, 1975.

Tec, Nechama. *Dry Tears: The Story of a Lost Childhood*. New York: Oxford University Press, 1984.

————. *When Light Pierced the Darkness: Christian Rescue of Jews in Nazi-Occupied Poland.* New York: Oxford University Press, 1986.

TENT, JAMES F. *In the Shadow of the Holocaust: Nazi Persecution of Jewish-Christian Germans.* Lawrence: University Press of Kansas, 2003.

TODOROV, TZVETAN. *The Fragility of Goodness: Why Bulgaria's Jews Survived the Holocaust.* Princeton, NJ: Princeton University Press, 1999.

TOOZE, ADAM. *The Deluge: The Great War, America, and the Remaking of the Global Order, 1916–1931.* New York: Viking, 2014.

————. *The Wages of Destruction: The Making and Breaking of the Nazi Economy.* New York: Penguin, 2006.

TRUNK, ISAIAH. *Judenrat: The Jewish Councils in Eastern Europe under Nazi Occupation.* New York: Macmillan, 1972.

————. *Lodz Ghetto: A History.* Bloomington: Indiana University Press, 2006.

TSCHUY, THEO. *Dangerous Diplomacy: The Story of Carl Lutz, Rescuer of 62,000 Hungarian Jews.* Grand Rapids: William B. Eerdmans, 2000.

TURNER, HENRY ASHBY JR. *General Motors and the Nazis.* New Haven, CT: Yale University Press, 2005.

————. *German Big Business and the Rise of Hitler.* New York: Oxford University Press, 1985.

————. *Hitler's Thirty Days to Power.* Reading, MA: Addison-Wesley, 1996.

UNITED STATES HOLOCAUST MEMORIAL MUSEUM. *Historical Atlas of the Holocaust.* New York: Macmillan, 1996.

VAGI, ZOLTAN, ET AL. *The Holocaust in Hungary.* Lanham, MD: AltaMira Press, 2013.

VAN PELT, ROBERT JAN. *The Case for Auschwitz: Evidence from the Irving Trial.* Bloomington: Indiana University Press, 2002.

————. "Nazi Ghettos and Concentration Camps: The Benefits and Pitfalls of an Encyclopedic Approach." *German Studies Review* 37 (2014): 149–59.

VAN RAHDEN, TILL. *Jews and Other Germans: Civil Society, Religious Diversity, and Urban Politics in Breslau, 1860–1925.* Madison: University of Wisconsin Press, 2000.

VENTRESCA, ROBERT. *Soldier of Christ: The Life of Pope Pius XII.* Cambridge, MA: Harvard University Press, 2012.

VINCENT, C. Paul. "The Voyage of the St. Louis Revisited." *Holocaust and Genocide Studies* 25 (2011): 252–89.

VITAL, DAVID. *A People Apart: The Jews in Europe 1789–1939.* Oxford: Oxford University Press, 1999.

VOLKOV, SHULAMIT. *Germans, Jews, and Antisemites.* New York: Cambridge University Press, 2006.

WACHSMANN, NIKOLAUS. *KL: A History of the Nazi Concentration Camps.* New York: Farrar, Straus and Giroux, 2015.

WALLER, JAMES. *Becoming Evil: How Ordinary People Commit Genocide and Mass Killing.* New York: Oxford University Press, 2002.

WALTER, DIRK. *Antisemitische Kriminalität und Gewalt: Judenfeindschaft in der Weimarer Republik.* Bonn: J. H. W. Dietz Nachfolger, 1999.

WARD, JAMES MACE. *Priest, Politician, Collaborator: Josef Tiso and the Making of Fascist Slovakia.* Ithaca: Cornell University Press, 2013.

WASSERSTEIN, BERNARD. *The Ambiguity of Virtue: Gertrude van Tijn and the Fate of the Dutch Jews.* Cambridge, MA: Harvard University Press, 2014.

———. *On the Eve: The Jews of Europe Before the Second World War.* New York: Simon & Schuster, 2012.

WATSON, ALEXANDER. *Ring of Steel: Germany and Austria-Hungary in World War I.* New York: Basic Books, 2014

WATT, RICHARD M. *Bitter Glory: Poland and Its Fate 1918–1939.* New York: Simon and Schuster, 1979.

WEBER, EUGEN. *The Hollow Years: France in the 1930s.* New York: W. W. Norton & Company, 1994.

WEIKART, RICHARD. *Hitler's Ethic: The Nazi Pursuit of Evolutionary Progress.* New York: Palgrave Macmillan, 2009.

WEISS-WENDT, ANTON. *Murder Without Hatred: Estonians and the Holocaust.* Syracuse: Syracuse University Press, 2009.

WEISS-WENDT, ANTON, ED. *The Nazi Genocide of the Roma.* New York: Berghahn, 2013.

WEITZ, ERIC D. *A Century of Genocide: Utopias of Race and Nation.* Princeton, NJ: Princeton University Press, 2003.

WELZER, HARALD. *Täter: Wie aus ganz normalen Menschen Massenmörder werden.* Frankfurt am Main: Fischer Taschenbuch, 2007.

WESTERMANN, EDWARD B. *Hitler's Police Battalions.* Lawrence: University Press of Kansas, 2005.

WETTE, WOLFRAM. *Feldwebel Anton Schmidt.* Frankfurt am Main: S. Fischer, 2013.

———. *Karl Jäger: Mörder der litauischen Juden.* Frankfurt am Main: S. Fischer, 2011.

WHITESIDE, ANDREW G. *The Socialism of Fools: Georg Ritter von Schönerer and Austrian Pan-Germanism.* Berkeley: University of California Press, 1975.

WILDT, MICHAEL. *Hitler's Volksgemeinschaft and the Dynamics of Racial Exclusion: Violence against Jews in Provincial Germany, 1919–1939.* New York: Berghahn, 2012.

———. *An Uncompromising Generation.* Madison: University of Wisconsin Press, 2009.

WINSTONE, MARTIN. *The Dark Heart of Hitler's Europe: Nazi Rule in Poland under the General Government.* New York: I. B. Tauris, 2015.

WISTRICH, ROBERT S. *Antisemitism: The Longest Hatred.* New York: Pantheon, 1991.

———. *Hitler and the Holocaust.* New York: Modern Library, 2001.

WITTE, PETER, ET AL. *Der Dienstkalendar Heinrich Himmlers 1941/42.* Hamburg: Christians, 1999.

WOLF, HUBERT. *Pope and Devil: The Vatican's Archives and the Third Reich.* Cambridge, MA: Harvard University Press, 2010.

WÜNSCHMANN, KIM. *Before Auschwitz: Jewish Prisoners in the Prewar Concentration Camps.* Cambridge, MA: Harvard University Press, 2015.

WYMAN, DAVID S. *The Abandonment of the Jews: America and the Holocaust, 1941–1945.* New York: Pantheon, 1984.

———. *Paper Walls: America and the Refugee Crisis, 1938–1941.* New York: Pantheon, 1985.

WYMAN, MARK. *DP: Europe's Displaced Persons, 1945–1951.* Ithaca: Cornell University Press, 1998.

YISRAELI, DAVID. "The Third Reich and the Transfer Agreement." *Journal of Contemporary History* 6 (1971): 129–48.

ZIMMERMAN, JOSHUA D. *The Polish Underground and the Jews, 1939–1945.* New York: Cambridge University Press, 2015.

ZIMMERMAN, JOSHUA D., ED. *Contested Memories: Poles and Jews during the Holocaust and Its Aftermath.* New Brunswick: Rutgers University Press, 2003.

———. *The Jews in Italy under Fascist and Nazi Rule, 1922–1945.* New York: Cambridge University Press, 2005.

ZIMMERMANN, MOSHE. *Wilhelm Marr: The Patriarch of Antisemitism.* New York: Oxford University Press, 1986.

ZUCCOTTI, SUSAN. *The Italians and the Holocaust.* New York: Basic Books, 1987.

———. *Père Marie-Benoit and Jewish Rescue.* Bloomington: Indiana University Press, 2013.

———. *Under His Very Windows: The Vatican and the Holocaust in Italy.* New Haven, CT: Yale University Press, 2000.

INDEX